Advanced C++
Programming Styles and Idioms

James O. Coplien
AT&T Bell Laboratories

ADDISON-WESLEY

An imprint of Addison Wesley Longman, Inc.

Reading, Massachusetts • Harlow, England • Menlo Park, California
Berkeley, California • Don Mills, Ontario • Sydney
Bonn • Amsterdam • Tokyo • Mexico City

Pearson Education Corporate Sales Division
201 W. 103rd Street
Indianapolis, IN 46290
(800) 428-5331
corpsales@pearsoned.com

Library of Congress Cataloging-in-Publication Data

Coplien, James O.
        Advanced C++ programming styles and idioms / James O. Coplien.
            p.   cm.
        Includes bibliographical references and index.
        ISBN 0-201-54855-0
        1. C++ (Computer program language)   I. Title.
    QA76.73.C153C67   1992
    005.26'2--dc20   91-19806
                                                                            CIP

AT&T

This book was typeset in Times, Courier, and Helvetica by the author, using a Linotronic 200P phototypesetter and an Amdahl 5990 running the UNIX® System V Operating System.

Text printed on recycled and acid-free paper.

ISBN 0201548550

19 2021222324 PH   07 06 05 04

19th Printing   September 2004

*To Sandra,
Christopher,
Lorelei, and
Andrew Michael
with love*

S. D. G.

Obtaining Copies of the Book's Software Examples

The software for many of the book's examples has been made available on-line, on `netlib.att.com` where copies may be retrieved for personal, non-commercial use. The source can be retrieved by establishing an ftp connection to the netlib machine, using an anonymous login, and using your electronic mail address as the password. The files appear under the directory `netlib/c++/idioms`. Alternatively, the software can be retrieved through electronic mail (if you do not have ftp access) by sending electronic messages of the form

```
send index for c++/idioms
send 2-2a.c 2-2b.c 2-4.c 2-5.c from c++/idioms
```

to login `netlib@research.att.com`. The index file lists all available files.

Preface

This book is designed to help programmers who have already learned C++ develop their programming expertise. To understand how programmers achieve proficiency, we need to understand not only how people learn a new language (such as a programming language), but also how a language is used to solve software problems effectively.

Learning Programming Languages

Not everything you need to know about a product is described in the owner's manual. Before the arrival of our first child, my wife and I were admonished by a friend that no book, and no training, could completely prepare us for the art of parenting. We must of course learn minimal, essential skills. But the interesting, challenging, and rewarding aspects of raising a child go beyond this basic knowledge. For example, no book or "owner's manual" will help you understand why your three-year-old daughter rubs toothpaste in your one-year-old's hair, or why your children hang their socks in the refrigerator.

The same is true of programming languages. Programming language syntax shapes our thinking to a degree, but what we learn in the "owner's manual" about syntax alone only gets us started. Most of what guides the structure of our programs, and therefore of the systems we build, is the *styles* and *idioms* we adopt to express design concepts.

Style distinguishes excellence from accomplishment. An effective parenting style, or programming style, comes from personal experience or by building on the experience of others. A software engineer who knows how to match a programming language to the needs of an application, writes excellent programs. To achieve this level of expertise, we need to go beyond rules and rote, into convention and style, and ultimately into abstractions of concept and structure. It is in that sense that this book is "advanced."

The rules, conventions, and concepts of programming drive the structure of the systems we build: They give us a model of how to build systems. A model for problem decomposition and system composition is a *paradigm*, a pattern for dividing the world into manageable parts. C++ is a multiparadigm language. C programmers use C++ as a better C. Object-oriented advocates do everything polymorphically. In fact, a variety of approaches is usually necessary to express the solution to a software problem efficiently and elegantly.

Learning a programming language is much like learning a natural language. Knowledge of basic syntax lets a programmer write simple procedures and build them into nontrivial programs, just as someone with a vocabulary of a few hundred German words can write a story far richer than see-Dick-run. But mastery of language is quite another issue. That such stories are nontrivial does not make them elegant or demonstrate fluency. Learning language syntax and basic semantics is like taking a 13-hour course in German: It prepares you for the task of ordering a bratwurst, but not for going to Germany to make a living, and certainly not for getting a job as a German language journalist or poet. The difference is in learning the *idioms* of the language. For example, there is nothing in C itself that establishes

```
while (*cp1++ = *cp2++);
```

as a fundamental building block, but a programmer unfamiliar with this construct would not be perceived as a fluent C programmer.

In programming, as in natural language, important idioms underly the suitability and expressiveness of linguistic constructs even in everyday situations. Good idioms make the application programmer's job easier, just as idioms in any language enrich communication. Programming idioms are reusable "expressions" of programming semantics, in the same sense that classes are reusable units of design and code. Simple idioms (like the `while` loop above) are notational conveniences, but seldom are central to program design. This book focuses on idioms that influence how the language is used in the overall structure and implementation of a design. Such idioms take insight and time to refine, more so than the simple notational idioms. The idioms usually involve some intricacy and complexity, details that can be written once and stashed away. Once established, programming language idioms can be used with convenience and power.

The Book's Approach

Assuming a background in the basic syntax of C++, this book imparts the proficiency that expert C++ programmers gain through experience by giving a feel for the styles and idioms of the language. It shows how different styles let C++ be used for simple data abstraction, full-fledged abstract data type implementation, and various styles of object-oriented programming. It also explores idioms that the core of the C++ language does not directly support, such as functional and frame-based programming, and advanced garbage collection techniques.

The Book's Structure

Rather than taking a "flat" approach to learning the advanced features of C++ by organizing around language features, this book looks at these increasingly powerful abstractions from the perspective of the C++ features required to support them. Each chapter of this book is organized around a family of such idioms. The idioms progressively build on each other in successive chapters.

Chapter 1 provides a historical perspective on C++ idioms. It provides some motivation as to why idioms came about, and varying degrees to which different idioms can be thought of as part of the language or as outside the language.

Chapter 2 introduces the fundamental C++ language building blocks: classes and member functions. Though much of the material is basic, the chapter establishes idioms and vocabulary that recur in later chapters. It introduces compiler type systems, and their relationship to user-defined types and classes, from a design perspective. It also presents idioms that make const more useful.

Chapter 3 introduces idioms that make classes "complete" types. C++ has been evolving to automate more and more of the work of copying and initializing objects, but programmers still need to customize assignment and default constructors for most nontrivial classes. This chapter provides a framework for that customization. I call the idioms described in this chapter *canonical forms*, meaning that they define principles and standards to make the underlying mechanics of objects work. In addition to the most commonly used canonical form, idioms are presented to apply reference counting to new and existing classes. These are the first idioms of the book to go beyond straightforward application of the base C++ syntax. A variation on reference counting, counted pointers, is shown as a way to move C++ a step further away from the machine, abandoning pointers in deference to smarter, pointer-like objects. Lastly, the chapter looks at how to separate the creation of an object from its initialization. To someone familiar with basic C++, this might seem an unnatural idiom: C++ tightly couples these two operations. The need to separate them arises in the design of device drivers and in systems with mutually dependent resources.

Chapter 4 introduces inheritance; Chapter 5 adds polymorphism to inheritance to introduce object-oriented programming. Many new C++ programmers get "inheritance fever," using it at every occasion. While it is true that inheritance is used mostly to support the object paradigm, it has a distinctly separate application for software reuse. Introducing inheritance apart from polymorphism helps the reader separate the two concepts and avoids the confusion that often arises from trying to internalize two foreign concepts at once.

Chapter 6 approaches the constructs, styles and idioms of C++ from the perspectives of architecture and design. It examines what classes *mean* at the level of an application, high above the level of syntax. Appreciating the relationships between the design abstractions of an application, and between the classes and objects of its implementation, leads to systems that are robust and easily evolved. Another key to evolution is broadening designs beyond a specific application, to cover applications for a whole domain; guiding principles for domain analysis are an important part of this chapter. The chapter contains numerous rules of thumb about appropriate use of inheritance, an area of difficulty for inexpert C++ programmers. Readers who have been exposed to object-oriented design will appreciate the explanation in this chapter of how to transform the output of design to C++ code. Encapsulation as an alternative to inheritance, both for reuse and for polymorphism, is explored in the context of the C++ language.

Chapter 7 explores reuse of code and designs. Four distinct code mechanisms are explored, with particular attention devoted to the benefits and pitfalls of "inheritance fever." Idioms are presented to significantly reduce the code volume generated by parameterized type libraries using templates.

The remainder of the book stretches beyond native C++ into advanced programming idioms. Chapter 8 introduces exemplars, objects that take over many of the roles of C++ classes. Exemplars are presented as special objects that solve some common development problems, such as the "virtual constructor" problem. But exemplars also lay the groundwork for more powerful design techniques supporting class independence and independent development.

Chapter 9, which focuses on symbolic language styles, breaks with concepts many hold fundamental to C++ programming including strong typing and explicit memory management. The idioms of this chapter are certainly outside mainstream C++ development and are reminiscent of styles found in Smalltalk and Lisp. One might claim that those who want to program in Smalltalk should program in Smalltalk. Those who want Smalltalk in all of its glory should indeed use Smalltalk. However, the fact that the styles presented in this chapter are exotic does not mean that the need that the need for them is rare or esoteric. Sometimes we want a small portion of a system to have the flexibility and polymorphism of symbolic languages, and in those situations we need to step outside the bounds of the C++ philosophy while working in the confines of the C++ semantics and type system. This chapter regularizes such idioms so they do not have to be created from scratch each time they are needed.

Chapter 9 also presents idioms supporting incremental run-time update. Implementations of this idiom are necessarily dependent on many details of the target platform. The gist of this material is to familiarize the reader with the level of technology at which incremental loading issues must be worked. The example presented is typical and, as such techniques go, it is neither obtuse nor trivial. The code presented for incremental loading needs major reworking for platforms other than Sun work stations, and it may be found altogether unsuitable to some environments. None of the book's other idioms depend on this idiom, so it can be pursued or rejected on its own merits. The goal of Chapter 9 is *not* to change C++ into Smalltalk; this cannot, and should not, be done. These idioms are less compile-time type safe and generally less efficient than "native C++" code; what they offer is flexibility and an increased measure of automated memory management.

Chapter 10 covers dynamic multiple inheritance. Multiple inheritance is a controversial C++ feature, and discussion of this dynamic variation is separated out to avoid tainting other chapters. While static multiple inheritance as described in Chapter 5 has value, dynamic multiple inheritance avoids problems of a combinatorial explosion of class combinations. This approach has been found valuable in many real-life programs including editors, CAD systems, and database managers.

The last chapter discusses objects from a high-level, system view. The chapter raises the level of abstraction above chunks the size of a C++ class, to larger and more encompassing units of software architecture, organization, and administration. The chapter puts a number of important system issues in perspective, including scheduling, exception handling, and distributed processing. Some guidelines for modularization and reuse are also discussed, tying together the concepts of Chapters 6 and 7. Included in this discussion are considerations for library structure and maintenance.

In Appendix A, the basic C++ concepts are compared with their C analogues. Many readers will have already learned these basics or can find them in introductory texts. This material is included here for two reasons. First, it serves as a ready reference for those occasions when you need clarification of an obscure construct without having to go to a separate text. Second, C and C++ styles are viewed from a design perspective, showing how to mix procedural and object-oriented code. This is particularly important for C++ programmers working with a base of C code.

The examples in this book are based on Release 3.0 of C++, and have been tried under Release 3 of the AT&T USL Language System on many different hardware platforms, and under some other C++ environments as well. Many of the examples have been tried under GNU C++ Version 1.39.0 and Zortech C++ 2.0, though examples using features of the 3.0 release await forthcoming releases of these tools. Some code makes use of general purpose class libraries for maps, sets, lists, and others. Efficient versions of such libraries are available from many vendors, and adequately functional versions can be created from scratch for pedagogical purposes. The skeletons, and sometimes complete bodies, of many general-purpose classes can be gleaned from examples in the book. Key class names are listed in the Index.

Acknowledgments

This book owes much to many friends. The original impetus for the book came from Chris Carson at Bell Laboratories, and he if anyone is the book's godfather. I appreciate his initiative and support in starting this effort. The book reflects the guidance of Keith Wollman, my resourceful and accommodating editor, and Helen Wythe, the production supervisor. Lorraine Mingacci collaborated significantly with me on Chapter 6, and discussions with her about the rest of the book have been of immense value. The book owes much to a core team of thorough and relentless reviewers and contributors of ideas: Tim Born, Margaret A. Ellis, Bill Hopkins, Andrew Koenig, Stan Lippman, Barbara Moo, Bonnie Prokopowicz, Larry Schutte, and Bjarne Stroustrup. Alexis Layton, Jim Adcock, and Mike Ackroyd offered suggestions and insights to keep the book focused and balanced, and I am deeply grateful for their contributions. Many other improvements are owed to reviews by Miron Abramovici, Martin Carroll, Brian Kernighan, Andrew Klein, Doug McIlroy, Dennis Mancl, Warren Montgomery, Tom Mueller, Anil Pal, Peggy Quinn, and Ben Rovegno. Mary Crabb, Jean Owen, and Chris Scussel lent their expertise on the wonders of text formatting. Brett L. Schuchert and Steve Vinoski took painstaking effort to report the bugs that made it into early printings; their efforts have greatly improved the quality of subsequent printings. Credit goes to Corporate Desktop Services of Glen Ellyn, Illinois, for working out the final phototypesetting bugs. Many thanks to Judy Marxhausen for advice on special topics.

Much credit goes to AT&T managers for their encouragement and for their provision of time and resources to work on the book. Thanks to Paul Zislis and Ben Rovegno for support early on, and very special thanks to Warren Montgomery, Jack Wang, and Eric Sumner, Jr., for their support, ideas, and forbearance.

Students from many of my courses have been a good source of input and feedback on materials that would later be brought together in this book. Special thanks go to the students of the C++ courses I taught at AT&T Bell Laboratories, both in Naperville, Illinois and in Columbus, Ohio, in 1989.

Contents

LIST OF FIGURES

1

Introduction

Idioms are an important part of both natural and programming languages. This book focuses on idioms that make C++ programs more expressive, and language styles that give software its structure or its "character." C++ code can be written without these idioms, but it is styles and idioms that give programs much of their expressiveness, efficiency, and aesthetic value. They are a byproduct of years of language experience, iteration, and dialogue.

Individual idioms often have amusing but instructive origins. This introduction looks at two kinds of C++ idioms from the perspective of the history of the language: those that influenced its development and those supporting object constructs beyond the basic C++ model.

1.1 C++: An Evolving Language

C++ has been a language at the right time and the right place. The progenitor of C++, C-with-classes, was born in 1980—a landmark year for Smalltalk as well—and its growth was propelled by the explosion of the "object phenomenon" in the early 1980s. The language grew as the industry's understanding of objects grew. By the summer of 1983, C-with-classes had entered the academic and research world, initiating a dialogue that has continued to shape the language to this day.

By adopting a posture of flexibility and growth, C++ benefited from the experience of its own users and from the progress in object-oriented programming in the rest of the computing community. Programming languages were breaking new ground in multiple inheritance, encapsulation techniques, and other important areas. C++, for which standardization was to start only in 1989, had the flexibility to build on an ever-growing object-oriented language experience base.

1

The creation of the `protected` class scope is a specific example of how development experience influenced C++. The `friend` relationship was frequently used to grant derived classes permission to violate the encapsulation of their base class. This use of `friend` became common enough that the `protected` language facility was introduced. Such public feedback refined the C++ protection model to be one of the best of its time. Similar experience paved the road for multiple inheritance and templates in C++, and refined countless other details in the language.

The "place" of C++ in history is its foundation in C. C is among the most popular programming languages in the world today, with few contenders in its broad niche of systems programming. Just as C code was efficient and allowed close access to the machine, so would C++. As an improvement on Classic C, C++ offers compile-time type safety. That, and its efficiency, set C++ apart from other object-oriented languages in common use.

But these two evolutionary influences—the maturing object paradigm and the influence of the ever popular C language—were occasionally at odds. It was not (and still is not) the goal of C++ to be all things to all people, and design decisions were made to balance between the tradition of C and the new directions espoused by Smalltalk and Flavors. Most decisions were made in favor of mature or familiar technology: though C++ is culturally a product of the Smalltalk age, it traces its language technology to Simula (1967), Algol 68 (1968), and C (1973).

One important consideration in these decisions was where to bury the complexity of advanced features. Putting the complexity in the compiler simplifies development for the user: the compiler can automate mundane tasks associated with memory management, initialization, cleanup, type conversion, and I/O, among others. One principle that has guided C++ evolution is that the compiler should not be simplified at the expense of user convenience. But overloading the compiler with *too* much intelligence leads to a dilemma: it either constrains the user to a single model of some aspect of programming (a "tyrannical" language), or the language itself must grow to express a smörgasbörd of alternatives (an "anarchical" language).

1.2 Handling Complexity with Idioms

To provide the power of a high-level language while avoiding the inflexibility of a "tyrannical" language, C++ developed building blocks that programmers could use to code their own models of computation. Language features relying heavily on compile-time support (e.g., type conversion) were left in the language itself. However, other "language features"—including much of the memory management model, I/O, and some object member initialization—can be taken over by the user in advanced applications. Many common programming tasks became *idiomatic*, using C++ constructs to express functionality outside the language proper, while giving the illusion of being part of the language.

An idiom for object copying and memory management is a good example. When an object is assigned to another or passed as a function parameter, the compiler automatically generates code to assign or initialize the recipient object's fields one by one from those of the source object. That can be inefficient for large objects, and it can lead to anomalies for pointer data members: the compiler default provides a shallow copy, when a deep copy is sometimes desired. Both of these problems can be addressed with an idiom for reference-counted objects that separates a class into a memory management portion called a *handle* and an application portion called the *body*. Handle classes use programmer-supplied versions of code for assignment, initialization and cleanup of objects, code that the compiler automatically applies to manage memory as needed. That idiom is described in Chapter 3.

Another example is input/output, which (as in C) is not part of the language. But it is common to overload left shift and right shift operators to support a stream object idiom for input and output. All classes follow a single convention for I/O. Here, the complexity is not in the compiler, nor in the user application, but in a general-purpose library. The library is accessed through a `#include` file, which overloads operators to make it appear as though the logical shift operators were originally designed for I/O in C++.

The key to the success of these idioms is that they are transparent to the end user, as if they were part of the language itself. They provide the combined breadth and power of an "anarchical" language, with the transparency of a "tyrannical" language. The user is not constrained to use a memory mangement model that is completely general but prohibitively expensive, but can choose from a spectrum of alternatives. Tradeoffs for efficiency, C interface compatibility, and convenience of use are under programmer control. Less is more: The areas that C++ does *not* define give it a spectrum of flexibility difficult to achieve in languages with more highly integrated memory management models. C++ is not as rich in features as it is in *meta*-features, simple building blocks that can be combined to create a *gestalt* more powerful than the sum of the pieces alone.

These meta-features were the product not of a single, grand vision, but of practical experience gained first from academia and research, and later from exploratory development projects. C++ came to be a language with a "kit" of facilities to define powerful semantics for common programming tasks. Individual facilities of the language, such as constructors and overloaded operators, have some value in their own right, but they are low-level constructs. Idioms combining constructors and overloaded assignment provide the power of a high-level language. As with language features proper, many of these idioms came from users of early versions of C++. The evolution of the C++ language in light of object-oriented applications, and the evolution of applications to take advantage of new C++ features, has culminated in the language definition described in the *C++ Annotated Reference Manual* [1]. This specification is mature enough to serve as a basis for formal standardization. These idioms are in common enough use to be considered orthodox practices of everyday C++ programming.

Casual users of C++, or those who learned it as "a better C," may not stumble across these idioms on their own. The programming language does not force their use; it only provides the building blocks that make them possible. In that sense, the idioms are "advanced"—they go beyond the bounds of what the language enforces, or even encourages. The first goal of this book is to convey the orthodox idioms of C++ as programming tools in their own right. It is organized around idioms, introducing supporting language features as necessary, instead of the other way around. This organization helps first-time C++ programmers move on to advanced (idiomatic) constructs more quickly, and provides a framework so those familiar with the syntax can move on to more powerful semantics.

1.3 Objects for the Nineties

The orthodox idioms described above are rooted in the C heritage of the C++ language. Another class of idioms has risen from a growing and increasingly experienced C++ user community, with influence from other programming language camps. C++ today is a language still culturally compatible with C, and is as strongly object-oriented as it can be without severing that compatibility. This is an important niche, bringing object-oriented constructs to the traditional C development culture of compilers, operating systems, and real-time control systems. C++ is rich with language support for object-oriented programming, though we have seen that much of this support comes through conventions, styles, and idioms. Many of these idioms are supported by language meta-features.

To be called an "object-oriented programming language" brought ever-increasing demands as the industry progressed. As C++ grew and changed, and the user community grew even more rapidly, users found they needed increasingly powerful constructs to keep up with new-found applications for object-oriented techniques. An example was the need for "virtual constructors," which required a degree of polymorphism more easily supported by weakly typed languages than by the strong C++ type model. Weak typing, or dynamic typing, is simulated in C++ by extra levels of indirection and idiomatic constructs. The complexity of most of these idioms can be encapsulated in the classes using them—they look just like ordinary classes to the application user, though they display type flexibility found in higher-level programming languages.

The idioms formed to support these advanced features are less idiomatic than those with roots in the development of C++ itself; that is, there are fewer meta-features supporting them. Much of this is owed to the C heritage of C++: C++ is C, and then some, but it cannot easily encompass the design philosophies of both C and Smalltalk at the same time. To *directly* support the type models of Smalltalk or Flavors would have required a major change in philosophy, and a major departure from the C++ model of the object paradigm. That, again, would raise the dilemma between "tyrannical" and "anarchical" languages. Experience has shown that these idioms can be effectively used without specific language support, encapsulating the details of their implementation in private class members.

In that context, the second thrust of this book is to present C++ idioms supporting what many claim necessary to complete the object model supported by C++ and its orthodox idioms. These idioms do not arise only for those wishing to emulate Smalltalk in C++: they address design and engineering issues in any strongly object-oriented C++ program.

1.4 Design and Language

As the language grew, so did the computer science community's appreciation of the relationship between object-oriented design and object-oriented programming language. Much early use of the object paradigm was as a programming tool providing abstraction, encapsulation, and flexibility beyond that offered by procedural design. More recently, objects (or, more precisely, *entities*, their application domain counterparts) have come to be appreciated as design constructs.

C++ followed this evolution closely. The C++ class concept was initially designed to reflect design concepts, with reuse (through private inheritance) an additional but secondary consideration. As the experience base grew, the C++ subtyping model grew to express the object and class relationships produced by object-oriented analysis and design. The strong compile-time C++ type model helps guard against common misuses of inheritance.

Design is not the focus of this book, though design considerations are woven into the text throughout. Design and programming have a close kinship in the object paradigm, and even though this book is about "programming," it cannot ignore serious consideration of design approaches. Chapter 6 focuses on design from a C++ language perspective; Chapter 7 looks at reuse, which is largely a design issue; and Chapter 11 looks at systemic issues beyond "find the objects" and appropriate use of inheritance. Like the language syntax, semantics, and idioms, these design approaches are the product of years of experience.

C++ finds itself in the midst of the popularity of object-oriented design and, as was discussed above, may owe much of its success to that. But too often object-oriented approaches are embraced to the exclusion of others. Other paradigms are not dead or any less relevant than before, but still can be applied if the discerning designer determines they are a good fit for a problem. Many C++ idioms presented in the following chapters have little to do with the object paradigm. For example, the functors of Section 5.6, the subsystem modularization techniques of Chapter 11, and the parametric reuse constructs of Chapter 7—these are still advanced uses of C++, all within the provisions and spirit of the language.

Hopefully, the C++ language descriptions, idioms, and styles of this book will give you an edge in advanced programming, giving you the benefit of the experience of others. The styles and idioms may apply off-the-shelf to C++ projects that you are now working on or that lie in your future. As Stroustrup has said, good programming and good design are the result of taste, insight, and experience. This book is not the last word on how to use C++ in large systems, by any means. Experiment, explore and build some to throw away.

References

1. Ellis, Margaret A., and B. Stroustrup. *The Annotated C++ Reference Manual.* Reading, Mass: Addison-Wesley, 1990.

2

Data Abstraction and Abstract Data Types

Typed programming languages came on the scene in the 1950s, not as the "best current practices" for good design or as system structuring tools, but as a means of generating *efficient* object code from program source. Over time, programming language type systems came to be regarded as having value in their own right for type checking and type safety of interfaces. In the 1960s, types matured to being on a par with procedures as program building blocks. These advances led to new and more abstract programming language notions and constructs, among them:

- *Abstract data types* (ADTs) which define the interface to a data abstraction without specifying implementation detail. An abstract data type may have different implementations to suit different needs or to work well in different environments.

- *Classes*, which are implementations of abstract data types. Language support for classes first came with Simula 67.

- Advanced programming language type systems, that gave ADTs first-class standing as language abstractions. Operator overloading and other programming language advances gave ADTs a new level of expressiveness and power. Such facilities first appeared in the languages Bliss, Algol 68, and Simula, and became more refined in Mesa and Clu.

In C++, the built-in or *indigenous types* give us compile-time interface checking and efficient code generation: `int`, `short`, `long`, `float`, `double`, `long double`, `char`, and pointers. These abstractions come prepackaged in every C++ environment, ready to serve as counters and indices, and as building blocks for numerical analyses, symbol processing, and so forth. The C++ class allows us to

7

combine related data, their operators, and closely coupled functions, creating a single program unit supported by the language. These classes have the same power and convenience as the built-in types: they can be used to declare or dynamically create new instances, and their use is subject to type checking. The interface to a class can be managed separately from its implementation, the class interface serving as a specification of an ADT.

Just because something is a class, however, does not mean it can be treated with the same generality as a built-in type like int or double. The class designer must provide constructs to dovetail a new class into the compiler type system. For example, the compiler can be "taught" how to convert between a built-in double and an instance of a user-defined Complex class. The compiler can also be "taught" how to generate efficient code to create, assign, and copy instances of a class. With more work—most of it "cookbook"—a class can be turned into a user-defined type we call a *concrete data type*. That gives class objects the power to be declared, assigned, and passed as parameters exactly like variables of the built-in types of C and C++.

A class is a useful design and implementation abstraction even without the mechanisms making it a concrete data type. It is little work to make a class into a concrete data type, and the extra convenience of concrete data types usually makes the effort worthwhile. But "plain" classes are a good starting point, and the class basics covered in this chapter will have you well on your way to building nontrivial class types. Chapter 3 builds on this chapter to elaborate basic class types into concrete data types.

This chapter starts by introducing the *class* construct, perhaps the most fundamental abstraction mechanism in C++. We will discover how functions and data are combined into a class in a way that is "inside-out" from the C way of doing things. Constructs for graceful initialization and destruction of class variables are described next. This chapter also introduces other C++ constructs and concepts often associated with classes: inline functions, constant member functions and constant objects, static member functions, and member function pointers.

2.1 Classes

The C++ class construct is closely related to the C struct. C++ accepts C language style struct declarations and maintains their C language semantics. The class keyword is usually used to emphasize that a structure is being used as a user-defined data type, not simply an aggregation of data. That is, when both data and functions are grouped together, class is used; when only data are grouped, struct is used instead. Functions grouped in a class are called *member functions*; they are "members" of the class containing them. A C++ struct may have member functions just like a class, but more commonly retains its C language sense of being an unintelligent data record. Formally, the only difference between class and struct in C++ is in their default access rights, as described below. Figure 2-1 shows the similarity between C structs and C++ classes when used as data encapsulation mechanisms.

Unlike C, C++ introduces a new type into a program for each tagged structure or class; it is as though a typedef were inserted after the declaration:

C code:

```
struct EmpLabel {
   char name[NAME_SIZE];
   char id[ID_SIZE];
   int gender:1;
      . . . .
} foo;

typedef struct EmpLabel Employee;

struct EmpLabel fred;
Employee lisa;
```

C++ code:

```
struct Employee {
   char name[NAME_SIZE];
   char id[ID_SIZE];
   int gender:1;
      . . . .
} foo;



struct Employee fred;
Employee lisa;
```

In C++, the tag and type are synonymous, whereas in C they are separate names.

C++ structs behave as classes whose members are publicly exported by default, whereas classes' members are private to the class by default. The access can be changed using the keywords private, public, and protected. The appearance of one of these three keywords, followed by a colon, designates the protection for the members following it, to the end of the class or up to the next such designation. The default protection is in effect prior to the appearance of the first such designation. The protection attributes have the following semantics:

- public members of an object are accessible to any function having access to the declaration of that object's class and scope access to the object itself.

- protected members of an object are accessible only to the member functions of that object's class or of its derived classes. A derived class object cannot access the protected fields of a base class object, not even of an object of its *own* base class. A derived class member function may access protected members only of the base class portion of an object of its own class.

- private members of an object are accessible only to member functions of that object's class.

C code: **C++ code:**

```
struct {                                  struct {
   char name[NAME_SIZE];                     char name[NAME_SIZE];
   char id[ID_SIZE];                         char id[ID_SIZE];
   short yearsExperience;                    short yearsExperience;
   int gender:1;                             int gender:1;
   unsigned char dependents:3                unsigned char dependents:3;
   unsigned char exemptions:4;               unsigned char exemptions:4;
} foo;                                    } foo;

struct {                                  class {
   char name[NAME_SIZE];                  public:
   char id[ID_SIZE];                         char name[NAME_SIZE];
   short yearsExperience;                    char id[ID_SIZE];
   int gender:1;                             short yearsExperience;
   unsigned char dependents:3                int gender:1;
   unsigned char exemptions:4;               unsigned char dependents:3;
} bar;                                       unsigned char exemptions:4;
                                          } bar;
```

Figure 2-1. Analogy Between C structs and C++ classes

The encapsulation provided by private and protected can be violated using the friend mechanism, if so desired. Protection will be discussed in detail later. (See Chapter 3; see also the entry for "protection" in the Index.)

Though classes can be thought of as syntactic extensions of structs, we tend to think of classes more in terms of what they communicate about a program's design. Structures are used to package related data in any program structuring technique. For example, in functional decomposition (see Appendix F), each level of functions has its own data, and a struct might be used to associate the related data (or to create several groupings of related data) at a given level. The data structures generated in functional decomposition do not necessarily reflect the states of abstractions in the application, but rather reflect artifices of the implementation strategy.

C++ classes offer two things beyond C structs: typing and abstraction. Classes are used to create new *user-defined types* in a C++ program—the types we call abstract data types. Classes serve as type building blocks because they capture the activity of a collection of data along with its representation. For example, consider a Complex number class:

```
class Complex {
public:
friend Complex& operator+(double, const Complex&);
        Complex& operator+(const Complex&) const;
friend Complex& operator-(double, const Complex&);
        Complex& operator-(const Complex&) const;
friend Complex& operator*(double, const Complex&);
        Complex& operator*(const Complex&) const;
friend Complex& operator/(double, const Complex&);
        Complex& operator/(const Complex&) const;
        double rpart() const;
        double ipart() const;
        Complex(double=0.0, double=0.0);
private:
        double realPart, imaginaryPart;
};
```

Here, the class offers a way of capturing not only the relationship between realPart and imaginaryPart, as a struct might do, but also between the representation of a complex number and its behaviors, or operations. C language constructs cannot capture these relationships in a convenient and intuitively satisfying way, but can represent them only through programming conventions.

Classes help the programmer provide higher-level programming constructs than either functions or structs alone support. These constructs serve as *abstractions*, and what they abstract typically relates closely to the application for which the program is being written. The use of classes emphasizes this mapping from application domain abstractions to solution domain abstractions in a way that data structs alone cannot.

Good designers might think in terms of abstract data types and write code in terms of structs and functions. In that case, the structure of a good C++ program is the same as the structure of a good C program, just turned "inside out." This is called *object inversion*, and will be investigated in the next section.

2.2 Object Inversion

Many programs have libraries or modules organized around a data structure. Take, for example, a simple stack. The data for the stack may be put in a struct, and there may be several procedures closely tied to that structure, which operate on variables declared from that structure.

In C++, we turn things inside out. We view the functions as *belonging* to the structure because of their close coupling to the structure and its data. Instead of passing a `Stack` structure to each of its associated procedures, we put the procedures *inside* the `struct` along with its data. These functions are called member functions or *operators*. Other languages (most notably, Smalltalk) call them *methods*. Figure 2-2 shows the `Stack` example done in this style. (This code, though functional, is too simple to be realistic and is presented for pedagogical purposes only. Things have been kept simple by making the stack a fixed size, its elements of a homogeneous type, and for only one specific type at that—`longs`.)

Note that the C++ member functions, such as `Stack`'s `push` function (called `Stack::push`) do not dereference a structure pointer, and do not even show any explicit access to the class object that would correspond to the `struct` in the C implementation. This is because C++ creates another level of scope for `classes`, and the functions can be thought of as living *inside* instances of the structure. Each declaration of a `Stack` "variable" allocates space somewhere in memory, just as it does for `structs`. For example, the instance q in `main` of the C++ program corresponds to memory on the run-time stack. This instance is called an *object* of class `Stack`. Member functions of `Stack` are applied to its objects (e.g., `q.initialize()` or `q.push(1)`). Expressions in these functions referring to members of class `Stack` use the data of the object (here, q) for which the member function was called.

Member functions access their objects' data through an implicit parameter pointing to the object for which the function is called. The parameter's name is `this`. Though `this` is passed transparently as a parameter, it is accessible directly to the programmer. The `this` parameter performs the same function as the `struct Stack` pointer parameter does in the C functions; the pointer is so commonly needed that the compiler provides it automatically. Furthermore, the compiler automatically prepends an implicit `this->` qualifier to class member references within member functions. Inside `Stack::initialize`, the expression `sp = -1` means `this->sp = -1`. Dereferencing `this` explicitly is legal but tedious, verbose, and usually redundant. The following two C++ code fragments are equivalent:

```
void Stack::initialize() {        void Stack::initialize() {
    sp = -1;                          this->sp = -1;
}                                 }
long Stack::top() const {         long Stack::top() const {
    return items[sp];                 return this->items[this->sp];
}                                 }
```

C code:

```c
#define STACK_SIZE 10


struct Stack {
    long items[STACK_SIZE];
    int sp;
};

void Stack_initialize(s)
struct Stack *s;
{
    s->sp = -1;
}



long Stack_top(s)
struct Stack *s;
{
    return s->items[s->sp];
}

long Stack_pop(s)
struct Stack *s;
{
    return s->items[s->sp--];
}

void Stack_push(s, i)
struct Stack *s; long i;
{
    s->items[++s->sp] = i;
}

int main()
{
    struct Stack q;
    long i;
    Stack_initialize(&q);
    Stack_push(&q, 1);
    i = Stack_top(&q);
    Stack_pop(&q);
}
```

C++ code:

```cpp
const int STACK_SIZE = 10;

class Stack {
private:
    long items[STACK_SIZE];
    int sp;
public:
    void initialize();
    long top() const;
    long pop();
    void push(long);
};

void Stack::initialize() {
    sp = -1;
}

long Stack::top() const {
    return items[sp];
}


long Stack::pop() {
    return items[sp--];
}

void Stack::push(long i) {
    items[++sp] = i;
}

int main()
{
    Stack q;

    q.initialize();
    q.push(1);
    long i = q.top();
    q.pop();
}
```

Figure 2-2. Corresponding C and C++ Code for a Stack Implementation

Notice the `const` designation on the member function `Stack::top`. This is an assertion that the member function does not modify the object for which it is called (the object pointed to by `this`). The `const` construct is described in more detail in Section 2.9.

2.3 Constructors and Destructors

Two important ideas behind the design of the C++ language were that (1) variables should always be automatically initialized, and (2) classes should control their own memory allocation. Integration of these concepts into the language allows class authors to orchestrate allocation and deallocation so class users needn't worry about it. We define special member functions to take care of initialization and cleanup of objects, called the *constructor* and *destructor*, respectively.

The compiler has a special relationship with functions it recognizes as constructors and destructors, and it recognizes them by their distinctive names. A constructor member function has the same name as the class to which it belongs. The destructor's name is the name of the class preceded by a tilde ("¯"). Though the tilde and the class name are usually not separated by spaces, that is only a convention, not enforced by the language.

When using C++ in its "native" mode without any advanced idioms, you do not call constructors and destructors directly. The compiler automatically generates constructor and destructor calls to initialize variables when they need to be initialized, and to clean them up when they go away. For example, on entry to a function that has local class object variables, the constructors of those variables are automatically invoked, and their destructors are called automatically when the function returns. The constructor and destructor also work with memory management primitives `new` and `delete` to initialize and tear down dynamically allocated objects.

Note that constructors and destructors are member functions with *no* return type. This is because they are never really called directly, but the compiler generates code to call them as needed. One might be tempted to think that a constructor "returns" an object on completion. But constructors may just as well be asked to initialize an existing block of memory set aside for an object (for example, a global object) as to initialize a dynamically allocated object (for example, when `operator new` is used). How the object address flows in and out of the constructor is handled behind the scenes by the compiler. Using an uncommon language construct, constructors and destructors *can* be invoked at will for a specified object, which is useful for special cases of advanced memory management as described in Chapter 3. Most of the time, though, the automatically generated calls are the norm.

It is not necessary to have constructors and destructors for a class if you are just using classes for simple data aggregation or abstraction. You *do* need them if you want classes with dynamic internal structure to behave like natural types of the programming language. For example, the `Stack` example above has no constructors or destructors; it does, however, have an `initialize` function, and that function must be called explicitly to set things to a sane state. We can replace that function with a constructor so that `Stack` initializes its own internal structure, without users of `Stack` having to worry about it. First, we must change the class declaration

```
class Stack {
public:
    Stack();
    long top() const;
    long pop();
    void push(long);
private:
    long items[10];
    int sp;
};
```

and then replace the `initialize` function with the constructor

```
Stack::Stack() {
    sp = -1;
}
```

The `initialize` function no longer has to be called from the `main` program; the constructor is called *automatically* when `Stack` objects are created, as when the declaration of q is encountered. So the call to `initialize` can just be removed from `main`, and the program will work fine.

Let's now look at a more general stack class (Figure 2-3) that will allow us to explore constructors a little further, and to introduce destructors. The `Stack` currently has a fixed size of ten elements; we may want to create a `Stack` with fewer or more elements at declaration time. To do this, we define a constructor taking a parameter whose value will be taken by the constructor as the stack size. The constructor can dynamically allocate memory using the C++ new operator:

```
Stack::Stack(int size) {
    items = new long[size];
}
```

Because the constructor dynamically allocates memory, a destructor must be added to return the memory to the free pool when an object gets cleaned up. The destructor applies the `delete` operator to the dynamic memory pointer to

```
const int STACK_SIZE = 10;

class Stack {
public:
    Stack();       // one constructor
    Stack(int);    // another constructor
    ~Stack();      // destructor
    long top() const;
    long pop();
    void push(long);
private:
    long *items;
    int sp;
};
```

Figure 2-3. Declaration of a Stack with Constructors and Destructors

accomplish this:

```
Stack::~Stack() {
    delete[] items;
}
```

Here, the syntax delete[] items uses the brackets to inform the compiler that items points to a *vector* of longs, not just to a single dynamically allocated instance of a long.

Notice that there are now two constructors: both have the same name! The name Stack has become "loaded down" with two meanings; the term for this is *overloading*. This causes no confusion or ambiguity; if the context requires a constructor with an argument, then the one with the argument is called. Otherwise, the other constructor is called, and we can define it to make a stack of a default size 10. The compiler takes care of this automatically (this will become more clear in the discussion below). The new Stack class declaration is shown in Figure 2-3, and its implementation in Figure 2-4.

If a class does *not* have a constructor, then there is no guarantee of how objects of that class will be initialized. If a constructor-less class contains objects of classes that themselves have default constructors, then those objects will be properly set up and initialized, but other fields of the constructor-less object will have undefined contents. Consider the code in Figure 2-5 as an example. Objects of class B have no class objects as members, only instances of built-in C types (pointer to char and short). However, B's constructor takes pains to initialize all its objects' members. Instances of C have one class object member, B, and an int; objects of class D have only ints. The main program creates objects of classes C and D, and we note that all the

```
Stack::Stack() {
    items = new long[STACK_SIZE];
    sp = -1;
}

Stack::Stack(int size) {
    items = new long[size]; // like a typed sbrk or malloc call,
                            //   except constructor is called
                            //   if present
    sp = -1;
}

Stack::~Stack() {
    delete[] items;         // like free, except destructor
                            //   is called
}

long Stack::top() const {
    return items[sp];
}

long Stack::pop() {
    return items[sp--];
}

void Stack::push(long i) {
    items[++sp] = i;
}

int main()
{
    Stack q;            // call Stack::Stack()
    Stack r(15);        // call Stack::Stack(int)
    q.push(1);
    int i = q.top();
    q.pop();
}
```

Figure 2-4. A Stack with Constructors and Destructors

primitive type fields of objects of classes C and D go uninitialized. If these classes had constructors, and if the constructors specified initialization of these fields, then initialization would be complete.

As noted above, C has a B member. Because B has a constructor, the fields of C::b will be initialized every time a C object is created. The B::B constructor is called from a default constructor (one taking no parameters) that the compiler generates automatically for class C. The compiler must supply this constructor so it

```
class B {
public:
    B() { p = 0; s = 0; }
    int f();
private:
    char *p;
    short s;
};
class C {
public:
    int g();      // no constructor
private:
    int i;
    B b;
};
class D {
public:
    int h();
private:
    int j, k;
};
C gc;              // p and s initialized, i set to zero

int main() {
    C c;           // p and s initialized, i undetermined
    D d;           // j and k uninitialized
    int l = c.g();
}
```

Figure 2-5. Initialization of Primitive Type Class Members

has a place to call the constructor for C::b. However, the compiler-generated code initializes only members for which constructors exist, so only class object members are implicitly initialized in the absence of a constructor. Members declared as built-in types are *not* initialized automatically. This behavior is consistent with the lack of initialization for structures in C.

2.4 Inline Functions

The inline function modifier can be used to request that a function be expanded
inline. Inline expansion avoids the overhead of a function call by expanding the body
of the function at the point it is called. The compiler will attempt to inline expand the
code of a function that is declared as such before it is used, where the declaration and
use appear in the same source stream (i.e., part of the same source file or the closure
of source files #included by that file). Such inline expansion can result in large
savings of CPU time: one programmer found that making functions of a hardware
simulator inline sped up the simulator by a factor of four!

C preprocessor macros have long been used to simulate inline expanded functions
in C. Here, a macro is used to simulate an absolute value function:

```
#define abs(x)  (x < 0? (-x): x)

int main() {
    int i, j;
    . . . .
    i = abs(j);
    . . . .
}
```

Inline functions can replace such preprocessor macro definitions. Inlines are
preferable to macros because they obey the same type and scoping rules as functions.
They generate code as good as (and often better than) their macro counterparts (see
the exercises at the end of this chapter). In some environments, they provide for
better symbolic debugging than macros do. For example, some C++ environments
allow you to turn off inline function expansion with a compiler flag, so that all
functions compile into closed copies of subroutine code. This means that debuggers
can easily set breakpoints on those functions, something that usually cannot be done
with macros.

A function may be made inline by explicit use of the inline keyword on the
function definition:

```
inline int abs(int i) { return i < 0? -i: i; }

class Stack {
    . . . .
    long pop();
};

inline long Stack::pop() {
    return items[sp--];
}
```

A member function can be made inline just by making the definition part of the declaration; this approach is discouraged because it complicates program administration (see Section 2.11). However, the definition-with-declaration notation will be used in this book for the sake of clarity of presentation, without any intention of inline expansion. Here is an example of an inline expanded member function:

```
class Stack {
    . . . .
    long pop() { return items[sp--]; }   // inline expanded
};
```

The definition of an inline function (and, of course, an `inline` declaration of the function) must occur in the source text before any call to that function. The appearance of an inline declaration for a function, after any call to the function, is an error. Consider the following example:

```
class C {
public:
    inline int a() { return 1; }
    int b()        { return 2; }   // also inline
    int c();
    int d();
    int e();
};
inline int C::d() {      // Error: C::c called before
    return c() + 1;      //     inline declaration, below
}

inline int C::c() { return 0; }

int C::e() {
    return c() + 5;      // C::c call inline expanded
}

int main() {
    C o;
    int i = o.d();       // C::d inline expanded,
                         //     but nested C::c call not
}
```

Various C++ implementations have their own restrictions on inline expansion. For example, a compiler may not expand functions with loops (though the first iteration of the loop may be expanded), or recursive functions (though the initial iterations of a partial recursive function may be expanded). Functions that exceed a compiler-dependent complexity threshold may not be expanded.

Inline functions are not a performance panacea. Improved performance often comes at the expense of increased code size; the expansion factor depends on the C++

environment you are using. The 80/20 rule applies: look for that 20 percent of the code where your program spends 80 percent of its time, and inline expand functions called from inner loops. Identifying good inline function candidates in a program's "hot spots" is one convenient and effective way to improve performance.

2.5 Initialization of Static Data Members

C++ classes may have static data members; they parallel the construct of static member functions. Static data members are declared in the class interface, usually in a header file (usually a file with a .h suffix, though this varies from system to system). The definitions of these data, with an optional initializer, should be in a .c file (or .C, .CPP etc., depending on what suffix your system uses for C++ program source files), not in a header file. An example is shown in Figure 2-6.

Static data members reduce the number of global names in a program. They also bestow some useful properties of ordinary data members on objects and values that are not replicated one per object—for example, access control rules. They are a boon for library providers in that they avoid polluting the global name space and thereby allow easier writing of library code and safer use of multiple libraries.

These reasons apply to functions as well as objects, and static member functions are a companion concept to static member data. They are described next.

2.6 Static Member Functions

Early experience with C++ revealed that *most* of the names that ought to be local within a library were in fact function names. It was discovered that nonportable code such as:

```
((X*)0)->f();
```

was used to simulate static member functions. This "trick" will fail under some implementations of dynamic linking, and no reasonable semantics are guaranteed by the language.

Declarations in header files:

```
struct X {
    X(int, int);
    . . . .
};

struct s {
    static const int a;
    static X b;
    . . . .
    int f();
};
```

Definitions in a .c file:

```
const int s::a = 7;
X s::b(1,2);
int s::f() { return a; }
```

Figure 2-6. Initialization of Static Data Members

C++ static member functions are like global functions whose scope is within a class. They are as efficient as global function calls, and marginally more efficient than usual member function calls:

```
class X {
public:
    // ...
    void foo() { fooCounter++; . . . . .}
    static void printCounts() {
        printf("foo called %d times\n", fooCounter);
    }
private:
    static int fooCounter;
};

int X::fooCounter = 0;

int main() {
    printCounts();      // error (unless there really
                        //         is such a global function)
    X::printCounts();   // fine
}
```

The most common use of static member functions is to manage resources common to all objects of a class. Static member functions usually operate on static class data. For example, a class may contain counts of how many times its member functions are called; each member function would increment its own `static int` peg count. One or more static functions would be used to reset, retrieve, or print the values of such counts.

Another potential use of static member functions might be to group together a related collection of functions that should not be treated as an object. The relationship between such data might be weaker than what ties together most object member functions, and they do not relate to a design-level resource (Chapter 6). In some sense, this models the Ada concept of a package. Such constructs will be further explored in Chapter 11.

2.7 Scoping and const

In C, the `#define` construct is used to replace constant values (so-called *manifest constants*) with symbolic names. It is more in the spirit of C++ to use `const` symbols for this purpose. They can usually be used wherever a `#define` constant would have been used in C. C++ constants can be scoped, so constants peculiar to a class do not pollute the global name space, a point where macros fall down.

Constants used local to a file can be declared and defined within that file; they are invisible to other files in the same program:

```
const int MAX_STACK_SIZE = 1000;
const char *const paradigm = "The Object Paradigm";
```

Constants may be shared across source files by declaring them `extern`. These declarations can be placed in a commonly included header file:

```
extern const double e;
```

and a *single* definition of the value placed in a convenient program source file (.c or .C or .cpp, etc., file):

```
#include <math.h>
extern const double e = exp(1.0);
```

The syntax for `const` static members complicates declaration of symbolic constants inside a class. In particular, the value of static member constants may not be bound at compile time. That means such a value may not be used to declare the size of an array:

```
static const int SIZE1 = 10;

class C {
    . . . .
    static const int SIZE2;
    char vec1[SIZE1];      // O.K.
    char vec2[SIZE2];      // illegal, SIZE2 not known
};

const int C::SIZE2 = 10;
```

To overcome this shortcoming of const, we use a construct that is a synonym for const: enums are immutable, symbolic integer values that serve some roles const ints cannot fulfill. An enumerated type in C++, as in C, is usually defined as a collection of symbolic integer constants that can be used in switch and if statements, but whose underlying integer value is not of interest. It is equally valid to assign these symbols specific values in the enum declaration, giving them the sense of symbolic constants. Here, we create a "constant" named StackSize inside class Stack:

```
class Stack {
public:
    void push(int);
    int pop();
    int top() const;
private:
    enum { StackSize = 100 };      // const simulation
    int rep[StackSize], sp;
};

void Stack::push(int el) {
    if (sp >= StackSize) error("stack overflow");
    else rep[sp++] = el;
}
```

2.8 Initialization Ordering of Global Objects, Constants, and Static Class Members

C++ guarantees that variables are initialized in the order of their appearance within a given source file; however, there is no guaranteed ordering of global class object initialization across source files. This holds for all global class object variables, but it is especially noteworthy for static class members because initialization of global class objects may depend on the validity of their class's static constant values.

Open assumptions about ordering of initialization can lead to subtle bugs. For example, consider a simple header file, **Angle.h**, containing the following declarations:

```
#include <math.h>
#include <stdio.h>

extern const double pi;

class Angle {
public:
    Angle(double degrees) {
        r = degrees * pi / 180.0;
    }
    . . . .
    void print() {
        printf("radians = %f\n", r);
    }
private:
    double r;
};
```

Now consider the source file, pi1.c, containing the definition of the constant pi:

```
#include <Angle.h>
extern const double pi = 4.0 * atan(1.0);
```

and a source file, pi2.c, containing application code:

```
#include <Angle.h>

Angle northeast = 45;

int main() {
    Angle northeast2 = 45;
    northeast.print();
    northeast2.print();
    return 0;
}
```

When compiled and run on my system, this program generates output

```
radians = 0.000000
radians = 0.785398
```

because pi has not been initialized by the time the constructor for northeast is called.

If there is a valid need to orchestrate the ordering of such initializations, the technique presented in Section 3.7 can be used. It is better to avoid these dependencies where possible, particularly in library code that is to be used by others.

2.9 Enforcement of const for Class Object Member Functions

The 2.0 release of the C++ language brought some new applications of const. In earlier releases of C++ it was possible to change the value of a const class object by calling a member function on it. This has been reported as a problem and as a bug many times.

If we were to disallow calls of member functions for const objects, this by itself would render const objects useless. To make the language complete, the 2.0 release introduced const member functions, member functions that may be called for a const object. The compiler guarantees that a const member function does not modify the object for which it is called (unless a conscious effort is made to thwart the compiler's enforcement efforts; see "Logical const-ness" below). It also guarantees that only const member functions are applied to const objects. An example can be found in Figure 2-7. The use of const as a suffix to the parameter list of a function declaration was designed to be consistent with the use of const as a suffix to *. Because of separate compilation, we cannot rely on the compiler by itself—without user-provided clues—to detect when a member function that modifies its object is called for a const object.

Logical const-ness and Physical const-ness

The *state* of an object—the values of all its member data—controls how its member functions act. There are three components to an object's state:

1. Data that reflect an application state (for example, remembering the arrival of a transient message or signal);

2. Data that are loosely coupled to states in the application but are artifices of the solution (Stack::sp, for example);

3. Supporting data for debugging and administration that are not otherwise tied to the semantics of the application (for example, a count of how many times a function has been called).

This is not a perfect categorization; data such as reference counts can be thought of as being in either the second or third category, and other states may straddle the first two categories. However, it helps underscore an important consideration of how member functions interact with const objects.

```
struct s {
    int a;
    f(int aa) { return a = aa; }
    g(int aa) const { return aa; }
    //    h(int aa) const { return a = aa; }
};

void g()
{
    s o1;
    const s o2;
    o1.a = 1;
    //    o2.a = 2;
    o1.f(3);
    //    o2.f(4);
    o1.g(5);
    o2.g(6);
}

/*
Remove the //s and the compiler should generate these messages:

"", line 5: error: assignment to  member s::a of const struct s
"", line 13: error: assignment to  member s::a of const s
"", line 15: warning: non const member function s::f() called
              for const object
*/
```

Figure 2-7. const Member Functions

As an example, consider a class BinaryTree, with a member function findNode that returns a copy of a node according to some criteria. The algorithm might be tuned to rebalance the tree when node search time becomes excessive, using a threshold based on the number of nodes in the tree. One would expect findNode to be a const member function, but its need to rebalance the tree occasionally will cause the compiler to complain if it is declared as such: const member functions may not modify their objects' data.

Such cases do not appear to be common, and there is a straightforward work-around for cases where this is necessary. The trick is to access the local object through a pointer that is an alias for this:

```
T BinaryTree::findNode(String key) const {
    . . . .
    if (needReBalance) {
        // put comment here to explain why const
        // is violated
        BinaryTree *This = (BinaryTree*)this;
        . . . .
        This->left = This->left->left;
        . . . .
    }
}
```

Another way of thinking about the solution is to create a *reference* to this that behaves as an alias for it, but with fewer protection properties:

```
T BinaryTree::findNode(String key) const {
    . . . .
    if (needReBalance) {
        typedef BinaryTree *BinaryTreePointer;
        const BinaryTreePointer &This = (BinaryTree*)this;
        . . . .
        This->left = This->left->left;
        . . . .
    }
}
```

The second form emphasizes that This is just a constant alias for this. The generated code will likely come out the same as that in the first case. If the function is inline, one of these approaches may produce less code, depending on the compiler implementation.

A String class illustrates a counterpoint to the example above. A String has an obvious implementation as a pointer to a dynamically allocated block of memory containing a vector of characters. A member function String::getChar may be defined to remove and return the last character of a string. This member function may not change the state of the object itself—that is, the contents of the pointer do not change. The *logical* state of the object is nonetheless modified, so getChar should not be declared a const member function, even though the compiler would allow it.

2.10 Pointers to Member Functions

There are times when we want to change the behavior of a function at run time; member function pointers are one way to do that. Consider an application where a class represents a component called a filter in an electrical circuit, made up of an inductor, capacitor, and resistor in series.[1] This filter is a particular kind of circuit called an RLC circuit (where R, L and C are engineering notations for resistors, inductors, and capacitors respectively). A common problem is to determine the step response of the filter. The step response of a filter is the output it generates when an abrupt, instantaneous change in voltage is applied to it. We want to create an object that models the filter's behavior. The constructor of the class requires parameters specifying the filter's inductance, capacitance, resistance, initial current and voltage, and so forth. A class member function will calculate the current flowing through the circuit as a function of time. The behavior of the component over time may vary in one of three distinct ways: overdamped, underdamped, or critically damped. Which of these modes of operation the circuit adopts can be determined from the constructor parameters.

Each of the three modes is governed by a formula specifying the current as a function of time. An understanding of these formulas is not necessary to appreciate the example, but here is a summary for those who are interested. For the overdamped case,

$$i(t) = A_1 e^{s_1 t} + A_2 e^{s_2 t}$$

For the critically damped case,

$$i(t) = e^{-\alpha t}(A_1 t + A_2)$$

For the underdamped case,

$$i(t) = e^{-\alpha t}(B_1 \cos \omega_d t + B_2 \sin \omega_d t)$$

where

$$s_{1,2} = -\alpha \pm j\omega_d$$

---

1. Thanks to Don Stein, who inspired some good ideas for this section.

$$\alpha = \frac{R}{2L}$$

$$\omega_0 = \frac{1}{\sqrt{LC}}$$

$$\omega_d = \sqrt{\omega_0^2 - \alpha^2}$$

Those who have studied physics will recognize these equations—and can use the following code—to model the characteristics of a mass connected to a spring in a medium of some viscosity. Analogues in other domains exist as well.

We want the class to give the appearance of having a single current function, but one whose internal behavior differs greatly as a function of context.

In C++, we can declare a pointer to a member function, and use that variable to call a function provided the pointer has been suitably initialized. A member function pointer must specify both the type of the class containing the member function, as well as the signature (interface) of the function itself; even function pointers are type checked. We can reassign a given function pointer to address several different functions during program execution, where all the functions pointed to have the same parameter types and return type.

Here are some function declarations, and declarations of function pointers that can be used to address them:

Function Declarations	Compatible Pointer Declarations
| ```
int String::curColumn();
int String::length();
int String::hash();
``` | ```
int (String::*p1)();
``` |
| ```
char Stack::pop(int);
``` | ```
char (Stack::*p2)(int);
``` |
| ```
void Stack::push(char);
``` | ```
void (Stack::*p3)(char);
``` |
| ```
int PathName::error(int,
         const char* ...);
``` | ```
int (PathName::*p4)(int,
         const char* ...);
``` |

Here are some initializations using the above declarations:

```
p1 = &String::length;
p2 = &Stack::pop;
p3 = &Stack::push;
p4 = &PathName::error;
```

And here is how those functions might be called:

```
int main() {
    String s;
    Stack t;
    PathName name, *namePointer = new PathName;
    p4 = PathName::error;

    int m = (s.*p1)();
    char c = (t.*p2)(2);
    (t.*p3)('a');
    (name.*p4)(1, "at line %d\n", __LINE__);
    (namePointer->*p4)(3, "another error (%d) in file %s",
        __LINE__, __FILE__);
    return 0;
}
```

We can also declare pointers to class object data members:

```
class Table {
public:
    sort();
    . . . .
};

class X {
public:
    Table t1, t2;
    . . . .
};

int main() {
    Table X::*tablePointer = &X::t1;
    X a, *b = new X;
    (a.*tablePointer).sort();      // a.t1.sort()
    (b->*tablePointer).sort();     // b->t1.sort()
    tablePointer = &X::t2;
    (a.*tablePointer).sort();      // a.t2.sort()
    (b->*tablePointer).sort();     // b->t2.sort()
    return 0;
}
```

How, then, might we code the electrical circuit model? Figure 2-8 shows a class used to characterize the response of an RLC circuit. Parameters to the class constructor include the values of the resistor (r), inductor (l), and capacitor (c), as well as the initial current flow in the circuit. We can create an object of this class, and then invoke the current member function with a time parameter to see the value of the current flow at any point in time.

However, the "member function" current is not a function at all, but a function pointer set up by the constructor. The constructor makes a decision about which response function to use based on the parameters supplied for the circuit, and arranges for current to point to the right function. Here is the code for the constructor, which initializes the current function pointer:

```
SeriesRLCStepResponse::SeriesRLCStepResponse(
    double r, double l, double c, double initialCurrent) {
    R = r; L = l; C = c; currentT0 = initialCurrent;
    alpha = R / (L + L);
    omegad = sqrt(frequency()*frequency() - alpha*alpha);
    . . . . calculation of a1, b1, a2, b2, etc . . . .
    if (alpha < frequency()) {
        current =
            &SeriesRLCStepResponse::underDampedResponse;
    } else if (alpha > frequency()) {
        current =
            &SeriesRLCStepResponse::overDampedResponse;
    } else {
        current =
            &SeriesRLCStepResponse::criticallyDampedResponse;
    }
}
```

And here is a simple application using the RLC circuit class:

```
int main()
{
    double R, L, C, I0;
    cin >> R >> L >> C >> I0;
    SeriesRLCStepResponse aFilter(R, L, C, I0);
    for(time t = 1.0; t < 100; t += 1.0) {
        cout << (aFilter.*(aFilter.current))(t) << endl;
    }
    return 0;
}
```

Often in C++, what can be done with function pointers can be done more elegantly in other ways. Another way of handling the above example is by using objects called *functors*, where each function is replaced by an object. That technique relies on

```
#include <complex.h>
typedef double time;

class SeriesRLCStepResponse {
public:
    complex (SeriesRLCStepResponse::*current)(time t);
    SeriesRLCStepResponse(double r, double l,
        double c, double initialCurrent);
    double frequency() const { return 1.0 / sqrt(L * C); }
private:
    complex underDampedResponse(time t) {
        return exp(-alpha * t) * (b1 * cos(omegad * t) +
            b2 * sin(omegad * t));
    }
    complex overDampedResponse(time t) {
        return a1 * exp(s1 * t) + a2 * exp(s2 * t);
    }
    complex criticallyDampedResponse(time t) {
        return exp(-alpha * t) * (a1 * t + a2);
    }
    double R, L, C, currentT0, alpha;
    complex omegad, a1, b1, a2, b2, s1, s2;
};
```

Figure 2-8. Class Characterizing the Response of a Resonant System

virtual functions, and will be described in detail, using this same example, in Section 5.6.

2.11 Program Organization Conventions

Years of C++ programming experience have resulted in some coding and program organization conventions that have been solidified by Kirslis [1] and others. Most of these are "obvious" and straightforward, but it is useful to cover them once again here for uniformity's sake.

Class *declarations* are usually kept in a header file. A header file is a C++ source file whose name has a .h suffix. The file has an obvious name; for a Stack class, the file would be called Stack.h. The term "declaration" here implies those things that are of interest to a *user* of a class, not just to the person who is implementing the class. The class implementation's source is kept mostly in C++ source files having a .c suffix (for example, Stack.c).

Class declarations are ordered so the `public` part comes first (it is important and the part most people care about), followed by the `protected` and finally the `private` sections of the class interface. Inline functions are generally broken out from the interface but kept in a header file, after their class declaration, using the `inline` keyword. Separating the inline function bodies from their declaration unclutters the class interface. For an optimal separation, inline function definitions can be put in their own header file, which is `#included` either from the bottom of the class header file, or from the application code. This organization also makes it easier to change an existing non-inline function into an inline, or vice versa. The whole header file is encased in some conditional compilation directives that help administer nested `#includes`:

```
// Stack.h version 1.4

#ifndef _STACK_H
#define _STACK_H 1
class Stack {
public:
    Stack();       // one constructor
    Stack(int);    // another constructor
    ~Stack();      // destructor
    long top() const;
    long pop();
    void push(long);
private:
    long *items;
    int sp;
};

inline void Stack::push(long i) {
    items[++sp] = i;
}
#endif _STACK_H
```

Exercises

1. Using the C++ template facility, rewrite the `Stack` example so it can be used to create stacks of any type.

2. Augment the St ack class so that when you say

    ```
    #include <stdio.h>
    . . . .
    Stack interactiveStack = stdin;
    ```

    a Stack will be created, taking its elements from the stream *stdin* (or any stream thus specified) until an end-of-file is reached.

3. The UNIX open routine takes a const char* argument that specifies the name of the file to open. Sketch out how you would create header file declarations and code for a library, so that you could do any of the following:

    ```
    String group("/etc/group");
    FILE *f = fopen("input", "r");
    int fd1 = open("/etc/passwd", O_RDONLY);
    int fd2 = open(group, O_RDONLY);
    int fd3 = open("outfile", O_CREAT, 0640);
    int fd4 = open(fd2, O_NDELAY);
            // (hint: fcntl(2), fcntl(5))
    int fd5 = open(f, O_RDONLY);
    ```

4. The Curses package [2] is a portable simple window system used by UNIX editors and game programs. Look at the Curses manual page for your local installation. Change the struct (it might be called _win_st or WINDOW) into a class, complete with declarations for member functions like addch, getch, addstr, getstr, move, clear, erase, etc.

5. Complete the preceding exercise to make an operational Window class. The member functions can invoke Curses functions to get their work done.

6. Using preprocessor macros, we can define what is effectively an inline function that will add a ".c" suffix to an instance of a String abstract data type:

    ```
    // + has been defined as a string catenation operator
    #define addsuf(s) (s + ".c")
    ```

    (a) Define a C++ inline function to do the same thing.

    (b) Write a small C++ program to use both approaches.

    (c) To that program, add a second call to the macro version and observe the number of bytes of growth in program size.

(d)   Replace the second macro invocation by a (second) invocation of the inline function, noting the new size of the program. Explain the difference between the two size increases.

7.   Can a constructor tell if it is being invoked via a new operator, or on an object whose space has been preallocated? Why or why not?

8.   Write an efficient stack class without fixed bounds on the size of the stack.

☐

References

1. Kirslis Peter A., "A Style for Writing C++ Classes," *Proceedings of the USENIX C++ Workshop*. Santa Fe: USENIX Association Publishers (November 1987).

2. Strang, John. *Programming with Curses*. Newton, Mass.: Reilly and Associates, 1986.

3

Concrete Data Types

Concrete data types are types that you as a programmer can create. You can define the data representation of these types in terms of primitive C types, and in terms of other abstract or concrete data types you have created. You can define your own operators on those types—what their names are, and how they behave. You can even redefine what it means to apply C operators like +, −, *, and / on those types. In short, the types you create are as concrete as the built-in C types int, char, double, and so forth.

Concrete data types should be distinguished from the class implementations described in the previous chapter in that concrete types are well behaved anywhere a built-in C type (like **int**) is well behaved. Concrete data types follow a specific form using class members to augment the C++ compiler's type system so the compiler can generate efficient and safe code for arbitrarily complex abstractions. We will call this form the *orthodox canonical class form*—"canonical" meaning it gives a framework of rules for the compiler to follow in code generation, and "orthodox" meaning that it is the form most directly understood and supported by the language itself. This is the preferred way of doing things in C++; it gives the programmer a high degree of flexibility and helps eliminate surprises. ADTs can be implemented without the full baggage of the canonical class form and used in limited applications; however, this baggage comes fairly cheaply, and it is usually worth the investment to use them in all but the most trivial cases.

This chapter starts by introducing the orthodox canonical form itself. It then describes C++ data hiding facilities that support information hiding inside classes. Overloading, which is necessary to most canonical forms and useful when building classes like complex number types, is described next. A user must specify how objects of existing types can be converted automatically into objects of a new class, and Section 3.1 describes how to specify such type conversions.

The remainder of the chapter discusses three important aspects of dynamic memory management, which is a key issue in most object-based programs. Idioms to reduce the cost of copying objects, using reference counting, will be introduced. The language facilities for taking control of system memory allocation and deallocation algorithms and data structures are described next. Lastly, the relationship between object creation, and object initialization, are explored, with examples of how to treat them as separate events.

3.1 The Orthodox Canonical Class Form

The orthodox canonical class form is one of the most important C++ idioms, and is a common theme that underlies much else presented in this book. If you follow this "recipe" in formulating your classes, then the variables created from your classes can be assigned, declared, and passed as arguments just like any C variable.

Let's say you want to create a class `String` providing straightforward operations like `length`, catenation, and so forth. You would, of course, define a new class with member functions for the operations on `String`, but the interface needs more than the string-specific operations to make it act as a full-fledged data type. *By convention*, its interface should be made from a pattern like the one in Figure 3-1. This `String` is intended to provide a data abstraction that hides the details of the C language representation of strings—that is, `char*`. The C string is "buried" in the private data of the class; it is directly accessed only by the class operators and member functions. Let's examine these member functions one by one to see how they should be implemented.

`String()`:

> This constructor initializes `String` objects to default values when no initialization context is provided. It is called the *default constructor*, or sometimes the *void constructor*. For `String`, the default action is likely to create a null (empty) string. (If this were a class like `ComplexNumber`, it would set the value to zero, etc.) The code is straightforward:
>
> ```
> String::String() {
>     rep = new char[1];
>     rep[0] = '\0';
> }
> ```
>
> This is the constructor that the compiler calls automatically to initialize members of a vector of objects. For example, this constructor

```
class String {
public:
    // the public user interface to a String:

    // redefine "+" to mean catenation, two cases:
    friend String operator+(const char*, const String&);
    String operator+(const String&) const;
    int length() const;        // length of string in characters
    . . . .                    // other interesting operations

    // boilerplate member functions:

    String();                  // default constructor
    String(const String&);     // constructor to initialize a new
                               //    string from an existing one
    String& operator=(const String&);   // assignment
    ~String();                 // destructor

    /*
     * These operators are typical of the kinds of customized
     * behaviors a user can define for a type.  These are
     * examples suitable for a String class.
     */

    String(const char *);      // initialize from a "C string"
private:
    char *rep;                 // implementation data and
                               //    internal functions
                               //    (here, represent internals
                               //    as a good old C string)

};
```

Figure 3-1. A String Using the Orthodox Canonical Form Idiom

initializes each member of the following vector:

```
String stringVec[10];    // each initialized
                         // with String::String()
```

If the user defines no constructors for a class, then the compiler will provide the default constructor on the programmer's behalf. That constructor will arrange to call the default constructor of all class members that are themselves class objects. (In the case of this String example, there are no such members.) However, if the compiler provides the code for the default constructor, then members without default constructors will be uninitialized (see Section 2.3, page 16).

```
String(const String&):
```

Given a `String` that has already been built (and possibly modified), this constructor should build an exact copy of it. The parameter is a *reference* to a `String`; here, that just means that this function has the actual object to work with (i.e., instead of just being given a pointer to it or a copy of it).

```
String::String(const String& s) {
    // leave room for '\0'
    rep = new char[s.length() + 1];
    // copy the old one's data into the new one
    ::strcpy(rep, s.rep);
}
```

(The invocation `::strcpy` means to invoke the function of that name that appears at the outermost (global) scope.) In general, this constructor has to copy *every* data item of the existing object into its corresponding place in the new one. We will call it the *copy constructor*, meaning it initializes an object by copying from a similar one. The term is slightly misleading, because it is often implemented to do a logical copy or so-called ''shallow copy'' of an object. (*Shallow copy* means to copy an object without physically copying objects referred to by the one being copied, while *deep copy* means to recursively copy lower level objects referred to by the object being copied.) The copy made by this constructor need not be a *physical* copy: it could be a logical copy but should behave externally as though it were a physical copy. This is useful for memory sharing and management strategies described later in this chapter. A more precise description for this constructor might be that it creates ''logical clones'' from existing objects, but the term ''copy constructor'' has come into common use.

A call to this constructor is generated by the C++ compiler when a `String` is passed by value as a parameter, and sometimes when one is returned as a value.

```
String& operator=(const String&):
```

The assignment operator is much like the copy constructor, with two minor exceptions. First, it has a return value—the constructor did not. If a member function is not a constructor, it must supply a return value if the caller is expecting one. It turns out that the most suitable type returned by an assignment operator is a *reference* to the current type, to save the overhead of creating an intermediate, temporary object. (Appendix D contains further discussion on the assignment operator.)

Second, because this object's contents are being replaced by some new contents (which is what assignment means), this function has the responsibility of getting rid of the old ones. The assignment operator must explicitly clean up any memory that it relinquishes a reference to while making way for a new value. Because the canonical form is being used, it is *guaranteed* that a constructor was called before operator=, given that all constructors do their job and suitably initialize rep. Therefore you *know* it is legal to clean up the old rep during assignment.

```
String& String::operator=(const String& s) {
    if (rep != s.rep) {  // special check for a = a
        // blow away the old rep:  square brackets
        //    tell compiler that a vector is being
        //    deleted
        delete[] rep;

        // just like String::String(const String&)
        int lengthOfOriginal = s.length() + 1;
        rep = new char[lengthOfOriginal];
        ::strcpy(rep, s.rep);
    }

    // have to return the result, too, which the
    // constructor didn't.  The result is a
    // reference to the object.
    return *this;
}
```

The variable this is the internal variable used by the compiler to point to the "current" object. The compiler provides it automatically for you, and it need not be (nor can it be) declared. The variable this is so special that it is a C++ reserved word that cannot be used as an ordinary variable name. Its type is a constant pointer to an object of some class— in particular, the class containing the member function. You should never try to assign to the variable this.

Note that redefining the semantics of assignment is a form of *overloading*: we are giving the assignment operator a meaning for Strings that is different from its meaning for other types. The default meaning of class object assignment is member-by-member assignment of the pieces of the object on the right-hand side into the corresponding pieces on the left-hand side of the assignment operator. What we do here is "catch" the assignment operator and take control away from the compiler, and redefine what assignment means. We can give assignment different meanings in different contexts. Programmers are responsible for preserving the intuitive meaning of assignment in the code they write; there is nothing in the language or compiler that will force you to do what makes sense!

To read why bitwise copy does not work—and why even member-by-member copy (as in the current version of C++—that is, Release 2.0 and later) does not always work without some help—see Appendix D.

The declaration of `operator=` causes it to return a reference to the type of which it is a member. This means that the expression *a* = *b* can itself be used on the left-hand side of (another) assignment. Such expressions are called *l-values*. This has the unfortunate side effect of making the following expression legal:

```
String a, b, c;
(a = b) = c;
```

The semantics of such a statement are confusing at best, and we may want to enforce against its use. An alternative form of assignment might be

```
const String& String::operator=(const String& s) {
    . . . .
}
```

The first `const` modifier prevents the result of the expression evaluation from further modification by other member functions, making the left-associative assignment illegal. This does come with the slight penalty of making potentially useful constructs such as

```
(a = b).put('c');
```

illegal.

`~String():`

The destructor must clean up any of the resources the object acquired through the execution of its constructors, or through the execution of any of its member functions along the way. Other member functions of `String` may have to keep track of other dynamically allocated resources in `String`'s member data so the destructor can find them and free them as appropriate. Here, the only dynamically allocated data item is the C string pointed to by `rep`. Again, because we are using the canonical form, we know that a constructor must have been called in order for the destructor to have been called, so we know `rep` does point to a string on the heap. The code is simple:

```
String::~String() {
    delete[] rep;
}
```

Note that destructors never take arguments. Any single class has at most one destructor.

String(const char*):

This constructor just creates a `String` from a C string. It is a constructor specific to `String`, and most types will have their own custom constructors to initialize instances from some context provided by the programmer. Constructors may have multiple arguments. A class may have several constructors with different argument combinations; the correct one is automatically chosen from context by the compiler. The code for this constructor is simple:

```
String::String(const char *s) {
    int lengthOfOriginal = ::strlen(s) + 1;
    rep = new char[lengthOfOriginal];
    ::strcpy(rep, s);
}
```

This is not part of the orthodox canonical form per se, but it is an ordinary user-supplied constructor whose semantics relate to the application. In addition to being a constructor to initialize a `String`, it is also a conversion operator that defines how to build a `String`, when a character pointer is provided where a `String` object is expected:

```
extern int hash(String);
    . . . .
hash("character literal");
        // String::String(const char*) is
        //     automatically called (and maybe
        //     String::String(const String&))
```

length():

The `length` operator is also specific to `String` and is simple to write:

```
int String::length() const {
    return ::strlen( rep );
}
```

This is not part of the orthodox canonical form per se, but it is an ordinary member function whose semantics relate to the application.

This `String` example describes an idiom, or pattern, to be followed in implementing any class. This form, for some class X, is characterized by the presence of the following:

- A default constructor (`X::X()`)

- A copy constructor (`X::X(const X&)`)

- An assignment operator (`X& operator=(const X&)`)

- A destructor (`X::~X()`)

☞ *When to use this idiom*: In general, you *must* use the orthodox canonical form if:

- You want to support assignment of objects of the class, or want to pass those objects as call-by-value parameters to a function, *and*

- The object contains pointers to objects that are reference-counted, or the class destructor performs a `delete` on a data member of the object.

You *should* use the orthodox canonical form for any nontrivial class in a program, for the sake of uniformity across classes and to manage the increasing complexity of each class over the course of program evolution.

Additional idioms later in this book build on the orthodox canonical form, and those idioms should be used if that is what the application suggests.

Pointers are common in object-oriented C++ programs, and most classes will meet the above criteria. For the sake of uniformity, most nontrivial classes should follow the orthodox canonical form. A "trivial" class in this context is one used as a C `struct` is used, for data aggregation (though it may contain member functions as a notational convenience). If member functions are used to control access to the data of a class, and if those data include pointers, it is a rule of thumb to use the orthodox canonical form.

Some departures from the canonical form can be used to invalidate selected default behaviors. Making the default constructor `private` makes it impossible to create instances of the class without providing a parameter designating a specific constructor. Copying does not make sense for some classes. For example, an object whose members are memory-mapped I/O registers in a microprocessor should not be copied and cannot be moved. It may not make sense to copy a graphics system's `Window` object. If it were legal to copy a `Window` object, it could be passed to a function by value, and every function call with a value `Window` parameter would cause a new `Window` to appear on the screen! Making those classes' `operator=` and copy constructor `private` guards against copying objects of those classes.

One category of classes commonly used in object-oriented designs is *container classes*, object types designed to hold collections of other objects. Examples of container classes include Sets, Lists, Queues, Dictionaries, Bags, and Stacks. Container classes should use this form or a variant thereof.

The orthodox canonical form underlies most concrete data types. Other canonical forms described later in the book build on this one.

3.2 Scoping and Access Control

A class can control accessibility of its members to functions other than its own member functions. This will be called "horizontal access control" by convention, evoking the image of a class controlling access to its members by its peers and neighbors. This is to be contrasted with "vertical access control," which pertains to access between base classes and derived classes. Proper horizontal access control management enforces encapsulation, guaranteeing that a class will be used in a semantically reasonable and consistent way by its clients. It also helps support abstraction, a notion important to the successful application of a user-defined type in a complex system. Later chapters in the book, particularly Chapters 5 and 6, will examine the interaction between access control, inheritance, and object-oriented programming.

Note that class `String` (Figure 3-1) has two labels in it, one `private` and the other `public`. Anything that follows a "`public:`" label (up to the following label) can be directly accessed from any C++ function. If a function has a pointer to a `String`, then it can use that pointer to call any of the functions, or access any of the data, that are labeled `public`.

A `private` member (one following a "`private:`" label) can only be accessed by a member function of its class. No private member can be directly accessed outside the class. There is one exception to this rule: the `friend` mechanism, which allows other functions to violate a class's encapsulation. A declaration of the form

```
friend class George;
```

empowers all member functions of class `George` to access the `private` and `protected` members of the class in which the declaration resides. For example,

```
class Sue {
    friend class George;
public:
    . . . .
};
```

declares that `George` is viewed by `Sue` as a `friend`, though it says nothing about how `George` views `Sue`. `George` is allowed to circumvent `Sue`'s encapsulation. A declaration of the form

```
friend Sally::peek(int);
```

is more selective; it gives only the named member function of class `Sally` access to the current class's private members.

Private member functions are useful for hiding algorithms peculiar to a class's implementation that are not published as part of the class interface.

Member functions can access any member of their own class, `private` or `public`. Protected members of a base class can be accessed by a member of a derived class only when they form part of a derived class object and are accessed as such.

By default, a `struct` behaves just like a `class` with all its members `public`:

C code:	C++ code:
```struct Stack { . . . . };```	```class Stack { public: . . . . };```

However, a `struct` may also designate protection for its members:

---

struct code: **class code:**

```
                                                class Stack {
struct Stack {                                  public:
    void push(int);                                 void push(int);
    int pop();                                      int pop();
    int top() const;                                int top() const;
private:                                        private:
    int rep[100];                                   int rep[100];
};                                              };
```

While a private datum is accessible to the member functions of its enclosing class, both for reading and writing, member function access can restrict outside users of the class to just reading it. For example, we may want to make a `String`'s representation available for use in a C language context (Figure 3-2). This is more efficient than creating a copy of `String`'s internal data for use outside the class. But it is also dangerous if abused as a sneak path to change `String`'s internal state.

Here is a syntactic alternative based on references:

```
class String {
public:
    . . . .
    String(const char *s): C_rep(rep) {
        rep = new char[::strlen(s) + 1];
        ::strcpy(rep, s);
    }
    const char* &C_rep;
    . . . .
private:
    char *rep;
};
```

```
class String {
public:
    String();                  // default constructor
    String(const String&); // copy constructor
    String& operator=(const String&);  // assignment
    ~String();                 // destructor
    String(const char*);    // create a String from a "C string"
    String operator+(const String&) const;
                               // redefine "+" to mean catenation
    int length() const;     // length of string in characters
    const char *const C_rep() {
        return (const char *const)rep;
    }
private:
    char *rep;
};

int main() {
    String s;
    . . . .
    printf("string is %s\n", s.C_rep());
}
```

Figure 3-2. A Class Publishing Its Internal Data

3.3 Overloading: Redefining the Semantics of Operators and Functions

We have shown how to take control of the assignment operator while preserving the high level semantics of assignment. We can also do this with most of the other C operators. Redefining what operators mean, called *operator overloading*, is important for user-defined types: We characterize types in terms of the operations on them. Consider the operators of the C language, and the types it supports—that is, the arithmetic types, with operations like +, −, *, and /. For convenience and clarity, we certainly want control over how these operators deal with operand objects from a user-defined Complex, Vector, or Matrix class. One advantage of C++ over C is the transparency of user-defined types such as Complex; they can be used just like ints and doubles. In C, even typedef does not really create a new type, because it does not affect how operators (for example, + and −) work. C++ has the power to do this, partly through concrete data types as described in this chapter, and partly through operator overloading.

There are other potential uses for overloading as well—less obvious than the arithmetic types example, but useful nonetheless. For example, we have designed this

String class to have a + operator, with the intended semantics of string catenation. So, the code on the left is interpreted the same as the code on the right (both are valid C++ given the declarations of Figure 3-2):

```
int main() {                          int main() {
    String a, b("this is b");             String a, b("this is b");
    String c("!");                        String c("!");
    a = b + c;                            a = b.operator+(c);
}                                     }
```

Because we can define operator+ to do whatever we want, we can define it to do catenation when applied to Strings. Here is the code:

```
String String::operator+(const String& s) const
{
    char *buf = new char[s.length() + length() + 1];
    ::strcpy(buf, rep);
    ::strcat(buf, s.rep);
    String retval( buf );
    delete[] buf;              // get rid of temporary storage
    return retval;
}
```

Notice that the function creates a new String on the fly; it actually calls String::String(const char*) to make a String object from buf, and that object becomes a local variable of operator+. Then, on return from operator+, a *copy* of that new object is returned to the function's caller; that copy is actually made with a call to String::String(const String&), the copy constructor.

There is some taste involved in using overloading. Overloading operator[] on a class that looks like a vector (below) is a reasonable thing to do; overloading operator= is necessary to the canonical form. Other uses, such as overloading arithmetic operators to have nonarithmetic semantics, have disputed usefulness. While they may help designers express their intent, they may also confuse casual readers of code. If these operators are idiomatically introduced for use in some context (e.g., operator+ on strings might mean catenation), limited use of these operators can be productive and improve flexibility. But they can also be abused (for some examples, see the exercises at the end of this chapter).

An Example: Overloading Subscripting

We can even overload such apparently unlikely operators as subscripting. Let's say that we want to be able to subscript Strings to pick individual characters out of them. After adding a declaration of the operator to the class declaration,

```
class String {
public:
    .  .  .  .
    char& operator[](int);
    .  .  .  .
};
```

we code the function itself. The code looks like this:

```
char& String::operator[](int index)
{
    return rep[index];
}
```

If we wish, this function can do range checking to make sure that index is positive and that it is less than length(). It can print an error message on a bounds error, and/or can return an EOF character if it detects this condition. Using these constructs, you can add error checking code to debug applications using Strings without having to change the application at all. The trouble-shooting code can be removed once the program is debugged; an even better idea is to leave it in the source and use #ifdefs to keep it from being compiled until it is needed again.

Because the return type of operator[] is declared to be a *reference* to character, it can be used on the left-hand side of an assignment. For more information on the details of references, see Appendix C.

You do not have to overload operator[] to take an integer argument; it can take arguments of any type, or it can be overloaded several times for several distinct types. If there are multiple declarations, the compiler will determine from context which one should be called. For example, we might overload subscripting to take a const char* parameter:

```
some_type operator[](const char *)     // associative array
```

This could be used as a member operator of a collection object such as a list or bag to retrieve an object by name. Or we could add such a member function to String to search for instances of indicated substrings.

As a more advanced example, consider overloading operator[] so the implementation can differentiate between its use as an *l*-value (left-hand side of an assignment) and its use to retrieve the value at a given index. We use a trick based on a version of operator[] that creates temporary return values of a dummy type. When the dummy object is created or appears in certain contexts (e.g., as the left-hand side of an assignment, or in a context where another type is expected), its own overloaded operators take control to yield the expected result. An example is shown in the File abstraction of Figure 3-3. When a File object is indexed in an *l*-value

```
class FileRef {
private:
    class File &f;
    char buf[1];
    unsigned long ix;
public:
    FileRef (File &ff, unsigned long i) : f (ff), ix (i) { }
    FileRef &operator=(char c);
    operator char ();
};

class File {
friend class FileRef;
public:
    File(const char *name) {
        fd = open(name, O_RDWR|O_CREAT, 0664);
    }
    ~File() { close(fd); }
    FileRef operator[] (unsigned long ix) {
        return FileRef(*this, ix);
    }
private:
    int fd;
};

FileRef& FileRef::operator=(char c) {
    lseek(f.fd, ix, 0); write(f.fd, &c, 1); return *this;
}

FileRef::operator char () {
    lseek(f.fd, ix, 0); read(f.fd, buf, 1); return buf[0];
}

int main() {
    File foo("foo");
    foo[5] = '5';
    foo[10] = '1';
    char c = foo[5];
    cout << "c = " << c << endl;
}
```

Figure 3-3. Overloading `operator[]` with Context Sensitivity

context, the specified byte of the file is overwritten. Otherwise, the specified byte of the file is fetched and returned as the value of the expression.

Invocation of operator[] on a File object yields a result of the hidden "dummy" type, FileRef. That object will either be assigned into as an *l*-value, or used for its value directly. Use of File::operator[] on the left-hand side evaluates to a FileRef object. Now with a FileRef object as a left-hand side, and a character as the right-hand side, FileRef::operator= is invoked where a write is done. When a File object is subscripted in any context where a character result is expected, the subscripting will again evaluate to an intermediate FileRef object and then will be converted to a char using FileRef::operator char. Code to read the file can be put in that conversion operator. Thus when the result of a subscripting operation is used as the target of assignment, a write is done; when it is used for its value, a read is issued.

Member Operator Overloading Versus Global Overloading

There are two kinds of overloading in C++: *member overloading* as shown in the above example, and *global overloading*, which is done at the outermost scope level. Assume that a and b are both declared as objects of class C. Class C has C::operator+(C) defined, so this is a case of member function overloading similar to the earlier example. In this program, a + b means a.operator+(b). In the alternative, we can *globally* overload the + operator:

```
C operator+(C,C) { . . . . }
```

This, too, applies to a + b, with a and b supplied as the first and second parameters to the function, respectively. Of these two forms, member overloading is preferred. Using this second form requires the use of friends; they take a bit away from the pleasing aesthetics of a self-contained class. The second form may be necessary to accommodate classes in an object code library, where the source cannot be modified and recompiled. Mixing the two forms should be avoided. If both forms are present for a given operator, with similar formal parameter types, then use of the operator can be ambiguous, perhaps fatally so.

However, one must use globally overloaded operators for symmetry, which is aesthetically pleasing in its own right. Consider the case of multiple, global, overloaded operator+ functions, all friends of class String:

```
class String {
friend String operator+(const char*, const String&);
friend String operator+(const String&, const char *);
public:
    . . . .
private:
    char *rep;
};

String operator+(const char* s, const String& S) {
    String retval;
    retval.rep = new char[::strlen(s) + S.length()];
    ::strcpy(retval.rep, s);
    ::strcat(retval.rep, S.rep);
    return retval;
}

String operator+(const String& S, const char *s) {
    String retval;
    retval.rep = new char[::strlen(s) + S.length()];
    ::strcpy(retval.rep, S.rep);
    ::strcat(retval.rep, s);
    return retval;
}
```

Using these declarations, both of the following "additions" work:

```
String s1;
"abcd" + s1;
s1 + "efgh";
```

It is impossible to make this work without global overloading. Because we cannot get "inside" the native C string type (viz. char*) to redefine its operations, we cannot support symmetry simply by defining class operators: the global friend function approach is necessary. When two consenting mature class types (as contrasted with indigenous types like int, char, etc.) want access to each others' private members, a friendship relationship can be arranged between those classes; a global friend function is usually not necessary. A friend conversion function may also be needed to smooth conversions between two classes where one class is in a library, and no source is available other than its class interface declaration. For example, we may want to change a `PathName` class so that the + operator could be used to add a `String` suffix. If `PathName` is in a library for which source is not available, global overloading must be used:

```
PathName operator+(const PathName &p, const String &s) {
    . . . .
}
```

3.4 Type Conversion

With additional constructors and operator definitions, we can give the compiler enough information to do automatic type conversion or promotion from context. For example, let's say that we want the following to work for the sake of uniformity:

```
#include <String.h>

extern "C" int strlen(const char *);

int main() {
    String s("1234");
    int j = ::strlen(s);        // same as j = s.length();
    . . . .
}
```

To make this work, we need to tell the compiler how to create a "primitive" (nonclass) type out of a type we have created. This can be done by using *operator* specifications. Here, we want the compiler to automatically convert a `String` into a `char*`, so we define an operator on `String` to do so:

```
class String {
public:
    operator const char*() const { return rep; }
    . . . .
};
```

(The first `const` states that memory pointed to by the return value should not be modified by code outside the class, and the second `const` says this member function does not alter the contents of the `String` object operated on.) Now, when the compiler sees a `String` in any context where a `const char*` makes sense, it will automatically call `String::operator const char*` to do the conversion. The operator just returns a pointer to an internal datum, which is already in the format that C language routines want. If conversion had been necessary, as much processing as needed can be put into the body of the operator. This is called the *member operator function* idiom.

As another example, let's say that whenever a `String` appears where an integer is expected, it decodes the string as though it were an ASCII representation of an integer and yields the result. The code might look like this:

```
class String {
public:
    . . . .
    operator int();
    . . . .
};

String::operator int()
{
    int retval;
    if (sscanf(rep, "%d", &retval) != 1) return 0;
    else return retval;
}
```

To elicit this function, the `String` must appear in a context where it can be interpreted as an integer. This can be done either implicitly (for example, by invoking the function in an actual parameter list where an `int` is expected) or explicitly, with a conversion:

```
#include "String.h"

int main()
{
    char buf[10];
    printf("enter number of bytes: ");
    scanf("%s\n", buf);
    String sbuf = buf;

    // explicit conversion to int:
    printf("read in value %d\n", int(sbuf));

    char *thing = new char[100];
    // explicit conversion to const char *const:
    ::strcpy(thing, (const char *const)sbuf);

    // implicit conversion to int:
    int charsLeftInThing = 100 - sbuf;
    . . . .
    return 0;
}
```

☞ *When to use this idiom*: Use this idiom only for conversion to built-in C types. If it is necessary to convert a `String` to some other class, such as a `ParseTree`, the conversion should be handled by `ParseTree`, not `String`.

To convert `Strings` to `ParseTrees`, a `ParseTree(const String&)` constructor should be added for class `ParseTree` when possible. `String` cannot know about every other class in the universe; classes that *care* about `String` should *worry* about it! For `ParseTree` to have free access to the `String` internals it needs for efficient conversion, a `friendship` relationship may be needed between the two classes. (For a simple class like `String`, this is not likely to be a problem, but it does come up in more involved data structures and types.)

Conversion operators should be introduced after due design consideration. Overly liberal use of conversion operators can cause combinatorial code explosion, and increases the risk of conversion ambiguities.

There may be exceptions to these rules of thumb; do what makes sense. Again, consider the example of providing a conversion from a `String` to a `ParseTree`. If `ParseTree` is provided in a library, with only object code and the header file containing its class declaration, then it may be awkward or impossible to make the changes inside class `ParseTree`. First, we may not know enough about `ParseTree` internals to express the conversion in terms of the private members of the class appearing in its declaration. This suggests that the conversion must be done in terms of the public interface of the class, so it might as well be done outside the class. Second, changing the interface of `ParseTree` without regenerating its library code may result in inconsistencies between "old" and "new" `ParseTree` code (generated from the two different interfaces). Lastly, making the change outside the class in terms of the class's public interface eases later transitions to new releases of the library for use by the same application code. We handle this conversion by modifying `String`:

```
#include "ParseTree.h"

class String {
public:
    . . . .
    operator ParseTree() { . . . . }
    . . . .
};
```

We already have seen how to convert some existing types into a `String`: One example is `String::String(const char*)` that builds a `String` from a

```
#include "Node.h"
class String {
public:
    . . . .
    String(Node);
    . . . .
private:
    . . . .
    String nodeWalk(const Node*);
};
String
String::nodeWalk(const Node *n) {        // infix node walk
    if (n == 0) return "";
    String retval = String("(") + nodeWalk(n->leftChild());
    retval = retval + " " + n->contents();
    retval = retval + " " + nodeWalk(n->rightChild()) + ")";
}

String::String(Node n)
{
    String temp = nodeWalk(&n);
    rep = new char[temp.length() + 1];
    ::strcpy(rep, temp.rep);
}
```

Figure 3-4. Constructor to Flatten a Node into a String

const char*. Additional constructors can be made to convert any type to a
String. For example, consider a class Node that represents an element in a binary
tree of character strings:

```
    class Node {
    public:
        Node();
        Node(const Node&);
        Node& operator=(const Node&);
        Node *leftChild() const;  // does not modify object
        Node *rightChild() const; // does not modify object
        char *contents() const;   // yields this node's contents
                                  // declared const because it
                                  // does not modify the object
    private:
        . . . .
    };
```

Figure 3-4 shows a constructor that flattens the tree under a Node into a parenthesized form. Another way of thinking about the constructor is that it knows how to make a String from a Node. It uses a helper function, nodeWalk, to traverse the tree.

3.5 Reference Counting: Making Variables Use "Magic Memory"

Compared to procedural programs, object-oriented programs more often bind their variables to objects allocated from the heap instead of to those statically declared as globals, automatics, or class members. This is largely because the lifetimes of object instances and their data are to the object paradigm as stack frames or activation records are to procedural programming. It is in objects that most data live, and their comings and goings should correspond to the lifetimes of the real-world entities they represent. Memory allocation and reclamation are important issues from this perspective. Because programmers have control over what happens to an object at the times it is created and destroyed, through constructors and destructors, they can introduce optimizations to improve the performance and memory utilization of individual classes.

One of the most common mechanisms is *representation sharing* and *reference counting*. This idiom can be generalized to any C++ class whose instances are copied. It is particularly useful for those classes that dynamically allocate memory. Consider the String class of the preceding section. Assignment causes the entire string to be replicated, almost doubling the memory requirements just to copy and store redundant information. We can add "smarts" to the class so that instead of making a copy, multiple variables share the same internal storage. The representation is itself an object, managing the shared data and an associated reference count. There are a number of different ways of doing this, and three variants will be presented here. The first is a general form that can be adopted for most abstractions. The second example shows how to defeat some inefficient memory copying introduced by the first approach. The last approach looks at how to automate some of the tedium for maintenance of such abstractions. Also, this section will show how to convert existing classes to use reference counting.

The Handle Class Idiom

The first technique is to encapsulate the original String (e.g., Figure 3-1) class in a containing class that acts principally as a storage manager. We call this class a *handle class* because it is used to access another class where the application intelligence lies.

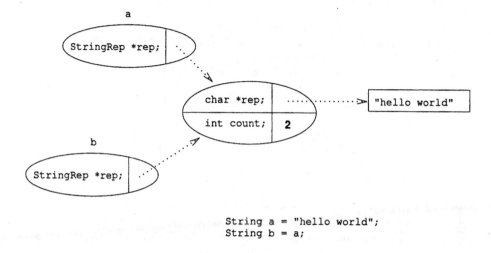

```
String a = "hello world";
String b = a;
```

Figure 3-5. Handle Class Strings with Reference Counting

The handle is viewed by the user as the actual class, but the work is done in the inner one. So we must do the following:

1. Rename class String to StringRep.
2. Add a reference count field to StringRep.
3. Create a class String that contains a pointer to a StringRep.
4. Arrange for String to forward most of its operations to StringRep, overseeing the sharing of representations when assignment is done.

Figure 3-5 shows what a new String looks like in memory. The String named a is initialized with the constant "hello world" and then b is assigned a's value. While a and b name separate String objects, both point to a shared representation containing most of the low-level data and intelligence for string operations. The representation carries a *reference count*, an integer telling how many String objects hold pointers to it. When the count goes to zero, the object can be freed.

Figure 3-6 shows the declaration of the new StringRep class. Its member functions are the same as they were for String before, except here they have been moved inline and made more concise. (These should be made inline in a given application only if performance analysis suggests that they should. For some applications, the size of the code generated may impose unacceptable costs.)

```
class StringRep {
friend String;
private:       // these are now accessible only to String
    StringRep()              { *(rep = new char[1]) = '\0'; }
    StringRep(const StringRep& s)  {
      ::strcpy(rep=new char[::strlen(s.rep)+1], s.rep);
    }
    StringRep& operator=(const StringRep& s) {
        if (rep != s.rep) {
          delete[] rep;
          ::strcpy(rep=new char[::strlen(s.rep)+1], s.rep);
        }
        return *this;
    }
    ~StringRep()             { delete[] rep; }
    StringRep(const char *s) {
        ::strcpy(rep=new char[::strlen(s)+1], s);
    }
    StringRep operator+(const StringRep&) const;
    int length() const     { return ::strlen(rep); }
private:
    char *rep;
    int count;
};

StringRep StringRep::operator+(const StringRep& s) const
{
    char *buf = new char[s.length() + length() + 1];
    ::strcpy(buf, rep);
    ::strcat(buf, s.rep);
    StringRep retval( buf );
    delete[] buf;            // get rid of temporary storage
    return retval;
}
```

Figure 3-6. A Class for a String's Representation

Now we need a new String class that uses StringRep to do all the string-related work, while handling much of the memory management itself; this class is shown in Figure 3-7.

Note that the "raw" constructors (those building a String from scratch—that is, not from another String) set the count field of the representation to one. Those operations that just copy another string (String(const String&) and operator=(const String&)) borrow the original's representation and increment its reference count. Anything that modifies or replaces the representation

```
class String {
public:
    String() {
        rep = new StringRep; rep->count=1;
    }
    String(const String& s) {
        rep = s.rep; rep->count++;
    }
    String& operator=(const String& s) {
        s.rep->count++;
        if (--rep->count <= 0) delete rep;
        rep = s.rep;  return *this;
    }
    ~String()               {
        if (--rep->count <= 0) delete rep;
    }
    String(const char *s) {
        rep = new StringRep(s);
        rep->count = 1;
    }
    String operator+(const String& s) const {
        StringRep y = *rep + *s.rep;
        return String(y.rep);
    }
    int length() const {
        return rep->length();
    }
private:
    StringRep *rep;
};
```

Figure 3-7. The `String` Interface to `StringRep`

must decrement the current representation's count and return it to free store if its count is nonpositive.

One advantage of this approach is that it leaves all the knowledge of "string-ness" in the internal class, leaving the outer class to deal largely with memory management. That means, for example, that this would be a good approach to convert an existing class to use reference counting. However, it can introduce some serious inefficiencies; for example, `operator+` does much redundant work in the interest of expressive simplicity. In this code, an invocation of `operator+` causes three heap allocations and may create some additional temporary objects on the stack. How to improve on this will be discussed in the following section.

We call `String` the *handle* class and `StringRep` the *body* manipulated by the handle. Use of two (or potentially more) classes where an instance of one serves as a manager for instances of the other is called the *handle/body class idiom.*

☞ *When to use this idiom*: The handle/body class idiom may be used to decompose a complex abstraction into smaller, more manageable classes. The idiom may reflect the sharing of a single resource by multiple classes that control access to it. Its most common use is for reference counting (see below).

The most common case of the handle/body class idiom is for reference counting, as it is with the `String` example. When the body class contains a reference count manipulated by the handle class, such use is called the *reference counting idiom.*

☞ *When to use this idiom*: Use reference counted objects for classes whose instances are often copied through assignment or parameter passing, particularly if the objects are so large or complex that copying is expensive. Use it when multiple logical copies of an object may exist, though the data themselves may not be copied—for example, a computer screen object that is to be passed between functions, or memory locations shared between processors, where each user wishes to hold their own copy of an object for access to that resource.

A More Conservative Method

The second approach starts from the ground up (more or less). It is "conservative" of real time and frugal with overhead. The `String` class accessed directly by the user is modeled after the original of Figure 3-1. Its representation (Figure 3-8) is expanded to include a count field as before and is accessed through one more level of indirection. The count and data pointer are grouped in a simple class with a single simple constructor and one simple destructor.

We can put in some "back doors" to save a copy for invocations of `String`'s `operator+(const String&)` member function. We create a new constructor that takes a reference to a character pointer as its argument; i.e., the pointer is passed in by reference, and the constructor takes over its value and nulls out the original (Figure 3-9).

```
class StringRep {
friend String;
private:
    StringRep(const char *s) {
        ::strcpy(rep = new char[::strlen(s)+1], s);
        count = 1;
    }
    ~StringRep() { delete[] rep; }
private:
    char *rep;
    int count;
};

class String {
public:
    String()                        { rep = new StringRep(""); }
    String(const String& s)         { rep = s.rep; rep->count++; }
    String& operator=(const String& s) {
        s.rep->count++;
        if (--rep->count <= 0) delete rep;
        rep = s.rep;
        return *this;
    }
    ~String() {
        if (--rep->count <= 0) delete rep;
    }
    String(const char *s)           { rep = new StringRep(s); }
    String operator+(const String&) const;
    int length() const              { return ::strlen(rep->rep); }
private:
    StringRep *rep;
};

String String::operator+(const String& s) const
{
    char *buf = new char[s.length() + length() + 1];
    ::strcpy(buf, rep->rep);
    ::strcat(buf, s.rep->rep);
    String retval( buf );
    delete[] buf;            // get rid of temporary storage
    return retval;
}
```

Figure 3-8. A More Efficient String Implementation

```
#include <string.h>
class StringRep {
friend String;
private:    // private so it does not pollute global name space
    typedef char *Char_p;
    StringRep(StringRep::Char_p* const r) {
        rep = *r; *r = 0; count = 1;
    }
public:
    StringRep(const char *s)
        { ::strcpy(rep = new char[::strlen(s)+1], s); count = 1; }
    ~StringRep() { delete[] rep; }
private:
    char *rep;
    int count;
};
class String {
public:
    String()                   { rep = new StringRep(""); }
    String(const String& s) { rep = s.rep; rep->count++; }
    String& operator=(const String& s) {
        s.rep->count++;  if (--rep->count <= 0) delete rep;
        rep = s.rep;
        return *this;
    }
    ~String() { if (--rep->count <= 0) delete rep; }
    String(const char *s)   { rep = new StringRep(s); }
    String operator+(const String&) const;
    int length() const      { return ::strlen(rep->rep); }
private:
    String(StringRep::Char_p* const r) {
        rep = new StringRep(r);  // call new constructor
    }
    StringRep *rep;
};
String String::operator+(const String& s) const
{
    char *buf = new char[s.length() + length() + 1];
    ::strcpy(buf, rep->rep);
    ::strcat(buf, s.rep->rep);
    String retval( &buf );  // call the new private constructor
    return retval;
}
```

Figure 3-9. Some Tricks to Optimize Catenation

Here, the code in `String`'s `operator+(const String&)` takes advantage of the special hook provided through the `StringRep` constructor `StringRep(Char_p* const)`, which is accessible because of the `friendship` relationship between the two classes. The two functions enter into an agreement whereby `String::operator+(const String&)` allocates the memory to hold the characters, a pointer to which is passed to the `String` constructor `String(const Char_p*)`, which then turns it over to the special `StringRep::StringRep(Char_p* const)` constructor which retains the pointer. The special `StringRep` constructor causes the original pointer in `operator+` (`buf`) to be zeroed out to ensure that no dangling references to the storage remain. All these provisions together avoid copying the string representation when building the `retval` object in `String::operator+`.

Counted Pointers

The counted pointers technique differs significantly from the preceding two approaches. This idiom came from work exploring general garbage collection techniques for C++. The idea is to make pointers into real objects. Every time a pointer is copied, its `operator=` or copy constructor is called, so the number of outstanding references to an object is tracked in a single representation object shared by multiple counted pointers. When a pointer goes out of scope, its destructor is called and the reference count is accordingly decremented. When the count goes to zero, the block is recovered, either on-the-spot, or by a scavenging routine (the former is done here.) The only trick is to take control of invocations of the –> operator on an object using operator overloading.

Overloaded `operator->` works differently from other overloaded C++ operators. For all other operators, the body defining the operator's implementation has final control over the value returned from the operation. For `operator->`, the return value is an intermediate result to which the base semantics of –> are then applied, yielding a result. So,

```
class A {
public:
    B *operator->();
};

. . . .
int main() {
    A a;
    . . . . a->b . . . .
}
```

means the following:

1. Invoke A::operator->() on object a;
2. Capture the return value from that invocation in a temporary, x, of type B*;
3. Evaluate x->b, yielding its result.

Here, b could be replaced by any member—data or function—of class B (not shown). If class B overloads operator->, then the above three steps are applied again.

Not only does this approach yield the advantages of the previous reference counting technique, but it has some further possibilities as well. Consider a program where counted pointers are the only kinds of class objects. (The term *class object* as used here means an object whose type is some class type; there are other objects as well, of types int, char, vectors, and other indigenous C types that are found in any C++ program.) First, counted pointers bring all the advantages of concrete data types: They can be passed as parameters, assigned, created, destroyed, etc. Second, they bring properties normally associated with pointers, such as addressing objects dynamically allocated from the heap. However, the objects are instantiated without using new and they are deallocated automatically without delete being invoked; that is, they have the same allocation behavior that we expect from automatic and static instances of class objects. For example, if String is implemented as a counted pointer (see below), and a String is embedded in class A, as follows,

```
class A {
public:
    A() : s("hello world")  { }
private:
    String s;
};
```

then every object created of class A will contain a counted String pointer, s, initialized to give the appearance of pointing to a String whose contents are "hello world". Copies of an object of class A have the appearance of containing a pointer to the same String as the original: We think of copying s as copying a pointer. However, it still has all the properties of a real reference-counted object. For example, changing its value causes its representation to become unshared. In other words, counted pointers act like pointers that have constructors, so they are initialized automatically to point to a newly allocated object when they come into scope.

Figure 3-10 shows how StringRep is implemented for a counted pointer. It is based on the previous example, but the processing of catenation has migrated from String to StringRep, closer to the information it manipulates. Also, a constructor to make a StringRep from a const char*, and a print operator, have been added for convenience.

```
class StringRep {
friend String;
private:
    StringRep()              { *(rep = new char[1]) = '\0'; }
    StringRep(const StringRep& s) {
        ::strcpy(rep=new char[::strlen(s.rep)+1], s.rep);
    }
    ~StringRep()             { delete[] rep; }
    StringRep(const char *s) {
        ::strcpy(rep=new char[::strlen(s)+1], s);
    }
    String operator+(const String& s) const {
        char *buf = new char[s->length() + length() + 1];
        ::strcpy(buf, rep);
        ::strcat(buf, s->rep);
        String retval( &buf );
        return retval;
    }
    int length() const       { return ::strlen(rep); }
    void print() const       { ::printf("%s\n", rep); }
private:
    StringRep(char ** const r) {
        rep = *r; *r = 0; count = 1;
    }
    char *rep;
    int count;
};
```

Figure 3-10. The "Inner Implementation" of a Counted String Pointer

Figure 3-11 depicts String, now devoid of an explicit length operation; any invocation of a length operation on a String is forwarded to the StringRep by operator->. The same is true for other member functions that might exist: strchr (search for character in string), hash, etc. Class String continues to do most of the memory management work and handling of the reference count inside the StringRep instance. Figure 3-10 shows an implementation of the catenation operator StringRep::operator+. It is expressed principally in terms of StringRep members, which saves a level of data indirection over the implementation of Figure 3-9. Because String forwards operator+ invocations to StringRep, this approach incurs the cost of an additional function call for each invocation of operator+. The cost can usually be optimized away using inline function expansion.

```
class String {
friend class StringRep;
public:
    String operator+(const String &s) const { return *p + s; }
    StringRep* operator->() const   { return p; }
    String() {
        (p = new StringRep())->count = 1;
    }
    String(const String& s)  { (p = s.p)->count++; }
    String(const char *s) {
        (p = new StringRep(s))->count = 1;
    }
    String operator=(const String& q) {
        // a little different this time for variety's sake
        if (--p->count <= 0 && p != q.p) delete p;
        (p=q.p)->count++; return *this;
    }
    ~String()          { if (--p->count<=0) delete p; }
private:
    String(char** r) {
        p = new StringRep(r);
    }
    StringRep *p;
};
```

Figure 3-11. The Public Interface of a Counted String Pointer

Now, instead of using a `String` as an instance, we use it like a pointer. (`String` is a class whose only representation is a pointer—think of it as a pointer with operators.) In fact, we now reference `Strings` *only* through these pointers. The only thing that is a little strange is that they do not appear to be declared as pointers:

```
int main()
{
    String a("abcd"), b("efgh");
    printf("a is "); a->print();
    printf("b is "); b->print();
    printf("length of b is %d\n", b->length());
    printf("catenation is "); (a+b)->print();
    return 0;
}
```

One advantage of counted pointers is that new member functions need to be added only to the body class. For example, most new string operations can be implemented as `StringRep` member functions: the handle class `String` gets these operations automatically through its `operator->`.

☞ *When to use this idiom*: Use counted pointers for relief from the burden of manually disposing of dynamically allocated memory. They can also be used when prototyping to relieve the burden of duplicating changes to the signature of a body class in its handle class. Use of counted pointers is determined largely by style and taste, though it is an important component of the symbolic idioms presented in Chapter 9.

Adding Reference Counting to Existing Classes

An existing class may be a good candidate for performance improvement by making it reference counted. A variety of obstacles can make this difficult: lack of access to source files, constraints on the size or layout of the class that would be upset by the addition of a count field, the need to use reference counting only part of the time, among other obstacles. For such classes, an additional level of handle class can be applied. Assume that class `Stack` already existed in a library as a non-reference-counted class, and that we needed to use reference counted stacks for part of the application. We create a new stack abstraction, named `CountedStack`, using the existing `Stack` class:

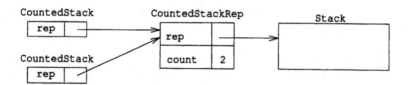

Here, the original `Stack` abstraction is used untouched, and two new classes are used to manage it. Class `CountedStack` takes care of memory management, while `CountedStackRep` serves as a simple data structure to add a level of indirection:

```
class CountedStack {
public:
    CountedStack(): rep(new CountedStackRep) { }
    int pop() { return rep->rep->pop(); }
    void push(int i) { rep->rep->push(i); }
    CountedStack(const CountedStack &c): rep(c.rep) {
        rep->count++;
    }
```

```
    CountedStack(const Stack &c):
        rep(new CountedStackRep(new Stack(c))) { }
    operator Stack() { return *(rep->rep); }
    ~CountedStack() {
        if (--rep->count <= 0) delete rep;
    }
    CountedStack &operator=(const CountedStack &c) {
        c.rep->count++;
        if (--rep->count <= 0) delete rep;
        rep = c.rep;   return *this;
    }
private:
    struct CountedStackRep {
        int count;
        Stack *rep;
        CountedStackRep(Stack *s = 0): count(1) {
            rep = s? s: new Stack;
        }
    } *rep;
};
```

Some additional work has been done here to allow `CountedStack` objects and `Stack` objects to be used interchangeably.

Envelope Classes for Memory Management and Singleton Letters

We showed above how to split `String` into two separate classes to reduce duplication of storage and object copying overhead. The outer `String` class was the handle class, with the `StringRep` class the body. Both classes were visible to the user and present in the global (class) name space. All classes containing pointers to dynamically allocated resources should be implemented as handle/body pairs or envelope/letter pairs if they are to be used as concrete data types (Chapter 3). Here, we show how many body and letter classes can be encapsulated in their respective handle and envelope classes to form a more cohesive abstraction.

The `String/StringRep` arrangement is one example of a *singleton letter class*. The envelope class, `String`, is designed to hold only one kind of letter, a `StringRep`. These two form a composite object that the application views as a single entity. The letter is *never* seen from outside the envelope. So instead of just putting an instance of the letter inside an instance of the envelope, we put the *class* of the letter inside the *class* of the envelope (Figure 3-12).

```
class String {
public:
    String()                        { rep = new StringRep(""); }
    String(const String& s)         { rep = s.rep; rep->count++; }
    String& operator=(const String& s) {
        s.rep->count++;
        if (--rep->count == 0)
            delete rep;
        rep = s.rep;
        return *this;
    }
    ~String() {
        if (--rep->count <= 0) delete rep;
    }
    String(const char *s)           { rep = new StringRep(s); }
    String operator+(const String&) const;
    int length() const              { return ::strlen(rep->rep); }
private:
    class StringRep {
    public:
        StringRep(const char *s) {
            ::strcpy(rep = new char[::strlen(s)+1], s);
            count = 1;
        }
        ~StringRep() { delete rep; }
        char *rep;
        int count;
    };
    StringRep *rep;
};
```

Figure 3-12. A Singleton Envelope Encapsulated as a Nested Class

---

☞ *When to use this idiom*: Use singleton letter classes when envelope/letter pairs are used for reference counting or whenever the interface of the letter should be visible *only* to the envelope. The idiom is most useful for stable abstractions, as changes to the letter will force recompilation of the envelope and all its clients more often than if the envelope and letter are maintained separately.

The coding of the member functions for this approach is no different from the previous version of String. This approach improves design encapsulation and makes for less pollution of the global name space than if two global classes are used as above. Its cost is that changes to the interface or data of the letter class will require more code recompilation.

Multiple letter classes can be nested inside a given envelope. Chapter 5 presents a simple token parsing class used to generate atomic token objects. The parsing class, GeneralAtom, is an envelope class for letter classes such as Punct, Name, and Oper. Unlike the StringRep class, which is invisible to the user, these letter classes may be used directly by an application. The letters could be declared in the public interface of the GeneralAtom envelope. Such nested classes must be accessed with a qualified naming syntax (e.g., GeneralAtom::Punct). Having too many letter classes inside an envelope class makes the envelope class interface more difficult to comprehend. Those applications where the letter classes are derived from the envelope class (e.g., where Complex, BigInteger, and DoublePrecisionFloat are derived from Number) obviously cannot use the nested class technique.

3.6 Operators new and delete

C++ provides a way for the programmer to take control of memory allocation. This control may be important for the kind of "magic memory" necessary to make class objects run as efficient concrete data types on a given platform. It also makes it possible to control memory allocation on a class-by-class basis in a way that is integrated with the language type system. By default, programs written under most C++ implementations ultimately use malloc and free, the C memory allocation primitives, to manage free store in the user process address space. There may be several reasons to partially or totally circumvent the use of these primitives:

- Memory may need to be statically engineered, as in an embedded system such as a telecommunications or flight guidance system, and objects may need to be allocated from a fixed pool.

- The performance of malloc and free may not be adequate for the user's purposes. A tailored algorithm can outperform the default primitives, particularly when there are large numbers of small objects.

- The existing environment may provide no memory management routines, so the programmer must supply them.

Memory on the free store is allocated by applying operator new to a type specifier. You can say

```
new int;
```

```
// stddef.h to get size_t
#include <stddef.h>

struct Head {
    long length;
    struct Head *next;
};

static Head pool = { 0, 0 };

static Head *h = (Head *)HEAP_BASE_ADDRESS;

/* fast dumb first-fit allocator */

typedef char *Char_p;

// NEXT LINE IS MACHINE AND COMPILER DEPENDENT:
const long WRDSIZE = sizeof(void*);

void* operator new(size_t nbytes)
{
    /* First, look in free list */
    if (pool.next) {
        Head *prev = &pool;
        for (Head *cur = &pool; cur; cur = cur->next) {
            if (cur->length >= nbytes) {
                prev->next = cur->next;
                return (void*)(Char_p(cur) + sizeof(Head));
            } else prev = cur;
        }
    }
    /* Nothing on free list, get new block from heap */
    h = (Head*)(((int)((Char_p(h)+WRDSIZE-1))/WRDSIZE)*WRDSIZE);
    h->next = 0;
    h->length = nbytes;
    h = Char_p(h) + nbytes + sizeof(Head);
    return (void*)(Char_p(h) - nbytes);
}

void operator delete(void *ptr)
{
    Head *p = (Head *)(Char_p(ptr) - sizeof(Head));
    p->next = pool.next;
    pool.next = p;
}
```

Figure 3-13. Simple First-Fit Allocator for operator new

which allocates one object of type int, or

```
new int[10];
```

which allocates a vector of ten objects of type int. When you invoke new on a type, the compiler arranges for the return value to be a pointer of an appropriate type—in both the above cases, of type int*. The assignment

```
int *ia = new int[ size ];
```

allocates a vector of a user-specified size and sets ia to point to it. The dynamically allocated collections of integers created here are uninitialized, as are dynamically allocated instances of all built-in types. Class objects allocated with new are initialized by their constructors.

To return a vector of objects to free store, you say

```
delete[] ia;
```

which takes the value in ia, previously returned by a call to new, and returns the memory it addresses to free store. The brackets [] should be used when deleting dynamically allocated vectors of objects, and *must* be used to delete a vector of objects for which destructors must be called. A single object, as would be allocated with

```
ia = new int;
```

is freed by saying

```
delete ia;
```

Let's first look at the case where we decide to take over memory management entirely. We may do this either to incorporate a faster memory management algorithm or because we are running C++ in an environment without underlying memory management support (for example, a stand-alone program on an outboard microprocessor). We can achieve either of these ends by redefining the operators new and delete. Customized versions of operator new and operator delete are shown in Figure 3-13. This allocator uses a simple algorithm that keeps heterogeneous blocks on a single list and uses first-fit retrieval to satisfy memory requests. While on the free list, blocks are treated as though they are instances of struct Head, a data structure to maintain free list links.

Now whenever a C++ function performs a new or delete, the overloaded operators will be called instead of the ones in the standard library. The memory management algorithm used by the overloaded versions of the operators can be anything you want; those illustrated in Figure 3-13 are designed to use a heap storage block starting at HEAP_BASE_ADDRESS and extending indefinitely far into upper memory.

```
// a dumb string (not a concrete data type)
// to demonstrate new/delete

class String {
public:
          String() { rep = new char[1]; *rep = '\0'; }
          String(const char *s) {
              rep = new char[::strlen(s)+1];
              ::strcpy(rep,s);
          }
          ~String() { delete[] rep; }
   void*  operator new(size_t);
   void   operator delete(void*);
          . . . .      // other interesting operations
private:
          static String *newlist;
          union {
              String *freepointer;
              char *rep;
          };
          int len;
};
```

Figure 3-14. Declaration of a String with Custom Storage Management

Another common trick is to customize memory allocation on a class-by-class basis. This can have advantages even when running under an operating system with its own memory management primitives, because the user can supply an algorithm that is smarter about the behavior of a particular class than the general purpose operating system primitives could be. Classes for frequently allocated small objects (four to ten bytes in size as a rule of thumb) when converted to use this approach, can speed up a program by an order of magnitude over the default malloc-based memory allocation primitives. It can also be less wasteful of memory, eliminating malloc's overhead of four to eight bytes per allocation.

For any given class, the object allocated is always of the same size. For class objects allocated dynamically using new, we might want to preallocate the memory in chunks whose size is a multiple of the class's object size. Each class can have its own pool of objects exactly the right size to satisfy operator new requests.

Figure 3-14 declares a String with its own allocation operators; these operators override whatever new and delete semantics exist at the global level. The public interface of String is otherwise the same as it would be without specialized storage management. The union in the implementation of the String allows a block of storage to be treated either as an active String object, in which case the union

```
String *String::newlist = 0;

void String::operator delete(void *p) {
    String *s = (String *)p;
    s->freepointer = newlist;
    newlist = s;
}

void* String::operator new(size_t size) {
    if (size != sizeof(String)) {
        // this check is needed for cases when class
        // derivation is used (Chapter 4) and the
        // derived class has no operator new.
        // String::operator delete above will field
        // this over-sized block when it is reclaimed.
        return malloc(size);
    } else if (!newlist) {
        newlist = (String *)new char[100 * sizeof(String)];
        for (int i = 0; i < 99; i++) {
            newlist[i].freepointer = &(newlist[i+1]);
        }
        newlist[i].freepointer =0;
    }
    String *savenew = newlist;
    newlist = newlist->freepointer;
    return savenew;
}
```

Figure 3-15. Operators new and delete for the String class

contents are interpreted as pointing to the string's representation, or as a block of storage on a free list, in which case the union contents are interpreted as a link in a free list. There is a private, static datum newlist that serves as the head of the free list.

Figure 3-15 shows the new and delete operators for the String class; these override the default storage management system when String objects are built. The expression

```
new String
```

causes memory to be allocated for a String object, followed by an invocation of the String constructor to initialize that object. Within the constructor, memory for the string representation itself is allocated from the heap as a character vector; this does not interact with String's operator new but uses the system default. The implementation shown here maintains a linked list of memory blocks, each the size of

```
class String {
private:
          static String *newlist;
          union {
               String *freepointer;
               char *rep;
          };
          int len;
public:
          enum { POOLSIZE = 1000 } ;
          String() { rep = new char[1]; *rep = '\0'; }
          String(const char *s) {
               rep = new char[::strlen(s)+1];
               ::strcpy(rep,s);
          }
          ~String() { delete[] rep; }
     void *operator new(size_t);
     void operator delete(void*);
          . . . .    // other interesting operations
};
```

Figure 3-16. Class Declaration for String with Static Memory Pool

a String instance; deallocation of a String object causes it to be put onto the list, and requests for new instances are satisfied by removing blocks from the list. When the list is exhausted, a new pool of 100 String objects is allocated all at once, based on the knowledge that it is cheaper to call malloc once to ask for a large number of bytes than to call it many times with small requests.

The String abstraction hides these memory allocation details, and this String can be used with exactly the same source programs that would be used if no special storage management were being done. In the following code, the compiler interprets the invocation of new String as a request for storage from String's operator new if it is present, and from ::operator new (the system default) if it is not:

```
int main() {
    String *p = new String("abcdef");
    delete p;
    return 0;
}
```

A slightly modified allocator works in applications where operator new and operator delete use statically allocated memory. In fact, the code is simpler in

```
String* String::newlist = 0;
static unsigned char memPool[String::POOLSIZE * sizeof(String)];
static const unsigned char *memPoolEnd =
    memPool + String::POOLSIZE + sizeof(String);

void String::operator delete(void *p) {
    String *s = (String *)p;
    s->freepointer = newlist;
    newlist = s;
}

void* String::operator new(size_t size) {
    if (size != sizeof(String)) {
        // this check is needed for cases when class
        // derivation is used (Chapter 4) and the
        // derived class has no operator new
        return ::malloc(size);
    } else if (newlist == memPoolEnd) {
        StringOutOfMemory();
        return 0;
    } else if (!newlist) {
        newlist = (String*)memPool;
        for (int i = 0; i < POOLSIZE-1; i++) {
            newlist[i].freepointer = &(newlist[i+1]);
        }
        newlist[i].freepointer = memPoolEnd;
    }
    String *savenew = newlist;
    newlist = newlist->freepointer;
    return savenew;
}
```

Figure 3-17. Operators for `String` with Static Allocation Pool

that it triggers an error condition (by invoking a system recovery routine, for example) when the preallocated blocks are exhausted, instead of trying to allocate more blocks and add them to the pool. Such an implementation is shown in Figures 3-16 and 3-17.

Vectors of all types are allocated by using the global `operator new`. Even if `String` had its own `operator new`, the invocation

```
String *sp = new String[25];
```

results in the allocation of a single block of memory of size `25*sizeof(String)` bytes, and that block is allocated by `::operator new`. This is because the object being allocated is a vector; vectors are C artifacts, not C++ class objects.

3.7 Separating Initialization from Instantiation

It is sometimes important to separate *instantiation*—the process of allocating basic resources for an object—from *initialization*—the process of configuring an object's state. This is important for initializing or re-initializing objects in stand-alone microprocessor systems. It is also useful when initializing mutually referential objects.

As an example of the first case, consider a real-time control system running on a stand-alone microprocessor. The system is initialized by an initialization subsystem that specifies the exact order in which constructors are called for global objects. For example, global tables referenced from read-only memory (ROM) need to be initialized early, at specific addresses, so initialization code in ROM can use them. The memory size and location for these objects is predetermined, but the contents are initialized at run time. If the system incurs a correctable fault at run time, it may wish to reinitialize corrupted objects in place, leaving others alone. A faulty peripheral can be replaced without stopping the CPU (an important consideration in continuously running systems), and the constructor for the peripheral's object can be invoked after the peripheral has been replaced. Other objects continue to refer to the peripheral object at its original address.

As an example of the second case, consider an editor with an `Editor` and a `Window` class, each having members pointing to an instance of the other. Each expects the other to exist as context for its own initialization, so there is an "after you/after you" circular dependency. This could be solved by splitting initialization between the constructor and a member function, handling the mutual reference in the member function after both objects had been allocated and (partially) initialized. However, this is contrary to the reason we have constructors in the first place—to guarantee *automatic* initialization without the programmer having to remember to call an initialization function, and it results in a constructor whose execution leaves an only partly initialized object.

This "patch-up" approach is clumsy and unsatisfying, and we would sooner express the separation of creation and initialization using straightforward provisions of the programming language. This section shows that, without taking a "patch-up" approach, you can bootstrap objects of both classes by first instantiating both, and then initializing both.

Such an approach is outside the "usual" set of good C++ programming practices and some cautions are in order. In C++, tying initialization and instantiation together removes the user from worrying about invoking an explicit initialization routine when an object comes into existence. The other side of the coin—object cleanup and destruction—has similar problems, so this approach should be used only when circumstances demand it. An example will be presented here, and the issue will be explored further in Chapter 9 in conjunction with more advanced idioms.

```
#include <stddef.h>

void *operator new(size_t, void *p) { return p; }

struct S {
    S();
    ~S();
};

char buf [sizeof(S)][100];
int bufIndex = 0;

void f() {
    S a;      // automatic allocation/initialization

    S *p = new S;           // explicit allocation
                            // operator new finds the store
                            // automatic initialization
    delete p;               // explicit deletion
                            // automatic cleanup

    S *ppp = new (buf) S;   // explicit allocation in buf
                            // automatic initialization
    ppp->S::~S();           // explicit cleanup

    // "a" automatically cleaned up/deallocated
    //    on return from f()
}
```

Figure 3-18. Explicit Allocation and Deallocation in Objects

Consider the code of Figure 3-18. Here, we overload `operator new` to take an extra parameter: the memory address at which the object is to be placed. The body of this `operator new` simply returns its argument. This version of `operator new` will be called only when an extra parameter is supplied to `new`, directing it where to place an object, using the syntax

        . . . . new (*object-address*) *Type(params. . . .);*

Such an invocation thwarts the automatic memory allocation semantics of `new`, and reduces to just a call of the constructor for an object whose location is known. We can similarly ask that a destructor be applied to an object without relinquishing its storage by calling a destructor directly:

    object-address -> *Type* :: ~ *Type* ();

The overall effect is that allocation takes place first, and then initialization follows as an independently requested activity. The code may specify that the object be

```
#include <iostream.h>
#include <stddef.h>

void *operator new(size_t, void *p) { return p; }

class Foo {
public:
    Foo() { rep = 1; }
    Foo(int i) { rep = i; }
    ~Foo() { rep = 0; }
    void print() { cout << rep << "\n"; }
private:
    int rep;
};

struct { int:0; };   // machine-dependent alignment
char foobar[sizeof(Foo)];

Foo foefum;

int main()
{
    foefum.print();
    (&foefum)->Foo::~Foo();    // cause premature cleanup of
                               // object with global extent
    foefum.print();            // undefined results!
    Foo *fooptr = new(foobar) Foo;
    fooptr->Foo::~Foo();
    fooptr = new(foobar) Foo(1);    // unrelated to earlier
                                    //    allocation
    fooptr->Foo::~Foo();       // cause premature cleanup
                               // do NOT delete fooptr
    fooptr = new Foo;
    delete fooptr;
}
```

Figure 3-19. Explicit Allocation and Deallocation into Preallocated Memory

allocated anywhere it chooses: an arbitrary pointer could have been supplied instead of buf.

NOTE: Care must be taken not to delete an object allocated this way: It will confuse the memory manager into thinking that some local storage actually came from the heap, and general insanity is likely to ensue.

Figure 3-19 presents another example, where foobar is being used as a single global object of type Foo. The space is set aside for the object at compile time; this may be done so the code can be run on a primitive microprocessor platform that has no operating system with support for dynamic memory allocation. Or, there just may be some computation that needs to be done in `main` or elsewhere to generate values that are to be supplied to `Foo`'s constructor when `foobar` is initialized. Also in this example, the same storage (`foobar`) is reused for two unrelated objects of class `Foo` at different times.

The premature cleanup of object `foefum` in Figure 3-19 should not be done in programs where the environment invokes destructors for global variables on program exit; if it is, then `foefum`'s destructor will be called twice! This is safe only if `foefum` is reinstantiated (`new (&foefum) Foo`), if the platform does not invoke destructors at program exit, or if the object was allocated in memory not originally allocated to a class object (as with `fooptr` above).

Exercises

1. Describe the difference between `structs`, `classes`, abstract data types, and concrete data types.

2. List, compare, and contrast the abstraction mechanisms you know about in the C++ language.

3. Modify the `String` class so that substrings can be extracted from an existing string, leaving the existing string intact. For example:

   ```
   String s = "abcdefg";
   . . . .
   String t = s(j, k);
   ```

   In this example, j is the starting index with 1 indicating the first character of the string. If j is negative, it is an offset *back* from the string's *end*, with −1 being the last character of the string. (Null termination characters are a convention used at the lower C language level and are not present here.) The second parameter, k, indicates the number of characters to grab starting at the index j. If k is negative, then j is taken as the index of the rightmost end of the substring and characters are grabbed back to the left. (The substring is not transposed by this "backward grabbing.")

4. Consider how you would handle out-of-bounds cases in the previous exercise.

5. The "`X::X(const X&)`" constructor is part of the canonical form. One of its uses is to provide a mechanism to copy function call parameters onto the stack, making a "copy" of the caller's variable on the callee's

activation record. Show what would happen for an object of a class X which had an X::X(X) constructor, but not the canonical X::X(const X&).

6. Write a constructor for Node that takes the parenthesized String produced by String::String(Node) and produces an entire tree from it.

7. Write a system memory allocator that uses only statically engineered memory—that is, memory whose location and size are fixed by the program before run time. What do you do when memory is exhausted?

8. What happens if operator new allocates a larger block of memory than is called for by the size of its class? Can you think of uses for this? What if it allocates a smaller block than is called for?

9. Augment the printf function you wrote for the exercise in Appendix A (or augment your local C printf code) so it takes a %S format and a corresponding String argument.

10. Show that if all classes follow the canonical form given above for the String that uses operator-> (Figure 3-11), then a C++ program need never use any pointers to class objects at the application level (that is, outside the classes that themselves use operator->).

11. Consider the following code:

```
class String {
public:
    . . . .
    String(char* s)  { . . . . }
    operator const char*() const { . . . . }
    . . . .
};

extern "C" {
    int open(char*, int ...);
}

int open(String, int ...);
```

Exactly what happens in each of the following cases? Why? Are they semantically identical? Why or why not? (Try running a program with some trace statements to help understand what is going on.)

```
int i = open("abcd", O_RDONLY);
int j = open(String("abcd"), O_RDONLY);
String abcd = "abcd";
int k = open(abcd, O_RDONLY);
```

This exercise may help you understand how to avoid some ambiguities in your own designs. In general, overloading needs to be treated as a *system* design issue, so that one person's declarations do not interfere with those of another.

12. Take a sizable C++ program and change it so that its classes' destructors assign zero to the value of this (if your compiler supports it). Compare the performance of the original program with the modified one. Can you explain the difference?

13. Show another way to implement the strlen (String) function using approaches from Section 3.3, instead of using a conversion member function.

14. Start with the String class on page 38. Add an overloaded operator& () yielding a StringPointer object as a result. Objects of StringPointer are to be used in a program wherever a String* would otherwise be used. Complete the implementation of StringPointer, including overloaded operator-> () and operator* (). Make such changes to String as are necessary. Where would you use these two classes? Compare and contrast with the approach discussed starting on page 65.

15. Create a class Int with an overloaded operator+ so that

```
Int i = 0, j = 0;
j = i + 25 + 15 + 14 + 2;
```

means *bit* 25 ored with *bit* 15 ored with *bit* 14 ored with *bit* 2—that is, 0200140004. Likewise, arrange for − to turn bits *off*. Where could this be used? What problems does it create? (This problem was suggested by an example in Lippman[1].)

☐

References

1. Lippman, Stanley B. *A C++ Primer*. Reading, Mass: Addison-Wesley, 1989.

4

Inheritance

Inheritance is a language feature used to express special relationships between classes. It takes classes as programming language abstractions and arranges them into hierarchies that are abstractions in their own right. These higher order abstractions establish a foundation for object-oriented programming, which is covered in the next chapter.

Inheritance is commonly used in two ways. In one role it can be an abstraction mechanism, a tool to organize classes into hierarchies of specialization. In another role, it can be thought of as a reuse mechanism, a way to create a new class that strongly resembles an existing one. In both cases, you can think of it as a way for one class to subcontract or delegate some of its tasks to another.

One useful way of thinking about inheritance is as an abstraction mechanism. In C, functions are the abstraction mechanism for algorithms, and `structs` are the primary abstraction mechanism for data. The C++ concept of a class combines these two into an abstract data type and its implementation. In C++, adorning these abstractions a little more gives them the full appearance and power of types, just like built-in types in the language that "come with the compiler." That is a powerful abstraction technique in its own right. Inheritance goes one step further, providing a mechanism to collect related classes together into a high level generalization that characterizes all of them. Classes with similar, compatible behaviors can be organized in an inheritance hierarchy. The class at the top of the hierarchy serves as an abstraction of all those below it, shielding the programmer from the details of their variations.

In the sense that inheritance means building new abstractions from old ones, where one class inherits data and member functions from another, C++ is like most object-oriented languages. But in C++, inheritance commonly defines type compatibility as well. That is, two types may be so closely related that an object of one type may be used where an object of the other type is expected. Inheritance is used to express these relationships, and compiler type checking allows compatible classes to be used interchangeably. As shall be discussed in Chapter 6, publicly deriving class B from class A implies that objects of class B can be used where objects of class A are expected. The original, or "parent" class at the top of an inheritance hierarchy is called the *base class*. The immediate parent class of any class is called its base class in C++; other programming languages sometimes call it a *superclass*. The new class that inherits properties of the parent class, as a "child," is called the *derived class*; other languages sometimes call it the *subclass*. A child may in turn be the parent of a "grandchild" class; such hierarchies can be arbitrarily deep, though they are not usually more than three or four deep in practice.

Classes in an inheritance hierarchy can be viewed as different forms of an abstraction characterized by the base class, and code written in terms of the base class can use any of its other forms interchangeably. This *polymorphism*—the ability of a program to treat many forms of a class as though they were one—is a powerful abstraction mechanism that shields the programmer from the implementation details of derived classes. We might use inheritance to relate classes that corresponded to similarly acting resources, producers, consumers, and so forth, appearing in the application. Inheritance helps manage the structure of large systems when used this way as a design aid.

Another way to think of inheritance is as a means to define a new class as an incremental refinement of an existing one. If you need a new class that behaves much as an existing class does with a slightly modified implementation, then inheritance is a powerful way to express that. Inheritance allows you to base a new class on an existing one, tweaking just what you want to tweak, and *sharing* the rest of the class. (You can think of it as an alternative to conditional compilation of source using #if or #ifdef, or as an alternative to run-time decisions; see Section 7.9.) The new class can inherit the properties of an existing one, customizing it by overriding selected member functions in the new class.

Inheritance can thus be used in two significantly different ways:

1. To reflect some semantic relationship between classes. This relationship might be the result of evolution, where one class's member functions are used to refine or specialize some properties of an existing base class while inheriting the rest. Or this use of inheritance may capture a strong similarity between two existing abstractions, so strong that a derived class object can serve where a base class object is expected. This kind of relationship is usually implemented using:

   — Public inheritance
   — Member functions that are virtual

2. To reflect code sharing. Though a class may not exhibit all the properties of its base class, it may be close enough that the reuse gains make inheritance worthwhile. Although a `Queue` and a `CircularList` are not interchangeable, they may have enough code in common that inheritance could profit common evolution of the two abstractions. This kind of relationship is usually implemented using:

    — Private inheritance
    — Member functions that are not virtual

However, these implementation guidelines are not hard and fast, and are mentioned here to give a flavor of what lies ahead, and to set some context for where this chapter fits in with those that follow. The rules for choosing between `public` and `private` are more design considerations than implementation issues, and they are handled separately as such in Chapter 6. Discussion of virtual functions is deferred until Chapter 5, where object-oriented programming is introduced. Of the examples in this chapter, `PathName` exemplifies the code-sharing approach, while the `Imaginary` number class and `Telephone` examples model semantic design relationships between classes.

Also deferred to Chapter 5 is the discussion of the *inheritance canonical form*. The discussion must be delayed because an appreciation of the finer points is predicated on an understanding of virtual functions and multiple inheritance, both of which are explored later. Discussion of multiple inheritance is left for the section on object-oriented programming. There is little use of multiple inheritance without virtual functions, so presenting contrived examples of multiple inheritance here is not useful.

4.1 Simple Inheritance

We introduce and illustrate inheritance with a `Complex` number class, as shown in Figure 4-1. Complex numbers are useful in physical sciences and engineering applications as a generalization of rational numbers, imaginary numbers, real numbers, and integers. The code for `Rational` numbers, `Imaginary` numbers, and so forth, can be constructed by incrementally modifying the code for `Complex`. These classes are a perfect candidate for inheritance.

```
class Complex {
public:
    Complex(double r = 0, double i = 0): rpart(r), ipart(i) { }
    Complex(const Complex &c): rpart(c.rpart), ipart(c.ipart) { }
    Complex& operator=(const Complex &c) {
        rpart = c.rpart; ipart = c.ipart; return *this;
    }
    Complex operator+(const Complex &c) const {
        return Complex(rpart + c.rpart, ipart + c.ipart);
    }
    friend Complex operator+(double d, const Complex &c) {
        return c + Complex(d);
    }
    friend Complex operator+(int i, const Complex &c) {
        return c + Complex(i);
    }
    Complex operator-(const Complex &c1) const {
        return Complex(rpart - c1.rpart, ipart - c1.ipart);
    }
    friend Complex operator-(double d, const Complex &c) {
        return -c + Complex(d);
    }
    friend Complex operator-(int i, const Complex &c) {
        return -c + Complex(i);
    }
    Complex operator*(const Complex &c) const {
        return Complex (rpart*c.rpart - ipart*c.ipart,
                    rpart*c.ipart + c.rpart*ipart);
    }
    friend Complex operator*(double d, const Complex& c) {
        return c * Complex(d);
    }
    friend Complex operator*(int i, const Complex& c) {
        return c * Complex(i);
    }
    Complex operator/(const Complex &c) const { . . . . }
    . . . .
    operator double() {
        return ::sqrt(rpart*rpart + ipart*ipart);
    }
    Complex operator-() const { return Complex(-rpart, -ipart); }
private:
    double rpart, ipart;
};
```

Figure 4-1. A Simple Complex Class

Here is a simple Imaginary number class *derived from* Complex:

```
class Complex {
friend class Imaginary;
public:
    . . . .
};
class Imaginary: public Complex {
public:
    Imaginary(double i = 0): Complex(0, i) { }
    Imaginary(const Complex &c): Complex(0, c.ipart) { }
    Imaginary& operator=(const Complex &c) {
        rpart = 0; ipart = c.ipart; return *this;
    }
};
```

Note that we have made Imaginary a friend of Complex. The classes in this inheritance hierarchy are written together as a package. There are some efficiencies and notational conveniences to be gained by coupling the classes together. As a general rule, classes should avoid exporting their internal structure, even to derived classes—inheritance is not a license to violate encapsulation. On the other hand, this example illustrates how good base class design might be influenced by the classes derived from it, and vice versa. Iteration and prototyping are important to achieve optimal class and inheritance structures.

The dependencies across levels of the class hierarchy become clearer in this example as it is fleshed out. Consider the following application code:

```
int main() {
    Complex a(42,2);
    Imaginary b = 2;
    Complex c = a - b;
    // c is Complex(42,0)
    return 0;
}
```

Here, the result returned by Complex::operator- is statically typed as a Complex, but returns a value that is in fact a real number. This raises two issues. The first is peculiar to arithmetic types in C++, caused by the dualism between built-in types such as double and user-defined classes such as Complex and Imaginary. We would *like* double to fit somewhere in the Complex hierarchy, and in particular we would like to derive double from Complex (a double is just a *kind* of Complex, after all). But because double is a built-in type and not a class, we cannot build it into the inheritance hierarchy, so there is no convenient way to tell the compiler that double and Complex are type compatible. The best we can do is to arrange for automatic type conversion from doubles to Complexes (Section 3.4), but that forces the overhead of Complex on all double computations. The alternative is to replace each use of double with a full-fledged class:

```
class Double: public Complex {
    // a Double is a kind of Complex
public:
    Double(double r = 0): Complex(r) { }
    Double(const Complex &c): Complex(c.rpart) { }
    Double& operator=(const Complex &c) {
        rpart = c.rpart; ipart = 0; return *this;
    }
    . . . .   // operations optimized for Doubles
};
```

That solves the first issue. The second problem is more general: Here we have a Complex member function, supplied an Imaginary parameter, from which we expect a Double result. In general, most classes in this inheritance hierarchy need to know about many of the others. The full solution to this problem is beyond the scope of this chapter, but its resolution using object-oriented programming is presented in Section 5.5.

Tailoring Complex Operations for Imaginary Semantics

The class Imaginary inherits most operations from its parent class. However, we want to ensure that an Imaginary object always has a zero real part. The class Imaginary *redefines* operations that might otherwise invalidate that assumption. For example, assignment of a Complex to an Imaginary needs special handling so the Imaginary does not end having a real part. We could deal with that either by issuing a run-time error, or by zeroing the real component when the assignment is done. Here we do the latter. The conversion loses information (the real part is discarded), but that is consistent with the loss of the fractional part in the coercion of a double to an integer.

The only other base class member function that could give the rpart field a nonzero value is Complex::Complex(double,double), but it is not inherited by Imaginary. Constructors of the base class are not inherited by the derived class.

Reuse of Base Class Code in the Derived Class

Inheritance lets `Imaginary` reuse the code of `Complex`'s arithmetic operator member functions. We have created a new type that accomplishes most of its work through the member functions of an existing type. It is safe to do this because imaginary numbers are complex numbers, too; they are just special *kinds* of complex numbers. For example, here we add an `Imaginary` to a `Complex` yielding a `Complex`:

```
int main() {
    Complex c = Complex(1,2);
    Imaginary k = -1;
    Complex sum = c+k; // legal: c.operator+(const Complex&)
    // sum is Complex(1,1)
    return 0;
}
```

Though `Complex::operator+` takes a `Complex` as a parameter, an `Imaginary` is a *kind* of `Complex`, a fact the compiler knows because of the inheritance relationship between the classes. Everything that a `Complex` provides in its interface is inherited by `Imaginary` in its interface. A C++ public inheritance declaration captures that relationship, permitting objects declared of type `Imaginary` to be supplied wherever a `Complex` is expected. Inheritance thus defines type compatibility between similar classes.

Tuning Derived Class Member Functions for Efficiency

The `Complex` member functions work fine when applied to an `Imaginary`, but they do some unnecessary work. For example, invoking `operator double`, which returns the magnitude of the complex number as a `double`, multiplies two pairs of numbers and returns the square root of their sum. That algorithm works for an `Imaginary`, but the algorithm can be simplified and made more efficient for `Imaginary` numbers if it is known that the real part will always be zero. We may add a version of `operator double` to class `Imaginary`:

```
Imaginary::operator double() {
    return ipart;
}
```

This new version will be invoked for variables declared as Imaginarys, while the original version will still be used for Complexes:

```
int main() {
    Imaginary i = -1;
    Complex j = Complex(0, -1);
    double a, b;
    a = double(i);    // Imaginary::operator double
    b = double(j);    // Complex::operator double
    // both yield 1
    . . . .
}
```

The examples we have seen so far depict at most one derived class for each base class. Of course, multiple classes may be derived from a single base. In Figure 4-2, we share the common attributes of several types of telephones in a common base class. Note that no objects of class Telephone are made; abstract telephones do not exist as living abstractions. Class Telephone exists only as scaffolding, or as a template after which specific kinds of telephones are patterned. Below, we investigate some primitive mechanisms to control where objects of Telephone can be instantiated. However, class Telephone has the knowledge of how to do things with phones in general; for example, it knows how to look at variables that capture terminal or call context information, or other system information, to determine the state of a call associated with its phone. Furthermore, we assume it can do this in a phone-independent way; that is, it uses the same mechanisms for POTSPhones (*Plain Old Telephone Service* phones) as for ISDNPhones (*Integrated Services Digital Network* phones, digital phones with advanced features). That means we can write the following:

```
POTSPhone phone1, phone2;
. . . .
if (phone1.isTalking()) phone2.ring();
```

The POTSPhone class *inherits* the ring and isTalking operations from class Telephone—just as if the operations had been physically copied into the derived classes. It realizes code reuse without code duplication.

```
class Telephone {
public:
    void ring();
    Bool isOnHook();
    Bool isTalking();
    Bool isDialing();
    DigitString collectDigits();
    LineNumber extension();
    ~Telephone();.
protected:
    LineNumber extensionData;
    Telephone();
};

// POTS is Plain Ordinary Telephone Service

class POTSPhone: public Telephone {
public:
    Bool runDiagnostics();
    POTSPhone();
    POTSPhone(POTSPhone&);
    ~POTSPhone();
private:
    // these are details of the phone's wiring
    // connections in the telephone office
    Frame frameNumberVal;
    Rack rackNumberVal;
    Pair pairVal;
};

// ISDN is Integrated Services Digital Network

class ISDNPhone: public Telephone {
public:
    ISDNPhone();
    ISDNPhone(ISDNPhone&);
    ~ISDNPhone();
    void sendBPacket();
    void sendDPacket();
private:
    Channel b1, b2, d;
};

class PrincessPhone: public POTSPhone {
    . . . .
};
```

Figure 4-2. A Base Class Common to Two Derived Classes

4.2 Scoping and Access Control

We have explored how to use inheritance to combine existing types to make new
ones. If we are concerned about encapsulation and information hiding, then we must
explore how inheritance affects the access of class members, both between classes
related by inheritance, and between classes where one provides a service used by
another. The access of members between classes related by inheritance is denoted
here as *vertical access*, with respect to classes viewed as being "above" and
"below" each other in the inheritance hierarchy. Accessibility of class members to
the outside world we call *horizontal access*, a relationship between classes viewed as
peers in the program structure. Inheritance raises questions about member access that
do not arise for simple class protection as described in Section 3.2. For example: Is a
class member accessible to member functions of its derived class? Are class members
accessible to a third class using the services of an object of one of its derived classes?

"Vertical" Access Control and Inheritance

A class can control which of its members are made available to a derived class. A
derived class cannot access its base class `private` members. Consider the
following code:

```
class A {
public:
    A();
    ~A();
    . . . .
private:
    int val;
};

class B: public A {
public:
    B();
    ~B();
    . . . .
    void func();    // cannot access A::val
};
```

No member function of B may access val, even though a val instance is present in
every B object. There is a "firewall" along the vertical (inheritance) scoping
dimension, preventing access of `private` base class members from the derived
class. Derived classes have no more right to violate base class encapsulation than any
other class.

Making this member `private` makes it inaccessible to other classes using either class A or class B. If val is made `public`, then it is accessible to member functions of B (or anyone else). If we want to make one or more of A's members accessible to B without making them public, we can make them `protected`:

```
class A {
public:
    A();
    ~A();
    . . . .
protected:
    int val;
};

class B: public A {
public:
    B();
    ~B();
    . . . .
    void func();     // can access A::val
};

class C: public B {
public:
    C();
    ~C();
    . . . .
    void func2();    // can access A::val
};
```

Here, val still behaves as though it were `private` to the whole world, *except* to member or `friend` functions of its derived classes.

To restrict access to val so that it is legal only from the derived class B and not from C, we can use the `friend` construct:

```
class A {
friend class B;
public:
    . . . .
private:           // totally walled off, except for friends
                   //    and members of A
    int val;
};
```

```
class B: public A {
public:
    . . . .
    void func();      // can access A::val
};

class C: public A {
public:
    . . . .
    void func3();     // cannot access A::val
};
```

Here, derived class B has a special relationship to A that permits access of base class private fields from the derived class; class C is barred from such access. Making a base class member protected is similar to making all the derived classes friends of the base class. All classes have access to their base class's protected members, so the base class does not need to be modified each time a new derived class requires access to such members. With friends, the addition of each new derived class requires a new friend clause in the base class. On the other hand, protected status gives indiscriminate permission to all derived classes, while friendship can be granted on a class-by-class basis. A protected member is accessible to a friend or member function of the derived class, but only if accessed through a pointer, reference, or object of the derived class. This is why Imaginary was made a friend of Complex in Figure 4-1 instead of giving the base class variables protected status. In particular, the derived class assignment operator must access members of a base class object passed as a parameter:

```
Imaginary &Imaginary::operator=(const Complex &c) {
    rpart = 0;
    ipart = c.ipart;
    return *this;
}
```

Had the base class members rpart and ipart been protected, a compile-time error would have resulted.

For additional examples, let's consider creating a PathName class from the String class from Chapter 3, recalled here:

```
class String {
public:
    String()                    { rep = new StringRep(""); }
    String(const String &s)     { rep = s.rep; rep->count++; }
    String(const char *s)       { rep = new StringRep(s); }
    ~String()            { if (--rep->count <= 0) delete rep; }
```

```
    String &operator=(const String &s) {
        s.rep->count++;
        if (--rep->count <= 0) delete rep;
        rep = s.rep;
        return *this;
    }
    String operator+(const String&) const;   // elsewhere
    operator const char* () const { return rep->rep; }
    String operator()(int,int) const;
                // substring, from Exercises in Chapter 3
    int length() const           { return ::strlen(rep->rep); }
protected:
    StringRep *rep;
};
```

PathName can inherit the properties of String as follows:

```
class PathName: public String {
public:
    PathName(const String&);
    PathName() : baseNameRep(""), String() {  }
    PathName(const PathName &p) : String(p),
        baseNameRep(p.baseNameRep) { /* empty */ }
    PathName &operator=(const PathName &p) {
        String::operator=(p); // assign base class part
        baseNameRep = p.baseNameRep;
        return *this;
    }
    ~PathName()     { /* empty */ }
    String baseName()    { return baseNameRep; }
    String prefix();
    String suffix();
    String fullPathName() { return *this; }
    String dirName() {
        return (*this)(0,length() - baseName().length());
    }
    String changeBaseName(const String &newFile);
private:
    String baseNameRep;
};
```

A user can invoke any `public` String member function on a PathName object because PathName is publicly derived from String. Let's say that we want to prevent the user from performing substring operations on PathNames. This keeps users from modifying the path components except through other, higher level member functions that operate on paths in terms of their component directories instead of characters (for example, changeBaseName). One way would be to trap the access at run time and print a message:

```
class PathName: public String {
public:
    . . . .
    String operator()(int,int) {
        printf("illegal PathName substring\n");
        return String("");
    }
    . . . .
};
```

However, the invalid invocation is not detected until run time; we would rather announce the error at compile time. A compile-time guarantee against invoking operator()(int,int) for PathName objects is enforced if PathName redefines the protection of the substring operator to make it inaccessible. This says that though operator()(int,int) is a valid operator on Strings, it is not so for PathNames. But that means that PathNames do not inherit the properties of Strings, at least, not all of them.

If we want to restrict exactly which part of the String interface is made accessible to code using objects of class PathName, then private inheritance must be used. The following code says that only the const char* conversion operator of String should be "brought down" as part of the interface of class PathName:

```
class PathName: private String {
public:
    String::operator const char*;    // from base class
    . . . .    // other PathName member functions
};
```

This is called an *access specifier*. It does not change the implementation of the operator or create a new operator; it just makes the operator part of PathName's public interface, instead of being hidden by the private derivation. Other operators and member functions—for example, operator()(int,int)—remain private to String and are not published in the interface of PathName. If the following code appears outside String or PathName

```
PathName p;
. . . . p(1,3) . . . .
```

the compiler issues a fatal error stating that the operator is private. However, the base class String::operator()(int,int) is still accessible to any of PathName's member functions.

"Horizontal" Access Control and Inheritance

The above constructs are used to control what is accessible to a derived class from a base class. These same constructs, as well as others, can be used to control what base class operations are made available to users of a class.

While a base class has some control over which of its members are accessible to a derived class, the derived class has some control over what part of the base class interface is made accessible to the clients of the derived class. There are two mechanisms supporting this: one is to use different modes of inheritance that tell how a derived class publishes base class members, and the other is to use access specifiers on a member-by-member basis.

The most common construct used to control access to inherited members is *public derivation* (also called *public inheritance*). For a base class A and a derived class B:

```
class A {            // base class (superclass)
public:
       . . . .
};

class B: public A {
public:
       . . . .
};
```

then all `public` members of A are available as members of B. If you say instead:

```
class A {            // base class (superclass)
public:
       . . . .
};

class B: private A {
public:
       . . . .
};
```

then no members of A are accessible as members of B to users of class B. This is called *private derivation* or *private inheritance*. However, member functions of class B still have access to `public` and `protected` member functions of class A (see below).

If a class is privately derived from some base class, we may make selective parts of the base class `public` interface accessible in its `public` interface. To do this requires use of the second approach to control access to inherited members, that of

access specifiers. We did this with `String` and `PathName` above. Consider the
class:

```
class List {
public:
    virtual void *head();
    virtual void *tail();
    virtual int count();
    virtual long has(void*);
    virtual void insert(void*);
};
```

and, privately derived from it, another new class:

```
class Set: private List {
public:
    void insert(void *m);
    List::count;       // access
    List::has;         //        specifiers
};
```

Here, `Set` uses the functionality of `List` for implementation, but uses private
inheritance to hide certain `public` member functions of its base class (`head` and
`tail`) because they do not make sense as set operations. Everything else is inherited
as is, except for `insert`, whose semantics for `Set`s differ from those of `List`s. (A
list may have duplicate copies of an element; a set may not.)

Notice that you *cannot* do the opposite. For example, the following is illegal:

```
class Set: public List {
private:
    List::head;        // illegal
    List::tail;        // illegal
public:
    void insert(void *m);
};
```

The compiler generates an error message for this code. Public derivation of `Set` from
`List` asserts that the interface of `Set` has everything that `List` has in its interface.
This means that anything a `List` object can be expected to do, a `Set` object should

```
class A {               // base class (superclass)
public:
    void f(int);
    void g(void*);
    . . . .
};

class B: public A {     // derived class (subclass)
public:
    void f(double);
    void g(int);
    . . . .
};

void B::g(int k) {
    f(k);                 // B::f(double) with promotion
    A::f(k);              // A::f(int);
    this->A::f(k);        // A::f(int);
    ::f(k);               // illegal: no global f
}

int main() {
    A *a;
    B *b;
    int i;
    . . . .
    a->f(1);              // A::f(int)
    a->f(3.0);            // A::f(int) with coercion int(3.0)
    b->f(2);              // B::f(double) with promotion double(2)
    b->f(2.0);            // B::f(double)
    a->g(0);              // A::g(void*)
    b->g(0);              // B::g(int)
    b->g(&i);             // error:  B::g hides A::g
}
```

Figure 4-3. Inheriting Functions of the Same Name but Different Signatures

be able to do as well. The C++ type system takes advantage of this, and accepts a Set object anywhere a List object was expected if public derivation is used. But for private inheritance, that would lead to anomalies such as

```
void *listhead(List l) {
    return l.head();
}
```

```
void f(int j) { . . . . }
class A {                 // base class (superclass)
public:
    void f(int);
    . . . .
};

class B: public A {       // derived class (subclass)
public:
    void f(double);
    void g(int);
    . . . .
};

void B::g(int k) {
    f(k);                 // B::f(double) with promotion
    A::f(k);              // A::f(int);
    this->A::f(k);        // A::f(int);
    ::f(k);               // ::f(int);
}

int main() {
    A *a;
    B *b;
    int i;
    . . . .
    a->f(1);        // A::f(int)
    a->f(3.0);      // A::f(int) with coercion int(3.0)
    b->f(2);        // B::f(double) with promotion double(2)
    b->f(2.0);      // B::f(double)
    b->A::f(7.0);   // A::f(int) with coercion int(7.0)
    b->g(10);       // B::g(int)
}
```

Figure 4-4. Access to Functions of the Same Name in Different Scopes

```
int main() {
    Set s;
    void *p = listhead(s);
    return 0;
}
```

Is the invocation l.head() valid or not? If the compiler allowed this, it would be a surprise to the programmer who specified that head should be private for Set objects, and constitutes a violation of encapsulation. Because listhead may be compiled separately from main, the compiler has no opportunity to provide compile-time diagnostics in the example above. As a safeguard against this situation, the compiler disallows the possibility for its existence, making it illegal to make access to a symbol more restrictive in a publicly derived class than in a base class.

These seemingly detailed linguistic arguments have a more convincing analogue in object-oriented design, and this issue will receive thorough treatment in Chapter 6.

Public derivation should be used almost universally. Private derivation is usually done for reuse of base class code by the derived class. Most of the time, other reuse constructs are preferable to private inheritance (Chapter 6). Unfortunately, private derivation is the default (if neither keyword is specified), so you should take conscious care to make most derivations public.

Note that there is no way for a base class to *force* its operations to be accessible as members of its derived classes: That is under the control of the derived class.

A derived class may define a member function with the same name as a function that already exists in its base class. Seen from outside the class, this new member function hides the base class definition, even if the functions differ in number or type of arguments and return values. An example of this can be found in Figure 4-3. From within member functions of class B itself, the only way to refer to A's member function f is with full class scope resolution, namely A::f.

If some code accesses a class object using a base class pointer or reference, it can invoke only base class member functions through that pointer. However, if a member function is invoked directly on an instance of the derived class using dot notation (object.function), then a derived class member function is chosen over a base class member function of the same name.

A user of the class can explicitly choose to override the scoping and invoke a member function at a particular level. Consider the example of Figure 4-4, slightly modified from the previous example by adding a global f(). The global function, which has an exact argument match for the call f(6) is ignored in deference to B::f(double), which hides the global one. The global f is explicitly invoked using the scope resolution operator in the call ::f(5).

Controlling Instantiation with Inheritance and Access Control

Sometimes, a base class exists only as a framework on which to build derived classes. For example, the above Telephone class serves as the framework for some real telephone types with specialized behaviors: ISDNPhone for a kind of digital phone, and POTSPhone for "plain old telephone service" telephones. Class Telephone declares what is common to the behaviors of all such telephones, as defined by the semantics of their member functions. It may also serve to hold implementation details common to all telephones (e.g., a phone number) independent of their type.

Using C++ protection constructs, a class offers its interface as a framework for derived classes, while preventing the creation of instances of itself. Consider the following `Telephone` example:

```
class Telephone {
public:
    ~Telephone();
    void ring();
    . . . .
protected:
    Telephone();
private:
    . . . .
};

class ISDNPhone: public Telephone {
    . . . .
};

class POTSPhone: public Telephone {
    . . . .
};
```

Notice that `Telephone::Telephone()` is `protected`. This suggests that its constructor cannot be "called" except from a derived class. The semantics of such a declaration are that an object of class `Telephone` cannot be declared. An abstract telephone cannot exist on its own: Only specific, real-world telephones like `ISDNPhone` and `POTSPhone` can actually be declared and instantiated. Properties common to all "general" or "abstract" phones are part of the "particular" phones; the constructor for the base class is implicitly called when a derived class is instantiated. But an object of the base class cannot be instantiated on its own.

Actually, the protection against making an object of type `Telephone` is not perfect here: One can be created in member functions of any subclass of `Telephone`, or in any `friend` functions of class `Telephone` if such should exist.

Section 5.4 in the chapter on Object-Oriented Programming describes more powerful language constructs that more directly and accurately communicate the design intent of an abstract base class.

4.3 Constructors and Destructors

Constructors and destructors are special member functions that automatically initialize new class objects as they come into existence and orchestrate cleanup of objects at the end of their lives. An object of an inherited class contains data members contributed by several different classes, and the constructors and destructors of all those classes contribute to the initialization and destruction of that object. This section looks at constructors and destructors in the context of inheritance: their order of execution, and mechanisms for one class to parameterize a base class constructor.

Order of Execution of Constructors and Destructors

When inheritance is used, an object is manipulated by member functions of its own class and all parent classes above it. Each object has multiple constructors and destructors, which means that initialization and cleanup logic are distributed instead of centralized in a single member function. It is important that each constructor is called to do its part of initialization and that each knows which constructors came before it so that it knows what states can be safely used.

Constructors of classes in an inheritance hierarchy follow a predictable pattern of execution. The compiler automatically orchestrates the execution of base class constructors and constructors for objects embedded inside the object being built. The code in the body of the constructor is only half the story: the compiler also supplies its own code to allocate memory and invoke related constructors as appropriate.

Memory is dynamically allocated when an object is created using the `new` keyword, invoking either the class's own `operator new` function if one exists, or the global `::operator new` otherwise. If the object is not being dynamically allocated using `new`, the constructor uses the memory provided by the variable it is constructing (automatics and globals) or that has been set up beforehand in some other way (for example, by a constructor in a derived class).

If a constructor belongs to a derived class, its first job is to call its base class constructor. A constructor does this automatically without the programmer having to code it; however, the programmer can exercise some control over how the constructor is called (see below). That constructor, seeing that memory is already allocated, in turn calls its base class constructors.

Next, a constructor initializes any of its own data members that are class objects by invoking their constructors. These objects are ordinarily initialized using their default constructor (Section 3.1); this can be changed with an initializer list, as described below.

After a constructor has arranged for its base class and member objects to be initialized, the user-supplied constructor body is executed. The body may assign new values to the previously initialized fields. The body should also initialize all data members that are of a built-in type such as `int`, `short`, `long`, `char`, and `double`, as well as any pointers.

When a constructor completes, it returns control to the point where it was called. When a base class constructor completes, it returns to the derived class constructor from which it was invoked, and initialization of the derived class object ensues from that point. The last thing to be executed is the initialization code in the class at the leaf (most derived class) of the inheritance hierarchy.

When a constructor is compiled, the compiler usually adds implicit code to handle C++ memory management, member function dispatching, base class constructor calls, and initialization of data members which themselves are class objects. Users can normally ignore the presence of this code. Because such code is installation and version dependent, you should not come to rely on its details, anyhow.

Destructors execute in the reverse order of constructors: first, the destructor of the object's class; second, destructors of non-static member objects; and third, destructors of base classes. If the class of the operand (the class at the leaf of the inheritance hierarchy) has (or inherits) an `operator delete`, then that function is called to reclaim memory instead of the system default. Freeing memory for the operand object itself is the last thing done before the destructor returns.

Passing Parameters to Constructors of Base Classes and Members

Let's look at the syntax for the constructor `Imaginary::Imaginary(double)` on page 89. Note that the body of this constructor is empty; it is executed just for its side effects. If the user had written a simple definition for this constructor,

```
Imaginary::Imaginary(double d) {
    ipart = d;
}
```

then the compiler would have arranged for the default base class constructor— `Complex::Complex()`—to be called at the head of `Imaginary::Imaginary` before the assignment was done. This makes it possible for `Imaginary` to assume that the `Complex` class is completely initialized, and that `Complex`'s data can be used to build the `Imaginary` class.

The `Imaginary` constructor's formal parameters are of potential use to its base class constructors, and the programmer has the flexibility to direct the compiler to call a specific base class constructor. In the example on page 89, the programmer explicitly specified that `Complex(0,i)` be invoked prior to the execution of `Imaginary::Imaginary(double)`.

It should also be noted that the `Complex::Complex(double,double)` constructor (Figure 4-1) specifies how `rpart` and `ipart` are initialized. The following two behave almost identically:

```
Imaginary::Imaginary(double a,        Imaginary::Imaginary(double a,
                     double b)                             double b)
{                                         : rpart(a), ipart(b)
    rpart = a;                         {
    ipart = b                              /* empty */
}                                      }
```

It is possible to reduce redundant copying if the constructor is called directly as on the right, compared to invoking assignment as on the left. This is more pronounced in the `PathName` example, where the elements to be copied into the new object are character strings and not just simple machine words:

```
PathName::PathName()                  PathName::PathName()
{                                         : baseNameRep(""), String()
    rep = String("");                     { /* empty */ }
    baseNameRep = String("");
}
```

Also, `baseNameRep` must be initialized before it is assigned to anyhow; in the left-hand example, the constructor `String::String()` is invoked on `baseNameRep` after the base class `String` is initialized, and before `PathName` constructor statements are executed. Note that this means `rep` is doubly initialized, too—once in the implicit call of the base class constructor, and once explicitly in the constructor for `PathName`.

In the constructor `PathName(const PathName&)`, we see a similar construct. The base class constructor `String::String(const String&)` is explicitly directed to be called with `p` as a parameter. It is invoked before any of the code of the `PathName` constructor is executed.

Another example of one constructor providing parameters for the invocation of the constructor of its base class is the declaration of class `Square` in the `Shapes` example in Appendix B. A square is a special case of a rectangle. The only distinction between the two is in the way they are made: `Square` needs only one parameter, not two, describing the length of a side. This is handled in the constructor simply by having it use the `Rectangle` constructor:

```
class Square: public Rect {
public:
    Square(Coordinate ctr, long x): Rect(ctr, x, x) { }
};
```

This new abstraction, which has all the power and behaviors of a `Rectangle`, was created with four lines of code.

4.4 Class Pointer Conversion

We can use the properties of inheritance to gain architectural leverage that simplifies the design and maintenance of a large system. Much of the power of inheritance is in its support for general application code to treat objects of classes in an inheritance hierarchy as plug-compatible abstractions. All such objects can be treated as though they were instances of the class at the root of the tree. This is called *polymorphism* (*poly*=many, *morphe*=form); many different forms of objects can be treated as if they were the same. This means application code can ignore the implementation details for specific kinds of `Telephones` (for example, `POTSPhones` and `ISDNPhones`), and just treat them all as `Telephones`. (Where some application code does need to address the peculiar functionality of a specific kind of phone, it can reach into lower levels of abstraction and do what it must.) This section and the next will lay some groundwork for a much more elegant and powerful approach to be presented in Chapter 5.

This programming power is based on conversion between pointers to objects of classes related by inheritance. You will find that most C++ programs access their objects by pointers, as objects are frequently allocated from the heap. C++ pointer variables offer two kinds of flexibility not found in ordinary instance variables. First, a base class pointer can point to an object of any class in the derivation hierarchy underneath it. Second, member functions invoked through a pointer are selected at run time instead of compile time, if the functions are declared to be *virtual*. These two properties are fundamental to object-oriented programming, which is covered in Chapter 5. If a class reference variable is bound to an object, then member functions called through that variable also receive polymorphic treatment; however, pointers are the more common case. Direct application of member functions to an object using the dot operator (for example, officePhone.ring) does not provide this flexibility.

In general, if we declare a pointer to an object of some class *C*, we can use that pointer to hold the address of an object of any of its descendant classes—that is, of a child, grandchild, or other *n*-th generation derived class. You *cannot* always go the other way. So, for example, a Telephone* can be used to point to *any* Telephone, ISDNPhone, or POTSPhone object. Something thought to be a Telephone can point to a POTSPhone because the features of the former are "covered" by the latter. It is illegal to go the other way because not all POTSPhone behaviors may be covered by Telephone: they are not common to all telephones. The error can be detected at compile time.

You *can*, with an explicit cast, convert a base class pointer into a derived class pointer. The cast tells the compiler you know something about the type of the object that the compiler does not. Claiming to know more than the compiler does is frequently dangerous, particularly if such assumptions are based on disjoint segments of code throughout the program.

If a base class member function applies equally well to objects of all derived classes, then a general base class pointer can be used to apply the member function to any object in the hierarchy, without having to know the exact type of the object at compile time. One example of where this is particularly useful is for functions outside the telephone class hierarchy that apply general telephone class operations to telephone objects, without having to know what kinds of telephone they are manipulating. Here, a ringPhones function takes a heterogeneous vector of pointers to Telephones as a parameter:

```
void ringPhones(Telephone *phoneArray[])
{
    for (Telephone *p = phoneArray; p; p++) {
        p->ring();
    }
}

int main()
{
    Telephone *phoneArray[10];
    int i = 0;
    phoneArray[i++] = new POTSPhone("5384");
    phoneArray[i++] = new ISDNPhone("5010");
    phoneArray[i++] = new ISDNPhone("0");
    phoneArray[i++] = new POTSPhone("5383");
    phoneArray[i++] = 0;
    ringPhones(phoneArray);
    . . . .
}
```

This will work: `Telephone::ring` is invoked for each of the telephone objects put in `phoneArray`. But this approach cannot take advantage of any data or member functions that are customized for the derived classes, because `ringPhones` only knows what is knowable about the base class `Telephone` at compile time. To illustrate, let's add the following class `OperatorPhone` with its own customized `ring` operation, and then run a slightly modified `main` program:

```
class OperatorPhone: public ISDNPhone {
public:
    OperatorPhone();
    OperatorPhone(OperatorPhone&);
    ~OperatorPhone();
    void ring();     // special ringing needed for operator
};

int main()
{
    Telephone *phoneArray[10];
    int i = 0;
    phoneArray[i++] = new POTSPhone("5384");
    phoneArray[i++] = new ISDNPhone("5010");
    phoneArray[i++] = new OperatorPhone("0");   // has its
                                                // own ring
    phoneArray[i++] = new POTSPhone("5383");
    phoneArray[i++] = 0;
    ringPhones(phoneArray);
    . . . .
}
```

Because `ringPhones` knows only that the vector elements are `Telephones`, it invokes `Telephone::ring` on each of the phones. While our intent may be for it to call the special `ring` function for `OperatorPhone`, the compiler does not have enough context to do that. We'll see in Chapter 5 how the compiler can provide that context automatically by using virtual functions. A "poor man's" alternative is to embed a *type selector field* in each object, as described below.

4.5 Type Selector Fields

A *type selector field* is a base class data member whose value indicates the type of the object containing it. The *virtual function* mechanism described in Chapter 5 is preferred over type fields. Type fields still are used in advanced idioms, and they are introduced here both anticipating such use and to provide a logical model of the model virtual functions automate.

```
class Telephone {
public:
    enum PhoneType { POTS, ISDN, OPERATOR, OTHER } phoneType()
        { return phoneTypeVal; }
    void ring();
    Bool isOnHook();
    Bool isTalking();
    Bool isDialing();
    DigitString collectDigits();
    LineNumber extension();   // not overridden below
    ~Telephone();
protected:
    LineNumber extensionData;
    PhoneType phoneTypeVal;
    Telephone();
};

class POTSPhone: public Telephone {
public:
    Bool runDiagnostics();
    POTSPhone(): phoneTypeVal(POTS) . . . . {
        . . . .
    }
    POTSPhone(POTSPhone &p): phoneTypeVal(POTS) . . . . {
        . . . .
    }
    ~POTSPhone();
private:
    Frame frameNumberVal;
    Rack rackNumberVal;
    Pair pairVal;
};

class ISDNPhone: public Telephone {
public:
    ISDNPhone(): phoneTypeVal(ISDN) . . . .     { . . . . }
    ISDNPhone(ISDNPhone &p): phoneTypeVal(ISDN) . . . . {
        . . . .
    }
    ~ISDNPhone();
    void sendBPacket();   // send a packet on the B channel
    void sendDPacket();   // send a packet on the D channel
private:
    Channel b1, b2, d;
};
```

Figure 4-5. Telephone Objects with Type Selector Fields

In Figure 4-5 we find a new rendition of `Telephone` using a type field to discriminate between different types of telephone objects. This field is present in objects for all kinds of phones, so we can always look at an object pointed to by a `Telephone*` and ascertain its type. Note that the constructor for each derived class of `Telephone` deposits its identification in the new field.

Now we can rewrite `ringPhones`:

```
void ringPhones(Telephone *phoneArray[])
{
    for (Telephone *p = phoneArray; p; p++) {
        switch (p->phoneType()) {
        case Telephone::POTS:
            ((POTSPhone *)p)->ring(); break;
        case Telephone::ISDN:
            ((ISDNPhone *)p)->ring(); break;
        case Telephone::OPERATOR:
            ((OperatorPhone *)p)->ring(); break;
        case Telephone::OTHER:
        default:
            error( . . . . );
        }
    }
}
```

The proper `ring` operation is now called independent of the class of the phone. It even has some foresight built into it; the first two cases could just have invoked `p->ring()`, since neither `POTSPhone` nor `ISDNPhone` have a custom `ring` operation. But written as is, it works; furthermore, even if a `ring` operation is added to `POTSPhone` or `ISDNPhone`, this code continues to work.

This code, as written, relies on a type field whose contents are manipulated at run time, to decide what function should be called for a given object. However, the compiler "knows" an object's class when it is created, so the compiler could generate code to associate type information with every object at run time. If such an annotated object were to exist at run time and a member function `ring` were to be applied to it, then the compiler could use the object's type information to automate the decision of which `ring` operation to call. This is how C++ virtual member functions work. Virtual functions are usually preferred over type fields, and will be discussed further in Chapter 5. It is a rule of thumb in the C++ community that type fields should be avoided; so, as written, this code is for instructive purposes only.

Type fields are used in advanced idioms presented later in the book, such as simulating multimethods (selecting a function at run time based on the types of multiple parameters) as in Section 9.7; another use can be found in the functors example of Section 5.6. An extensible type field idiom is described in some detail in Stroustrup [1].

Let's look at the shortcomings of the type selector field approach. When run-time operator selection is managed manually at the source level, as with the `switch` statement in `ringPhones`, program evolution becomes tedious and cumbersome. Even though the code does not need to be rewritten if we add a `ring` operator to `POTSPhone`, it needs to be recompiled under most C++ implementations. Consider, too, what it would take to add a new phone class: `ringPhones` would have to be modified, as well as *all* similar functions. The type discriminant enumeration in the base class would need a new element, and the coder of the new class would need to take care to initialize its type field in all its constructors. Everything touched by these changes would have to be recompiled and retested.

Exercises

1. Discuss uses of private inheritance.

2. Discuss ways of simulating data abstraction and inheritance in C.

3. Consider software structures that use the handle/body idiom for memory management and run-time flexibility; that is, the application class makes use of an auxiliary class inside itself, containing most of the implementation details. This is sometimes done to distance applications from changes to the implementation—for example, a change in the structuring of its data. The overall function of the object can be split between the handle and the body, just as functionality is split between the base and derived class under inheritance.

   Inheritance can be implemented two ways: by deriving from the outer handle class, or by deriving from the inner (''body'') classes, keeping the same envelope for all of them. Explore and discuss these two alternatives and the tradeoffs between them. Are there other alternatives?

4. Compile the following program:

   ```
   #include <iostream.h>

   class ZooAnimal {
   protected:
       int zooLoc;
   public:
       int cnt;
   };
   ```

```
class Bear: public ZooAnimal {
public:
    int find(ZooAnimal*);
};

int
Bear::find( ZooAnimal *pz ) {
    if (cnt) cout << zooLoc;
    if (pz->cnt) cout << pz->zooLoc;
}
```

What happens when you try to compile it? What does this tell you about the C++ protection model as it relates to objects and classes? Can you circumvent this protection? If so, how? *(See Lippman [2].)*

5. Define the classes that would be present in an elevator control system, with multiple elevators working together. What operations should be defined for the classes in this system? Are all of your classes "general nouns"? Why or why not?

6. Analyze (or compile and run) the following program:

```
class A {
public:
    A(int i = 0) { a = i; }
    A& operator=(A& x) { a = x.a; return *this; }
protected:
    int a;
};

class B: public A {
public:
    B(int i = 0): A(i) { b = i; }
    B& operator=(B& x) { b = x.b; return *this; }
private:
    int b;
};

int main() {
    B b1, b2(2);
    b1 = b2;
}
```

What is the resulting value of b1.a? What does this tell you about how you have to implement assignment when inheritance is used? How would you fix the problem in this instance?

□

References

1. Stroustrup, B. *The C++ Programming Language*, 2nd ed. Reading, Mass.: Addison-Wesley, 1991, ch. 13.

2. Lippman, Stanley B. *A C++ Primer*. Reading, Mass.: Addison-Wesley, 1989.

5

Object-Oriented Programming

Object-oriented programming is a program implementation style with roots in the encapsulation and abstraction of abstract data types. A programming language and development environment support abstract data types through a *type system*—the "stuff" that does type checking and ensures that double precision addition machine instructions are generated if you say a + b, where the addends are declared to be double precision. Languages with type systems were initially created to generate code that was more efficient than code compiled from untyped programs, but "type safety" was also an important consideration.

Most type systems live in the compiler and its associated tools; all the factors mentioned above are traditional compiler concerns and have no presence as such in a running program. However, the compiler may do some type conversion or optimization that makes some aspects of the type system visible at run-time. Consider the simple sequence

```
int i;
double d;
. . . .
d = i;
```

where the compiler needs to generate code to convert an integer to a double at *run* time. The degree of similarity between integers and double precision numbers makes such a conversion possible and natural; to a degree, the two types are "plug-compatible." In languages like C, all types are predetermined, and the compiler knows all operators applicable to these types, can interpret them in context, and can generate code directly to perform operations or convert between types.

Enter classes, where the programmer defines new types (for example, concrete data types, as in Chapter 3) and relationships between them (for example, using inheritance, as in Chapter 4). C++ makes it possible to construct systems using the organizing principle of hierarchies, a natural abstraction tool of the human mind.

117

These hierarchies and types are outside the domain of what the compiler knows, so it needs help from the user to provide the degree of "plug-compatibility" expected between similar classes.

The number of distinct class hierarchies in a large system may be cognitively manageable even when the number of individual classes is not. To use the power of hierarchy, programmers need to be able to work effectively along the top layers of the hierarchy without delving into derived classes. This principle applies to design and coding alike. Code written in terms of the high-level abstraction `SignedQuantity` may actually be dealing with values of classes `Complex` or `InfinitePrecision` at run time, where the latter two classes are in the inheritance tree under `SignedQuantity`. If the programmer writes

```
void afunction(SignedQuantity &c, SignedQuantity &d) {
    . . . . c + d . . . .
}
```

then the addition operation from the appropriate class must be selected from context at run time. This outstrips the compile-time type system, but for the sake of performance and type safety, run-time support can pick up where compile-time support left off. *This is the essence of object-oriented programming.* A new type system emerges based on the encapsulation of abstract data types, arranged in hierarchies, with run-time type support.

C++ strikes a balance between a compile-time type system component that preserves code efficiency and a run-time component offering flexibility and "plug-compatible" software parts. The language provides the basics needed for object-oriented programming, but maintains constructs for cultural compatibility with C.

Object-oriented programming is in some sense just a programming trick using indirection, a trick good programmers have been using for years. Two points are worth emphasizing: the importance of language support for these techniques and the even greater importance of the design principles behind them.

First, C++ takes such practices out of the realm of tricks and gives them first-class language standing which means that programs are more readable, writable, and maintainable. That is often good enough. But to make these tricks work effectively in C++ requires that the programmer be skilled in a few canonical forms and language idioms beyond those manifest in the syntax. C++ provides an extra level of indirection for functions: programmers needing an extra level of indirection in data, for increased flexibility or more general abstraction in another dimension, need a few additional idioms. Such idioms are described in this chapter. They are among the most important idioms in this book.

Second, the tricks themselves are not as important as the design and architectural principles they support. Good software is less the result of optimal syntax as of the well-trained and insightful thought processes of its craftspersons. In that context, this chapter lays a foundation for the design practices to be discussed in Chapter 6, where we find the ideas with the greatest leverage of any in the book. But the programmer and designer must remember that the design techniques are most effectively leveraged with the idioms discussed below.

5.1 C++ Run-Time Type Support: Virtual Functions

Class inheritance, described in the preceding chapter, gives the programmer the power to organize code in new ways supporting software reuse. Code common to several classes can be factored into a base class, and derived classes can augment the behaviors of the base class to create more refined or specialized abstractions. A variable declared as a base class pointer can be used to address an object of any of its derived classes and can invoke any of the common (base class) member functions of that object. This provides a degree of *polymorphism*: the same pointer can be used to manipulate objects of several different forms. A programmer may declare a pointer that can validly point to any object from a set of classes in an inheritance tree. Using that pointer, all such objects can be manipulated equivalently without knowledge of their particular class: Each is treated in terms of its *general* type, the base class of the hierarchy (Figure 5-1).

Inheritance allows us to apply a common set of member functions to objects whose classes are related to each other as siblings and cousins in an inheritance hierarchy. However, if inheritance alone is used to support polymorphism, it extends only to functions whose *implementations* are shared by the classes of interest. If a derived class has its own variation on the implementation of a base class member function, inheritance alone will not cause the derived class version to be selected when a function is invoked on an object of that class through a variable declared in terms of its base class. The pointer is typed to know about the base class, and it is ignorant of the structure or even the existence of derived classes. Consider a salary administration program using class Employee in the context of Figure 5-1. If the program understands Employees in general but is ignorant of SecurityGuards and Managers, it knows only how to give *default* raise treatment to any object in the Employee hierarchy. It simply does not have the context to do anything smarter.

We want the base class to have a robust interface that characterizes the *behaviors* of the abstraction it represents, expressed in the names, return types, and parameter types of its member functions. Member functions public to the base class either become part of the derived class interface, or are replaced in the derived class by a more suitable function with the same logical behavior. All base class behaviors apply

```
class Employee {
public:
    double salary() { return sal; }
    double computeRaise() { return 25; }
    Employee(double salary) { sal = salary; }
private:
    double sal;
};
```

```
class Manager: public Employee {
public:
    double computeRaise() { return 100; }
    Manager(double salary):
        Employee(salary) { }
};
```

```
class SecurityGuard: public Employee {
public:
    double computeRaise() { return 50; }
    SecurityGuard(double salary):
        Employee(salary) { }
};
```

```
Manager *boss1 = new Manager(2000);        // valid
double boss1Salary = boss1->salary();      // yields 2000
Employee *boss2 = new Manager(2300);       // valid
double boss2Salary = boss2->salary();      // returns 2300

double boss1Raise = boss1->computeRaise();  // yields 100
double boss2Raise = boss2->computeRaise();  // yields 25
```

Figure 5-1. A Weak Form of Polymorphism Using Inheritance.

When the type of the pointer exactly matches the type of the object, the right result is returned. When a general base class type pointer is used to address a derived class, only the base class functions are invoked: that another function of the same name resides in the object's class is invisible to the pointer.

to objects of all derived classes, so the base class represents the behaviors of all the classes derived from it.

We did this with inheritance in Chapter 4 by defining the ring member function differently for different kinds of telephones. A derived class may *override* the implementation of its base class member functions—that is, it may provide its own implementation of a function appearing in its base class public interface. Overriding a base class function of a given name with a derived class function of the same name is a way to fine-tune implementation, while preserving the fundamental meaning of the function as named. Applying the ring operator to telephones of different classes has the same meaning for all of them, though the details of the implementation differ according to the phone type.

We want the compiler to make the interchangeability of these objects as transparent as possible. The compiler knows that a suitably named function appears in the interface of the base class, but we want it to arrange to automatically call the function from the appropriate derived class—the class from which the object was originally created. We want the selection of the function to be determined by the *object's class*, not by the declaration of the pointer used to address it. As a result, the programmer can truly treat all objects of *any* of these classes equivalently, and the right thing will happen: `Managers` will get managerial raises, even though the raise administration program invokes `computeRaise` knowing only about `Employees` in general at compile time.

This capability is called *run-time operator identification* and, together with inheritance, it provides a form of polymorphism that gives the designer and programmer a flexible toolkit to create high-level software components. A style of programming that uses this capability uniformly on concrete data types is called *object-oriented programming*; it is the most straightforward way of supporting object-oriented design in C++.

Run-time operator identification applies only to references or pointers to class objects. Why? Because only variables declared to be pointers or references may be used to refer either to an object of their class or to an object of some subsequently derived class. One rationalization for this might be that it is only through the use of pointers that type information is lost: If you want to invoke a member function directly on an instance, then you must have a declaration of the object's class in hand, and such invocations are compile-time bound. However, if a pointer to an object exists distant from the point of initial object creation, it is not necessary for the user to pass along all the baggage of the type's details to any part of the program that touches the object.

Let's revisit the `Telephone` example from Chapter 4 and do it *right*, using the object paradigm. Actually, few changes are necessary. The original is recalled in Figure 5-2.

Note that we are using the version of the classes without the embedded "type identification" information that was present in Chapter 4 (page 110). We do not need it here—the compiler takes care of it automatically. We declare some base class member functions `virtual` and can provide customized versions of the same function in derived classes. The compiler generates code for virtual member function calls that causes the right derived class version of the function to be chosen at run time, based on the type of the object. Whenever an object is constructed from a class with virtual functions, the compiler arranges to deposit the "type field" of the class into the object. (The details of implementation vary across compilers, but all *conceptually* reduce to use of a type field as shown in Section 4.5. The field is for the compiler's use, and the language has no provision to make it accessible to the programmer.) Furthermore, the compiler arranges to do that more efficiently than can be done by hand, and in a way that has a smaller impact of change. For example, a program with a manually administered type field needs widespread edits and recompilation when a new derived class is added. When virtual functions are used, all

```
class Telephone {
public:
    void ring();
    Bool isOnHook() isTalking(), isDialing();
    DigitString collectDigits();
    LineNumber extension();
    ~Telephone();
protected:
    Telephone();
    LineNumber extensionData;
};
class POTSPhone : public Telephone {
public:
    Bool runDiagnostics();
    POTSPhone();
    POTSPhone(POTSPhone&);
    ~POTSPhone();
private:
    Frame frameNumberVal;
    Rack rackNumberVal;
    Pair pairVal;
};
class ISDNPhone : public Telephone {
public:
    ISDNPhone();
    ISDNPhone(ISDNPhone&);
    ~ISDNPhone();
    void sendBPacket(), sendDPacket();
private:
    Channel b1, b2, d;
};
class OperatorPhone : public ISDNPhone {
public:
    OperatorPhone();
    OperatorPhone(OperatorPhone&);
    ~OperatorPhone();
    void ring();    // special ringing needed for operator
};
class PrincessPhone : public POTSPhone {
    . . . .
};
```

Figure 5-2. A Telephone Example

that needs to be recoded or recompiled in most C++ environments is source code referring directly to the new class. *It is a bad idea to manually place a type identification field in a class.* It makes the program difficult to evolve.

The first step to making the Telephone class object-oriented is to make its member functions virtual. We make base class functions virtual to tell the compiler that the behavior and implementation of those functions will be sensitive to what class they are being applied to, and that the base class cannot foresee the needs of all derived classes that might be created over the life of the program. That gives us the freedom to provide new implementations of those functions in classes derived from the base where the virtual function declaration appears. So there may be any number of different versions of a given virtual function, as many as one for each class in the inheritance hierarchy under that base.

The base class usually defines a body for a virtual function, which may be inherited by a derived class as a default if it chooses not to override its implementation. If the derived class does not override the function, then the derived class behaves as if the base class class function were part of its interface. If the function is overridden in one or more derived classes, then the derived class version overrides the base class version. What distinguishes virtual functions from other functions is that the derived class function *always* prevails—even when the derived class object appears in a context where an object of the base class is expected.

Virtual functions cause the compiler to arrange for run-time support so that for derived class objects, the function from the appropriate derived class is called when invoking a function declared virtual in the base class. We want the operation to suit the type of the object to which it is applied, *not* to be inferred from the type of the pointer used to invoke it (Figure 5-3). Here's how the base class looks with the virtual declarations:

```
class Telephone {
public:
    virtual void ring();
    virtual Bool isOnHook();
    virtual Bool isTalking();
    virtual Bool isDialing();
    virtual DigitString collectDigits();
    virtual ~Telephone();
    LineNumber extension();
protected:
    LineNumber extensionData;
    Telephone();
};
```

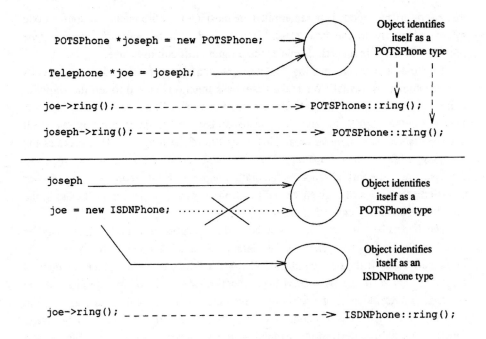

Figure 5-3. Virtual Function Run-Time Identification.

The identity of the operator that is invoked tracks the type of the object being
pointed to, not the type of the pointer, when the function is virtual

Nothing other than adding the `virtual` key words needs to be done to the base class. The `virtual` keyword must be added where the function is *declared* in the class declaration, not where the function is *defined*.

In the design of a base class, we may create functions that we would never expect to be overridden in the derived class. For example, the member functions `isOnHook`, `isTalking`, and `isDialing` are thought of as ordinary member functions that could be implemented as straightforward base class member functions without any help from derived classes. That is, those functions are not just placeholders, they provide default behaviors suitable to all derived classes. However, experience shows that base class member functions often need to be overridden in derived classes as the system evolves, and it is good for the sake of uniformity to declare them virtual in the first place. Even if no advantage is ever taken of their run-time properties, the run time overhead cost is negligible: Making a function virtual typically adds about 15 percent to the cost of a function call. If function calls constitute 10 percent of a program's execution profile, the ubiquitous use of virtual functions will cause about a 2 percent performance drop. However, virtual functions need to be compared to what the alternative implementations would be without them. Programs written in C are likely to use switch or if statements where C++ programs would use virtual functions to select from among alternatives at run time. Some applications (for example, a Scheme interpreter written in C++ [1]) have found virtual functions *faster* than using the switch/case approach.

Now we can rewrite applications using the new behavior. To refresh our memories, here's the old ringPhones function:

```
void ringPhones(Telephone *phoneArray[])
{
    for (Telephone *p = phoneArray; p; p++) {
        switch (p->phoneType()) {
        case POTS:
            ((POTSPhone *)p)->ring(); break;
        case ISDN:
            ((ISDNPhone *)p)->ring(); break;
        case OPERATOR:
            ((OperatorPhone *)p)->ring(); break;
        case OTHER:
        default:
                error( . . . . );
        }
    }
}
```

A much simpler version is now appropriate:

```
void ringPhones(Telephone *phoneArray[])
{
    for (Telephone *p = phoneArray; p; p++) p->ring();
}
```

If p points to an OperatorPhone object, then p->ring() will invoke OperatorPhone::ring(). If it points to any other kind of object in this Telephone hierarchy, then Telephone::ring() will be invoked instead, since no other class redefines the default behavior of telephone ringing.

Note that this works only if the function is declared virtual in the base class. Consider the following:

```
Telephone *digitalPhone = new ISDNPhone;
. . . .
digitalPhone->sendDPacket();     // wrong, won't find function
```

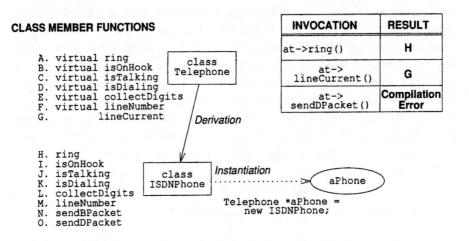

CLASS MEMBER FUNCTIONS

A. virtual ring
B. virtual isOnHook
C. virtual isTalking
D. virtual isDialing
E. virtual collectDigits
F. virtual lineNumber
G.   lineCurrent

H. ring
I. isOnHook
J. isTalking
K. isDialing
L. collectDigits
M. lineNumber
N. sendBPacket
O. sendDPacket

INVOCATION	RESULT
at->ring()	H
at->lineCurrent()	G
at->sendDPacket()	Compilation Error

Figure 5-4. Inheritance of the Virtual-ness of Functions

This example does not work, because sendDPacket is not declared in base class Telephone. Even if sendDPacket had been declared virtual in its own class, it still would not help (though that would allow virtual behavior with the derived classes of ISDNPhone). For run-time operator identification to occur, the member function must be virtual. A member function can become virtual in one of two ways. A member function is virtual if it is declared virtual in the class used to declare the pointer through which the operation is invoked. A member function is also virtual if a member function of the same name with the same type and parameters appears higher in the inheritance hierarchy (Figure 5-4). The virtual-ness of a function is inherited by derived classes all the way down an inheritance hierarchy.

Another way of thinking about the virtual keyword is that it creates a new kind of declaration for something different than a member function. Virtual member functions may be thought of as being not functions but as declarations of *names* of functions. Ordinary (nonvirtual) member function declarations are functions; they bind directly to function bodies at compile or link-edit time. Virtual functions do not. When a virtual function name is invoked at run time, its name is used to bind the call to a function. In this sense, virtual functions are analogous to method selectors in Smalltalk, and the member function bodies are analogous to Smalltalk methods.

5.2 Destructor Interaction and Virtual Destructors

Notice that the destructor `Telephone::~Telephone` is also virtual; this seems a bit unusual, since we do not normally think of *calling* a destructor. But, it really *is* important that it be virtual. Consider the following code:

```
class Telephone {
    . . . .
    ~Telephone();
    . . . .
};


Telephone *digitalPhone = new ISDNPhone;
. . . .
delete digitalPhone;
```

What happens? The `delete` invocation has no idea that the object is an `ISDNPhone`, and there is nothing in `Telephone` giving any indication that destructor invocations are to be looked up at run time. So the `Telephone` destructor is the one called. This means that if the `ISDNPhone` constructor allocated resources intended to be freed by the `ISDNPhone` destructor, they would *not* be and would become "garbage."

If the destructor of the base class `Telephone` is declared virtual, then at run time the code looks up the destructor suitable to the type of the object operated on:

```
class Telephone {
    . . . .
    virtual ~Telephone();
    . . . .
};


Telephone *digitalPhone = new ISDNPhone;
. . . .
delete digitalPhone;    // works, calls ISDNPhone::~ISDNPhone()
```

The object's own destructor is then invoked, causing the appropriate cleanup actions to occur. Of course, the base class destructor `Telephone::~Telephone()` will still be called immediately afterwards, following normal C++ destructor behavior (Section 4.3).

5.3 Virtual Functions and Scoping†

Making a function virtual may effectively change its scope. This can cause subtle changes in program semantics that are important to consider when building an inheritance hierarchy.

First, it is important to note that any function that is to receive run-time operator identification treatment *must* have exactly the same *signature* as the virtual function in its base class. The signature of a function is made up of its name, an ordered specification of its parameter types, and the function return type. (In C++, the return type is not formally used as part of the signature to resolve calls of overloaded functions, but it is still part of the function's characterization). Changing the return type of a virtual function is illegal:

```
class Number {
public:
    virtual float add(const Number&);
    Number(double);
    . . . .
};

class BigNumber: public Number {
public:
    virtual double add(const Number&);  // illegal
    BigNumber(double);
    . . . .
};
```

This change is illegal because an invocation of the add operation on some object yields an expression whose type is not compile-time knowable, so it is impossible to generate code to handle the return value:

```
void someFunction(Number &num) {
    Number a = 10, *num;
    . . . . num->add(a) . . . .      // double or float?
};
```

Another way to "break" virtual function behavior is to change the parameter list of the function in the derived class. It is legal to do so, but what results is two distinct functions with no relationship to each other: One function *hides* another of the same name, at a higher level in the inheritance hierarchy. For example, consider the

---

† See Sections 3.2 and 4.2 before reading this section.

```
class Number {           // base class
public:
    virtual void add(int);
    . . . .
};

class BigNumber : public Number {    // derived class
public:
    void add(double);
    . . . .
};

int main() {
    Number *a;
    BigNumber *b, bo;
    . . . .
    a->add(1);               // Number::add(int)
    a->add(3.0);             // Number::add(int) with
                             //     coercion int(3.0)
    b->add(2);               // BigNumber::add(double) with
                             //     promotion double(2)
    b->add(2.0);             // BigNumber::add(double)
    b->Number::add(7.0);     // Number::add(int) with
                             //     coercion int(7.0)
    bo.add(8);               // BigNumber::add(double)
                             //     promotion double(8)
    bo.add(9.0);             // BigNumber::add(double)
    bo.Number::add(9);       // Number::add(int)
    bo.Number::add(10.0);    // Number::add(int) with
                             //     coercion int(10.0)
    return 0;
}
```

Figure 5-5. Signature Changes Breaking the Inheritance of Virtual-ness

program in Figure 5-5, where BigNumber::add(double) completely hides a function of the same name in the base class, so it is inaccessible to users of the derived class. This would also be true if BigNumber::add were declared to be virtual.

Scoping and virtual functions can interact in other subtle ways. Consider the following code:

```
#include <iostream.h>

class A { public: virtual void f(int); };
void A::f(int) { cout << "A::f\n"; }
class B: public A { public: void f(double); };
void B::f(double) { cout << "B::f\n"; }
class C: public B { public: virtual void f(int); };
void C::f(int) { cout << "C::f\n"; }

int main ()
{
    A *a;
    B *b;
    C *c = new C;
    c->f(2);        // C::f
    c->f(2.0);      // C::f with coercion
    b = c;
    b->f(2);        // B::f with promotion
    b->f(2.0);      // B::f
    a = c;
    a->f(2);        // C::f
    a->f(2.0);      // C::f with coercion
    return 0;
}
```

There is a virtual function defined in the root base class A, a nonvirtual with a different signature in the middle class B, with the virtual redefined in the leaf class C. What is noteworthy is that a virtual high in the class hierarchy can be hidden by a member function in the middle of the hierarchy. One way to think about this is that an object of class C carries with it C::f(int), but the visibility of C::f(int) changes with the type of the pointer addressing it. This counters our intuition, which would hold that making a function virtual ensures that the same function is called on an object no matter how it is referenced. Most C++ systems now warn that such overloaded functions hide a virtual function with the same name, appearing above it in inheritance structure.

5.4 Pure Virtual Functions and Abstract Base Classes

Consider again the `Telephone` example of Chapter 4, where a `protected` constructor made it impossible to create a `Telephone` instance (page 104). Instances were to be created only from derived classes: things like `POTSPhones` (Plain Ordinary Telephone Service telephones), `VideoPhone`, `ISDNPhone` (Integrated Services Digital Network phone), and so forth. We cannot actually *do* anything with an abstract `Telephone`! Why? Because we cannot write code (the `ring` member function) to ring phones in general, only code that knows how to ring a particular kind of phone. POTS phones get ringing voltage applied; digital ISDN phones get a message sent to them to generate ringing and to illuminate a lamp.

C++ has a syntax to succinctly capture the semantics of member functions such as `ring` in the declaration of the function itself. First, we recognize that such a function should be virtual: We want system software using all different kinds of `Telephone` objects to be able to invoke their `ring` member function without having to know their implementation details or their exact type. Second, we know we cannot write a general, default body for such a function, so we bind its body to the null pointer:

```
class Telephone {
public:
        virtual void ring() = 0;      // pure virtual function
        Bool isOnHook();
        Bool isTalking();
        Bool isDialing();
        virtual DigitString collectDigits();
        LineNumber extension();
        virtual ~Telephone();
        Telephone();                  // public again
        . . . .
};
```

Such a function is called a *pure virtual function*; it serves as a placeholder to assert that telephones, in general, can be rung, though we cannot state—in general terms— how to do it. They are "pure" in the sense that they have no body, but only an interface or pure signature.

Now it is impossible to create an object of class `Telephone` simply because the compiler would not know what to do with one if a `ring` operation were ever performed on it. Such a class is called an *abstract base class* or a *partial class*: It is abstract or partial in the sense that it defines some behaviors without defining their implementations. It imposes an obligation on its derived classes to define a set of member functions. As such, the class defines a type—an abstract data type—without defining implementation. An abstract base class is a specification of an abstract data type (ADT), and no more, if all its member functions are pure virtual.

Pure virtual functions specify more than the hidden constructor did in Chapter 4 (page 104). First, they declare that their class cannot be instantiated, or used as a formal parameter type or function return type. The hidden constructor had these properties, too, with the loophole that a base class object could be created from within a derived class member function. Second, pure virtual functions specify which functions must be overridden in a derived class if the derived class is to have any instances.

A body *can* be provided for a pure virtual function. A pure virtual with a body can be called using the scope resolution operator:

```
#include <iostream.h>

class Base {
public:
    virtual void pure() = 0;
};

class Derived: public Base {
public:
    void pure() { cout << "Derived::pure" << endl; }
    void foo()  { Base::pure(); }
};

void Base::pure() { cout << "Base::pure" << endl; }

int main() {
    Derived d;
    d.Base::pure();
    d.foo();
    d.pure();
    Base *b = &d;
    b->pure();
    return 0;
}
```

When run, this program produces the following as output:

```
Base::pure
Base::pure
Derived::pure
Derived::pure
```

If the body of Base::pure is removed, a link-edit-time error results.

This could be useful in the `Window` example. `Window` could insist that its derived classes provide their own version of `clear` but could still provide basic `clear` functionality common to all window types. For example, `Window::clear` might position the cursor to the middle of the screen when invoked as the final action of a derived class `clear` member function.

5.5 Envelope and Letter Classes

The handle/body class idiom supports design techniques offering greater flexibility, better performance, and reduced impact-of-change over the orthodox canonical form alone (Chapter 3). The envelope/letter is a technique using a pair of classes that act as one: an outer ("handle" or "skin") class that is the visible part, and an inner ("body") class where implementation details are buried. The handle is said to *forward* requests made of it to the body inside it. The two together form a *composite object.* Here, we introduce an extension of the handle/body idiom called the *envelope/letter* idiom that adds flexibility and encapsulation above what handles and bodies alone provide.

The handle/body idiom adds a level of run-time indirection to object interactions. The increased flexibility owes largely to this run-time binding and indirection. Though there are multiple objects, the appearance to the user is that there is a single object—the handle—which orchestrates the entire operation of the composite. This separation may be used to divorce a memory management veneer from the "real semantics" of an inner object for advanced memory management, as in the `String` example in Section 3.5. This separation also supports other garbage collection techniques and run-time class and object replacement schemes described in Chapter 9.

The envelope/letter class idiom is a special case of the handle class idiom, used when the handle class and body class share the same behaviors but when the body class behaviors specialize or augment the behaviors of the handle class. A handle class is called an envelope when used this way, and a body class is called a letter. The two classes are related in much the same way that a base class (the role played by the envelope) relates to a derived class (played by the letter), but with more run-time flexibility than found in inheritance. A letter class is derived from its envelope class, but its instances are also contained in envelope instances.

Envelope/letter class communities are usually more self-contained than classes in an inheritance hierarchy. Most letter classes are accessed only through their envelope. The same is largely true for classes in an inheritance hierarchy, with the exception that invocation of derived class constructors may be widespread in program code. Letter class constructor invocations tend to be localized to code of the envelope class.

☞ *When to use this idiom*: Sometimes we want more flexibility than is possible with C++ compile-time binding. Such flexibility may be motivated by the need to take over some traditional compile-time functions such as object/class association. Envelope/letter classes can provide more polymorphism and run-time type support than inheritance with virtual functions alone can. This can simplify and generalize user interactions with a package of related classes. It can also reduce impact of change on coding and recompilation.

The relationship between envelopes and their letters can be thought of in two ways. First, the envelope may be envisioned as delegating some of its functionality to a collaborating letter object. Secondly, the letter may be thought of as being in the envelope's employ, logically encapsulated inside the envelope. This second model of envelopes and letters is well suited to enforcing encapsulation, with strong analogies to the examples in Section 3.5.

The following section will look at envelopes and letters as they can be paired to provide more powerful object-oriented programming idioms than the single, compile-time classes "native" C++ offers. The section starts by motivating the need for run-time association between an object and the properties usually associated with its class. It then moves on to a special case of this idiom: how to conveniently bring objects into existence without knowing their exact class. This approach is expanded into an alternative allowing variable-sized objects without an extra level of indirection. A notational convenience is described to provide relief from duplicated code for envelopes and letters. The section closes with a refinement of envelopes and letters using C++ nested classes.

Envelope Classes and Delegated Polymorphism

In pure object-oriented programming languages like Smalltalk, variables are run-time bindings to objects that act like labels. Binding a variable to an object is like sticking a label on it. Assignment in these languages is analogous to peeling a label off one object and putting it on another. Variables in these languages have little or no type information associated with them, and little is done at compile time to enforce type compatibility. The objects themselves, of course, have operations, member functions, and attributes that together constitute type information, so type checking can still be done at run time. Languages with this property are at some disadvantage because of the type surprises that can arise at run time. But such languages offer a high degree of flexibility useful for prototyping and program evolution, and provide a basis for advanced memory management techniques. The C++ type model does not have this much run-time flexibility for two reasons: its early binding of symbols to addresses and its early enforcement of type compatibility.

In C and C++, variables are synonyms for addresses or offsets instead of being labels for objects. Assignment does not mean relabeling; it means overwriting the old contents with new ones. We compensate for this by manually adding a level of indirection, accessing objects through pointers. Though variable names are still associated with a piece of storage, the storage is "only" a pointer, so the association between the name and the "real" object is easily changed by overwriting the pointer. However, programming with pointers is sometimes awkward. Memory management becomes more difficult: Dangling pointers are a possibility. Accessing all objects through pointers makes the use of some programming language features inconvenient, particularly the use of operator overloading:

```
class Number {
public:
    Number();
    virtual Number *operator*(const Number&);
    . . . .
};

class Complex: public Number {
public:
    Complex(double,double);
    Number *operator*(const Number&);
    . . . .
};

class Integer: public Number {
public:
    Integer(int);
    Number *operator*(const Number&);
    . . . .
};

Number *numberVector[5], *numberVector2[5], *productVector[5];
. . . .
numberVector[0] = new Complex(0,10);
numberVector[1] = new Integer(0);
numberVector[2] = 0;
numberVector2[0] = new Integer(10);
numberVector2[1] = new Complex(10,10);
for (int i = 0; numberVector[i] && numberVector2[i]; i++) {
    // terrible (but necessary) syntax:
    productVector[i] = *numberVector[i] * *numberVector2[i];
}
```

The second complication is that the C++ compiler makes sure an object will be able to satisfy the member functions applied to the variable declared to address it. This is done through the compiler's enforcement of a *type system*. "Type system" as used in this sense has only a tenuous relationship to conceptual abstractions in the application, which can be thought of as formal types that the program reflects in its class structure (see Section 6.1). Type systems have proven useful in preventing errors; the C++ type system catches type mismatches at compile time. The C++ type system is conservative in its interpretation of the class structure and, by inference, in its view of the relationship between design abstractions: It catches all real misuse of application domain types but may block some valid application uses as well.

The loose variable-to-object binding and strong run-time type systems of symbolic languages help relieve the programmer from the burden of declaring compatibility between types. We often want to treat a collection of classes interchangeably, regarding all objects of these classes as though they belong to the same class. Virtual functions provide this functionality for pointer and reference variables. But pointers are fragile—they have been called "the GOTOs of data"—and they do not integrate well with overloaded operators. In the Number example above, pointers allow us to treat all the quantities as Numbers at the expense of clumsy syntax. What we really want to do is treat everything as a number, and let each object itself wield its expertise about how to handle things:

```
int main() {
    Number c(1.0, -2.1);
    Number r(5.0);
    Number product = c * r;
    r = 0;
    return 0;
}
```

One problem with this is that the objects have to figure out what their class is at run time: c becomes a Complex, r becomes a DoublePrecisionFloat, and product becomes whatever it is supposed to become. (The first two could in theory be done at compile time with a prescient compiler, but the third one would, in general, have to be done during execution.) But objects of different classes take different amounts of storage, so for an object to change its class, it would have to change its size, which is a quantity known at compile time. The binding of objects to virtual functions is done during object initialization and cannot be changed; this, also, gets in the way of an object changing its own type. Another problem is that once an object's class is set, the object may need to "change its mind" about what its class should be. For example, the initial definition of product suggests it should be a complex number; there may be no need to keep its Complex identity after being set to zero.

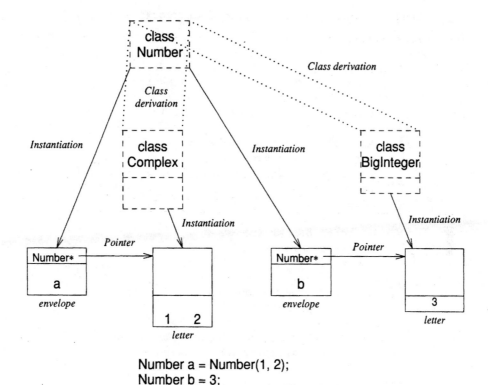

Number a = Number(1, 2);
Number b = 3;

Figure 5-6. Polymorphic Numbers

What we really want is a run-time association between an object and its class. Furthermore, we want variables to have loose association with the class of their objects—that is, to allow variables to "take on different types" over the course of execution. A collection of classes implementing such a flexible number package is illustrated in Figure 5-6 through Figure 5-8, and is discussed below.

To preserve reasonable semantics, all classes whose instances masquerade as numbers must have a Number-like signature. We express this in C++ by stating that such classes must be able to take Number as an abstract base class. A hierarchy of numeric types can be built under Number. Objects of these classes must be packaged in an "envelope" that preserves the identity (address, if you will) of a quantity as its value—and potentially, its type—change as operations are applied to it. This "envelope" has the same signature as the objects it holds, and the same class Number can do double duty as an abstract base for the "letter" classes, and as an "envelope" shielding representational details from the user. This model is illustrated in Figure 5-6, with sample code shown in Figure 5-7.

```
struct BaseConstructor { BaseConstructor(int=0) { } };

class Number {
public:
    Number() { rep = new RealNumber(0.0); }
    Number(double d) { rep = new RealNumber(d); }
    Number(double rpart, double ipart) {
        rep = new Complex(rpart, ipart);
    }
    Number operator=(const Number &n) {
        n.rep->referenceCount++;
        if (--rep->referenceCount == 0) delete rep;
        rep = n.rep;
        return *this;
    }
    Number(const Number &n) {
        n.rep->referenceCount++;
        rep = n.rep;
    }
    virtual Number operator+(const Number &n) {
        return rep->operator+(n);
    }
    virtual Number complexAdd(const Number &n) {
        return rep->complexAdd(n);
    }
    virtual Number realAdd(const Number &n) {
        return rep->realAdd(n);
    }
    void redefine(Number *n) {
        if (--rep->referenceCount == 0) delete rep;
        rep = n;
    }
    . . . .
protected:
    Number(BaseConstructor) { referenceCount = 1; }
private:
    Number *rep;
    short referenceCount;
};
```

Figure 5-7. Partial Implementation of a Number Class

```
class Complex: public Number {
public:
    Complex(double d, double e): Number(BaseConstructor()) {
        rpart = d;  ipart = e;
        referenceCount = 1;
    }
    Number operator+(Number &n) { return n.complexAdd(*this); }
    . . . .
    Number realAdd(Number &n) {
        Number retval;
        Complex *c1 = new Complex(*this);
        RealNumber *c2 = (RealNumber*)&n;
        c1->rpart += c2->r;
        retval.redefine(c1);
        return retval;
    }
    Number complexAdd(Number &n) {
        . . . .
    }
private:
    double rpart, ipart;
};
```

Figure 5-8. Partial Implementation of a Complex Class

Following the reference-counted object idiom of Section 3.5, most memory management intelligence for Number objects is in the envelope class, while the application semantics are in the letter class (Figures 5-7 and 5-8). Constructors build the appropriate kind of letter object for the parameters provided. Assignment and the copy constructor use the reference counting idiom introduced in Section 3.5, where referenceCount is the member datum that counts outstanding references to the shared representation. Operations are forwarded from Number to the letter maintained "inside" it, as shown in the implementation of operator+ and other operators in Figure 5-7.

The Number class of Figure 5-7 serves both as the class of the "universal number" objects seen by the user, as well as base class for the letter classes; some of its member functions reflect special services provided to the derived classes. The special constructor Number::Number(BaseConstructor) initializes instances of Number that form the base class part of letter classes. It supplants the default constructor `Number::Number()` to avoid infinite recursion arising from the creation of a new instance of a `Number` derived class from within `Number::Number`.

The member functions `complexAdd`, `realAdd`, and `redefine` are application-specific member functions provided as services to the derived classes; however, they are not `protected` because they are invoked across instances. Any `Number` object must be prepared to receive an instance of any other "kind" of number object as an operand to one of its operations. Consider the following code:

```
Number aComplex(1.0, 2.0);
Number aReal(3.0);
Number result = aComplex + aReal;
```

When aComplex's `operator+` operation is invoked with aReal as a parameter, it forwards the request to its letter object. That invokes `Complex`'s `operator+` with aComplex as its operand and the value of aReal as a parameter. `Complex::operator+` in turn invokes the `complexAdd` operation on its parameter, passing `*this` (the value of aComplex) as a parameter. Control is now inside `Number`'s `complexAdd`, which just forwards the call to `RealNumber`'s `complexAdd`. With `friendship` access to both objects, the `complexAdd` member function of `RealNumber` generates an appropriately typed result and returns it.

That summarizes how such flexibility works in the steady state. How such polymorphic objects initially come into being will be elaborated further in the next section.

Simulating the Notion of "Virtual Constructors"

An important design guideline of object-oriented design (Chapter 6) is that each class should know how to take care of its own business. Much of the power of object-oriented programming is in the polymorphism that comes from combining inheritance and virtual functions. Inheritance and virtual functions used together enable a user to communicate with an object exclusively through the interface defined by its base class. The compiler provides the "magic" that dispatches member function calls to the appropriate derived class member function at run time. C++ constructs isolate the user of a family of classes from knowing the details of the number and nature of derived classes, as well as from the implementation details of these classes.

In C++, however, there is one exception to this that falls short of what programmers using pure object-oriented languages hold as fundamental. Consider a class Number from which BigNumber and Complex are derived, and where most derived class operations (member functions) also appear as virtual operations in the base class. A user who has a pointer or reference to a Number can bind it to an object of class Number, BigNumber, or Complex, and can interact happily with any of them using the virtual functions of Number. Users do not need to know the details of the Number class hierarchy to treat all their instances equally, accessing them in terms of the properties they inherit from Number.

How did such a pointer come to refer to an object of a derived class in the first place? Where was the object made, and what information was at the disposal of the creator to indicate which derived class to use? The user could not have generated a new BigNumber or new Complex; this would violate the principle that the user not know about the details of the structure of derivation or of low-level classes. It could not have come from a third party, since the third party should have no more business knowing about Number's derived classes than our user does. So the pointer must come from inside the Number/BigNumber/Complex combination itself. We might reason that the Number constructor created a BigNumber because its parameter was larger than some threshold, or perhaps that a sqrt operation inside Number created a Complex when invoked with a negative value.

When a user says new Number, then, we conclude that Number's constructor is concocting a BigNumber or a Complex and arranging for the operator new return value to point to one of those. But this cannot be; consider the following code:

```
Number::Number() {
        if (some condition)
            this = new BigNumber;    // illegal
}
```

Assignment to this is illegal in C++; its typical intended use is satisfied by the more restrictive capabilities of operator new.

A solution: We can use a third party abstraction as an agent to do business with Number/BigNumber/Complex on behalf of the client creating the object. An object of class Number, used as an envelope class, can fill the role of this agent. Each Number instance points to a letter object created from one if its derived classes—for example, a BigNumber or Complex. This pointer is declared as a Number*:

```
class Number {
private:
    Number *rep;
    . . . .
```

Number's member functions are forwarded to the object pointed to by the private rep field:

```
public:
    Number operator*(const Number &n) {
        return rep->operator*(n);
    }
    . . . .
```

The letter's member function declarations are exactly like those of Number, their base class. The private rep field is initialized by the envelope constructor, which constructs either a BigNumber or a Complex, depending on some condition, and puts a pointer to the resulting object into the private rep field.

Take for example a Number class that we would like to store on an output stream (the ostream type of the common C++ iostreams library). But we may also wish to initialize a Number from an istream (input stream)—that is, to give Number the ability to read one of itself back in, creating a new object in the process. So there could be a constructor of the following form:

```
class Number {
public:
    . . . .
    Number(istream& s) {
        char buf[10];
        s >> buf;
        switch( numParse(buf) ) {
        case COMPLEX:
            rep = new Complex(buf);
            break;
        case FLOAT:
            rep = new DoublePrecisionFloat(buf);
            break;
        . . . .
        }
    }
private:
    enum NumType {COMPLEX, FLOAT, BIGINT};
    NumType numParse(char *);     // determine type of number
    Number *rep;
};
```

(Of course, in real life, rep would be assigned within the body of numParse to avoid duplicated knowledge between it and Number::Number(istream&) about all numeric classes.)

The class now appears to build different kinds of objects on the fly, whose properties are determined by context provided to the constructor (here, the contents of a stream of bytes from a file or other source).

This gives classes the run-time flexibility that virtual functions give objects, a capability that has come to be known as *virtual constructors*. Virtual constructors are a step towards simulating classes as full first-class objects in C++, using C++ as if it were a single-hierarchy system (composed uniformly of objects, instead of having classes that are not objects but "something else"). Such flexibility will be more fully exploited and expanded in Chapter 8 when exemplars are discussed.

☞ *When to use this idiom*: The virtual constructor idiom is used when the type of an object needs to be determined from the context in which the object is constructed. Examples include building a window object of the right type and size as a function of the screen used by the program, or creating objects from interactive or unformatted file input.

The example below is from the architecture of an `Atom` class used to represent atoms (indivisible lexical tokens) in a text parsing scheme. `Atom` does much of the lexical legwork for a simple parsing system. Here is the base class definition, where all member functions are declared as virtual:

```
class Atom {
public:
    Atom() {}
public:     // union of signature of all Atoms
    virtual ~Atom() {}
    virtual long value()    { return 0; }
    virtual String name()   { return String("error"); }
    virtual operator char() { return 0; }
    virtual Atom *copy() = 0;
};
```

Note that `Atom::copy` is *pure virtual*: It has a specification of " = 0" following its declaration. Classes derived directly from `Atom` inherit this function as pure virtual, unless they provide a function body for it. This means that `copy` *must* be defined in all classes directly derived from `Atom` if objects are to be instantiated from those classes; this is necessary for proper operation of this idiom. `Atom::copy` has no body, which implies that it is impossible to create an `Atom` object; only derived classes that contain or inherit a `copy` member function with a body can be instantiated.

```
class NumericAtom : public Atom {
public:
    NumericAtom(): sum(0) { }
    NumericAtom(String &s) {
        sum = 0;
        for (int i=0; s[i] >= '0' && s[i] <= '9'; i++) {
            sum = (sum * 10) + s[i] - '0';
        }
        s = s(i, s.length()-i);
    }
    NumericAtom(const NumericAtom &n) { sum = n.value(); }
    NumericAtom()              { sum = 0; }
    long value() const         { return sum; }
    Atom *copy() const {
        NumericAtom *retval = new NumericAtom;
        retval->sum = sum; return retval;
    }
private:
    long sum;
};
```

Figure 5-9. A Class for a NumericAtom Lexical Atom

Let's take a look at the letter classes that do most of the "real work"; they are self-contained and can be understood without knowing the details of the envelope class. Figure 5-9 shows class NumericAtom, the class that handles numeric atoms. The constructor NumericAtom::NumericAtom(const String&) parses an integer from its String parameter, "eating" the characters from the string as it goes. The second constructor is a simple copy constructor. The value function returns the integer value.

Note that as a class representing a numeric quantity, NumericAtom redefines Atom's value operation but leaves the character conversion function operator char to take on the default behavior of returning a null character. That means that a user of these classes must know from context whether invocations of functions like operator char or value make sense; it would not do to make them pure virtual, since there is no point in redefining them in many of the derived classes. The copy member function makes a physical copy of the object, returning an Atom*. This satisfies the need for a single operation that will duplicate any Atom. The copy function alleviates the need for a "type field," as will be described below.

```
class Name : public Atom {
public:
    Name(): n("") { }
    Name(String& s) {
        for (int i=0; s[i] >= 'a' && s[i] <= 'z'; i++) {
            n = n + s(i,1);
        }
        s = s(i, s.length()-i);
    }
    Name(const Name& m) { n = m.name(); }
    ~Name() {}
    String name() const { return n; }
    Atom *copy() { Name *retval = new Name;
                    retval->n = n; return retval; }
private:
    String n;
};

class Punct : public Atom {
public:
    Punct(): c('\0')        { }
    Punct(String& s)        { c = s[0]; s = s(1,s.length()-1); }
    Punct(const Punct& p) { c = char(p); }
    operator char() const { return c; }
    ~Punct() {}
    Atom *copy() { Punct *retval = new Punct;
                    retval->c = c;  return retval; }
private:
    char c;
};

class Oper : public Atom {
public:
    Oper(): c('\0') { }
    Oper(String& s) { c = s[0]; s = s(1,s.length()-1); }
    Oper(Oper& o)   { c = char(o); }
    ~Oper() {}
    operator char() const { return c; }
    Atom *copy() { Oper *retval = new Oper;
                    retval->c = c; return retval; }
private:
    char c;
};
```

Figure 5-10. Classes Name, Punct, and Oper

The letter classes Name, Punct, and Oper are each implemented analogous to NumericAtom (Figure 5-10). The envelope class is called GeneralAtom; its job is to orchestrate the creation of all objects from derived classes of Atom:

```
class GeneralAtom : public Atom {
public:
    GeneralAtom(String&);
    GeneralAtom(const GeneralAtom& a) { realAtom=a.copy(); }
    ~GeneralAtom()      { delete realAtom; }
    Atom *transform()   { Atom *retval=realAtom; realAtom=0;
                          return retval;}
    Atom *copy() const { return realAtom->copy(); }
public:    // union of signature of all Atoms--necessary
           // if GeneralAtom is to be used as though it
           // were an instance of one of its derived classes
           // (i.e., for when transform() isn't used)
    long value()     { return realAtom->value(); }
    String name()    { return realAtom->name(); }
    operator char() { return realAtom-> operator char(); }
private:
    Atom *realAtom;
};
```

As the envelope, GeneralAtom is the only class the user transacts business with directly: Objects from all the rest of the classes are treated as letters placed inside objects of the envelope class. The GeneralAtom class can be given a character string as a constructor parameter (GeneralAtom::GeneralAtom(String&)), and will analyze the string, creating and retaining a pointer to an object from the appropriate derived class of Atom:

```
GeneralAtom::GeneralAtom(String &s) {
    if (!s.length()) realAtom = 0;
    else switch(s[0]) {
    case '0': case '1': case '2': case '3': case '4':
    case '5': case '6': case '7': case '8': case '9':
        realAtom = new NumericAtom(s); break;
    case ',': case ':': case ';': case '.':
        realAtom = new Punct(s); break;
    case '*': case '/': case '+': case '-':
        realAtom = new Oper(s); break;
    default:
        if (s[0] >= 'a' && s[0] <= 'z') {
            realAtom = new Name(s);
        } else
            realAtom = 0;
    }
}
```

Here is a simple invocation of this code:

```
Atom *lexAtom(String& s) {
    GeneralAtom g(s);
    return g.transform();    // for subsequent efficiency
}
void parse(String& s) {
    for (Atom *a = lexAtom(s); a; a = lexAtom(s)) {
        . . . .
    }
}
```

An envelope class instance can be used in one of two ways: as a scaffold—that is, a temporary object to build a specific object in a general context—or as the actual object that will be passed around the program and live out its life as though it were the real thing. Note that when a GeneralAtom is built, the resulting object pointer from operator new can be declared to be of type Atom*; that can validly point to a GeneralAtom because GeneralAtom is derived from Atom and can exhibit all the same behaviors. Deriving both the envelope and the letters from the same base class is an important part of this idiom; it asserts that either (or both) stand in for the same design concept. But instead of using the GeneralAtom object pointer, it would have done just as well to use the pointer to the internally generated "letter" object of class Oper, Punct, NumericAtom, etc. The program would work the same in both cases; in the latter case, the envelope functions only as a scaffold to get the letter object built. In the case where it is used as scaffolding, the envelope does not need to be perfectly faithful to the behaviors of Atom's derived classes; its signature does not need to reflect all the signatures of all the types it is to represent.

These envelope class objects must be transitory in nature *unless* their signature is a union of the signature of all classes for which they are to be envelopes. In the example, an envelope can be used almost anywhere that the "real" class can, at the expense of one more level of indirection. The indirection can be eliminated by replacing the contents of an existing Atom* that points to a GeneralAtom, with the results of invoking the transform operation on that pointer, at which time the envelope can be discarded.

If the envelope class does indeed field all the operations one would ever want to invoke on the letter classes, then transform would be invoked only to avoid the extra indirection, thereby improving performance. Those willing to live with the extra indirection can freely use instances of the envelope class as automatic variables, or as initialized objects with global extent. A key benefit of the envelope/letter idioms is that it completely hides the dynamic nature of object creation from the user, while preserving the expected object interface. If one didn't want or need that transparency, then it would suffice to bury the initialization logic in a global function or in a public static member function of the class.

Note that if a constructor such as

```
GeneralAtom::GeneralAtom(const GeneralAtom&)
```

is called, it has to obtain a copy of the object that was passed to it as a parameter. This might have been done by putting a "type field" in every derived class of Atom, which GeneralAtom would use to call the appropriate constructor, with suitable casting, to clone the object. Here we dealt with the issue using a virtual function, copy, instead. The only change that needs to be made to Atom or GeneralAtom when a new derived class is added, is to the GeneralAtom constructor GeneralAtom(String&) itself.

Another Approach to Virtual Constructors

This section presents another way to express "virtual constructors," to create objects whose exact type and size are not known when the constructor is entered. Instead of using an envelope/letter idiom with an extra level of indirection, this approach modifies the type of the object in place. The approach builds on a buddy system memory allocation scheme and is called the *buddy system virtual constructor idiom*. As an example, we show a class that takes a byte stream from an incoming message link and turns it into an appropriately typed object, based on the contents of the message.

This mechanism can also be used to make variable-sized objects—that is, objects of a given class that extend their size to allocate space for a vector based at the end of the object. The approach described here has some aesthetic advantages over that presented in Stroustrup [2].

☞ *When to use this idiom*: This idiom best applies when object size is not known ahead of time. This includes applications where object size cannot be determined by the object's class alone (for example, variable-length messages). It is useful where the performance cost of an extra level of data indirection cannot be afforded, or for places where pointers cannot be used (objects in shared memory, audit strategies requiring pre-engineered buffers, etc.)

This idiom will not commonly be used for concrete data types. It goes beyond what C++ implementations assume as common use, though the example below is portable and makes no assumptions about C++ environment implementation details. The idiom is most useful for highly dynamic system resources such as the message buffer example elaborated here.

Consider a base class LAPD (*L*ink *A*ccess *P*rotocol for *D*ata) used in a networking application. LAPD is a subset of the common HDLC (*h*igh-level *d*ata *l*ink *c*ontrol) protocol used for the level 2 (data link layer) of ISO (*I*nternational *S*tandards *O*rganization) protocols. From LAPD, we can derive a class characterizing the next higher level of protocol. Here, we assume that there are several different message types that conform to the X.25 level 3 (network layer) protocol built on the LAPD level 2 protocol. These different message types represent different communications functions: alerting, connect, setup, acknowledgement, and others.

At the heart of this approach is an overloaded operator new that allows a base class constructor to overlay its object with a derived class object. When the base class constructor is called with a stream of characters from the data link as a parameter, the right kind of message object is built in dynamic memory.

Let's look at a scheme to handle this through selected overloading of operator new. First, a globally overloaded operator new arranges for the LAPD constructor to call one of its derived class constructors, specifying that it should build the object at the address of the base class object. Second, class LAPD has its own operator new that arranges to build the object in a predetermined buffer guaranteed to be large enough to hold the largest of messages:

```
// this operator allows one object in the LAPD
// hierarchy to overlay itself with an instance
// of one of its derived classes

inline void *operator new(size_t, LAPD *l) { return l; }

unsigned char bigBuf[4096], *bigBufPtr = bigBuf;

class LAPD {
public:
    void *operator new(size_t) { return (void*) bigBufPtr; }
    LAPD(const char *buf) {
        . . . .
        (void) new(this) Setup(buf);
        . . . .
    }
    LAPD() { /* no-op */ }
};

class Setup: public LAPD {
    . . . .
};
```

An invocation of the form

```
LAPD *msg = new LAPD(buf);
```

calls LAPD::operator new to allocate memory for the object, in preparation for invoking the constructor. The memory for the object is taken from the buffer pointed to by bigBufPtr. The LAPD constructor is then called, with the value of this set up to point where bigBufPtr was initialized. The LAPD constructor might decide that a Setup message is called for by examining the contents of buf, and it invokes the globally overloaded operator new to allocate memory for the derived class object. The globally overloaded operator new just returns the address that was supplied as a parameter, after which the Setup constructor is called. The value of this in the LAPD constructor is thus passed into the value of this inside the Setup constructor.

The problem with this approach is that the memory needs to be allocated before the derived class constructor is called, and the compiler can't know in advance how much memory will be needed. This problem is overcome by allocating all messages at the bottom of a large pool of memory and having the derived class constructor adjust the address of the bottom of the pool to be just beyond the end of its own data:

```
inline int round(int a, int b) { return ((a+b-1)/b)*b; }
class Setup: public LAPD {
friend LAPD;
private:
    SetupPacketBody body;
    Setup(const char *m): LAPD() {
         . . . .
         bigBufPtr += round(sizeof(Setup), 4);
    }
};
```

This trick works well, but creates a problem regarding memory fragmentation.

To solve the fragmentation problem, we use a variation of the buddy system memory management algorithm. This algorithm has been popularized by Knuth [3], though Knuth credits the approach to Harry Markowitz and Kenneth Knowlton from work in the early 1960s. Knuth's exposition forms the basis for the code in this chapter.

In the buddy system, a request for a block of a given size is satisfied with a block whose size is the next largest power of 2. Unused blocks are maintained on a free list. If a newly freed block adjoins a previously freed block, the two are coalesced into one, minimizing memory fragmentation. The interesting property of the buddy system approach is that the address of an adjoining block can be inferred from the address and size of a newly freed block, making it easy to determine whether blocks can be coalesced.

Instead of looking for a nearest-fit block, the approach presented here uses the buddy system to do "worst fit"—to take the largest available block to satisfy a request for a message buffer. However, the allocation algorithm is suspended after this block is identified, and the "virtual" constructor execution is allowed to proceed before the allocation process has been completed. When the message parsing is finished, the object size is known, and control is returned to the buddy system allocator to split the large block down so the enclosing memory block is the next largest 2^k block enclosing the object.

Now, when the block is freed, it enjoys the benefits of the buddy system's collapsing of adjacent blocks into a single, larger block. Memory fragmentation is greatly lessened, provided that the memory pool is much larger than the size of the largest message, and the full flexibility of "virtual constructors" is preserved.

Figure 5-11 shows the interface to the LAPD base class. The interfaces to the new and delete operators are shown, as are the constructor taking a const char* that applications will use to build messages. A default constructor is supplied; this will be invoked from the derived class constructors. It must be defined as a no-op because it is invoked on a previously initialized object. It is also worth noting that constructors for this base class object are called twice—LAPD(const char*) at the direction of the user, and LAPD() from the derived class—so any class object members of LAPD set from the first constructor will be reinitialized to their default values by the second. In other words, this base class should not contain class object instances.

Much of the internal data of the class are devoted to storing the fields of a LAPD header and to defining fields for dynamic memory management. Since many of the memory management fields are put to use only after the object has been returned to the free list, their space is shared with application instance space using a union. One field, tag, must be present in such objects whether active in an application or on the free list; it is this tag that the buddy system garbage collector looks at to determine whether the associated block of memory is allocated.

Figure 5-12 shows a class used to manage memory buffers for messages. The buddy system has its own data structures hidden to the application, and those structures need to be initialized before the application allocates memory for message buffers. So the memory allocation implementation was put in its own class instead of being distributed throughout the message classes themselves. A single, global instance of LAPDMemoryManager, simply called manager, serves to manage the memory for all LAPD messages.

```
class LAPD {
friend class LAPDMemoryManager;
public:
    virtual int size() { return 0; }
    void *operator new(size_t);
    void operator delete(void *);
    LAPD(const char *const);
protected:
    LAPD() { /* no-op */ }
private:
    // as in buddy system, each node can either be a
    // free block or allocated.  allocated blocks
    // don't need the memory info linked list overhead
    union {
        struct {
            unsigned char flag;
            struct {
                unsigned int sapi:6;
                unsigned int commandResponse:1;
                unsigned int zero:1;
                unsigned int tei:7;
                unsigned int ext:1;
            } address;
            unsigned char control;
        } header;
        struct {
            LAPD *linkf, *linkb;
            unsigned short size;
        } minfo;
    };
    // both allocated blocks and freelist blocks
    // need this bit for garbage collection
    unsigned char tag;   // buddy system allocated tag
    int performCRCCheck() { /* . . . . */ }
};
```

Figure 5-11. Class LAPD

```
inline int round(int a, int b) { return ((a+b-1)/b)*b; }


// This class could be nested in LAPD.
// It is used to build a singleton object
// used to manage message memory.  The main reason
// it was made a class in its own right was for
// the sake of initial conditions in the buddy
// data structures.
class LAPDMemoryManager {
friend LAPD;
public:
    LAPDMemoryManager();
    LAPD *largestBlock();
    void allocateResizeBlock(int);
    void deallocateBlock(LAPD, int);
private:
    enum { MessageBufSize=4096, Log2MessageBufSize=12 };
    unsigned char availBuf[
        (1+Log2MessageBufSize)*round(sizeof(LAPD),sizeof(LAPD*))];
    // avail contains objects that serve as list heads to free
    // poll lists of objects of different sizes, all 2**k
    LAPD *avail;
    int savej;      // save context across calls of
                    // largestBlock and allocateResizeBlock
    unsigned char buf[MessageBufSize];
    LAPD *buddy(int k, LAPD *l) {
        char *cp = (char *) l;
        return (LAPD*)(long(cp) ^ (1<<(k+1)));
    }
};

static LAPDMemoryManager manager;     // singleton object
```

Figure 5-12. Message Memory Management Class

The interface of the memory management class contains a default constructor, which simply initializes buddy system data structures:

```
LAPDMemoryManager::LAPDMemoryManager() {
    // Data structure initialization, per Knuth
    LAPD* buf = (LAPD*)this->buf;
    avail = (LAPD*)availBuf;
    avail[Log2MessageBufSize].minfo.linkf = 0;
    avail[Log2MessageBufSize].minfo.linkb = 0;
    buf[0].minfo.linkf = buf[0].minfo.linkb =
                            &avail[Log2MessageBufSize];
    buf[0].tag = 1;
    buf[0].minfo.size = Log2MessageBufSize;
    for (int k = 0; k < Log2MessageBufSize; k++) {
        avail[k].minfo.linkf = avail[k].minfo.linkb =
                                        &avail[k];
    }
}
```

The buddy system allocation algorithm is split into two member functions and modified so that an object can be grown after passing the first phase of allocation. The largestBlock member function returns a pointer to the largest available block in the buddy system free pool:

```
LAPD*
LAPDMemoryManager::largestBlock() {
    for (int k = Log2MessageBufSize; k >= 0; --k) {
        if (avail[k].minfo.linkf != &avail[k]) {
            savej = k;
            return avail[k].minfo.linkf;
        }
    }
    return 0;
}
```

The private vector avail contains objects that serve as list heads to free pool lists of objects of different sizes, all even powers of 2. The normal buddy system algorithm searches this vector looking for a block of the smallest size at least as large as the desired space, and then repeatedly halves the block for a best fit to the requested amount of space. Because the LAPD class does not know at the outset how much space it will need, the algorithm is modified to return the largest available block. Arrangements to halve it to size will be made between the memory manager and derived classes of LAPD.

The deallocateBlock member function returns a block to the free store, coalescing it with adjacent free blocks if such exist. It follows directly from Knuth.

```
void
LAPDMemoryManager::allocateResizeBlock(int sizeNeeded) {
    // mostly from Knuth Volume 1
    int k, j = savej;
    // Round up to next 2**n
    for (int i = 1; i < Log2MessageBufSize; i++) {
        k = 1 << i;
        if (k > sizeNeeded) break;
    }
    LAPD *l = avail[j].minfo.linkf;
    avail[j].minfo.linkf = l->minfo.linkf;
    l->minfo.linkf->minfo.linkb = &avail[j];
    for (l->tag = 0; j - k; ) {
        --j;
        LAPD *p = (LAPD*)(((char *)l) + (1 << j));
        p->tag = 1;
        p->minfo.size = j;
        p->minfo.linkf = &avail[j];
        p->minfo.linkb = &avail[j];
        avail[j].minfo.linkf = p;
        avail[j].minfo.linkb = p;
    }
}

void
LAPDMemoryManager::deallocateBlock(LAPD *l, int k) {
    for (;;) {
        LAPD *p = buddy(k,l);
        if (k==Log2MessageBufSize || p->tag == 0 ||
                                p->minfo.size != k) {
            break;
        }
        p->minfo.linkb->minfo.linkf = p->minfo.linkf;
        p->minfo.linkf->minfo.linkb = p->minfo.linkb;
        ++k;
        if (p < l) l = p;
    }
    l->tag = 1;
    l->minfo.linkf = avail[k].minfo.linkf;
    avail[k].minfo.linkb = l;
    l->minfo.size = k;
    l->minfo.linkb = &avail[k];
    avail[k].minfo.linkf = l;
}
```

Figure 5-13. Block Allocation Routines for Class LAPD

The `allocateResizeBlock` member function carries out the remainder of the buddy system algorithm, simply following the Knuth algorithm (Figure 5-13).

In the private implementation of `LAPDMemoryManager`, we find a `savej` member that is used to retain the value of an index into `avail` across the two phases of the allocation algorithm. The index can be used to determine the size and location of a block being worked on. We also find a specification of the buffer size, and the value of its binary log, used in the allocation algorithms. The buffer itself, `buf`, is encapsulated in the memory manager object. The freelist list head vector is called `availBuf`, declared as an anonymous vector of bytes but accessed through the pointer `avail` as though it were a vector of LAPD objects. Last, we find a copy of the buddy function, used to identify adjacent blocks that might be coalesced together. The code for buddy is slightly nonportable; a `char*` pointer is cast to a `long` to perform the exclusive-OR operation supporting the buddy system scheme. Adjustments may be needed for platforms where pointers are longer than `long`s.

That lays the groundwork for message memory management; this software can reside in a library hidden from the user, with one exception that will be discussed below. An application programmer creates a message class by deriving it from LAPD, as is done for the `Setup` and `Conn` classes in Figure 5-14. The code is straightforward except for the call to `allocateResizeBlock` within the constructor, which starts the second phase of the buddy algorithm to adjust the block size to the actual size of the message.

Note that in the design of the message classes, we distinguish between the *body* of the message (at ISO Protocol Level 3), and the abstraction corresponding to the same data "in flight" through the network, including their header and trailer bits, etc. Here, the former is called `SetupPacketBody`, and the latter just `Setup`. Figure 5-14 shows a similar configuration for a class to handle `Conn` (connection) messages.

Now we can show how a message might be built. An application program captures a byte stream from an incoming data link, and passes it as a parameter to the constructor of LAPD (Figure 5-14). `LAPD::LAPD(const char*)` needs to determine the message type so the appropriate derived class constructor can be invoked. The invocation may look like this:

```
LAPD *message = new LAPD(bytepointer);
```

That invocation will invoke an `operator new` to allocate storage for the object. The one that gets called is the one specifically defined for class LAPD, and all it does is call on the memory manager for the address of the largest block it has and returns

```
class Setup: public LAPD {
friend LAPD;
private:
    struct SetupPacketBody {
        unsigned char rep[4096];
    };
    SetupPacketBody body;
    int size() { return sizeof(Setup); }
    Setup(const char *m): LAPD() {
        manager.allocateResizeBlock( size() );
        ::memcpy(&body, m+sizeof(header), sizeof(body));
        . . . .
    }
};

class Conn: public LAPD {
friend LAPD;
private:
    struct ConnPacketBody {
        unsigned char rep[4096];
    };
    ConnPacketBody body;
    int size() { return sizeof(Conn); }
    Conn(const char *m): LAPD() {
        manager.allocateResizeBlock( size() );
        ::memcpy(&body, m+sizeof(header), sizeof(body));
    }
};
```

Figure 5-14. Call Setup and Connect Level 3 Protocol Classes

that value:

```
void* LAPD::operator new(size_t /* unused */) {
    return manager.largestBlock();
    // gets finished up in derived class constructor }
```

The allocation now complete, the LAPD constructor can go about the business of determining the message type and invoking the appropriate derived class constructor. For the sake of example, assume that the fourth byte of the message (the data after the header) is used to determine the message type (Figure 5-15). On identifying the message type, the LAPD constructor directly invokes the appropriate derived class

```
LAPD::LAPD(const char *bits) {
    ::memcpy(&header, bits, sizeof(header));
    performCRCCheck();

    // Determine type of message based on fourth
    // octet (byte) of message contents field
    switch((bits + sizeof(header))[3]) {
    case SETUP:
        (void) ::new(this) Setup(bits); break;
    case CONN:
        (void) ::new(this) Conn(bits); break;
    case ALERT:
        (void) ::new(this) Alert(bits); break;
    . . . .

    default:
        error("invalid message"); break;
    }
}
```

Figure 5-15. Body of Constructor to Build Message Objects

constructor (Section 3.7). The syntax

```
(void) new(this) derived_class(arg)
```

causes the overloaded new definition to be invoked:

```
// this operator allows an object in the LAPD
// hierarchy to overlay itself with an instance
// of one of its derived classes

inline void *operator new(size_t, LAPD* l) { return l; }
```

In other words, the derived class will be forced to allocate its instance at the same location where the base class instance resides, so it will just overlay the existing instance. Remember, this is at the bottom of the largest available block known to the memory allocator.

If there is additional refinement of message types, a class derived from LAPD may defer more detailed message processing to one of its derived classes. For example, Setup::Setup may overlay the current Setup instance with an instance of one of its own derived classes. Eventually the refinement stops, and a derived class constructor will call the memory manager's allocateResizeBlock member function to finalize the block size and reorganize the free memory lists.

Deallocation of memory is more straightforward. Every message uses `LAPD::operator delete` to free its storage, which in turn simply calls the memory manager's `deallocateBlock` member function to do buddy system reclamation of the block:

```
void
LAPD::operator delete(void *l) {
    manager.deallocateBlock((LAPD*)l, ((LAPD*)l)->size());
}
```

Variable-Sized Objects The above example can be extended to create variable-sized objects of a given class, apart from any concern for matching an object size to some class along a line of inheritance. This might be useful in the message application where messages of a given type have different body sizes.

The approach originally proposed for this purpose by Stroustrup [2] can no longer be used, because assignment to `this` is illegal in C++ 2.0 and later releases. One reason for introducing `operator new` in C++ was to provide a more general solution to this problem. A class can arrange for all its instances to be of a specified size:

```
class LAPD {
public:
    // make all LAPD objects 128 bytes big
    void *operator new(size_t) { return ::new[128]; }
    . . . .
};
```

However, this approach has several pitfalls. First, `operator new` has no access to the constructor parameters, so an object sizing parameter could be passed only through global data. Second, the constructor executes too late to make any decisions about the size of the object: `operator new` completes before the constructor body executes. Third, there is no obvious way to adjust the object size in any but the base class.

Using the buddy system algorithm described above, we can solve these problems. As with the original class `LAPD`, the sizing of the object is left until the last moments of object initialization. The memory manager is notified how many *total* bytes are to be allocated for the object, so the object can grow by an arbitrary amount over the size dictated by its class. In Figure 5-16, class `Conn` has a previously computed value `bodySize` that contains the size of the message body. That size can be used to compute the total object size. The body is copied into `bodyStorage`, which behaves like a variable-sized vector, by the `memcpy` call in the constructor. After the

```
class Conn: public LAPD {
friend LAPD;
private:
    struct ConnPacketBody {
        unsigned char rep[4096];
    } *body;
    int bodySize;
    int size() { return sizeof(Conn) + bodySize; }
    Conn(const char *m): LAPD() {
        . . . .
        ::memcpy(bodyStorage, m+sizeof(header), bodySize);
        body = (ConnPacketBody*) bodyStorage;
        manager.allocateResizeBlock( size() );
    }
    char bodyStorage[1];
};
```

Figure 5-16. A Dynamically Sized Conn Class

object is set up, the memory allocator is told to fix the object to be of size `size()`, which includes the storage for the message body.

A word of caution: Classes using this technique require more disciplined use than do concrete data types. These classes do not create ordinary objects that can be created in any context. They can be instantiated only in a pre-allocated memory block whose address is passed to their constructors.

En Masse Delegation and Envelope Classes

Dynamic, run-time simulation of inheritance can be done with something like *delegation*. Delegation is to object instances what inheritance is to classes: the ability to share code and automatically use one abstraction's code to field requests made of another. Delegation is based on a run-time relationship between one object's member function and the context provided by another object. The programming languages Actors[4] and self[5] support delegation.

In C++, inheritance relationships are compile-time bound. C++ does not directly support delegation—its type system would have to be more run-time intensive—but many aspects of delegation can be simulated by forwarding one object's member function calls to another. This forwarding can be done at the granularity of a class, the same used for inheritance. One might want to simulate inheritance using member function forwarding to realize the behavioral advantages of subtyping, as well as the flexibility of run-time symbol bindings. However, the administrative work to put the "boilerplate" in place can become tedious:

```
class A {
public:
    void a();        // peculiar to A
    void b();        // peculiar to A
    void c();        // peculiar to A
    A(char *r) {
        cp = new char[::strlen(r)+1]; ::strcpy(cp,r);
    }
private:
    char *cp;
};

class B {
public:
    void a()        { delegate->a(); }    // tedious
    void b()        { delegate->b(); }    // tedious
    void c()        { delegate->c(); }    // tedious
    void d();       // peculiar to B
    B(char *r = "")  { delegate = new A(r); }
private:
    A *delegate;
};
```

Had we used inheritance to achieve subtyping, the inherited member functions would have come along for free. Here, replicating A's interface in B is tedious both for initial coding and for evolution: Any interface change must be coordinated between the two classes.

Much of the inconvenience of replicating the interface can be relieved in C++ by overloading the -> operator to take over the semantics of dereferencing pointers to the outer object. The implementation technique is the same as that used for counted pointers (page 65). This allows one object to transparently "forward" operations to another:

```
class A {
public:
    void a();        // peculiar to A
    void b();        // peculiar to A
    void c();        // peculiar to A
    A(char *r) {
        cp = new char[::strlen(r)+1]; ::strcpy(cp,r);
    }
private:
    char *cp;
};
```

```
class B {
public:
    // explicit forwarding of a, b, c unnecessary
    void d();          // peculiar to B
    A *operator->()   { return delegate; }
    B(char *c = "")   { delegate = new A(c); }
private:
    A *delegate;
};
```

The object delegated to can be changed at any time by changing the value of the `delegate` pointer.

Now, operators can be freely added to class A without worrying about coordinated changes in B. Three other factors are noteworthy:

1. Except for its constructor, code for B does not have to be recompiled if A changes.

2. The syntax for declaration and use of these objects takes some getting used to:

    ```
    int main() {
        B aBInstance("hello world\n");
        aBInstance.d();   // dot notation (rarely used)
        aBInstance->a();  // arrow notation
        // no delete of aBInstance:  it is not a pointer
        return 0;
    }
    ```

    This approach puts the burden on the user of the class to remember whether a member function is forwarded or not, and to use the appropriate syntax. If this is a troublesome inconvenience, then `operator->` should not be used and each member function should be treated individually as in the "tedious" example above. If all functions are forwarded, then of course the syntax for all member function calls is uniform.

    Many of these inconveniences would disappear if we were able to overload `operator.`, but it is one of the few C++ operators that may not be overloaded.

3. We must use arrow notation, not dot notation, to invoke the "real" member functions in the inner class. Dot notation is used only for functions that are never delegated but that are defined in the outer class.

4. If operators (such as the arithmetic operators) are overloaded as class members of A, then they must be defined in B as well:

```
int A::operator+(const A &a) const {
    int q;
    . . . .
    return q;
}

int B::operator+(const A &a) const {
    return delegate->operator+(a);
}
```

Another example appears in Figure 5-17. Here, a SeaPlane class delegates its functionality either to a Boat or a Plane, depending on its "mode."

☞ *When to use this idiom*: Use this idiom in envelope/letter class pairs that change frequently, to avoid redundant update of the signature of both envelope and letter class interfaces. This idiom also underlies other advanced idioms, such as the symbolic idioms of Chapter 9.

Iterators and Cursors

Collection classes, such as sets, lists, and trees, are commonly used utilities in C++ programs. A collection class may be shared between several classes; for example, a resource list in a simulation program might be shared by its producer, its consumer, and a simulation control class. All of these classes might want to visit each element on the list in succession, for different reasons: the producer, to change the state of a previously queued item; the consumer, to look for an item with a certain priority or characteristic; the simulation controller, to print out the contents of the queue on demand.

All of these scans are *nondestructive* scans: In themselves, they do not affect the state of the list. If these scans are interleaved, then it is crucial that they not modify data internal to the list. However, the data needed to successively visit each list

```
class Vehicle {
public:
    virtual int mpg()       { return 0; }
    virtual void takeOff() { hostVehicle->takeOff(); }
    virtual void swim()     { hostVehicle->swim(); }
    Vehicle(Vehicle *host) { hostVehicle = host; }
private:
    Vehicle *hostVehicle;
};

class Plane: public Vehicle {
public:
    int mpg() { return 10; }
    Plane(Vehicle *v) : Vehicle(v) { }
};

class Boat: public Vehicle {
public:
    int mpg() { return 3; }
    Boat(Vehicle *v) : Vehicle(v) { }
};

class SeaPlane: public Vehicle {
public:
    SeaPlane(): Vehicle(0) {
        currentMode = boat = new Boat(this);
        plane = new Plane(this);
    }
    ~SeaPlane() { delete boat;  delete plane; }
    void takeOff() { currentMode = plane; }
    void swim() { currentMode = boat; }
    Vehicle *operator->() { return currentMode; }
private:
    Vehicle *boat, *plane, *currentMode;
};

int main() {
    SeaPlane seaPlane;
    cout << seaPlane->mpg() << endl;
    seaPlane->takeOff(); cout << seaPlane->mpg() << endl;
    seaPlane->swim(); cout << seaPlane->mpg() << endl;
}
```

Figure 5-17. A SeaPlane Class Modeling En Masse Delegation

member are private to the list itself. Several objects (producer, consumer, and controller) can each traverse the list independently if they keep their own copy of the "list position" state. This state is kept in an object called an *iterator* or *cursor*, that lets the holder walk through an aggregate one element at a time.

Iterators are special kinds of handle classes. Unlike the handle classes from earlier in the chapter, iterators are helper classes that supplement, but do not replace, the body class interface. Iterators are usually declared `friends` of their body classes.

Consider the `Queue` class shown at the end of this chapter. When compiled and run, this program produces as output

```
1 2 3
leaving: 1 2 3 4 5
6 7 8 9 10 11 12
leaving: 6 7
8 9 10 11 12
leaving: 8 9
```

The `Queue` iterator acts as a "cursor" that walks through the `Queue`, one element at a time. Each cursor instantiated for a `Queue` object is independent from the others, and no use of an iterator affects the `Queue` itself.

The code must work even if the `Queue` changes between uses of the iterator. None of `Queue`'s state can be remembered by `QueueIterator` across invocations of its member functions.

Here, the iterator is initialized from a `const` reference to a `Queue`, to help ensure the `Queue` exists before an attempt is made to traverse it.

5.6 Functors: Functions as Objects

In Section 2.10 (page 29 and following), we saw how class member function pointers could be used to provide several different versions of a function through the same function interface. However, the syntax for calling a member function "parameterized" in this way was awkward:

```
. . . . afilter.*(afilter.current)(t) . . . .
```

and much of the orchestration of the approach was based on obscure constructs of the C++ language. Using inheritance with virtual functions, we can make things cleaner.

Recall that the example in Section 2.10 was based on the application of an impulse of current to an electrical network consisting of an inductor, a capacitor, and a resistor. Depending on the parameter values for these components, the circuit might react in one of three ways. For each of those responses, a separate function was used.

What is proposed here is that each different type of response be encoded in its own *class* instead of its own function. We can think of this in terms of an advanced architectural construct called a *functor*. Logically, functors are functions that behave like objects (or objects that behave like functions): They serve the role of a function, but can be created, passed as parameters, and otherwise manipulated like objects. The implementation in C++ is straightforward: Each functor is a class with a single member function. A functor object can be used to characterize each of the three possible step responses of the circuit.

☞ *When to use this idiom*: Use this idiom whenever you would be otherwise tempted to use function pointers, particularly member function pointers.

What does this buy us? First, using inheritance, we can factor common code into a base class. These formulas contain subexpressions that may be complex enough to be cast as functions in their own right. In this particular example, subexpressions such as $\omega 0$ appear in several of the formulas, and relate crisply to well-defined constructs in the application domain. These are natural to factor out as common piece parts. Furthermore, such use of inheritance provides a language construct to tie related functions together: All the functors that can be used interchangeably in a given context will have a common base class.

Second, using virtual functions with inheritance, we can gain the same kind of run-time flexibility that we achieved with function pointers. Instead of selecting a function pointer as the designated value through which the "real" function is invoked, we designate a pointer to the appropriate functor object. We invoke the function as though it resides in the base class, and the "indirectness" that selects the right function at run time is handled by the virtual function mechanisms of C++.

There is one difficult implementation issue with which we must struggle. We can easily design the three classes corresponding to overdamped, underdamped, and critically damped response, and we can make the base class that contains what is in common to all three. What remains is to invent a mechanism to decide *which* of the three functors to create. In the function pointer example, we had the luxury of having all the data at hand inside the constructor, and we could use those data to decide which function to select. Here, with functors, the behavior itself is identified with the

```
#include <complex.h>
typedef double time;

class SeriesRLCStepResponse {
public:
    virtual complex current(time t) {
        return object->current(t);
    }
    double frequency() const { return 1.0 / sqrt(L * C); }
    SeriesRLCStepResponse(double r, double l,
        double c, double initialCurrent, short isenvelope=1);
protected:
    double R, L, C, currentT0;
    double alpha;
    complex omegad, a1, b1, a2, b2, s1, s2;
private:
    SeriesRLCStepResponse *object;
};

class UnderDampedResponse: public SeriesRLCStepResponse {
public:
    UnderDampedResponse(double r, double l, double c, double i):
        SeriesRLCStepResponse(r,l,c,i,0) { }
    complex current(time t) {
        return exp(-alpha * t) * (b1 * cos(omegad * t) +
                b2 * sin(omegad * t));
    }
};

class OverDampedResponse: public SeriesRLCStepResponse {
public:
    OverDampedResponse(double r, double l, double c, double i) :
        SeriesRLCStepResponse(r,l,c,i,0) { }
    complex current(time t) {
        return a1 * exp(s1 * t) + a2 * exp(s2 * t);
    }
};

class CriticallyDampedResponse: public SeriesRLCStepResponse {
public:
    CriticallyDampedResponse(double r, double l, double c,
                                                double i) :
        SeriesRLCStepResponse(r,l,c,i,0) { }
    complex current(time t) {
        return exp(-alpha * t) * (a1 * t + a2);
    }
};
```

Figure 5-18. Base Functor Class and Classes for Three Simulation Modes

object being created; by the time any constructor is running, it will be too late to make any decisions about what object to create. Enter the envelope/letter idiom, simulating virtual constructors, providing an extra level of indirection to support the illusion of dynamically typed object creation.

Figure 5-18 shows the classes used to model the resonant circuit. `SeriesRLCStepResponse` serves both as a base class for each of the letters and as the envelope itself. As a base for the letter classes, it provides a virtual member function, `current`, which will be redefined on a case-by-case basis by the derived classes. The base class has `protected` data for properties common to all its derived classes.

As an envelope class, it has a pointer named `object` that points to the letter, where the particulars of individual response types are handled. This field is `private`, so it is not exported to the derived classes. The envelope forwards calls of its `current` member function to the letter's `current`, a virtual function, whose behavior will be bound at run time.

Figure 5-18 depicts the functor classes for each of the three alternatives of circuit operation. For a given circuit simulation, a single object of one of these classes will be instantiated. Each class has two public member functions: its constructor, necessary to gather the parameters for current evaluation, and `current` that yields a current value as a function of time. The `current` function is declared virtual in the base class `SeriesRLCStepResponse`.

We now return to the base class constructor, where most of the interesting work is done (Figure 5-19). The constructor evaluates its arguments to ascertain the circuit's mode of operation, and then binds the base class's `object` field to a newly created "response" object of the appropriate derived class of `SeriesRLCStepResponse`.

Note that the constructor can work in one of two modes: It can be called either to make an object that will serve as the envelope, or to make the base class part of a derived class. If called with its `isenvelope` parameter set to 1, the constructor behaves as if the object were an application object in its own right. The object will act as an envelope that analyzes the circuit parameters and will create a letter object modeling the circuit's behavior. If `isenvelope` is 0, then the constructor assumes it is being called from one of the derived classes, in which case its only job is the calculation of ω_d. The value of `isenvelope` defaults to 1 for the convenience of users of the class; derived classes must override the default with their specification of parameters to be passed to the base class constructor.

```
SeriesRLCStepResponse::SeriesRLCStepResponse(
       double r, double l, double c, double initialCurrent,
       short isenvelope) {
   R = r; L = l; C = c; currentT0 = initialCurrent;
   alpha = R / (L + L);
   . . . .
   // calculation of a1, b1, a2, b2, etc
   . . . .
   if (isenvelope) {
       if (alpha < frequency()) {
           object = new UnderDampedResponse(
                                     r, l, c, initialCurrent);
       } else if (alpha > frequency()) {
           object = new OverDampedResponse(
                                     r, l, c, initialCurrent);
       } else {
           object = new CriticallyDampedResponse(
                                     r, l, c, initialCurrent);
       }
   } else {
           omegad = sqrt(1.0/(L*C) - (alpha*alpha));
   }
}
```

Figure 5-19. Constructor for Circuit Response Class

The `main` program is straightforward:

```
int main() {
    double R, L, C, I0;
    cin >> R >> L >> C >> I0;
    SeriesRLCStepResponse afilter(R, L, C, I0);
    for (time t = 1.0; t < 100; t += 1.0) {
        cout << afilter.current(t) << endl;
    }
    return 0;
}
```

It simply creates a `SeriesRLCStepResponse` object with suitable parameters, then repeatedly invokes the `current` operation with different values of time. From the user's perspective, ease of use is the same as for the implementation in Section 2.10. However, this implementation is more straightforward and represents a more aesthetic design. Most conventional uses of function pointers can be implemented using C++ virtual functions, producing code that is easier to understand, debug, and maintain.

Functional and Applicative Programming

The above approach offers a good conceptual model of functors, but functions still do not look like objects as we want them to. Using C++ overloading, we can bring functions and objects closer together at the syntactic level, rounding out the functor idiom.

In addition to providing a `current` function, we provide access to the same function using `operator()` (the "call" operator):

```
class SeriesRLCStepResponse {
public:
    virtual complex operator () (time t) {
        return current(t);
    }
    virtual complex current(time t) {
        return object->current(t);
    }
    double frequency() const { return 1.0 / (L * C); }
    SeriesRLCStepResponse(double, double,
                          double, double, short=1);
    . . . .
};
```

We can now use the filter as though it were a function that we had created as an object:

```
SeriesRLCStepResponse afilter(R, L, C, I0);
for (time t = 1.0; t < 100; t += 1.0) {
    cout << afilter(t) << endl;
}
```

This may just look like syntactic sugar, but it does have some powerful applications. Consider the domain of *applicative programming*, where functions are the primary abstraction: Functions are treated like values. The main thing one does with a function is apply it, usually to the result of another function. The result of a function application may be a data value, or it may be another function!

Here, we discuss an application of functors to a simulation of electronic circuit filters. A filter is an electronic device that passes signals of a specified frequency range, and stops other frequencies from getting through. For example, your television tuner contains *band-pass filters* that select the signals for individual channels to let them through to the screen while rejecting the rest. You might put a *notch* filter on your antenna lead-in to selectively "notch out" the frequency from a nearby radio transmitter that interferes with your television picture. We will model some of the behaviors of such filters using functor objects. Each object is initialized with filter characteristics that customize the filter's response. A functor object takes an input, massages it, and generates an output as a result.

To model filters as functors, it is useful to think of them as mathematical abstractions. You can think of an electronic filter as implementing a mathematical function: a continuous mapping of input values to output values. If we apply an input to a filter, the filter transforms it and produces an output, just as a mathematical function would. We represent that function as a tangible abstraction, an object, just as a real-world electronic filter is a tangible entity.

We also model voltage values as functions. For the application here, the voltages will be constant both in magnitude and frequency, but one can imagine that they might in reality be more dynamic.

In the applicative paradigm, one *applies* a function (i.e., a function value) to an input value to yield a result. Applying a filter to a voltage would yield another voltage. However, what is the result of applying one function to another, or, in our case, of applying one filter to another? Consider an algebraic application of the sine function to the subtract $\pi/2$ function, independent of any numeric quantities. The result, instead of being a value, is itself the function cosine:

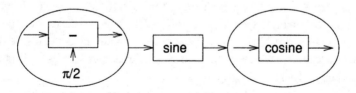

When functions are values, they can be operated on by other functions to produce yet other functions. We can treat filters in the same way. Ultimately applying a filter to a voltage value will of course produce an output value with a voltage and a frequency.

Figure 5-20 shows a general applicative value class used both to represent voltage values and to serve as the base class for electronic filter classes. It exports a type, Type, that is used by each filter class to determine the type of the filter driving it, so it can synthesize an instance of a new filter class from itself and its driving filter.

```
typedef double Frequency;
typedef double Voltage;

class Value {
public:
    enum Type { T_LPF, T_HPF, T_BPF, T_Notch, T_Data };
    virtual Type type() { return T_Data; }
    virtual Frequency f1() { return omega1; }
    virtual void print() {
        cout << "Value " << volts << " volts at frequency " <<
            omega1 << endl;
    }
    virtual Value *evaluate(Value* = 0) {
        return this;
    }
    Value(Voltage v=0, Frequency w1=0): volts(v), omega1(w1) {
    }
private:
    Frequency omega1;
    Voltage volts;
};

Value Zero(0);

Value *zero = &Zero;
```

Figure 5-20. An Applicative General Electronic Signal Value

Each filter publishes its type via the `type` member function. (The discussion of why a type field is used here instead of a virtual function is taken up below.) All values and all filters have at least one frequency; for values, this is their characteristic frequency, and for filters, it specifies a cutoff point. A `print` member function is present to generate printable results. Lastly, we provide an `evaluate` member function, which causes a value or filter to return its output voltage if it is already driven by an input signal.

Figure 5-21 shows the `Filter` abstraction. It overrides all the member functions of its base class, `Value`. Some of the functions (`evaluate`, `operator()`, and `print`) are made pure virtual functions by class `Filter` forcing its derived classes to provide their own versions. It adds a member function, `f2`, for use by filters having two cutoff frequencies instead of just one, and a private datum `omega2` to store the value. Class `Filter` also adds a pure virtual member function overloading the function call syntax, `operator() (Value*)`; it is this operator that allows the object to be "called" as though it were a function. If the application requires, multiple overloaded `operator()`s may be provided with different parameter lists.

```
class Filter: public Value {
public:
    Filter(Frequency w1, Frequency w2 = 0):
        Value(0, w1), omega2(w2), cachedInput(0) {
    }
    virtual Value *evaluate(Value* = 0) = 0;
    virtual Value *operator()(Value*) = 0;
    virtual void print() = 0;
    Frequency f2() { return omega2; }
    Type type() {
        if (cachedInput) return cachedInput->type();
        else return baseType;
    }
protected:
    Type myType, baseType;
    Value *cachedInput;
private:
    Frequency omega2;
};
```

Figure 5-21. A General Electronic Filter Abstraction

We can derive a new class from `Filter` to model a *low-pass filter* (LPF):

```
class LPF: public Filter {
public:
    Value *evaluate(Value* input = 0) {
        Value *f = cachedInput->evaluate(input);
        if (f->f1()^ < f1()) return f;
        else return zero;
    }
    Value *operator()(Value*);
    void print() {
        if (cachedInput) cout << "COMPOUND" << endl;
        else cout << "LPF(" << f1() << ")" << endl;
    }
    LPF(Frequency w1): Filter(w1), baseType(T_LPF) { }
};
```

Its `print` operation and constructor are straightforward. The `evaluate` member function propagates demand for evaluation to the filter (or value) connected to its input; the request propagates until a voltage value object is reached, and some signal value is eventually returned. That signal's frequency is evaluated to see if it falls within the passband of the filter (i.e., whether the signal should be passed on or absorbed) and the appropriate value is returned.

```
Value *
BPF::evaluate(Value *input = 0) {
    Value *f = cachedInput->evaluate(input);
    if (f->f1() > f1() && f->f1() < f2()) return f;
    else return zero;
}

Value *
BPF::operator()(Value* f) {
    switch(f->type()) {
    case T_LPF:
        if (f->f1() > f2()) return this;
        else return new BPF(f1(), f->f1());
    case T_HPF:
        if (f->f1() < f1()) return this;
        else return new BPF(f->f1(), f2());
    case T_BPF:
        Frequency lowfreq = f->f1();
        Frequency highfreq = ((Filter*)f)->f2();
        if (f1() > lowfreq) lowfreq = f1();
        if (f2() < highfreq) highfreq = f2();
        return new BPF(lowfreq, highfreq);
    case T_Notch:
        cachedInput = f;
        return this;
    case T_Data:
        myType = T_Data;
        cachedInput = f;
        return evaluate();
    }
}
```

Figure 5-22. Bandpass Filter Implementation

More interesting is the definition of `operator() (Value*)` for this class:

```
Value*
LPF::operator()(Value* f) {
    switch (f->type()) {
    case T_Data:
        myType = T_Data;
        cachedInput = f;
        return evaluate();
    case T_LPF:
        if (f->f1() > f1()) return this;
        else return f;
```

```
    case T_HPF:
        if (f->f1() > f1()) return new Notch(f1(), f->f1());
        else return new BPF(f->f1(), f1());
    case T_BPF:
        if (((Filter*)f)->f2() < f1()) return f;
        else return new BPF(f->f1(), f1());
    case T_Notch:
        cachedInput = f;
        return this;
    }
}
```

The parameter is an input "value" (signal or filter) to which this filter is to be applied, and the return value will be either a signal or a filter-valued object depending on the input. The call operator classifies the input to the filter: If the input can be evaluated to a voltage (is of type T_Data), then it just sees if the signal's frequency is above its cutoff point and returns the value of the signal if it is. Otherwise, this member function attempts to return a new filter type that characterizes the combined behavior of itself and its input, just as the sine function returned a cosine function when presented with the appropriate input shifting function. For example, any combination of a low-pass filter and a high-pass filter will result in a band-pass filter, though the filter will be a degenerate one if the high-pass and low-pass filters pass no frequencies in common. If it is difficult to return a single primitive filter type under these conditions, the filter just returns itself, configured with another filter as an input. The resulting aggregate object will be passed around the simulation as though it were a single object. If the inputs are all later connected to Value objects, further invocations of evaluate will return a Value object instead of an aggregate (the answer will be a value, not a function).

Note that LPF::operator()(Value*) has a switch on the type of one of its parameters, something admonished against at the beginning of the chapter. The rationale behind the switch statement is that it prevents a proliferation of public, virtual member functions. If the operator()(Value*) function were redone using a virtual function approach, it would look like this:

```
Value *
Filter::operator()(Value *f) {
    return f->combineWithLPFoutPut(this);
}
```

(Note that the code has been moved up into the Filter class, as it will now be the same for all filter classes.) That is, LPF passes on the task of combining two functors to the other filter participating in the combination. Each existing case leg would require a new virtual member function somewhere—"`case T_LPF`" gives rise to:

```
LPF::combineWithLPFoutPut
BPF::combineWithLPFoutPut
HPF::combineWithLPFoutPut
Value::combineWithLPFoutPut
```

The total amount of code in these functions would be about the same as it is in the `case` legs. All else being equal, the `switch` solution has the advantage of fewer global functions than the `virtual` solution does. Both accommodate the addition of new filter types with equal ease (or pain).

The `virtual` function mechanism chooses functions based on the class of just one operand. In more general terms, what is desired here is the selection of a member function based on the types of *two* objects participating in an operation. This facility, not directly available in C++, is called *multi-methods*. Multi-methods will be brought up briefly again in Section 9.7.

We can define the classes for the remaining filter types (the implementation of BPF, the band-pass filter, is shown in Figure 5-22) and use them to construct and exercise a filter network simulation.

Figure 5-23 shows a simple main program to exercise the filter classes. We first create three filters, one each of a low-pass, high-pass, and band-pass. The low-pass filter passes signals with frequencies below 8000 Hz; the high-pass filter, signals above 1100 Hz; and the band-pass filter, frequencies between 1000 Hz and 10000 Hz. We apply the band-pass filter to the high-pass filter (line 7), and print it (line 8), yielding

```
BPF(1100,10000)
```

That is, the application of a band-pass filter functor to a high-pass filter functor results in a single filter-valued object, a band-pass filter passing frequencies between 1100 Hz and 10000 Hz, whose behavior is identical to what would have been presented by the original band-pass filter and high-pass filter in tandem. In line 9, that filter value is applied to a signal and printed, yielding

```
Value 100 volts at frequency 1260
```

That is, the signal's frequency (1260) falls in the pass band of the band-pass filter (1100-10000). In line 10, that filter is applied to a low-pass filter and the result is printed in line 11, and we have

```
BPF(1100,8000)
```

```
1   int main() {
2       Value *v = new Value(100,1260); // voltage at a frequency
3       BPF bpf(1000, 10000);    // a band-pass filter
4       HPF hpf(1100);           // a high-pass filter
5       LPF lpf(8000);           // a low-pass filter
6       Filter *a;               // a pointer to a filter
7       a = (Filter*)bpf(&hpf);  // apply a band-pass filter to a
8       a->print();              //   high-pass filter:  result?
9       (*a)(v)->print();        // apply to a voltage and print
10      a = (Filter*)(*a)(&lpf); // apply that to a low-pass
11      a->print();              //   filter:  whaddya get?
12      a = (Filter*)(*a)(v);    // now apply voltage to input
13      a->print();              //   of all that, and print
14      lpf(&hpf)->print();      // combine low- & high-pass
15      return 0;                //   filters
16  }
```

Figure 5-23. A Simple Program to Exercise Applicative Filters

This filter is applied to the same signal voltage as before (line 12), and it is still within the range of the filter:

```
Value 100 volts at frequency 1260
```

Lastly, we combine a low-pass and high-pass filter (line 14), and the result is printed as a band-pass filter:

```
BPF(1100,8000)
```

For an alternative syntax more in the spirit of applicative programming, we define a family of apply operators. These take a function object pointer as their first parameter, followed by parameters for the functor itself:

```
Value *apply(Value *object, Value *arg) {
    return (*object)(arg); }

Value *apply(Value *object, Value *arg1, Value *arg2) {
    return (*object)(arg1, arg2); }
```

For sake of convenience, let's also define a `printer` functor:

```
class Printer: public Filter {
public:
    Type type() { return T_Printer; }
    void print() { }
    Value *evaluate(Value*) {
        // error
    }
    Value *operator()(Value* v) {
        v->print();
        return 0;
    }
} printerObject;

Printer *printer = &printerObject;
```

We can now apply a low-pass filter to a high-pass filter, and apply the resulting filter to an input value, and take the output and amplify it by 3:

```
LPF *lpf = new LPF(w1);
HPF *hpf = new HPF(w2);
AMPLIFIER *amplifier = new Amplifier;
Value *inputValue, *three = new Value(3);

apply(
    printer,
    apply(
        amplifier,
        apply(
            apply(lpf, hpf),
            inputValue
        ),
        three
    )
);
```

which is semantically the same as

```
amplifier((*((*lpf)(hpf)))(inputValue), three)->print();
```

5.7 Multiple Inheritance

Sometimes a single thread of inheritance is not enough; we see that a new class needs to inherit properties from two or more parent classes. If we can decide at compile time what the parent classes are to be, we can use C++ *multiple inheritance* to combine the behaviors of multiple base classes in a single derived class. Multiple inheritance is a powerful feature, rich in semantics and able to directly express complex structures. It should be used sparingly, when single inheritance (or no inheritance at all) would lose important design information, not encapsulate change in the long term, or compromise the suitability of the solution to the problem.

Dynamic multiple inheritance, introduced as "mix-ins" in the Flavors language, is a useful construct to "tune" the behaviors of a type at run time. A user may want to combine the behaviors of selected base classes to create a derived class for a specific need, then create an object to fulfill that need in an application. In C++, derived classes must be declared at compile time for all possible combinations of derivations, and the program can choose the appropriate class at run time and create the object for the application. That can lead to a combinatorial explosion of derived classes. In Flavors, these types can be built more dynamically: the program can "mix in" the behavior of selected, lightweight base classes at run time to change the behavior of a basic class. A "poor man's" simulation of dynamic multiple inheritance is presented in Chapter 10. Static multiple inheritance is covered here.

A Window Abstraction Example

One common example in the literature is the use of multiple inheritance to support a terminal window/screen system. Here, we discuss a Window class used by a text editor to display file contents on a terminal:

```
class Window {
public:
    Window();
    virtual ~Window();
    virtual void addch(char) = 0;
    virtual void addstr(string) = 0;
    virtual void clear() = 0;
    virtual void scroll() = 0;
    . . . .
private:
    Color curColor;
};
```

The editor is to be portable across several terminals. There are two different kinds of derived classes of Window, one for each of two available windowing technologies.

The first is called `CursesWindow`, which is an implementation of `Window` using the Curses [6] package:

```
#include <curses.h>

class CursesWindow : public Window {
public:
    void addch(char);
    void addstr(string);
    void scroll();
    void clear();
    . . . .
private:
    WINDOW *cursesWindow;
};
```

The second is called `XWindow`, specifically designed for X work station windows [7]:

```
#include <X11/X.h>

class XWindow : public Window {
public:
    void addch(char);
    void addstr(const string);
    void clear();
    void scroll();
    . . . .
protected:
    Display *disp;
    Window window;
    XWindowAttributes windowAttributes;
    GC gc;
    Cursor theCursor;
    unsigned long whitePixel, blackPixel;
};
```

Most of the member functions of `Window` are virtual, which means they are actually implemented in the derived classes. The idea is that an object of type `CursesWindow` or `XWindow` can be instantiated and then passed through the editor and used as though it were type `Window`. Other C++ programs could be written to use the portable `Window` interface.

Although one goal is to provide a general `Window` facility for use by many programs, it is also desirable to tailor class `Window` to the needs of an editor. An `EditWindow` is a `Window` with attributes peculiar to an editor, such as line numbers of the first and last lines on the screen:

```
class EditWindow : public Window {
public:
    int topLine()     { return topLineVal; }
    int bottomLine()  { return bottomLineVal; }
    String fileName() { return fileNameVal; }
    . . . .
    void scroll();    // plays with topLineVal and
                      //   bottomLineVal in addition to
                      //   performing Window operations
private:
    int topLineVal, bottomLineVal;
    PathName fileNameVal;
    Editor *editorVal;
protected:
    Cursor theCursor;    // special editing cursor
};
```

EditWindow should be a derived class of Window but should also behave like a
CursesWindow or XWindow as appropriate. The question then arises about how to
set up the class derivation.

The answer is that we can create a class that inherits the properties both of
window technology and editor architecture, resulting in a single new window class we
can use for both:

```
class EditWnd_Curses:
    public EditWindow, public CursesWindow {
};

EditWnd_Curses aNewWindow;
```

In a simple sense that is enough: The new derived class inherits all the properties
of both of its parents. However, there are two problems:

- Some operations on the new class are ambiguous. For example, what does it
  mean to invoke aNewWindow.scroll()? Should the scroll operations of
  both parents be performed? In what order?

- The class has a single grandparent (Window) common to both its parents: should
  its instance data be included in an EditWnd_Curses instance just once, or
  twice?

Regarding the first point, C++ is unlike most object-oriented programming languages in that it makes no default assumptions about how to treat such ambiguities. The language tosses that problem back to you, the programmer, allowing you to address it using existing language constructs. This saves the complication of additional language features to handle this issue. Object-oriented programming languages embedded in Lisp have concepts called *wrappers* and before- and after-methods to deal with this ambiguity. The C++ solution preserves the full power of pre- and post-condition constructs that exist in Lisp-like languages. Regarding the second point, C++ has something called a *virtual* base class that emulates CLOS semantics of a single instance of a class with multiple appearances in the inheritance directed acyclic graph (DAG).

Note that these are not just programming language artifacts, but they relate to genuine ambiguity in the application structure. Resolving such name conflicts is a design issue, though C++ can express the design decision in the code.

C++ is defined such that *declaration* of conflicting operators is legal. Only the *use* of conflicting operators in an ambiguous way causes a fatal compilation error. So while it is good advice to be aware of this problem at design time, the compiler can identify all conflicts after coding is complete. The next section describes in detail how to resolve these conflicts. A discussion is also included on duplicated data for classes inherited along multiple lineages.

Member Function Ambiguities

Member function names from multiple base classes may clash in a derived class, and the user can add code to resolve such conflicts. The member function `CursesWindow::clear` conflicts with `Window::clear`; since the latter does nothing (it is just a placeholder), we can ignore it and forward the operation to `CursesWindow`. However, the `scroll` member functions of class `EditWindow` and class `CursesWindow` also compete for the `scroll` functionality of `EditWnd_Curses`. Both must be invoked, and the order of invocation may be significant. The derived class `EditWnd_Curses` resolves the ambiguity by providing a `scroll` operation of its own, overriding the base class `scroll` functions. The derived class `scroll` calls the base class member functions in the order we want them to be invoked:

```
class EditWnd_Curses: public EditWindow, public CursesWindow {
public:
    void clear()   { CursesWindow::clear(); }
    void scroll() {
        EditWindow::scroll();
        CursesWindow::scroll();
    }
    . . . .
};
```

```
EditWnd_Curses aNewWindow;
```

Invocations of the `scroll` member function on instances of `EditWnd_Curses` are no longer ambiguous; the class itself fields the operation. It specifies the implementation of `scroll` to be a sequence of calls to `scroll` functions in base classes for that object. It is not incumbent on the derived class function to call its base class counterparts—the member function could have contained any code we had liked—but execution of all potentially ambiguous operators in a specified order is a common idiom in object-oriented programming languages. In C++, this idiom relies on no special language features.

Data Ambiguities

One resolves data ambiguities in much the same way as function ambiguities. Consider:

```
class EditWindow: public virtual Window {
public:
    . . . .
protected:
    Cursor theCursor;
};
```

```
class XWindow: public virtual Window {
public:
    . . . .
protected:
    Cursor theCursor;
};
```

```
class EditWnd_X: public EditWindow, public XWindow { };
```

EditWnd_X has two members called `theCursor` in the above code:
`EditWindow::theCursor` and `XWindow::theCursor`. Then

```
EditWnd_X::refresh() {
    . . . .
    // error:  EditWindow::theCursor or XWindow::theCursor?
    . . . . this->theCursor . . . .;
    . . . .
}
```

is illegal because it is ambiguous. Such ambiguities can be resolved with explicit qualification:

```
this->EditWindow::theCursor; // EditWnd_X's EditWindow's
                             //   cursor
this->XWindow::theCursor;    // EditWnd_X's XWindow's cursor
```

Virtual Base Classes

The second problem is the multiple appearance of one class in the ancestry of another, multiply derived class. We solve this problem by making some of the base classes *virtual*. This means that even if class `Window` appears several times in the derivation directed acyclic graph (DAG), then its data will appear only once in an instance of the class `EditWnd_Curses`:

```
class Window {
    . . . .
};

class EditWindow : public virtual Window {
    . . . .
};

class CursesWindow : public virtual Window {
    . . . .
};

class XWindow : public virtual Window {
    . . . .
};

class EditWnd_Curses :
    public EditWindow,
    public CursesWindow
{
    . . . .
};
```

By default, data of a base class that can be traced as a parent through multiple lineages will appear in the derived class object as many times as the class appears in the ancestry. If one class is declared to be virtually derived, it states willingness to share base class data with others derived from the same base, should that base be implicated as a virtual parent multiple times. If all paths from a base class through the inheritance DAG to the derived class start by passing through a virtual derivation, then there will be one copy of the data. If there is a mixture of virtual and nonvirtual derivations, then there will be one copy of the data for each nonvirtual derivation, plus one copy for all virtual derivations combined.

Note that classes can violate each other's encapsulation if they share a common, virtual base class and both appear in the same multiple inheritance DAG. This shouldn't come as a surprise, since these classes expressed a willingness to share their base class data by using virtual derivation. Whether base class variable folding takes place is under programmer control—it is neither the default nor is it mandatory as in other programming languages.

Avoiding Redundant Base Class Function Calls for Virtual Base Classes

Now that we have the information of just a single `Window` object in a `CursesWindow` or `XWindow` instance, we ask related questions about the behavior of member functions. Look again at how we resolved the member function ambiguity above:

```
void EditWnd_Curses::scroll() {
    EditWindow::scroll();   CursesWindow::scroll();
}
```

We find a similar thing for `refresh` and other operations on windows. It may make sense to call all parents' like named functions in a reasonable order. But say that each of `EditWindow::scroll` and `CursesWindow::scroll` in turn went to *their* parent class, `Window`, to solicit its participation in the scrolling activity:

```
void EditWindow::scroll() {
    . . . .      // stuff peculiar to EditWindow
    Window::scroll();
}

void CursesWindow::scroll() {
    . . . .      // stuff peculiar to CursesWindow
    Window::scroll();
}
```

Note that when the `scroll` operation is applied to an object of class `EditWnd_Curses`, `Window::scroll` is invoked twice; this may not be what we want. For the clear function, this is a slightly inefficient inconvenience. For scrolling, it may actually be an error. We would like to be able to control the sequencing of Window::scroll calls relative to the execution of code for the derived classes CursesWindow and EditWindow.

We can fine-tune the sequencing using a programming convention. The code peculiar to EditWindow is broken out into a separate member function, _scroll:

OLD: **NEW:**

```
class EditWindow:                    class EditWindow:
          public Window {                      public Window {
public:                              public:
   void scroll() {                      void scroll() {
      . . . . // local logic              _scroll();
      Window::scroll();                    Window::scroll();
   }                                    }
   . . . .                           protected:
};                                      void _scroll() {
                                           . . . . // local code
                                        }
                                        . . . .
                                     };
```

The same is done for CursesWindow. Now the derived class can be more selective about when and in what order it orchestrates the activities of its parent classes:

```
class EditWnd_Curses: public EditWindow,
                      public CursesWindow {
public:
   void scroll() {
      // these four can now be in any
      //    order the programmer wishes
      EditWindow::_scroll();
      CursesWindow::_scroll();
      _scroll();        // perhaps, optional
      Window::_scroll();
   }
protected:
   void _scroll() {
      . . . . // any additional work the derived
             //    class has to do
   }
   . . . .
};
```

Here, the member function EditWnd_Curses::scroll indicates that the base class `EditWindow` should do its scrolling function first, followed by `CursesWindow`. `EditWnd_Curses` then invokes its own scrolling logic (if any), which has been similarly separated into `EditWnd_Curses::_scroll`. Last, the base class `Window::_scroll` is invoked to tie everything together. Any other ordering could have been specified by the programmer.

The introduction of the ancillary `_scroll` function we call the *multiple inheritance function ambiguity idiom*.

Virtual Functions

Virtual functions are useful in multiple inheritance structures as they are for single inheritance. The behavior is an intuitive extension of what happens in single inheritance: The function called is determined by the type of the object itself, not by the type of the pointer to the object.

Consider the `Window` classes above as an example. A variable declared to be a `Window*` can point to an instance of any class in the hierarchy. That pointer can be used to invoke a member function, and if the function is virtual, the function called will be determined by the kind of window object pointed to. Assume that the member function `scroll` is declared `virtual` in the base class:

```
class Window {
public:
    . . . .
    virtual void scroll() = 0;
    . . . .
};
```

Invocations of the virtual `scroll` operation are be dispatched to the correct object at run time:

```
int main() {
    EditWnd_X anXEditWindow;
    EditWnd_Curses aCursesEditWindow;
    Window *windowPointer = &anXEditWindow;
    windowPointer->scroll();  // calls EditWnd_X::scroll
    windowPointer = &aCursesEditWindow;
    windowPointer->scroll();  // calls EditWnd_Curses::scroll
    return 0;
}
```

This follows the pattern of how virtual functions work in the single inheritance case.

Casting Pointers to Objects with Multiple Inheritance

Consider the following in light of the above classes EditWindow, XWindow, and EditWnd_X:

```
EditWnd_X *pe = new EditWnd_X;
XWindow *px;
. . . .
px = (XWindow*)pe;    // px now contains a different
                      //     physical address than pe
px = pe;              // same result as previous
pe = 0;               // pe set to integer zero
// pe = px;           // error, cast needed
pe = (EditWnd_X*)px;  // pe is restored to original value
```

Here, a single EditWnd_X object is initially created with pe pointing to it. We cast pe into a pointer to an XWindow and copy the value to px. Since C++ allows a class object pointer to address any publicly derived class of its declared base type, the cast is legal and has intuitive semantics at the C++ language level. However, what happens "underneath" to make this work is not intuitive, and bears examination.

In multiple inheritance, the representations of different "parts" of the object start at different places in memory. If px is assigned the value of pe, px must point to the "XWindow part" of the original EditWnd_X object so members can be properly dereferenced. This has interesting side effects; consider the following:

```
void an_X_function(void *p1, void *p2) {
    if (p1 == p2) printf("p1 == p2\n");
    else printf("p1 != p2\n");
}

EditWnd_X *pe = new EditWnd_X;
XWindow *px = 0;
px = pe;
an_X_function(pe, px);
```

The test for equality in an_X_function will fail under most C++ implementations. Casting from one class pointer to another and then to a third type (here, void*) is not guaranteed to yield the same result as casting directly from the class pointer to the third type. This is somewhat analogous to casting a float such as 1.2 to an integer, and then to a double, where the result differs from casting the value directly from a float to a double.

Null pointers are treated specially; casting between pointers of different types within a C++ program guarantees that comparison with the null pointer will still succeed:

```
EditWnd_X *pe = 0;
XWindow *px = 0;
if (px == 0) . . . .     // test succeeds
px = pe;
if (px == 0) . . . .     // test succeeds
```

5.8 The Inheritance Canonical Form

It is important to design for evolution, to structure a program to evolve through changes in requirements and technology. A properly tuned inheritance structure can go a long way in easing long-term maintenance. Class inheritance conventions make programs easier to understand, and ensure proper operation of objects that are treated polymorphically.

Figure 5-24 offers a canonical form for C++ class derivation. One should consider making all derivations virtual by default. The rationale behind this relates to the semantics of multiple inheritance in C++, and how many copies of Base instance data should reside in any object that can trace its lineage to Base through multiple independent paths. Consider a base class Window, which has two kinds of derived classes: those to reflect window system dependencies and those to reflect application dependencies. On one hand, we want different kinds of windows for Microsoft Windows than we do for windows based on the X Window System; both behave similarly from an application viewpoint, but are implemented differently. Likewise, we want a special kind of window for use by a word processor, and another for an editor, depending on how we present the user interface. We might use an inheritance DAG like this, then:

```
class Window {
    . . . .
private:
    short windowID;
};

class XWindow: public Window {
    . . . .
};

class MSWindow: public Window {
    . . . .
};
```

```
class Base {
public:
    // class Base follows the orthodox canonical form
    Base();
    Base& operator=(const Base&);
    virtual ~Base();
    Base(const Base&);
private:
    . . . .
};

class Derived: [virtual] [public | private] Base {
public:
    Derived();
    Derived& operator=(const Derived&);
    ~Derived();
    Derived(const Derived&);

    void foobar() {
        . . . .
        _foobar();
        . . . .
        Base::foobar();
        . . . .
    }
protected:
    void _foobar() { . . . . }
};
```

Figure 5-24. The Inheritance Canonical Form

```
class WPWindow: public Window {
    . . . .
};

class EditWindow: public Window {
    . . . .
};
```

Now if we want the following,

```
class X_WP_Window: public XWindow, public WPWindow {
};
```

how many Window::windowID fields are there? The answer here is two. An analysis of the problem may suggest that that is the thing to do. There may be a WPWindowManager that keeps track of word processing windows, and a separate

`XWindowManager` that keeps track of X system windows, and each might want to have its *own* say about what the IDs of its window objects should be. That means that each object should have ID fields for each of the window empires that care about it—in this case, for each kind of window manager. Something similar would be done if class `Window` had constructs to maintain itself on a linked list:

```
class Window {
public:
    . . . .
    void insert(Window*);
    . . . .
private:
    Window *previous, *next;
    . . . .
};
```

If each window empire (for example, the application empire and the implementation technology empire) wanted to "own" the linked-list-edness of `Window`, the virtual derivation would not be used. Unfortunately, this decision is made when we do the first level of (single!) derivation, *not* when the multiple derivation is done. Careful consideration and good foresight, insight (and sometimes, hindsight) can help avoid restructuring the inheritance structure over the course of program evolution. We will not always guess perfectly, but it is worth the effort to consider these issues carefully up front.

The following banking application classes, from a short application at the end of the chapter, are a good example of when virtual derivation should be used. We have a base class `Account` and derived classes `CheckingAccount` and `SavingsAccount`:

```
class Account {
public:
    virtual void print_statement() = 0;
    . . . .
protected:
    // Common low-level file access functions for
    // use by derived classes
    void file_read(const char *);
    void file_write(const char *);
private:
    AccountNumber accountNumber;
};

class CheckingAccount: public virtual Account {
    . . . .
};
```

```
class SavingsAccount: public virtual Account {
    . . . .
};
```

Consider the following derivation:

```
class CheckingSavingsAccount: public CheckingAccount,
                              public SavingsAccount {
    . . . .
};
```

Here we use virtual derivation for the following reasons:

- Each account object has its own identity (its account number); we do not want `CheckingSavingsAccount` to have two separate account numbers.

- The derivation is being done to combine behaviors, not to combine states (and certainly not to replicate the state the objects share in common).

Again, foresight is needed at the level of the initial derivations at the top of the class DAG. Deferring these decisions to the time multiple inheritance is needed may lead to design rework, and will certainly trigger widespread recompilation of code.

The canonical form example above has also taken special pains to break up calls from a derived class member function to a base class member function of the same name. The "rule" is that for such functions, those parts of the function that deal locally with the derived class are broken out into the `protected` section. The sequencing of these pieces, and their interaction with the base, are orchestrated in the body of the "real" member function of the derived class. These steps are also taken to support multiple inheritance, as was taken up more specifically in Section 5.7. Such steps need be taken only when a derived class function is calling a base class function of the same name, and virtual derivation is a possibility in the future.

☞ *When to use this idiom*: Use of this idiom should be tempered by two considerations. First, virtual derivation from the base is unnecessary if you know for sure that multiple inheritance will never be used. Second, virtual derivation may affect performance, and the tradeoff between generality and conservation of microseconds needs to be weighed.

Here are some other guidelines for creating inheritance structures:

1. When using public inheritance, most base class member functions should be declared `virtual`. This declares that the derived class is a specialization of the base class. It ensures that the base class customizations will override the base class defaults behavior even

when a derived class object appears in a context where a base class object is expected. For example, if `SunWindow` is derived from `Window`, we want to be able to provide a `SunWindow` where a `Window` is expected. In order for the compiler to actually invoke `SunWindow` member functions, the functions must be declared `virtual` so the compiler can arrange to select the right function at run time.

2. When using private inheritance, most base class member functions should *not* be declared virtual. (This will be discussed further in Section 7.5.)

3. Virtual inheritance cannot be used if you plan to cast base class pointers to derived class pointers. This is something that should be done rarely if at all: It usually suggests that a nonvirtual function needs to be made virtual, or that a virtual function needs to be added to the classes in a hierarchy.

4. Use virtual derivation if you are not particularly concerned about performance or if there is a chance that the class you are developing will participate in multiple inheritance, subject to the following considerations:

   (a) Look at the state information in the base class. If it is something you would want to duplicate on a per-instance basis, particularly under multiple inheritance, then you do not want to use virtual derivation.

   (b) If part of the class data fit this criteria, and part do not, then rethink the design. Is multiple inheritance the right expression of what you want to do?

   (c) Are you willing to allow the encapsulation of the base class to be violated? Virtual derivation allows violation of encapsulation in subtle ways.

Exercises

1. Discuss inheritance when used with polymorphism as an abstraction mechanism.

2. Virtual functions can be thought of as supporting object-oriented programming based on a class architectural model related to abstract data types. Polymorphic functions, which can take an argument of any type as long as their behavior (signature) is what is expected, support object-oriented programming based on a procedural architectural model. A commonly cited example is a polymorphic sort function that can sort a vector of any kind of objects. Can you do polymorphic functions in C++? How? Contrast the C++ approach with approaches in other object-oriented programming languages.

3. *Templates* (Chapter 7) in C++ are a way of creating polymorphic functions; they are a way of providing compiler support for functions that are to work with any reasonable type or set of types. Where would you use templates instead of inheritance and virtual functions? What are their advantages over virtual functions? Are they more limiting than virtual functions? Why or why not?

4. Use a debugger to trace the function calls in the following program, which uses the Atom structures described in this chapter:

```
Atom *lexAtom(String& s) {
    GeneralAtom g(s);
    return g.transform();
}

void parse(String& s) {
    for (Atom *a = lexAtom(s); a; a = lexAtom(s)) {
        . . . .
    }
}
```

5. Reimplement the LAPD message handling of classes in Section 5.5 so that no buffer copying is necessary. (Pass pointers to constructors of classes that correspond to different kinds of messages and different levels of the protocol.)

6. Implement the Amplifier class for Section 5.6.

7. Design and implement a set of classes to do symbolic algebra in C++ using the functors idiom. Try adding a differentiator and integrator that will do symbolic calculus on formulas with unbound variables. The classes should employ Newton's method, a Runge-Kutta integration, etc. as appropriate when all boundary conditions and parameters are supplied.

□

Queue Iterator Example

```
class Queue {
friend class QueueIterator;
public:
    void *leave() {
        void *retval;
        if (head == tail) retval = 0;
        else {
            if (--head < 0) head = max - 1;
            retval = rep[head];
        }
        return retval;
    }
    void *first() { return rep[head]; }
    void enter(void *v) {
        if ((head + 1) % max == tail) { /* error -- full */ }
        if (--tail < 0) tail = max - 1;
        rep[tail] = v;
    }
    int empty() { return head == tail; }
    Queue() { rep = new void*[max]; head = tail = 0; }
private:
    enum Constants { max = 10 };
    void **rep;
    int head, tail;
};
class QueueIterator {
public:
    QueueIterator(const Queue& q): queue(q), current(q.head) { }
    int next(void* &i) {
        if (current == queue.tail) {
            return 0;
        } else {
            if (--current < 0) current = Queue::max - 1;
            i = queue.rep[current];
            return 1;
        }
    }
    void reset() { current = queue.head; }
private:
    const Queue &queue;
    int current;
};
```

```
int main() {
    int one=1, two=2, three=3, four=4, five=5, six=6,
        seven=7, eight=8, nine=9, ten=10, eleven=11, twelve=12;
    void *i;
    Queue a;
    a.enter(&one);
    a.enter(&two);
    a.enter(&three);
    QueueIterator qi = a;
    while (qi.next(i)) printf("%d ", (int)(*((int*)i)));
    printf("\n");
    a.enter(&four);
    a.enter(&five);
    a.enter(&six);
    printf("leaving: "); i = a.leave();
    printf("%d ", (int)(*((int*)i)));
    i = a.leave();
    printf("%d ", (int)(*((int*)i)));
    i = a.leave();
    printf("%d ", (int)(*((int*)i)));
    i = a.leave();
    printf("%d ", (int)(*((int*)i)));
    i = a.leave();
    printf("%d\n", (int)(*((int*)i)));
    a.enter(&seven);
    a.enter(&eight);
    a.enter(&nine);
    a.enter(&ten);
    a.enter(&eleven);
    a.enter(&twelve);
    QueueIterator qj = a;
    while (qj.next(i)) printf("%d ", (int)(*((int*)i)));
    printf("\nleaving: ");
    i = a.leave();
    printf("%d ", (int)(*((int*)i)));
    i = a.leave();
    printf("%d\n", (int)(*((int*)i)));
    qj.reset();
    while (qj.next(i)) printf("%d ", (int)(*((int*)i)));
    printf("\nleaving: ");
    i = a.leave();
    printf("%d ", (int)(*((int*)i)));
    i = a.leave();
    printf("%d\n", (int)(*((int*)i)));
    return 0;
}
```

Simple Banking Account Application Classes

```
#include <fstream.h>
class Account {
public:
      Account();
      Account(double penalty, double minimum,
                           const char *name = "Account");
      ~Account();
      virtual void deposit(double) = 0;
      virtual void withdraw(double) = 0;
      virtual void print_statement() = 0;
protected:
      void file_write(const char*);
      void file_read(char*);
protected:
      void _deposit(double);
      void _withdraw(double);
      void _print_statement();
private:
      double penalty;
      double minimum;
      double balance;
      char* name;
      ifstream fpr;
      ofstream fpw;
};
class InterestAccount : virtual public Account {
protected:
      InterestAccount(double penalty,
                       double interest, double minimum,
                       char* s = "InterestAccount");
      ~InterestAccount();
public:
      void deposit(double);
      void withdraw(double);
      void print_statement();
      double calculate_interest();
protected:
      void _deposit(double);
      void _withdraw(double);
      void _print_statement();
private:
      double interest;
};
```

```
class SavingsAccount : public InterestAccount {
public:
     SavingsAccount(double penalty,
                    double interest,
                    double minimum,
                    char* s = "SavingsAccount");
     ~SavingsAccount();
private:
};

class CheckingAccount : virtual public Account {
public:
     CheckingAccount(double penalty,
                     double minimum,
                     const char* s = "CheckingAccount");
     void deposit(double);
     void withdraw(double);
     void print_statement();
protected:
     void _deposit(double);
     void _withdraw(double);
     void _print_statement();
private:
};

class InterestCheckingAccount : public CheckingAccount,
                                public InterestAccount {
public:
     InterestCheckingAccount(double penalty,
          double interest,
          double minimum,
          const char *s = "InterestCheckingAccount");
     void  deposit(double);
     void  withdraw(double);
     void  print_statement();
protected:
     void _deposit(double);
     void _withdraw(double);
     void _print_statement();
private:
};
```

References

1. Russo, V. F., and S. M. Kaplan. "A C++ Interpreter for Scheme," *Proceedings of the C++ Workshop*. Denver: USENIX Association Publishers (October 1988).

2. Stroustrup, B. *The C++ Programming Language*, 1st ed. Reading, Mass.: Addison-Wesley, 1986, p. 165.

3. Knuth, Donald E. *Fundamental Algorithms*. Vol. 1, *The Art of Computer Programming*, 2nd ed. Reading, Mass.: Addison-Wesley, 1973, pp. 460-461.

4. Agha, G. A. *Actors: A Model of Concurrent Computation in Distributed Systems*. Cambridge: MIT Press, 1986.

5. Ungar, David, and Randall B. Smith. "Self: The Power of Simplicity." *SIGPLAN Notices 22*,12 (December 1987).

6. Strang, John. *Programming with Curses*. Newton, Mass: Reilly and Associates, 1986.

7. Mansfield, Niall. *The X Window System: A User's Guide*. Reading, Mass.: Addison-Wesley, 1991.

6

Object-Oriented Design

No activities so influences the quality of a product as do architecture and design. This is neither a new phenomenon nor unique to software or digital systems: The same has been true for decades in circuit design, and for millennia in the architecture of buildings. It is early in the life cycle, during architecture and design, that a system's long-term sustaining structure is put in place; this structure includes facilities to ease repair and enhancement. Architecture and design also make major contributions to aesthetics—giving a system both elegance and beauty. A well-designed structure will endure nature well and accommodate evolution gracefully; a poorly-designed structure will fall victim to the elements early in its life, perhaps even collapsing under its own weight.

In earlier chapters of this book, we have discussed the syntax and semantics of inheritance and virtual functions in C++: the foundations of object-oriented *programming*. Here, we take time to step back and look at things from the perspective of *design* and even from the more remote perspective of architecture. The key to evolvable, understandable programs is to base them on a good design, and the key to a good design for a C++ program is to understand what things make good classes, objects, and member functions, and what things do not.

The object paradigm is well-suited to structuring a wide variety of complex systems. Most complex software applications can be characterized by abstractions that objects and classes capture well: resources, events, and the "tangibles" of the application domain. Other techniques, such as functional decomposition or data flow analysis, work well in some domains but are not as broadly applicable. Object-oriented analysis is a good starting point for most systems; other techniques may work well as implementation strategies to complement object-oriented aspects of the implementation.

Object-oriented system construction techniques go beyond the technical issues of administering structure, providing a tool to communicate with customers and to capture their expectations for the final product. Mismatch of expectations is the downfall of many systems, both technological and sociological.

The object paradigm, like any paradigm, embodies a set of architectural rules and guidelines. These rules constrain the activities of design and programming, but it is these constraints that keep design and long-term maintenance from going awry. These constraints serve first to create and manage abstractions; as with any design approach, it is the building of abstractions that makes it possible to tackle complexity. The object paradigm's abstraction techniques focus on the terminology, resources, and abstractions that live in the *application* world; the abstractions in many other design approaches focus on the *solution* or *implementation* view of a product. Happily, the object paradigm provides an implementation technology—object-oriented programming—that can directly capture the structure of these abstractions in an implementation. This complete tie—from application analysis to design to implementation—helps the implementation structure parallel the abstractions that are fundamental, stable, and inviolate to the application (to the degree anything in software, or the real world, can be said to be that stable). This parallelism between the stable aspects of the characterization of the problem and the structure of the solution is the cornerstone of the object paradigm's support for system evolution. We call this the *isomorphic structure principle*, and it is central to the ability of objects and classes to encapsulate change.

The design techniques described in this chapter are not formal; most techniques in practice are not. The human mind is the best "tool" to support these techniques; other tools may be used to leverage the output of a design across an entire development community.

This chapter approaches software from the perspective of formulating design abstractions, showing how the C++ language can directly capture these abstractions in source code. It also introduces some "unwritten rules" of C++ programming that provide techniques and guidance to make object-oriented C++ programs flexible, efficient, and elegant. The chapter opens by adding some precision to the definition of class, object, type, and entity, and their relationships to each other. Using that foundation, the chapter takes a diversion into the design process itself. The remainder of the chapter discusses design rules for building class abstractions and structuring relationships between them. Having built a basis in object-oriented design in this chapter, we will move on to more advanced idioms in ensuing chapters.

6.1 Types and Classes

Classes are often characterized as a way of creating new types and introducing them into a programming language. And most (though not all) languages are said to have the notion of "type," which attaches an intuitive set of properties to variables in the language. For example, we know that integers can be added, subtracted, multiplied, and divided; in a language having string variables, we know they can be catenated, searched for a substring, and so on.

Let's bring some historical perspective into our discussion here. The concept of *type* was initially created as a formalism based on set-theoretic properties. Thus the *type* Integer meant the set of all integers; it conveyed the valid operations on members of that set, and properties, such as closure, that applied to that set. One set, called a *subset*, might be contained in another set. Each of those sets characterizes a type. The type characterizing the smaller set is said to be a *subtype* of that for the larger set. For example, Integer is a subtype of Real, because the set of reals contains the set of integers.

Enter programming languages, which initially tried to model mathematical expression in their syntax. It is common folklore that one of the earliest programming languages had as its goal the direct expression of FORmula TRANslation. FORTRAN's functions were to model mathematical functions; its types, mathematical types. *The goal was to model the abstractions of the problem domain directly in the programming language.* Much of early digital computing focused on engineering and mathematical domains, and their entities and types were reflected in the variables and types of the languages of the day. However, programming languages had to make some representational and behavioral concessions to reality: number sets could not be truly infinite, for example, but were constrained in practice by the word size of the machine.

Eventually, "types" became notational conveniences that lost most of their theoretical heritage. For example, many languages (including C, C++, and versions of FORTRAN through FORTRAN66) allow you to perform arithmetic on characters. This has dubious formal foundations in application semantics but is tremendously useful in real programming. Most functions in most programs do not rigorously implement mathematical functions (unambiguous mappings from a domain onto a range), so the formal roots have been lost.

The concept of *class* is old as well, going back at least to *Principia Mathematica* at the turn of the century [1]. In that work, classes are described as "merely symbolic or linguistic conveniences, not genuine objects as their members are if they are individuals." This captures much of what the term retains in its meaning today, and it overlaps today's meaning of "type" as well.

In C++, you can create your own classes and use them in the traditional programming language sense of being types. You can define conversions between any two class types that make sense for the application you are modeling. While it may make sense to define conversion from a `double` to a user-defined `Complex`, it may not always make sense to convert, say, a `List` to a `Set`, or an `Apple` to an `Orange`. These are issues tackled during design, and programming languages can offer only limited help. Such issues are better treated from a design perspective, using design rules that promote proper semantics and good design aesthetics.

So we have types, which have a heritage in the application domain, and classes, which express the corresponding solutions. For good object-oriented design, we want application domain *entities* to map onto the objects, and types to map onto the classes of the solution domain, as Figure 6-1 illustrates. Application domain entities are notions that we care about in our application: transactions, money, accounts, and tellers in a banking system; phones, calls, lines, and switches in a telecommunications system. We generalize these individual entities into *types*—that is, we can talk about transactions, accounts, phones, or calls in general, without talking about Joe's account at the Downtown Bank or Jane's home phone in particular. These application domain concepts are mapped onto software abstractions in the solution domain: types become *classes*, and entities become *objects*.

This model, while the most appropriate for C++, is not the only possibility. The concepts of both entities and types could be implemented as objects if a class were itself an object, as in self [2] or Smalltalk. The same programming language construct can be used to capture both entities and types from the application domain; when used to represent types, such objects are called *prototypes* or *exemplars*. The latter term is preferred in this book, as the word "prototype" has become an overloaded term (Section 6.2). Exemplars serve as models from which new objects are made, either by copying or by executing an ordinary member function to manufacture and return a new instance. A C++ idiom modeling an exemplar approach to object-oriented programming in C++ is described in Chapter 8.

In addition to the relationships shown in Figure 6-1, there are other relationships between application domain types that must be captured in the solution domain. If one type is a specialization of another—as a `DigitalPressureMeter` and `AnalogPressureMeter` are each specializations of the more abstract `PressureMeter`—we can capture that by using inheritance in the solution. Publicly deriving class `DigitalPressureMeter` from `PressureMeter` causes it to exhibit `PressureMeter`'s properties, capturing the application domain relationship between the two abstractions. We can put a `Spring` object inside our `AnalogPressureMeter` just as we find in the real world. Most of the time, such transformations are just this straightforward; it is this isomorphism between the problem domain and the solution domain that makes object-oriented design so powerful. A good mapping between these two worlds supports graceful evolution by encapsulating change. We reflect the structure of the application in the structure of our classes. The overall structure of the real world changes less often than the details of the behaviors of its parts (which are reflected in changes to member functions) or of

CONCRETE ⟵⟶ ABSTRACT

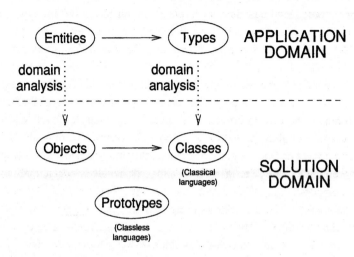

Figure 6-1. Domain Set Relationships

how parts are implemented (as may be reflected in the internal data structures or algorithms of a class).

Public inheritance is the language construct used to capture application domain specialization relationships in C++. Public inheritance, information hiding, and virtual functions are the pillars of object-oriented programming. By publicly deriving class `AnalogPressureMeter` from `PressureMeter`, we assert that class `AnalogPressureMeter` will exhibit all `PressureMeter` behaviors in its public interface. The code would look like this:

```
class AnalogPressureMeter: public PressureMeter {
public:
    . . . .
    // whatever is public in PressureMeter acts almost as
    // though it were declared here, from the perspective
    // of a user of an AnalogPressureMeter object
    . . . .
private:
    . . . .
};
```

However, the default mode of derivation in C++ is *private derivation*, which declares that base class member functions are available only from *within* the derived class, and are *not* made available to clients of the derived class. Private inheritance is less a design support technique than an implementation technique for reuse, and it will be discussed separately as such in Section 7.5. An overview of the differences between public and private inheritance can also be found at the beginning of Chapter 4.

Object relationships in the real world are more complex than can be expressed by specialization and containment alone, and a vocabulary of terms has arisen to describe these relationships. There is nothing sacred, magical, or even particularly scientific about these terms, but they do serve a purpose in communicating about object relationships. Borrowing from cognitive science and entity-relationship information modeling, we use the term IS-A to designate specialization: A `DigitalPressureMeter` IS-A `PressureMeter`. The term HAS-A is used to describe containment: an `AnalogPressureMeter` HAS-A `Spring`. But what about other relationships? How is an `AnalogPressureMeter` LIKE-A[1] `AnalogVoltMeter`? What are the relationships between `Manager`, `Secretary`, `DeptHead` (Department Head), `VicePresident`, `AdminAsst` (Administrative Assistant), and `CopyMachine`? In the spirit of object-oriented design, we want to capture these application relationships in the structure of our implementation. Properly capturing these relationships in an object-oriented programming language requires some additional insight, supported by language idioms, to create a program structure that evolves gracefully over time. This chapter will provide you with such idioms.

Object-oriented programming languages break new ground in the IS-A relationships in the problem domain. Inheritance is a technique that helps organize abstractions according to their IS-A relationships, while facilitating reuse of common properties across similar classes. But there are opportunities for reuse unrelated to IS-A and only weakly related to properties of the application. C++ is also expressive for coding solution domain optimizations and code reuse. This chapter will help designers distinguish between these two kinds of relationships. Balancing the structure between solution domain concerns and application domain concerns is an

---

1. The English language article disagreements that arise in the use of these terms are usually forgiven—that is, there is no "`LIKE-AN`."

engineering consideration crucial to system maintainability and to architectural aesthetics.

Failure to preserve close relationships between application domain formalisms, and solution constructs, can lead to an inflexible implementation that is difficult to understand. This problem becomes particularly menacing when classes are related to each other by subtyping (or IS-A), as discussed throughout this chapter. Before discussing that, though, let's lay more groundwork in the basics of object-oriented design.

6.2 The Activities of Object-Oriented Design

A deep understanding of the application is the key to the success of any design using any technique. A design that uses object-oriented techniques is certainly no exception, but object-oriented techniques make the job easier because the system building blocks are derived from things the *user* sees in the application (such as telephones and accounts), *not* from things the implementor uses in the solution (databases, relays, and disk drives). Implementors may still use the algorithms and tools that are common in their line of business, but such tools always operate in the context of things the user understands.

It is crucial that the designer of an object-oriented system (or of any system) have a good working relationship with the end user to validate assumptions about the system's purpose and operation. Prototyping and iterative development can help here. Using objects as units of throw-away helps developers iterate through several possible designs before committing to a final strategy. Once the major abstractions are understood from the evaluation of customer needs, developers can start to use development quality tools to take implementation forward.

These activities lead to a development process substantially different from traditional top-down or structured design techniques. This difference is important, and learning to develop iteratively using customer vocabulary is a mind-set change that must be mastered for successful object-oriented design.

Keeping that idea in mind, here are the activities of object-oriented design:

- *Identify the entities in your application domain.* Entities may be resources, events, or other well-defined "crisp" areas of specialization or expertise. Entities are often nouns of the problem statement provided by application end users. If the user expects "an X" to be in your application, then make X an entity. For example, if a knowledgeable customer of a flight control software package expects there to be a rudder on an airplane, then there should be a Rudder entity in the design of your flight control software.

At this level of consideration, whether an entity is a general "class" entity or a specific instance is not critical. Further differentiation between these two levels of abstraction takes place as the entities are transformed into implementation structures.

There are no hard and fast rules about what makes "good" entities, and there is no single "right" partitioning of a system into entities. There are, however, some rules of thumb we can apply as "litmus tests" for the quality of an abstraction:

— Is it easy to identify and name the behaviors of an entity? If not, consider whether the supposed entity might better be a function or some other abstraction.

— Do the entity's behaviors relate to each other, and to the entity, in an intuitively satisfying way?

— Is the abstraction too big, or too little? (Some designers consider the interface too large if it cannot be described on one side of a 3 x 5 card [3].)

— Pre-ordained hardware architectural components, and the software interfacing directly with them, are usually good candidates for entities.

— If you cannot think of two good, significantly different implementations of an entity, then a broader abstraction is probably needed.

Section 6.5 will investigate further rules of thumb to identify useful entities.

• *Identify the behaviors of the entities.* Each entity provides some service to the application, either by the set of tasks it performs or through other entities it contains. These services are the *responsibilities* of the entities to the application. All needed services and responsibilities must be identified and associated with the proper entities.

"Good" behaviors are crisp, clear, and concise. Thinking of them as the member functions they will become, behaviors should seldom require more than one or two parameters. Perhaps the most important factor in object-oriented design is choosing behaviors that are broad enough to serve a wide variety of systems within a given application domain, without creating an abstraction that is too large to understand or too vague to allow for efficient implementation. (For more on identifying "good" behaviors, see Section 6.5.)

- *Identify relationships between entities, particularly subtyping (IS-A) relationships.* If an entity is a specialized case of a more general entity, that relationship should be noted; it can be used to advantage in the implementation stage. A useful tool to aid in this activity is the *transaction diagram*, described in Chapter 11. Other important relationships, such as containment of one entity within another, will be discussed in more detail later in this chapter.

- *Create a C++ design structure from the entities.* The initially defined entities are good candidates for C++ classes and objects. Specific entities will map onto objects in a running program; generalizations of entities (types) become classes. The names of such classes should reflect the semantics of their application domain counterparts.

    Subtyping relationships are most often reflected as inheritance hierarchies in the implementation, with most of their member functions virtual. Sometimes, entity subtyping relationships are more suitably implemented using *forwarding* instead of inheritance. Forwarding is described later in this chapter.

    Some application domain entities may map not onto classes or objects in the implementation but onto abstractions from other paradigms. For example, traditional database technology may be adequate to model some data abstractions discovered during analysis of the application.

- *Implement.* The details of class data structures are filled in, new private functions added as utilities within classes, and the member functions themselves written. Unit testing of member functions and classes may occur at this stage.

- *Fine-tune.* Some functions may be declared as `inline` for efficiency, in places where a function call or argument copying overhead is too expensive. You may find commonality between some implementations, which did not manifest itself in the analysis phase (that is, in the first three activities). Here, you can use private derivation for code reuse.

- *Test.* Black-box testing proceeds as for any system.

Note that these activities are not sequential *steps*—that is, they are not a recipe for doing things in a prescribed sequence moving progressively toward an implementation. The activities are performed in a back-and-forth order, sometimes even in parallel, until iteration comes to a minimum and the system converges on stability. The key to a successful implementation is to iterate and to discard mistakes, starting over where improvement is needed.

In object-oriented development, the boundaries between traditional development steps become fuzzy. Early implementation (prototyping) can add depth and insight to the design phase, just as some design decisions may prescribe some implementation. While analysis and design still may be viewed as having distinct focuses, the two have much the same structure under the object paradigm and separating them has limited value.

Note also that the technique focuses on the products of the design themselves more than on the interactions between the pieces. Interactions between objects are, of course, important; they are what get the job done. But the architectural integrity of a system comes from the structure of its interfaces; object interfaces create structures that tend to encapsulate change well and evolve gracefully.

The system partitioning resulting from an object-oriented analysis of a system is much different from the structure resulting from traditional functional decomposition techniques that focus on interactions between system pieces. In functional decomposition techniques, functions are artifacts of design decisions deferred at higher levels: They are created out of analysis of the interactions between higher level components. These increasingly low-level design decisions often have only obtuse or complex ties to the application. If we focus first on the software abstractions, and second on the interactions, the design will evolve gracefully over time. It will also be easier to understand.

Consider this social analogy to object-oriented design: Your boss selects you and several other people to work as a team to solve a problem. The boss—the system designer—chooses you for your expertise, for the functions and services you offer to that team. The boss gives the team an objective and lets you have a go at it; there is no specification of exactly how you are to interact. You are all autonomous objects interacting with each other to accomplish the overall system task.

6.3 Object-Oriented Analysis and Domain Analysis

The activities of object-oriented design are techniques to analyze a problem and decompose it into abstractions that encapsulate expertise on facets of the problem at hand. It is important to look beyond the application at hand, broadening the abstractions to suit the entire domain of the application. Adding this perspective to the design activities characterizes a new set of activities collectively called *domain analysis.* As always, the terms "design" and "analysis" are intentionally fuzzy, with no special significance beyond casual English usage.

Why Broaden the Design Scope?

Let's say we have a contract for the autopilot software design for a Sopwith 123 airplane. We can find good abstractions—rudders, ailerons, motor, and so forth—and actually put them together to control the takeoff, flight, and landing of the plane.

Instead of designing just for the Sopwith 123, we want to broaden our abstractions as if we weren't designing for the Sopwith, but for a hypothetical, abstract Sopwith-like plane. The hypothetical "abstract plane" represents the characteristics of the *domain* we are interested in. We want to do this for three reasons:

1. Broadening our design scope prepares us to deal with new abstractions later that are similar to those in the application at hand. A company filling contracts for Sopwith 123 flight control software is likely to get contracts for similar airplanes in the future. We want to reuse Sopwith 123 software to satisfy the new contract.

2. Broadening our design scope helps the system evolve. If Sopwith comes out with a new motor, new hydraulics systems, or new compasses for the Sopwith 123, then we want to change our software as little as possible to meet the change in requirements. If the design abstractions minimize specific knowledge about the current motor, hydraulics system, compass, and so forth, then the impact of change will be lessened when new ones are introduced. One trick to help this evolution is to characterize abstractions in terms of their methods of interaction with other abstractions, instead of how they are implemented internally. If a compass interacts with the flight control hardware through three electronic signals, then we should characterize the compass in terms of the corresponding three properties. The new compass will likely have three pins as well, and our software might survive the change untouched.

3. Broadening our design scope helps the system best fulfill its intended use. The software industry has ceased to be surprised that delivered systems do not meet customer expectations. By broadening the scope of the system's abstractions, we enable the system to "cover more requirements ground." If the final system misses the mark on some customer expectation, a broad design can more easily accommodate the deviation from intended behavior than can a design optimized from a single perspective.

How to Broaden the Domain

How do we broaden an abstraction for resilience in light of change? One way would be to "fatten" class interfaces to provide all reasonable services. For example, should our system structure assume the plane has one motor, or that it may have several? We may add some "fat" to the initial design by making the central power plant abstraction be a vector of motors; the Sopwith 123 would be a degenerate design using a single-element vector. Here, the overhead and generality of a vector are extra baggage for the Sopwith 123 but can tremendously simplify a multi-motor design. Classes with behaviors added for the sake of generality are said to have *fat interfaces.*

Making fat interfaces is a longstanding generalization technique. Procedural linear algebra libraries often contain routines taking tens of parameters, most of which often go unused. Such abstractions are difficult to learn and understand. But it is one of the few satisfactory techniques that could be used with procedural abstractions without compromising generality.

With object-oriented design, it is even better to do just the opposite: We can *remove* behaviors from an abstraction to make it more general. An analysis of the Sopwith 123's motor may discover dozens of levers that can be manipulated. But instead of making every lever visible in the interface of the motor abstraction, it is better to either collapse several of the levers into more abstract concepts, or to hide the appearance of individual levers. If the motor has two carburetors (devices that control the flow of fuel and air into the motor), the two may be combined into a single abstract carburetor device. Using *transactions* as a design tool can help discover such commonality; these are discussed in Chapter 11. If the Sopwith motor is unique in having a pressure relief valve for manual starting, our general characterization of a motor would not display that feature. So instead of fat classes, we want "skinny classes" that are general because of what they do *not* say about an entity or type.

Balancing the Breadth of the Design

How broad is broad enough? We can ask this question both for individual abstractions and for the domain driving the design of their interfaces. Given the Sopwith 123 as a target system, we can ask how far we should generalize:

- For all models of Sopwiths?
- For all biplanes?
- For all planes with one propeller?
- For all planes with propellers?
- For all planes?

- For all powered flying things?

- For all vehicles?

- For all control systems?

- For all C++ software projects?

There is a point at which generalization creates more problems than it solves, and where this point falls is a product of experience and the nature of the business for which the design is being done.

The Products of Balanced Designs

We broaden the design scope to improve reuse; but reuse of what? Most reuse efforts focus on reuse of code. More important, though, is to reuse the structure of a solution: to reuse architecture and design. If portions of a design can be reused, then much code can be reused as well. If a particular abstraction doesn't fit any existing implementations, the class hierarchy provides a framework for creating a new abstraction. The existing design must of course be general enough to make this work; the new application must be within the scope of the domain that was used for the existing design.

Reusable designs can be captured as *frameworks* and *libraries*; these are discussed in more detail in Chapter 11. Reuse issues will be revisited in detail in Chapter 7.

6.4 Object and Class Relationships

Recall the design activities of identifying relationships between entities, and how those relationships translate into an implementation. This section begins an extended discussion of relationships between the abstractions of object-oriented design. The topic is so important that it will occupy us for the remainder of this chapter.

In the previous section, we saw that relationships between entities can be mapped directly onto corresponding C++ class and object structures. Consider Figure 6-2 and Figure 6-3, which depict a community of entities (a company of individuals) that have certain relationships to each other. Let's assume that we want to design a software system that reflects these abstractions (e.g., an organizational communications system or management information system). Looking at the relationships between the individuals, we determine the relationships between the classes we would use to represent them in our software.

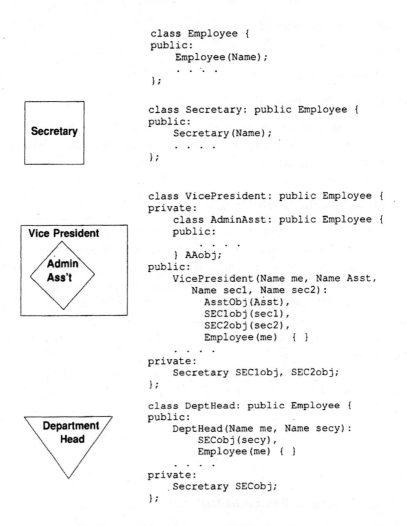

```
class Employee {
public:
    Employee(Name);
    . . . .
};

class Secretary: public Employee {
public:
    Secretary(Name);
    . . . .
};

class VicePresident: public Employee {
private:
    class AdminAsst: public Employee {
    public:
        . . . .
    } AAobj;
public:
    VicePresident(Name me, Name Asst,
        Name sec1, Name sec2):
            AsstObj(Asst),
            SEC1obj(sec1),
            SEC2obj(sec2),
            Employee(me)   { }
    . . . .
private:
    Secretary SEC1obj, SEC2obj;
};

class DeptHead: public Employee {
public:
    DeptHead(Name me, Name secy):
            SECobj(secy),
            Employee(me) { }
    . . . .
private:
    Secretary SECobj;
};
```

Figure 6-2. Type Relationships in an Organization

At least one other computer science discipline has an interest in defining relationships between real-world entities—namely, artificial intelligence. One AI tool is *semantic networks*, which have their own established vocabulary for relating entities to each other [4]. We borrow from that vocabulary here, because it is useful for discussions of software structure hierarchies as they reflect our models of the real world. Some of the relationships are described in the remainder of this section.

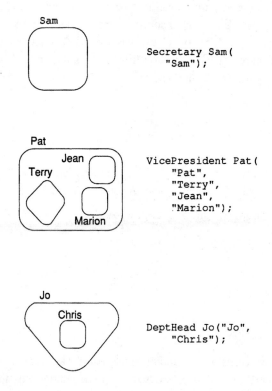

Secretary Sam(
    "Sam");

VicePresident Pat(
    "Pat",
    "Terry",
    "Jean",
    "Marion");

DeptHead Jo("Jo",
    "Chris");

Figure 6-3. Entity Relationships in an Organization

The IS-A Relationship

IS-A is the specialization relationship between types or classes. In the simple English sense, a Vice President *is an* Employee: Vice Presidents in general have all the characteristics employees in general have, but the reverse cannot be said. Another way of saying this is that a Vice President is a *kind of* Employee, but not all Employees are Vice Presidents. Or we can say that the set of all Employees contains the set of all Vice Presidents. So we can say that a Vice President in general IS-A Employee. Of course, a Secretary IS-A Employee, just as an Administrative Assistant IS-A Employee and a Department Head IS-A Employee.

We usually talk about IS-A relationships only in the class world (that is, not in the instance world). This relationship is more useful for discussing characteristics in general, not properties in particular. For example, we usually say that the chair you are sitting on is an entity of a specific type of chair, not that it IS-A chair. We do classify chairs using IS-A relationships: an (anonymous) red swivel chair with five legs and arms, as a type of chair, has an IS-A relationship to type Chair.

In C++, we represent IS-A relationships using public inheritance. Each of these classes is publicly derived from `Employee`:

```
VicePresident
DeptHead
Secretary
AdminAsst
```

That means that any accessible (`public`) characteristic of an `Employee` is also a characteristic of each of these more specific classes. In fact,

```
class Secretary: public Employee
```

can be read "`Secretary` IS-A `Employee`."

The HAS-A Relationship

HAS-A connotes containment and is interchangeable with *is-part-of* or *uses for implementation*. Unlike IS-A, which is solely a relationship for classes, HAS-A defines a relationship between two classes, between a class and an object, or between two objects.

Let's look first at the class level, and at `VicePresident` in particular. The Vice Presidents have gotten together and have created a position in the company designed to serve Vice Presidents alone—namely, the Administrative Assistant. What Administrative Assistants do is entirely at the direction of the Vice Presidents, and no one else in the management structure interacts strongly with Administrative Assistants (for the sake of the example, presume Administrative Assistants interact only with their principals, their own secretaries, and executives from other companies). Since it holds for all Vice Presidents, this relationship appears at the class level of generality. Class `VicePresident` HAS-A `AdminAsst`; we see the class *declaration* of the latter inside the former class declaration. This reflects *conceptual* ownership.

Now Vice Presidents do not create the notion of Secretaries, but it is clear in the English sense that Vice Presidents have secretaries. One clue in Figure 6-2 that Vice Presidents did not invent the notion is that Department Heads have secretaries, too (and Administrative Assistants may have their own secretaries). We say that an *instance* of VicePresident or DeptHead HAS-A Secretary. While there is no HAS-A relationship at the *class* level, there obviously is one at the *instance* level. Class Secretary stands alone as a concept in its own right; it is not, at the conceptual level, "owned" by any other class. Individual instances of Secretary are associated with their principals and are declared as members of classes derived from Manager.

HAS-A at the instance level may manifest itself as complete containment of one object *B* within another object *A*, or simply as object *A* containing a pointer to an object *B*, whether or not *B* is created by *A*. For example, class DeptHead could have contained only a pointer to a Secretary object in Figure 6-2. However, the state of the Secretary object still should be thought of as being part of the state of the DeptHead object. A HAS-A relationship still exists through a pointer between DeptHead and Secretary just as if the Secretary object had been embedded in DeptHead. If a pointer is used, however, we call it a HAS-A relationship only if there are no other holders of a pointer to the same instance (that is, if only one DeptHead object points to any given Secretary instance).

What if a C++ class contains a reference? A reference is an alias for an object elsewhere. If the reference is used for an object within the same class, then a HAS-A relationship exists without regard to the reference, and the reference does not change that relationship. Otherwise, a reference declaration states that the object may not be solely owned by the class containing the declaration, but that the object is accessible through another name. A HAS-A relationship may not exist.

Backing up a bit: Is it also true at the instance level that a VicePresident object (e.g., Pat) HAS-A AdminAsst object (Terry)? The answer is of course yes, *in addition to* the "conceptual ownership" relationship that exists between their classes in Figure 6-2. It is unusual to find a HAS-A relationship existing at the class level without existing at the object level, too. (However, one is coming just below— see if you notice it!)

Now let's extend the example a bit, introducing a new class Manager (Figure 6-4). We note IS-A relationships between VicePresident and Manager, as well as between DeptHead and Manager (a DeptHead IS-A Manager; a VicePresident IS-A Manager). Where does the concept of secretary now fit in? One might conclude that the *concept* of secretary is "owned" by managers, so we want to put the declaration of Secretary inside Manager. However, if different managers have different numbers of secretaries, then we wouldn't want to put a Secretary instance inside Manager, but rather declare one or more Secretary instances in each of the classes for specific manager types.

```
class Name { public: Name(const char *); . . . . };

class Employee {
public:
    virtual char *name();
    Employee(Name);
private:
    . . . .
};

class Manager: public Employee {
public:
    Manager(Name n): Employee(n) { }
protected:
    class Secretary: public Employee {
    public:
        Secretary(Name n) : Employee(n) { }
        char *name();
    };
};

class VicePresident: public Manager {
public:
    VicePresident(Name me, Name Asst, Name sec1, Name sec2):
        Manager(me), SEC1obj(sec1), SEC2obj(sec2),
        AsstObj(Asst) { }
private:
    Secretary SEC1obj, SEC2obj;
    class AdminAsst: public Employee {
        . . . .
    } AsstObj;
};

class DeptHead: public Manager {
public:
    DeptHead(Name me, Name secy): Manager(me), SECobj(secy) { }
private:
    Secretary SECobj;
};

Manager::Secretary Sam("Sam");
VicePresident Pat("Pat", "Terry", "Jean", "Marion");
DeptHead Jo("Jo", "Chris");
```

Figure 6-4. Some Code Mapping from Part of a Corporate Structure

The USES-A Relationship

A USES-A relationship is present if a member function or friend function of some class takes an instance of some other class—which it *uses*—as a parameter. There is also a USES-A relationship if logic within one class member function calls on the services of some other class. Note that there might be a USES-A relationship between a Vice President and a Department Head; the veep may "use" the Head to accomplish some task on their behalf. This is a USES-A relationship, not a HAS-A relationship, because the invocation of the services of the Department Head by the Vice President does not imply that a DeptHead object is included in the state of a VicePresident instance. DeptHead is not being used as a building block to implement a VicePresident; however, the two classes can collaborate through a USES-A relationship.

The CREATES-A Relationship

This is an unusual relationship in C++, certainly under the canonical forms we have studied so far, in that it is usually a relationship between an object and a class. An instance of one class, during the execution of one of its member functions, makes a request of some other class to create an instance; it invokes the new operator on the second class, causing its constructor to be executed. In short, it is like USES-A, but it is between an object and a class instead of between objects.

In Chapter 8, we will study exemplars in detail, using idioms that give the CREATES-A relationship more run-time flexibility. Using that idiom (which is *not* native to C++), we will find that CREATES-A is a relationship between two objects, one calling a member function of the other, without consideration for the class of either.

Putting Object and Class Relationships in Context

These four relationships capture the common logical connections between entities and types, and how they translate into classes and objects in an implementation. Depending on the application, language, and idiom used, other relationships may become important in the lexicon used to support project development.

These notions are informal, and one should be cautioned about attaching too much formalism to them. Each needs to be interpreted in context and used with judgment as a communication aid, not as a hard and fast design rule. For example, it is equally valid to characterize the interaction between Managers and Secretarys as a

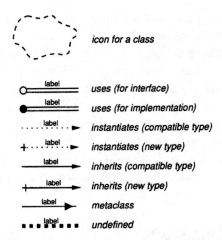

Figure 6-5. Icons for Class Relationships.

*From Grady Booch, **Object-Oriented Design with Applications**,*
Redwood City, Calif: Benjamin/Cummings, ©1991, p. 159. Reprinted by permission.

USES-A relationship as it was to use a HAS-A relationship above, particularly if the Secretarys are somewhat autonomous and have important interactions with other than their principals. If we adopt the view that it is *really* secretaries who run the organization, a much different structure arises.

A Graphical Notation for Class and Object Relationships

Booch[5] has developed a notation for communicating the structure of an object-oriented system design. The Booch design documentation technique has four components:

- *Class diagrams*, which document the structure of classes, their relationships to each other, and the general relationships of their instances;

- *Object diagrams*, showing the interaction between objects as they reference and contain each other, or pass each other as parameters;

- *State diagrams*, which view objects as finite state machines and document their state transitions as driven by member function invocations; and

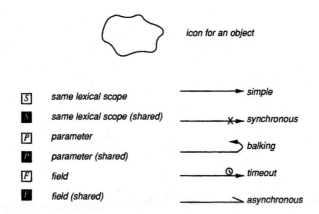

Figure 6-6. Icons for Object Relationships

From Booch, pp. 170-171. Reprinted by permission.

- *Timing diagrams*, which show the ordering of events across objects for part of the system.

The two most popular diagramming techniques are class and object diagrams, which use graphics to depict major relationships between classes or objects, as appropriate, in the system architecture. Each diagram has its own notation and set of icons: those for class diagrams are shown in Figure 6-5; those for object diagrams in Figure 6-6.

Figure 6-7 shows a class diagram for the Employee example discussed earlier in the chapter. The diagram captures the inheritance relationships between classes (with Employee and Manager as base classes), and it captures some relationships characterized by class-level generality (each DeptHead has a Secretary, and each VicePresident has a pair of secretaries; every object in class Secretary shares access to a single copy machine). (Note that the diagram does *not* capture the scoping of class Secretary inside class Manager.)

A corresponding object diagram is shown in Figure 6-8. Here, it becomes explicit that everyone who is a Secretary shares a Copier with the rest; Copier is a shared field of all objects of class Secretary. The object diagram does not show instances of Manager or Employee, because they do not have stand-alone instances. Secretary Jean is shown fielding phone calls for the vice president Pat: If callers wanting to speak with Pat find themselves talking to Jean, then it may be

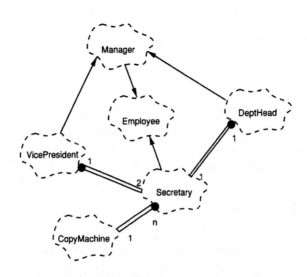

Figure 6-7. Class Diagram for Employee Organization Example

an indication that the class diagram needs to be changed to show that a
VicePresident relates to a Secretary in a way that is apparent in its interface:

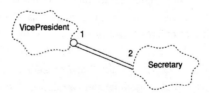

For a complete discussion of Booch's design notation, see Booch [5].

6.5 Subtyping, Inheritance, and Forwarding

Much of what can be said about inheritance has been said above about types; subtype
and type often become derived class and base class. But there are cases where this is
not so. Here, we examine common errors that create undesirable dichotomies
between type semantics of the application domain, and the inheritance or delegation
structure of the solution domain. The first two errors—"Losing Subtyping" and

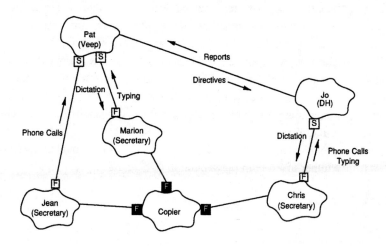

Figure 6-8. Object Diagram for Employee Organization Example

"Homonymic Types"—discuss the relationship between types and classes, and the pitfalls that arise there. "Class Independence" looks at how inheritance and delegation relate to encapsulation and how they might violate data abstraction. "Truly Semantic Member Functions" examines issues relating to both the "crispness" and encapsulation of member functions. The section closes with some special idioms to support multiple inheritance.

Inheritance for Its Own Sake: The Error of Losing Subtyping

> Insanity is hereditary—you get it from your children.

A good engineer designs with an eye to implementation. In the process of discovering application domain entities (or types), natural implementation strategies come to mind, including inheritance structures that we might be able to customize for a particular application. But such specific tuning may cut across class design relationships and can erode system structure. An example will illustrate.

Consider again a number-crunching application, for which we have created a Complex class (page 91). Its derived classes will include Double, BigInteger, and the class Imaginary, which will be the focus of the ensuing discussion. Complex efficiently supports reasonable operations: algebraic manipulations, computation of magnitude, assignment, perhaps printing to an output medium, and so forth. An Imaginary number is like a Complex but has no real part.

It is straightforward from an understanding of the application domain (mathematics) that the set of Imaginarys is a subset of the set of all Complexes. This suggests that Imaginary should be a subtype of Complex. Though all Imaginary numbers are *kinds* of Complex numbers, not all Complex numbers are Imaginary numbers.

A subtyping relationship in the application domain points to public inheritance of one class from another in a C++ implementation. We would expect to find:

```
class Complex {
public:
      .  .  .  .
};

class Imaginary : public Complex {
public:
      .  .  .  .
};
```

Note that this expresses the relationship Imaginary IS-A Complex; that Imaginary is a subtype of Complex; that the set of Imaginarys is a subset of the set of Complexes. Inheritance does not *force* those semantics in and of itself: It is incumbent on the programmer to maintain compatible semantics between classes in a hierarchy. Most of this can be achieved by maintaining compatible semantics between member functions of the same signature. Guidelines that help maintain such compatibility are the subject of much of the remainder of this chapter.

Given that the programmer adheres to such guidelines, the compiler can provide powerful safeguards, conveniences, and efficiencies through its type system. The compiler's notion of type compatibility is closely linked with design subtyping, with subset relationships between the design abstractions corresponding to classes, and with specialization of one class from another. It is this strong coupling that allows the programming language to express design relationships, and to provide a degree of enforcement of design rules.

The real data of Imaginary live in the base class Complex; we compute the magnitude of an instance of the derived class from data in the base class. The derived class also carries some extraneous baggage from the base class—the `rpart` field, which it knows is always zero.

It is good to have an eye to implementation when doing design, provided that implementation considerations do not get the upper hand. Here, implementation considerations might suggest that the overhead of an extra word in every `Imaginary` is unacceptable. An alternative implementation of `Imaginary` is better suited to this view and would look like this:

```
class Imaginary {     // no derivation from Complex
public:
    Imaginary(double i = 0): ipart(i) { }
    Imaginary(const Complex &c):  ipart(c.ipart) { }
    Imaginary& operator=(const Complex &c) {
        ipart = c.ipart; return *this;
    }
    Imaginary operator+(const Imaginary &c) const {
        return Imaginary(ipart + c.ipart);
    }
    Imaginary operator-(const Imaginary &c) {
        return Imaginary(ipart - c.ipart);
    }
    Imaginary operator*(const Imaginary &c) { . . . . }
    Imaginary operator/(const Imaginary &c) const { . . . . }
    operator double() { return ipart; }
    operator Complex() { return Complex(0, ipart); }
    Imaginary operator-() const { return Imaginary(-ipart); }
    . . . .
private:
    double ipart;
};
```

Two things are worth noting in this implementation. First, it performs algebraic operations more efficiently than its predecessor. But the second, more noteworthy, consideration is that `Imaginary` no longer inherits from `Complex`. Instead of having an IS-A relationship with `Complex`, it USES-A `double` instead.

Is it a problem for two different architectural structures to result from different solution domain optimizations of the same abstractions? The semantics of the two different versions are clearly the same. But something is lost in the optimized implementation, as it no longer captures the relationship between `Complexes` and `Imaginarys` in the application domain. The `Imaginary` as written still exhibits some properties of `Complexes` and maintains some degree of compatibility with them:

```
Imaginary::operator Complex, and
Imaginary::Imaginary(const Complex&)
```

arrange for that. But because the derivation is gone, we may not be able to treat `Imaginary` numbers as `Complexes` when it is useful to do so. For example, the conversion operators do not help the case where a `Complex*` is expected and an `Imaginary*` is provided.

The tradeoffs that need to be considered in this example and in similar applications are subtle and sometimes difficult. Acceptable solutions often come only through compromise. A solution for this example might be to derive both `Complex` and `Imaginary` from a `Number` abstract base class, without factoring any common data into the base class.

However, most abuses of inheritance come from lack of experience, are easily discerned, and have clear solutions. A programmer I once knew, as an object-oriented novice, characterized a low-pass filter class called `Filter` by deriving it from `Resistor`, `Capacitor`, and `Inductor` classes. It is *not* true that a `Filter` IS-A `Resistor`, nor is it a `Capacitor` or an `Inductor`. The set of `Inductors` does not contain the set of `Filters`. The "right" way to do this would be to embed an object of each of the constituent components inside the `Filter` object. Just as a filter contains a capacitor, inductor, and resistor in the application, so should the software `Filter` abstraction contain analogous component objects.

Here's another bad example:

```
class Shape: public Point, public Color {     // no
public:
    virtual void draw();
    virtual void rotate(const Angle&);
};
```

This asserts that a `Shape` IS-A `Color`, which of course is not true; nor is a `Shape` a `Point`. What *is* true is that a `Shape` HAS-A `Point` and a `Color`. One should, of course, do the following:

```
class Shape {
public:
    Shape(const Point&);
    virtual void draw();
    virtual void rotate(const Angle&);
private:
    Point center;          // center and color are attributes
    Color color;           //    of, or properties of, shapes
};
```

As one last example, consider the `String` and `PathName` classes presented in Section 4.2. If an existing library contains a `String`, we may be tempted to derive `PathName` from it. Public derivation would allow us to provide `PathName` objects where `Strings` were expected. For example, an existing hash function for `Strings` could be reused for `PathNames`. But public derivation gives `PathName` some member functions whose invocation could leave the object in an inconsistent state. The `PathName` constructor and its own operations can prevent illegal characters in its representation. However, if `PathName` inherits `operator[](int)` from `String`, then the following code violates the constraints `PathName`'s own operations try to enforce:

```
int main() {
    PathName batFile = "AUTOEXEC.BAT";
    batFile[0] = '*';    // illegal filename character
    . . . .
}
```

As was shown in Section 4.2, private derivation can be used to address these problems.

Problematic inheritance structures can be created by using *variance* as a basis for derivation. Variance builds one class on another based on a IS-LIKE-A relationship instead of an IS-A relationship. A close relative of variance is inverse inheritance, which has its advocates as a reuse tool. For example, a graphics package may contain class `Shape` with class `Circle` derived from it. Needing an ellipse, we might generalize `Circle` through inheritance, overriding its operations to yield an `Ellipse` class. These are both dangerous approaches, to be discussed below.

Incidental Inheritance: Homonyms in the Type World

We have been focusing on the semantic *behaviors* of application abstractions, and the classes that represent them, to drive system structure. Class behaviors should define a cohesive abstraction, and classes in the same inheritance hierarchy are grouped by the services they offer. Organizing by behavior is similar, but not equivalent, to organizing classes by external appearance. The difference between these two paradigms (models of organization) is that the first requires a deep understanding of the semantics of a class while the second can be done with simple lexical name comparison. Yet a third way to group classes is on the basis of their internal representation structure. This is similar to the second approach, except it looks inside the class, not at its interface. A `Line` class in a graphics program contains two `Point` objects; so does a `Rectangle`. We might conclude (incorrectly) that one should be a specialization of the other.

It is important to keep behavior properties in foremost consideration when designing class interfaces or grouping classes by inheritance. Liskov[2] defines criteria for proper arrangement of classes in inheritance hierarchies:

> What is wanted here is something like the following substitution property:
> If for each object o_1 of type S there is an object o_2 of type T such that for all programs P defined in terms of T, the behavior of P is unchanged when o_1 is substituted for o_2, then S is a subtype of T.

For example, some function (from the programs *P* of interest) that is written to manipulate objects (o_2) of type `Complex` (type *T*) when passed as parameters, should be able to accept objects (o_1) of type `Imaginary` (type *S*) as parameters. In a practical sense, it is safe to apply all *T* member functions to an *S* object, since all *P*s are unchanged when an *S* object (o_1) is substituted for a *T* object (o_2). This seems reasonable, since an `Imaginary` can be asked to do anything a `Complex` can do. Note that the converse is not true: a function designed to operate on `Imaginary`s cannot in general accept an object of type `Complex`. What would happen if you tried to access internal `baseNameVal` members of an arbitrary `Complex`?

This principle—called the *Liskov substitution principle*—is important to successful object-oriented design. It will be recalled several times throughout this book.

Some designers advocate using inheritance without conforming to the substitution principle. Sometimes, these uses are touted as subtyping driven more by implementation than by design. But such application can lead to misunderstandings that are the programming language analog of homonyms. Some of these abuses arise from attempting to apply the object paradigm "backward"—for example, to derive an `Ellipse` from a `Circle`, embellishing the latter to generalize into the former. Because such cases can clearly be identified as suspect by applying the Liskov substitution principle, they will not be dwelt on here. Most remaining abuses fall into the category of variance, which is an attempt to "inherit sideways" using an IS-LIKE-A rather than an IS-A relationship.

Sets and Lists as an Instructive Example   Consider an existing class `List`, which serves as a container for an ordered collection of objects; `List` makes no assumptions about the properties of the objects it contains (that is, it may be

---

2. Liskov [6], p. 25.

implemented as a list of void* objects). List might look like this:

```
class List {
public:
    void*   head();        // return front of list
    void*   tail();        // return end of list
    int     count();       // return list elements count
    Bool    has(void*);    // checks for membership
                           //     of element in list
    void    insert(void*); // add a new member to the list
};
```

Now let's say we want to construct a new class, Set, which looks like this:

```
class Set {
public:
    int     count();       // return set element count
    Bool    has(void*);    // check for membership of
                           //     element in set
    void    insert(void*); // add a new member to the set
};
```

Proud of how clever we are, we note a similarity between these two; we may even have tools to discover that class List exists and can serve as a basis for implementing Set. So we attempt to use inheritance accordingly:

```
class Set: public List {
public:
    void insert(void* m) {
        if (!has(m)) List::insert(m)
    }
private:
    // the following two lines are illegal C++ constructs
    List::head;    // head of a set is undefined
    List::tail;    // tail of a set is undefined
};
```

That is, to implement the semantics of sets where multiple insertions of the same value are considered redundant, we must redefine the insert(void*) member function. The count() and has(void*) operators are inherited as they stand. Our intent is to make head() and tail() inaccessible, since they are undefined for Sets, though they had meaning for Lists.

However, we are creating a serious problem here. Through derivation, we are saying that a Set IS-A List. In other words, we assert that anywhere a List object is expected, we can substitute a Set object. This simply is not true, nor is the reverse true. As a case in point, note their respective assumptions about treatment of multiple insertions of identical values: for Sets, insert is a null operation, for Lists it is not. Further, Sets do not have semantics for head() and tail() operations. C++ provides guidance in the latter case: the above declaration of Set, where List::head and List::tail are redefined as private, is defined as illegal in the language. If it were legal, it would have dubious semantics—especially if such functions were virtual.

So List and Set are almost *homonymic types*: They have the same signature but significantly different semantics. (If List did not have head() and tail(), the types would be perfect homonyms.) The problems that arise here motivated Liskov's guidelines for signatures of abstractions in an inheritance hierarchy, found at the beginning of this section.

Consider another example, taken from Sethi[7]. If class CircularList already exists, and we want to create a class Queue, we might do the following:

```
class CircularList {
public:
    int   empty();
          CircularList();
    void push(int);      // push at front
    int   pop();
    void enter(int);     // push at rear
private:
    cell *rear;
};

class Queue: public CircularList {
public:
          Queue() { }
    void enterq(int x)    { enter(x); }
    int   leaveq()        { return pop(); }
};
```

Note that Queue gets gratuitous push(int) and pop() operations, side effects of the derivation that are meaningless for Queues. The root of this problem can be traced to the use of public derivation. A good rule of thumb is that public derivation should be used for subtyping relationships; if the derivation is done for convenience or reuse, then private derivation should be used. Private inheritance (and superior alternatives) are explored in Chapter 7, as a means to code reuse.

A similar (though perhaps worse) set of problems arises when inheritance has the goal of reusing the *representation* of one type in another. For example, one may derive Set from List with the idea that the internals of Set will be the same as those of List; the operations might just interpret them a little differently. This obviously has no bearing on type and subtype models, and should be avoided. This is discussed further in Chapter 7.

Solutions Without Incidental Inheritance   More direct mechanisms often suffice when inheritance seems like a good solution. For example, reconsider the List and Set example from earlier in this section. You may have been disappointed that things did not work out well; there *was* a real opportunity for reusing some of the operations of List to implement Sets. It just turns out that public inheritance was the wrong way to do it. Here's another way:

```
class List {
public:
     void*  head();          // return front of list
     void*  tail();          // return end of list
     int    count();         // return count of list elements
     Bool   has(void*);      // checks for membership in list
     void   insert(void*);   // add a new member to the list
};

class Set {
public:
     int    count()          { return list.count(); }
     Bool   has(void* m)     { return list.has(m); }
     void   insert(void* m)  { if (!has(m)) list.insert(m); }
private:
     List   list;
};
```

We do need to explicitly "forward" Set's three operations to the internal list. Notice we need do nothing to invalidate head() or tail().[3]

This approach takes advantage of—reuses, if you will—the functionality of List to support the semantics of Set. Though there is some similarity between Lists and Sets, we hereby relinquish claims to any significant relationship between their types. Thought of in another way, this implementation points to a *design* that says

---

3. Liskov [6], sec. 3.2, p. 24.

nothing about the relationship between Sets and Lists. This implementation is reminiscent of *delegation*, which is based not on classes but on instances (page 160). C++ supports *forwarding* of operations from one class to another, which can be thought of as a weak form of delegation. A discussion of forwarding can be found in Section 5.5.

Inheritance with Addition and Overriding   Proper use of inheritance to implement subtyping according to the Liskov substitution criteria (see beginning of Section 6.5) can be achieved using *inheritance with addition*. Adding new member functions to a class intuitively reduces the number of objects it characterizes. For example, adding a speed calling function to a simple phone creates a new phone abstraction with more functions than the original: The set of speed calling phones is a subset of the set of all phones. Because existing operations are left intact, an object of the derived class can still be used where a base class object is expected—the superfluous operations of the derived class do not enter into the discussion. However, this also means that software manipulating such objects in terms of their base class interface will not be able to exercise the new member functions added at lower levels. In other words, the difference between SimplePhones and SpeedCallListPhones forces the programmer to deal with each on its own terms. A function declared to take a SimplePhone as a parameter will accept a SpeedCallListPhone, but it cannot be expected to exercise its speed calling features.

Using inheritance with addition, we can add new member functions in derived classes but cannot access those functions in terms of their base class interface. This is a quite restrictive model of inheritance and leaves no room for run-time dispatching of the new functions, from which the object paradigm derives much of its power. If the programmer must deal with every class in an inheritance hierarchy on its own terms, then inheritance offers no abstracting power. Programmers should be able to deal with a large collection of classes by treating them all as if they were instances of some class shared as a common ancestor.

Another extreme would be to use, as an abstract base, a class that is pure signature, devoid of any application semantics. Lacking semantics, we can guarantee that it has no semantic clash with derived classes. For example, the "universal base class" could have operations at, atPut, more, moreNow, and getNext, which access the object by its fields, or treat it as a serial aggregate. An at operation might take a string or enumerated value as a key to uniquely designate some internal value to be returned (in other words, associative retrieval). The atPut member function might take a key and a value as parameters, where the key would designate into which field the value was to be stored (associative store). Additionally, some atPut operations might be evaluated for their side effects, where special keys trigger the execution of internal member functions. Consider an associative array as a straightforward example:

```
class AssociativeArray {
public:
    void atPut(void *element, String key);
    void *at(const String&);
    . . . .
};

int main() {
    AssociativeArray a;
    a.atPut((void*)233, "AssociativeArray example");
    a.atPut((void*)230, "CircularList example");
    int circlistPage = (int)a.at("CircularList example");
                                // should return 230
    a.atPut((void*)10, "!size");   // change size of array
    a.atPut((void*)0, "!print");   // print the array
    int size = (int)a.at("!size"); // get the size
    . . . .
}
```

Here, we use the associative array to store page numbers of topics in a book. Retrieval is done by key. However, there are also special keys designated by a leading "!" that are used with at and atPut for their side effects: printing, changing and retrieving the size of the array, and potentially other requests.

This style of programming is often called *frame-based* programming, and is a style prevalent in cognitive science and is used in many symbolic language contexts. It results in base classes that present a "fat interface" that can be the union of the member functions of many, arbitrarily unrelated derived classes. This style of programming will be explored further in Chapter 8.

Such an interface is almost infinitely flexible; however, it does little to communicate or enforce the intents of design. This implementation is also likely to perform poorly, since it requires a string lookup for every operation. We want classes that are a happy medium, that communicate the general semantics of an interface without requiring any particular implementation. Such interfaces can be characterized in base classes that serve as "boilerplating" for implementations defined later in derived classes. A base class at the top of an inheritance hierarchy may never be used to create objects but will be used as the compile-time interface to objects of its derived classes. The base class characterizes the common behaviors of all the classes beneath it. For example, we may have a base class Window that declares itself to have the operations move(Point), addChar(char), clear(), deleteLine(), and the like. Derived classes of Window include CursesWindow, XWindow, MSWindow, and SunViewWindow. We would never instantiate a `Window` on its own; it doesn't know how to do anything! Instead, we instantiate only the derived classes. Base classes with this property are called *abstract base classes*. Abstract base classes for C++ are described in more detail in Section 5.4. For a set of windows, the framework might look like this:

```
class Window {
public:
     virtual void    addChar(char)        = 0;
     virtual void    clear()              = 0;
     virtual void    deleteLine()         = 0;
};

class CursesWindow: public Window {
public:
     void    addChar(char c) {  /* suitable algorithm */  }
     void    clear()         {  . . . . }
     void    deleteLine()    {  . . . . }
};

class XWindow: public Window {
public:
     void    addChar(char c) {  /* suitable algorithm */  }
     void    clear()         {  . . . . }
     void    deleteLine()    {  . . . . }
};

// etc.
```

All the member functions of class `Window` are pure virtual, and it has no data. Such classes are called *pure abstract base classes*—they characterize an abstract data type but say nothing about implementation.

Redefining base class members in a derived class is called *inheritance with overriding*. Member function semantics should be preserved when a base class member function is overridden in a derived class. Consider writing a virtual function in terms of the context surrounding it at its entry and on its return [8]. This context is the state of the current object, perhaps augmented with some external state information. On entry, a base class virtual function should assume no less about its context than its derived class counterpart, and on return it should assume no more. The entry criteria are based on the change of context when a base class member function is invoked on a derived class object, in which case the call is handled in the derived class member function. Because the derived class member function must be able to handle all requests made of the base class version, it can assume no more than the base class version does. The complement is true for the exit criteria: the derived class member function must accomplish at least what was expected of the base class version, though it may do even more.

If these criteria are met, the derived class member function is *semantically compatible* with the one in the base class. These criteria are clear in application domains where the relationships between types have a basis in formalism—for example, in a hierarchy of arithmetic types (reals, rationals, nonnegative rationals, cardinals, etc.). Establishing such criteria takes a little more work in the domains of graphics, business systems, telecommunications, and other areas where much of our work lies.

Note that pure virtual functions, in abstract base classes, are certain to satisfy these criteria. All they assume about the context in which they are invoked is that they are passed a given number of parameters of certain types. They have no code and therefore do not modify their context, and member function return types are all that is manifest of the context they leave on completion.

In the common case where a (non-pure) base class virtual function is overridden in the derived class, the two functions have at least some semantic difference—if they did not, the base class function could be used directly. However, the two functions should be semantically compatible as described above. Preserving the function name is no guarantee of compatible semantics. The designer must ensure that the derived class member function has the same semantics with respect to the derived class as the base class member function does with respect to the base class.

So there are two extremes of using inheritance. The first is abstract base classes, where the signatures of all classes in a hierarchy are the same but where new derived classes subtly change the semantics of their parents' operations. The other extreme, inheritance with addition, leaves existing implementations untouched, changing the interface in a strictly upward-compatible fashion. Unfortunately, most common uses of inheritance fall into neither of these extreme cases. Abstract base classes with no data and only pure virtual functions are rare. Good abstract base classes are designed to reflect the common behaviors of their derived classes. This design consideration usually leads to reuse: Common member functions and implementation data are factored into the base class. These common base class behaviors are often defaults that need to be overridden in derived classes. If care is taken to preserve a member function's semantics—behavior—from base class to derived class, all is well, and we achieve the desired architectural abstraction of inheritance hierarchies.

On the other hand, inheritance with addition has problems, too. If analysis of an application shows some function belongs only in a derived class, and not in its base class, then some architectural abstraction is lost. For example, consider a Shape library with fillable and nonfillable shapes, as illustrated in Figure 6-9. If we are to add a fill member function to color the interior of a shape, where should it go? If we put it in Shape, we have the choice of making it a pure virtual function or of giving it some default behavior. Making it a pure virtual function forces a fill member function to be defined in Line and other open shapes, which does not make

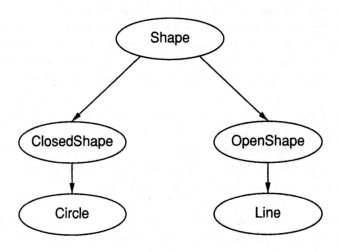

Figure 6-9. Yet Another Shape Library

sense. Default behaviors could be established in Shape::fill, but defaults that would make sense to Circle would likely not make sense to Line and its kin, so that is not right either. Defining fill as a pure virtual function inside ClosedShape is semantically the most proper, but it means that applications that care to fill objects must now see the interface of the ClosedShape class as well as that of Shape. That is one more class for the application to worry about, one more manual page to read, and one more interface whose changes the application is sensitive to. If ClosedShape and OpenShape were not originally in the inheritance hierarchy (which is likely, given that fill was not considered in the original design), then finding a semantically suitable home for the fill member function is even more difficult. What is usually done in this dilemma is to lie about the semantics a little, defining fill in Shape as a virtual function with a null body. A more severe alternative would be for Shape::fill to raise an exception.

Most real-world cases fall between the "clean" extremes of inheritance by pure addition, and abstract base classes, and are therefore subject to snaring by the subtyping trap. The example presented earlier in this section, where Set was derived from List overriding the insert(void*) member function, might be viewed as having failed for exactly this reason. Such mixed-up inheritance occurs frequently in programs where it is the cause of maintenance and evolution difficulties without ever being understood as such. The problem is known in the literature and in practice, but programming based on inheritance instead of subtyping perpetuates the problem. It is further aggravated by the use of polymorphism.

Note that problems arise only if virtual functions are used so related classes can be used polymorphically. Let's say that Set and List, implemented as they were on page 229, (using inheritance with overriding), were treated as completely unrelated classes. That is, Lists are treated as Lists, and Sets as Sets, and no attempt to substitute one for the other is ever made. Then the presence of overriding has no ill effect; it is a solution artifact unrelated to design properties of the application. The question of subtyping between these abstractions, and the implied ability to use one abstraction interchangeably with the other, never comes up in the application space. However, if the functions of List are virtual, and if that virtual-ness is used, then there is explicit use of the overriding property of inheritance, and problems can arise. The tight coupling between inheritance (which can reflect implementation similarity or application subtyping) and polymorphism (a solution domain construct used to support application domain subtyping) makes this issue a genuine problem.

Assume again that List and Set are treated as separate objects, the case where all goes well. The containment solution on page 231 is an example combining Sets and Lists without using inheritance. Instead, the Set object *forwards* requests to the List object embedded inside of it. Two types that cooperate closely, one forwarding some of its operations to another, seldom create subtyping assumptions. There are exceptions, particularly in advanced styles of C++ programming, and these will be explored later in the book. But in general, forwarding can support polymorphism, or the appearance of polymorphism, without the unnecessary entanglement of inheritance. The down sides of forwarding are that it has less compile-time type safety than inheritance, and captures less design information in the code than inheritance can.

Inheritance with Cancellation   Some object-oriented programming environments allow you to "subtract" or *cancel* base class properties in a derived class. C++ disallows cancellation in public inheritance. Compile-time enforcement of cancellation conflicts with the possibility for run-time conversion of a derived class object to an object of its base class. This can be illustrated with a code fragment:

```
class Base {
public:
    void function1();
    void function2();
};

class Derived: public Base {
private:
    Base::function1;     // cancellation (not valid C++)
public:
```

```
        void function3();
};
void f(Base *baseArg) {
    baseArg->function1(); // surprise: cancellation ignored
}
int main() {
    Derived *d = new Derived;
    f(d);
    return 0;
}
```

If cancellation were legal, the compiler would need to do intractably complete data flow analysis to guarantee no canceled properties of the object were ever used. The problem becomes more severe if the functions are virtual and separate compilation is used. One module, with access to the derived class declaration, creates a derived class object. That object is passed by base class pointer (a valid cast) to a function in another module, which does *not* have access to the derived class declaration and is unaware of the cancellation. The second module may invoke base class member functions on objects for which those functions had been canceled! For example, consider what would happen in the above code if function1 and function2 were virtual, and f had been compiled in a separate source file to which only the declaration of Base was visible.

Run-time enforcement of cancellation would overly complicate the language implementation and would require that each class object carry more baggage to designate those member functions it was masquerading as not having.

Base class data can be rendered inaccessible to a derived class and its clients, but they cannot be eliminated for, say, the sake of saving memory in derived class objects. As for virtual functions, a member function invocation that passes the type system at compile time is guaranteed to call *something* at run time, rather than giving a don't-understand-message response as in languages like Smalltalk. If the derived class provides no function of the corresponding name, then some parent class function of the same name and signature will be used.

Nonpolymorphic derivation is a slightly different story. As we saw earlier, compile-time cancellation through rescoping is disallowed by the language; for example,

```
class List {
public:
    void* head();
    void* tail();
    int count();
    long has(void*);
    void insert(void*);
};
```

```
class Set: public List {
public:
    void insert(void* m);
private:
    List::count;        // error
    List::has;          // error
};
```

is illegal. However, if a private derivation is done—effectively canceling *all* the public operations of the base class—the base class operations can be made accessible again one by one:

```
class Set: private List {
public:
    void insert(void* m);
    List::count;
    List::has;
};
```

Derivation with cancellation may be a hint that an inappropriate inheritance structure has been put in place—for example, with derivations reversed or askew in their parent/child relationship. In general, problems abound in the area of cancellation, and you should avoid it as a design technique, and even as a design accident, with great care.

The Need for "Truly Semantic" Member Functions

In object-oriented design and programming, the operations on an object correspond to some semantics in the real world. This is a stronger and deeper statement than saying that all objects be accessed by well-defined interfaces. Maintaining this semantic identity is important to the successful evolution of a design. Encapsulation is not so much a property of where data lie versus where operations are made visible as it is a property of how behaviors are organized.

We underscore this guideline with a couple of examples. The examples lay the groundwork for discussions in later sections concerned with the interplay between encapsulation and inheritance.

Example 1: get and set operations Programmers often adopt object-oriented guidelines of the form "public data are harmful; data should always be encapsulated and accessed via get and set operations." One problem with this is its expression in terms of internal data, which are a peculiarly solution domain concept. Another problem is that it says nothing about the holistic behavior of the object, or about the application domain type that inspired it. That it says nothing about the object as a whole, or its behavioral signature, brands the member function as a suspect artifice. That it says nothing of the application domain suggests that it is a solution domain invention. The latter alone is not a problem, but operations that cannot be tied to the application domain can hurt the class's ability to be understood and gracefully evolved.

Member function names should be crisp, semantically rich, and have a clear meaning or interpretation in the context of their class. The presence of get and set member functions is a red flag that the design should be rethought. What is the activity or responsibility of an object in retrieving an internal value? What is a client trying to achieve by setting the value of an internal state? Questions like these help relate the class member functions to the application, and help separate what a class needs to know from what is visible to its clients. Member functions that serve only as trapdoors to internal data do not preserve the encapsulation of a class by working within C++ scope rules: instead, they work within C++ scope rules to break encapsulation.

Example 2: public data   Of course, making class data public violates encapsulation. The appearance of a member object *B* in the public interface of another object *A* clutters the interface of *A* with the behaviors of *B*. It is unlikely that *B*'s behaviors express themselves in terms of *A*'s responsibilities to its community; *B* should be manipulated by *A*'s member functions. That leaves the interface of *A* uniform and "smooth" without the user having to go one level deeper to do what they want:

Not this:	This:

```
class Window {                  class Window {
public:                         public:
    Cursor cur;                     void moveCursor(int,int);
    . . . .                         . . . .
};                              private:
                                    Cursor cur;
                                };

int main() {                    int main() {
    Window win;                     Window win;
    win.cur.move(10,5);             win.moveCursor(10,5);
    . . . .                         . . . .
}                               }
```

Here, win.moveCursor is a crisper expression that win.cur.move, because it can be understood in terms of one abstraction instead of two.

Example 2 becomes more interesting under inheritance. Snyder [9] notes that most object-oriented languages allow derived classes to access the internal data of a base class, data not otherwise made public by that class. This is not the case in C++, which means that things are not as bad for C++ users as Snyder makes out in general. However, C++ users can still achieve the more popular semantics described by Snyder by giving data fields a `protected` attribute. The following section focuses on how this relates to violation of encapsulation.

Inheritance and Class Independence

Object-oriented design is based on data abstraction. Data abstraction, a generalization technique, usually goes hand-in-hand with *encapsulation*, an *information hiding* technique. That is, while data abstraction attempts to graciously hide gory details from you, it does not in itself prevent looking at internals if you wish. Encapsulation, on the other hand, fiercely guards against prying open an interface and looking at its insides. Abstraction relates more or less to the application domain, and encapsulation more or less to the solution domain.

Data abstraction and information hiding are neither necessary nor sufficient for object-oriented design, but they both are important components of good object-oriented practice, and are "good" independent of object-oriented programming. Further, they are interesting in light of ongoing dialogue about whether inheritance violates data abstraction.

There are three clear properties of data hiding that we wish to preserve, and that serve as "litmus tests" for violation of encapsulation or information hiding. We state them in terms of change; it is for the sake of program evolution that these techniques are important. By "change," we mean more than traditional models of editing an abstract data type's internal representation or proprietary functions—though such is certainly an obvious and common class of program evolution. Change must also account for inheritance, where differential changes can be applied to one class to define a new one.

1. Does a change to one class require reconsidering design decisions in other classes, or are they well contained?

2. Does some operation on a class (for example, an internal edit, or external application of inheritance or forwarding) have the potential of changing the semantics, or behavior, of that class? (One way of looking at this is asking what needs to be retested in light of a change.)

3. What is the effort (for example, recompilation cost) required to change some class? Is it proportional to the size of the class, the size of the class's

collaborators, the size of the program using the class, or the size of the project containing the class?

Here, we examine abstraction and data hiding only from the perspective of inheritance—that is, whether inheritance creates special problems or offers special opportunities.

C++ allows you to control the accessibility of base class members (data or functions) to a derived class. So it is the C++ programmer who implements semantics to enforce data hiding and encapsulation. Common public derivation has reasonable semantics to preserve encapsulation:

- Base class private members are not directly accessible to the derived class;

- Base class public members are accessible to the derived class no more and no less than they are accessible to any other code;

- Members public to the base class become part of the signature (public interface) of the derived class.

However, a serious issue remains. Although the data abstraction constructs of the C++ language limit the semantic scope of private data changes, the impact on recompilation is still severe. The following repercussions apply to most C++ environments:

- Changing the base class representation requires recompilation of code for all its derived classes.

- Adding a base class virtual function requires similar recompilation.

- Adding a base class nonvirtual function may not require recompilation of derived class code. However, if the new function hides another function of the same name (in *its* base class) then all code invoking a function of that name may require recompilation.

Another back door in C++ allows encapsulation to be broken. Let's assume that class Shape makes its center field protected—that is, center is accessible to "insiders" (derived classes) but intended to not be accessible to "outsiders:"

```
class Shape {
public:
    . . . .
    virtual void draw() = 0;
    virtual void move(Point) = 0;
protected:
    Point center;
};
```

Now, class `Ellipse` can inherit from shape and manipulate `center`. There is a conscious violation of encapsulation here, but to make too much of it would be silly, particularly if `Shape` is an abstract base class.

```
class Ellipse: public Shape {
public:
    . . . .
    virtual draw();
};

Ellipse anEllipse;
```

Now we can manipulate `anEllipse`, but we are prevented by the language from directly manipulating `center`. However, there is a way to cheat:

```
class Cheat: public Ellipse {
public:
    void cheat(Point p)  { center = p; }
};

Cheat anEllipse;
```

The derivation of `Cheat` from `Ellipse` violates the abstraction not of `Ellipse`, but of `Shape`. This is counter-intuitive, and violates the "principle of least surprise": nowhere in the addition of `Cheat` did the issue of `Shape` ever come up, yet the change violates `Shape`'s encapsulation. As a more insidious example, consider the following:

```
Point center;    // center of whole picture

class Circle: public Ellipse {
public:
    void incidentalCenterReference()   {
        . . . . center . . . .
    }
};

Circle aCircle;
```

Assume that the creator of `Circle` intended the reference to `center` to resolve to the `Shape::center` field of the `Circle` object. If `Shape` is ever reimplemented with the `center` field removed, renamed, or made private, then the same reference will be bound to the global `center`; it will compile without error, but with the wrong semantics. Inheritance violates abstraction here, but only because the provider of `Shape` gave `protected` status to some class members. This is a conscious compromise often done for performance tuning, memory optimization, or code reuse. The issue of `protected` fields and reuse will be taken up again in Chapter 7.

In general, although C++ classes can be kept linguistically independent with scoping constructs, the language semantics make it almost impossible to eliminate widespread ripple of impact of change. For small programs, where complete recompilation is acceptable, this is not an issue. In larger applications that benefit from limiting recompilation, ideally just to the code that changes, some programming styles and idioms should be applied to lessen the impact. Such idioms are described in Chapters 5 and 8.

6.6 Rules of Thumb for Subtyping, Inheritance, and Independence

Inheritance hierarchies where derived class functions override base class virtual functions are what give objects their power, but must be used with care. Such derivation should be limited to the following:

- Cases where a formal or strong intuitive subtype relationship exists between the base and derived class, and where overriding relates to a restriction on the boundaries of the subset of the base class objects represented by the derived class. A good, but not perfect, example is the derivation of Circle from Ellipse, whereby the rotate(Angle) operation is overridden. (Even this is not a *perfect* example, since from a pure type perspective, the rotate(Angle) operation defined for ellipses works perfectly fine for Circle and has no business being redefined. But we design in an imperfect world.)

- Cases where the base class semantics are compatible with those of the derived class. On entry, a base class virtual function should assume no less about its context than its derived class counterpart, and on return it should assume no more. Pure virtual functions, in abstract base classes, are certain to satisfy these criteria.

- Cases where, in effect, you are really doing inheritance with addition, and the function declaration is put in the base class interface for convenience. Subclasses may be annotated with their own peculiar operations. To the extent that it is safe and semantically sound to implement those operations in sibling classes (classes sharing a base class), including implementation as a no-op, then the function can be added as a virtual function in the common parent class with a body that does nothing. For example, a class Shape, with derived classes ClosedShape and OpenShape, might have a fill() operation. The base class would implement it as a no-op, and those semantics would be inherited by shapes where filling is a degenerate case. Only derived classes of ClosedShape would override it. Such a base class is said to have a *fat interface*; this practice should be used in moderation.

- Cases where the derived class and base class do *not* have an IS-LIKE-A relationship; they *should* have an IS-A relationship. If you discover two classes with an IS-LIKE-A relationship, find or create a base class common to both of them, which they can share as a parent.

We can also articulate some rules of thumb about data hiding in C++:

- C++ *requires* that design assumptions be revisited in light of changes within a class only if that class's exported symbol characteristics are changed. That is, a type is characterized by its signature (public interface), and signature consistency between the definition of a class and its use is enforced by the C++ compiler.

- It is difficult to tell whether a semantic change to a class invalidates design decisions in collaborating classes, even when the interface stays the same. However, programmer intuition is usually good in this area, and most well-behaved classes preserve containment for nonpublic data structures and algorithms.

- Guarantee the encapsulation of a base class by avoiding protected data; protected data smack of public data from the perspective of a derived class. However, always use protected data over `friends` or `public` data where applicable.

- Changing a class implementation, in general, requires that code be recompiled for classes that are derived from the changed class or which depend on its interface in any way. In a system that supports incremental loading of C++ code into a running program (as in a continuously running embedded system), any change to a class implementation will likely require that all extant objects of those classes be updated or replaced.

Another valuable rule of thumb: In general, member functions of classes to be put in a library should be made virtual even though they have no derived classes in their initial application. This allows for inheritance later, when a subtyping relationship between a new class and the library classes is discovered. Virtual functions must be used for C++ classes to benefit from object-oriented design techniques.

One might think about a similar rule of thumb that suggests that all derivations be done as virtual derivations, to support potential evolution to multiple inheritance in the future. However, that decision usually has to be left to the designer of the new child class, and cannot always be anticipated by the parents. In some sense, the virtual-ness of parent classes should be at the discretion of their descendants; however, C++ forces this decision to be made higher in the derivation hierarchy. This is a topic for ongoing language research.

Exercises

1. Show which of the relationships (IS-A, HAS-A, USES-A, etc.) have the following properties:

   (a) Transitivity

   (b) Associativity

   (c) Commutativity

2. Consider the following example:

   ```
   class CopyMachine {
   public:
         .  .  .  .
   };

   class Secretary: public Employee {
   public:
        Secretary(const char *n): Employee(n) { }
   private:
        static CopyMachine copyMachine;
   };

   Secretary Connie("Connie"), Terri("Terri");
   ```

   (a) What is the relationship between `Secretary` and `CopyMachine`? Between `Connie`, `Terri`, and `CopyMachine`?

   (b) If class `Manager` HAS-A class `Secretary`, and class `Secretary` HAS-A `CopyMachine` object, what is the relationship between `Manager` and `CopyMachines`?

3. Implement code for the `Account` examples of the chapter.

4. Implement an associative array whose only member functions are `at`, `atPut`, and the member functions from the orthodox canonical form.

5. Reimplement the associative array using enumerated values as keys. Compare the performance of the two associative arrays.

□

References

1. Whitehead, A. N., and Russell, B. A. W. *Principia Mathematica*. Cambridge, Mass.: Cambridge University Press, 1910.

2. Ungar, David, and Randall B. Smith. "Self: The Power of Simplicity." *SIGPLAN Notices 22*,12 (December 1987).

3. Beck, Kent, and Ward Cunningham. "A Laboratory for Teaching Object-Oriented Thinking." *SIGPLAN Notices 24*,10 (October 1989).

4. Brachman, Ronald J. "What IS-A and Isn't: An Analysis of Taxonomic Links in Semantic Networks." *IEEE Computer 16*,10 (October 1983).

5. Booch, Grady. *Object-Oriented Design with Applications*. Redwood City, Calif.: Benjamin/Cummings, 1991.

6. Liskov, Barbara. "Data Abstraction and Hierarchy." *SIGPLAN Notices 23*,5 (May 1988).

7. Sethi, R. *Programming Languages*. Reading, Mass.: Addison-Wesley, 1989.

8. Meyer, Bertrand. *Object-Oriented Software Construction*. Englewood Cliffs, N.J.: Prentice Hall, 1988, 257.

9. Snyder, Alan. "Encapsulation and Inheritance in Object-Oriented Programming Languages." *SIGPLAN Notices 21*,11 (November 1986).

7

Reuse and Objects

Reuse is something that is done to avoid duplication of effort over time and space. We can reuse ideas; we can reuse designs and major system interfaces; we can reuse source and object code. This chapter focuses on how the object paradigm and C++ in particular help construct reusable software.

Software reuse is a broad topic, and a complete treatment is beyond the scope of this book. Though object-oriented design and programming help reuse, it must be emphasized that reuse is a software engineering discipline, a craft with its own methodology and design rules. Reuse is not just "what happens" to a good design or implementation by coincidence or happenstance. True reuse is premeditated and can be ensured only through suitable design techniques, documentation, software management, and distribution mechanisms. Reuse should be contrasted with *software salvaging*, a reverse engineering practice to find code in an existing system that happens to suit one's purpose. It should also be distinguished from *software carryover*, which is what happens when a significant piece of software survives multiple releases of the system in which it is embedded. Salvaging and carryover have value, but cannot realize the same magnitude of benefits owing to a well-run reuse program.

This chapter focuses on language constructs and idioms for reuse in C++, with an eye to design considerations. Other sections of the book touch on reuse as well: Section 6.3 covers domain analysis, an important aspect of design for reuse. Chapter 11 looks at reusable software from a system perspective, including packaging issues. There are other aspects of reuse not covered here, such as documenting reusable software, organizing reusable software repositories, and using tools to peruse such repositories. For a more comprehensive portrayal of the sociological and project management reuse issues, see Tracz [1].

Code reuse is a solution domain issue. Inheritance is one reuse tool, providing a derived class the functionality of its base class without the overhead of the additional code. Object-oriented reuse brings claims of productivity, and reasonable gains can be and have been demonstrated.

Object-oriented design is sometimes confused with design for reuse under the object paradigm. One might think that if a class structure optimizes reuse, then it is the best possible object-oriented design making the most effective use of inheritance. One also might think that following the natural type relationships dictated by the application domain will naturally minimize duplication of code. Both are fallacies individually, but the greater danger is failure to distinguish between them at all.

We identify reuse opportunities by finding similar entities. We tend to reflect this commonality, and reuse code, through inheritance. But it is important to remember that inheritance is a solution domain concept, used both for reuse and to reflect subtyping. To determine how to reflect commonality in code, we need to understand relationships between objects: Do they have an IS-A relationship, or an IS-LIKE-A relationship? If the relationship is IS-A, then we should be looking for *design reuse*, not just code reuse. If the relationship is IS-LIKE-A, then there is potential for code reuse. However, care must be taken to *not* express IS-LIKE-A reuse with public inheritance. We saw in Section 6.5 that we might be tempted to inherit Sets from Lists to capitalize on some reuse. We were able to realize some reuse, but it fell apart when we tried to use a derived class object in a base class context. This "plug-compatibility" of objects is a focus of object-oriented design, and its relationship to reuse is incidental. Usually, a decision to use public derivation should still be driven by the considerations of Chapter 6.

Let's consider class Set, which IS-LIKE-A List. How does C++ express reuse of one of these class's code by the other? We found that Sets are "like" Lists; they both have properties of containers, and their signatures have much in common. We also discovered that it is not true that a Set IS-A List, or vice versa. It is important to note that while similarity between the implementations of two classes may point to a reuse opportunity, it may not be a good indicator that one should be derived from the other. The two classes may have a relationship that can be tied to the types of a system design if there is a third abstraction that captures what is common to the two. A Set IS-A Collection, and a List IS-A Collection, too, so Collection can serve as a base class for both, containing the code and data common to Set and List.

Code can also be shared by embedding an instance of one class in another, and forwarding the outer class's member functions to the inner one. A Set can be implemented in terms of a List this way, without using derivation. Hierarchies of *objects* (as opposed to hierarchies of classes) can realize reuse for abstractions that do not even have an IS-LIKE-A relationship. Such use is sometimes called *implementation hierarchy*.

Here we explore the interaction between subtyping and inheritance as it relates to reuse. We first explore where the subtype/derived class relationship is weak from the perspective of making generally reusable libraries. After that, we will look at reuse from the perspective of exactly what is being reused: design, code, or storage. All these have potential, but some have more potential than others, and some lend themselves well to object-oriented design or C++ while others do not. Design reuse is fundamental to successful reuse under the object paradigm. Code and storage reuse also have value, and some guidelines and hints are presented. Templates, which have perhaps the most promise for C++ code reuse, are discussed, and some refined reuse optimizations for templates are presented. We will also focus on the relationship between forwarding, inheritance, and reuse, as well as encapsulation and ADTs. Lastly, we will recap with some rules of thumb and generalizations.

7.1 All Analogies Break Down Somewhere

When inheritance is used to reflect IS-A subtyping between classes, software reuse is an incidental (but important!) benefit. The reuse in a class hierarchy is often driven by design considerations more than by reuse per se—that is, it relates to application domain subtyping as discussed in Chapter 6. But because object-oriented programming techniques are so tightly tied to the structures of object-oriented design, code reuse results from subtyping hierarchies as well. Though an Imaginary number class may be derived from Complex out of design considerations, Imaginary ends up reusing most Complex code as a side benefit. In this sense, object-oriented design is a valuable reuse tool, and the reuse of a base class's properties in a derived class is a valuable design tool. However, reuse is often used to justify strange applications of inheritance with little regard for subtyping. While that may have short-term reuse benefit, it may not encapsulate change in the long term.

Planning for reuse under the object paradigm must be rooted in analysis of the application domain during architecture and design. We want classes to be units of reuse, but we also want them to map accurately onto the application domain. A tension arises between class design well-suited to a particular application and a design for general reuse. One claim of the object paradigm is the isomorphism between the problem structure and the solution structure. When we identify entities during system analysis, we tend to fit them to the application at hand. This orientation to design creates classes suitable for use in a particular program or system, but not general enough for broad reuse. Taking the problem domain/solution domain isomorphism too literally can hamper software reusability. Effective reuse is based on broadening the scope of design to the entire domain (Section 6.3).

As an example, consider the classes we form in the design of a text editor. One of these classes will be `File`. We might formulate the signature of `File` based on what it needs to do to serve `Window`, `Editor`, `Keyboard`, `Session`, and other classes. One way of doing this is to anthropomorphize the classes, having designers playing the roles of the classes and acting out scenarios, or articulating what they perceive their needs to be from their perspective of the application world.

Design decisions made while formulating a class specifically for the editor can hurt its potential for reuse in several ways. One set of problems relates to the way `File` is envisioned by the designer: `File` might mean subtly different things in different applications. While we choose the semantics of `File` to mean "UNIX file," another more general view would make `File` an abstract base class with `UnixFile` as a derived class. That general view would lay a foundation for a much more broadly reusable `File` class, which could be augmented incrementally with derived classes like `VSAMFile`.

Another set of problems relates to exactly what a `File` needs to do. For an editor, a `File` needs to be able to be read and written. An advanced editor might put checkpointing capabilities in class `File` to support recovery from a system crash during an edit session. But a more generally reused `File` may need the ability to be checked for consistency, or to be compressed or encrypted, none of which may be supplied in the editor version. Also, the editor version may contain some baggage that a more general application would not want, such as checkpointing.

One could argue that failure to consider the union of all commonly useful operations on all commonly useful file types is a shortcoming in design. First, it is worth noting that design of a perfectly general file interface is an impossible job; the number of kinds of things that can be stored in a file, and the number of reasonably primitive operations that can be performed on it, is very complex. Consider for a moment what a UNIX file has to support to be useful in an editor, in a compiler (both source and object files), and in the operating system (I-nodes, operations on directories, etc.). Second, a "good" design does not have much "fat"—that is, code that is irrelevant to the application. So generality itself can be an albatross.

Some of these problems can be solved by expressing reuse at a high level of abstraction, and implementing the abstraction to suit the contexts of its use. For example, whether a `File` is made up of ASCII, EBCDIC, or FIELDATA characters can be deferred until `File` is actually used to do some work, instead of being encoded in the behaviors of `File` itself. One means to this end is *parametric polymorphism*, which C++ provides through its template feature. This raises the level of reuse, and puts the engineer closer to design issues than implementation issues.

The closer these tradeoffs can be bound to design decisions, the more flexibility and power will result.

Another way of raising the abstraction level of reuse is through abstract base classes. A class can use pure virtual functions to describe the framework of a reusable abstraction, and the functions can be filled in by the class user in the context where the abstraction is to be applied. Abstract base classes and frameworks for reuse are discussed further in Chapter 11.

7.2 Design Reuse

There is much contemporary common wisdom about the prospects of focusing on design instead of implementation as the "right" level of reuse. Integrating the taxonomies of application domain types with design for reuse results in classes whose interfaces should have carefully considered semantics, since it is semantics—not implementations—that are being reused. In his article on reuse myths, Tracz[2] provides some insight on the interaction between reuse and object-oriented design:

> The adaptability (and reuse potential) of a software component depends on the amount of domain analysis performed and the degree a module is parameterized to reflect this. Furthermore, the forms of parameterization provided by the programming language may not always support the degree or form of adaptability desired. Ada generics support reuse, but cannot replace inheritance. Classes alone aren't enough, either. While certain language features do help the development of reusable software, the language, in itself, is not enough to solve the problem.

By studying the domain as a whole instead of the application at hand, classes can be written for a broad class of applications. Good domain analysis is a difficult and time-consuming task, and a system design can afford a thorough domain analysis of only some of its classes. Particular attention should be paid to generalizing classes at the top of inheritance hierarchies, and to abstract base classes in particular. Derived classes may be more specific to individual applications. Those classes that are chosen as general, reusable abstractions should be carefully documented and published in a repository: If programmers cannot find a class, it will not be reused.

Design reuse may mean one of two things in this context: broad reuse of a well-defined package, or reusing the *signature* of a class—that is, the set of the class's behaviors that together form a reusable unit of semantics. Consider the ostensibly reusable `File` class once more. UNIX Operating System files can be created, deleted, sequentially read, and sequentially written. They can also be randomly read, checked for consistency in the event the file system crashes, renamed, compressed, etc. An editor may need only a small subset of these: For example, it would not need file consistency checking, nor perhaps compression, random I/O, or renaming. Carrying all this "baggage" along in the name of reuse adds to program complexity and size. Decomposing the `File` hierarchy into a collection of classes with finer granularity provides the user with options. By selecting the right level of class, a program can find an abstraction meeting its needs without adding too much additional baggage. Predicting how different applications will use an abstraction like `File`, and creating suitable tiers of functionality, is a fine point of design that takes time and hindsight to perfect.

Reuse of designs cuts down on time spent in the system design phase, a phase that is—or at least should be—a larger portion of the life cycle than coding. Given that we find a design to reuse, we may also be able to reuse portions of an existing implementation, those necessary to support our design. Or, we may choose to reimplement all or parts of it to best suit the engineering needs of our application, stubbing off those portions unneeded by an application. For example, a graphics support package would be implemented differently on different platforms supporting different primitives in hardware. Graphics applications could run unchanged on these various platforms, reusing the same design implemented in different ways: reuse of an application in different contexts. But these are less issues of reuse than of portability (i.e., reuse of application instead of library). More important to reuse are those aspects that support survivability across different applications.

Design savings from reuse may be offset in the near term by the time spent making new classes reusable for future projects. Time must be spent researching the application domain, documenting and publicizing new abstractions for general reuse later. A net savings of time invested results in the long term.

7.3 Four Code Reuse Mechanisms

Sometimes, we get lucky in a good design, and the reuse that results from subtyping-motivated inheritance is significant and gratifying. But with respect to reuse, inheritance is typically used as a fancy `#include` facility. It is a mechanism that incorporates selected parts of one class automatically into another. Its allure is that it does so while sharing object code as well as alleviating the need to copy source.

Code reuse is a solution domain phenomenon. How do we use the tools of object orientation to achieve reuse, without upsetting a set of classes that are well integrated with respect to the application domain? The first mechanism is forwarding, where a new object is built to collaborate with an existing object, and the two together act as one to fulfill a system role. This is particularly useful for classes having close IS-LIKE-A relationships but falling short of an IS-A relationship. The example of Sets and Lists in Section 6.5 again illustrates this. Forwarding naturally goes hand in hand with data abstraction; the Set class can call on the services of a List object embedded inside it (Section 6.5). Menus reusing the code of Windows is another example.

The granularity of design reuse is a class interface; class interfaces are the default units of reuse in inheritance. But what should the granularity of code reuse be? This, too, is often thought to fall along class partitionings, and classes as "natural" abstractions also serve as reusable blocks in an inheritance model. We will revisit inheritance shortly. However, forwarding selected member functions to an object of another class allows a finer granularity of reuse: that of individual member functions.

A second means of code sharing, not directly supported by C++ but found in Actors, self, and a handful of other languages, is delegation (page 160). In delegation, a member function applied to one object can transparently be forwarded to another, and data member references can be similarly deferred from one object to another. In delegation, two or more separate instances collaborate to appear as one. If one object delegates a member function to another, the second object's member function executes in the context of the first object's name space. Delegation is usually used in classless languages: It is to classless languages what inheritance is to classical languages. C++ uses inheritance as a technique for one object to run in the context of another (by a derived class being able to interact closely with the members of its base class), but C++ has no instance analogue to its class-based inheritance. If it did, it would have delegation.

Delegation has more run-time flexibility than inheritance. We simulate delegation in C++ with forwarding: an object of one class passing much of its work to another. This has the flexibility of delegation, though it does lose the context sharing found in languages with "real" delegation. For a Menu to reuse a Window, it need only contain a Window object. Many Menu member functions (move, refresh) can be implemented directly in terms of Window member functions. This works well in C++ in simple cases, and is a long-standing mechanism to support reuse without violating abstraction. However, problems can arise if the exact class of Window is not known at compile-time—that is, if we are to use a derived class of Window whose size and exact properties vary on a case-by-case basis. This is usually solved by embedding a pointer to the reused object (for example, by having Menu *point* to a Window), instead of an instance.

A third mechanism for solution-domain reuse is private derivation, where a derived class reuses the code of the base class for its own implementation, without including the base class interface as part of its own. Semantically, there is little difference between private inheritance, and embedding one class in another as a member. Private derivation may be used as a notational convention to document that reuse is intended, to distinguish from the use of one object by another to characterize its internal state. For example:

```
class Resistor { . . . . };

class Inductor { . . . . };

class Capacitor { . . . . };

// A low-pass filter (re)uses the off-the-shelf
// abstractions Resistor, Inductor, and Capacitor
// for its constitution;  reflect this with
// private derivation:

class LowPassFilter: Resistor, Inductor, Capacitor {
public:
    LowPassFilter(Resistor r, Inductor l, Capacitor c):
        Resistor(r), Inductor(l), Capacitor(c) { }
    . . . .
private:
    // private data do not reflect reuse, but
    // characterize the state of objects of the class:
    Frequency w0;
    Quality q;
    double High3dbPoint, Low3dbPoint;
};
```

This approach has severe limitations, though. The following is illegal because no class may appear as a direct base class twice:

```
class Arm { . . . . };

class Leg { . . . . };

// this is illegal:

class Robot: Arm, Arm, Leg, Leg {  // inheritance for reuse
private:
    Direction direction;           // members for
    Velocity velocity;             //    state variables
public:
    Robot();
};
```

The last reuse mechanism is *parameterization* (parametric polymorphism), which perhaps has the highest potential reuse leverage of all these mechanisms. The following section focuses on how C++ supports parameterization, and how programmer idioms can reduce redundant code produced by C++ parameterized types.

7.4 Parameterized Types, or Templates

The C++ template feature implements parameterized types. Templates define families of types and functions. Templates are an alternative to broad, shallow inheritance hierarchies constructed for code reuse. For example, let's assume we want to reuse the algorithms in a `Stack` implementation for stacks of all types (`int`s, `Window`s, and others). An inheritance approach would put all common code in a base class, with a derived class for each type of `Stack` we wanted to create (`intStack`, `WindowStack`, and so on). However, since the code inside `Stack` manipulates stacked elements, it seems natural to express these algorithms in terms of the types of things on the stack. That means that not much of the code can be in common across all `Stack` types, but that it will have to be rewritten on a case-by-case basis. We cannot even have a `Stack` abstract base class, because even the declarations of functions like pop and top are sensitive to what kind of stack it is.

An alternative is to implement `Stack` in terms of untyped, `void*` variables:

```cpp
class Stack {
private:
    struct Cell {
        Cell *next;
        void *rep;
        Cell(Cell *c, void *r) next(c), rep(r) { }
    } *rep;
public:
    void *pop() {
        void *ret = rep->rep;
        Cell *c = rep;
        rep = rep->next;
        delete c;
        return ret; }
    void *top() { return rep->rep; }
    void push(void *v) { rep = new Cell(rep, v); }
    int empty() { return rep != 0; }
    Stack() { rep = 0; }
};
```

Use of such a `Stack` is syntactically inconvenient, since it stores only `void*`s, which leads to lots of ampersands and casts in application code. More importantly, it forfeits much of what one wants in type safety. Even deeper problems can arise from the weak typing. Consider adding a `sort` member function to a class `List` implemented using `void*`. There is no convenient way for `List::sort` to compare any two elements for which it holds pointers; it hasn't the faintest notion of what they point to.

Higher level object-oriented languages like Smalltalk and CLOS get away with this by moving more type decisions to run time. Their polymorphism is less dependent on inheritance hierarchy than C++ polymorphism is. The benefit is a lower degree of coupling between such classes; the liability is the possibility of a "method not found" error at run time.

In C++, we can solve these problems without sacrificing either type safety or run-time efficiency. What we do in C++ is parameterize `Stack` with another type. The `Stack` of Figure 7-1 acts as a template for the manufacture of specific kinds of `Stacks`. The template is written in terms of some general type `T`, where `T` is assumed to have all the properties `Stack` requires of the objects it holds. When we want a `Stack` of objects of a specific type, we instruct the compiler to build one, and it will substitute the characteristics of that type for each appearance of the type parameter `T` in the body of the template. This is called *instantiating* one type from another, with a third as a parameter.[1] A `Stack` of `ints` can be instantiated from `Stack` with `int` as a parameter:

```
Stack<int> anIntegerStack;
```

We can now say things like

```
Stack<Window> windowManagerStack;

int main() {
    Stack<int> anIntStack;
    anIntStack.push(5);
    int i = anIntStack.pop();
    Window w(0,50,4,4,4);
    windowManagerStack.push(w);
    . . . .
}
```

When using templates, the following rules apply:

1. You cannot nest one parameterized class in another.

2. Static members within a parameterized class are peculiar to that instantiation of a type.

---

1. The use of the term is unfortunate; the same term is used for the creation of an object from a class. The two are implemented in C++ by separate programming language constructs, though one might imagine them to be related at a philosophical level.

```
template <class T> class Stack;

template <class T> class Cell {
friend class Stack<T>;
private:
    Cell *next;
    T *rep;
    Cell(T *r, Cell<T> *c): rep(r), next(c) { }
};

template <class T> class Stack {
public:
    T *pop();
    T *top() { return rep->rep; }
    void push(T *v) { rep = new Cell<T>(v, rep); }
    int empty() { return rep == 0; }
    Stack() { rep = 0; }
private:
    Cell<T> *rep;
};

template <class T> T *Stack<T>::pop() {
    T *ret = rep->rep;
    Cell<T> *c = rep;
    rep = rep->next;
    delete c;
    return ret;
}
```

Figure 7-1. A Stack Template

Classes are just one code abstraction that can be reused through parameterization; functions can be parameterized as well. A common example is the sort function, which needs to be able to sort a vector of any type (Figure 7-2).

Templates are by far the preferred code reuse mechanism in C++, and their main use is for constructing libraries of reusable code. However, it is important to understand that parameterization in C++ is based on reuse of *source* code, rather than object code. By contrast, much of the functionality of a base class can be reused by a derived class at the object code level; this has ramifications for overall code compactness and impact of change.

```
template <class S>
void sort(S elements[], const int nelements) {
    int flip = 0, sz = nelements - 1;
    do {
        for (int j = 0, flip = 0; j < sz; j++) {
            if (elements[j] < elements[j+1]) {
                S t = elements[j+1];
                elements[j+1] = elements[j];
                elements[j] = t;
                flip++;
            }
        }
    } while (flip);
}

int main() {
    Complex cvec[12];
    for (int i = 0; i < 12; i++) cin >> cvec[i];
    sort(cvec, 12);       // calls sort(Complex[], const int)
    for (i = 0; i < 12; i++) cout << cvec[i] << endl;
    return 0;
}
```

Figure 7-2. A Parametric sort using Templates

If enough of a class template's operations are insensitive to the type argument used to instantiate the class, then shared code can be cast in terms of void*s, and used as a foundation for other types that handle the casting where necessary. Consider a general List class template from which we want to instantiate several list classes. If the List template has a sort member function, then it is likely that each instantiation of List will create code for its respective sort, whether or not it is called. Assume that we do not want to sort lists and would just as soon not carry around the extra baggage of multiple copies of sort. We could do something like this:

```
class WindowList: private List<void*> {
public:
    Window *get() { return List<void*>::get(); }
    void add(Window *p) { List<void*>::add(p); }
    // no sort--remains private
};
```

```
class AddressList: private List<void*> {
public:
    Address *get() { return (Address*)List<void*>::get(); }
    void add(Address *p) { List<void*>::add(p); }
    // no sort--remains private
};
```

The implementation is tedious, but at least does not require that the entire get and add be redone for each new abstraction, and it does limit the copies of List<T>::sort to one.

This technique does not buy much if most of the template's member functions (or the ones we want to use) depend on the type parameter (as sort must if it is to compare two of the items on the list). Another place that source-level parameterization causes interesting problems is for library classes parameterized with *other* library classes. For example, assume class Set was implemented in terms of class List (Figure 7-3). Now, instantiation of a new type from Set requires that the source for both Set and List be at hand. If List in turn depends on another parameterized type, then its source needs to be at hand, and so on.

Set's use of List should be transparent to the user. The need to deal with the source of List, a class not appearing in the public interface of Set, is counterintuitive. This can lead to software administration surprises and requires special attention in user documentation. It seems to violate information hiding.

Another problem is that a good deal of List code will be duplicated for each Set that is instantiated. The differences between the List instantiations may be small, and some List code unused by Set will be generated on its behalf anyhow. This may also complicate software packaging: It means that the source for Set cannot be sold without the source for List. It is likely in this particular case that one would not be sold without the other anyway. However, in general, one type's use of another for its implementation should not be an overriding reason to make customers purchase source packages for both.

To provide the power of parameterization without the overhead of duplicated code from multiple copies of List, we use the *indirect template idiom*.

Figure 7-4 shows a List.h file defining a simple parametric List used to implement a new Set class. The ListItem class is a helper class that contains the item that has been inserted into the list, and a pointer for the linked list structure itself. List maintains a singly-linked list of these items as its internal representation of the list structure.

```
template <class ElementType> class Set {
public:
    void add(const ElementType& e) {
        if (!rep.element(e)) rep.add(e);
    }
    ElementType get() {
        return rep.get();
    }
    void remove(const ElementType&);
    int exists(const ElementType& e) const {
        return rep.element(e);
    }
    Set<ElementType> Union(const Set<ElementType>&) const;
    Set<ElementType> Intersection(const Set<ElementType>&)
        const;
    int size() const { return rep.size(); }
    void sort() { rep.sort(); }
private:
    List<ElementType> rep;
};
```

Figure 7-3. A Parametric Set Implemented in Terms of a List

In a separate file **Set.h**, we declare the template Set, using List for its implementation. We avoid instantiating a List class for each parameterized Set by adding a level of information hiding in two places. First, each particular kind of Set is derived from class SetBase. The SetBase interface has all the operations the Set object expects one of its *elements* to exhibit:

```
class SetBase {
friend ErsatzListElement;
private:
    virtual int comparelt(const void*, const void*)
        const = 0;
    virtual int compareeq(const void*, const void*)
        const = 0;
};
```

These operations are declared virtual and are decoupled from the type of object contained in the set: They communicate with the outside world only via the void* type. These operations will eventually be defined in the "real" class instantiated from the Set template, defined in terms of the type objects that the Set contains.

```
template <class T> class List;

template <class T> class ListItem {
friend class List<T>;
private:
    ListItem<T> *next;
    const T item;
    ListItem(const ListItem<T> *n, const T &i):
        item(i), next((ListItem<T>*)n) { }
};

template <class T> class List {
public:
    void sort();              // sort list in place
    void put(const T& t) { head = new ListItem<T>(head, t); }
    T get() {                 // get from head of list
        T retval = head->item;
        ListItem<T> *temp = head;
        head = head->next;
        delete temp;
        return retval;
    }
    int element(const T&) const;  // membership check
    . . . .                       // many other interesting operations
    int size() const;        // element count

    List(): head(0) { }      // default constructor
private:
    ListItem<T> *head;       // list head
};
```

Figure 7-4. The List.h File

The second trick is to wrap the list elements in another class, ErsatzListElement, which addresses them only through void* pointers:

```
class ErsatzListElement {
    // this is unparameterized, which means that there is one
    // List template instantiation to serve all Sets.
public:
    void *rep;
    int operator< (const ErsatzListElement& l) const {
        return theSet->compareIt(this,&l);
    }
```

```
      int operator==(const ErsatzListElement& l) const {
         return theSet->compareeq(this,&l);
      }
      ErsatzListElement(const void *v = 0): rep(v) { }
      ErsatzListElement(const SetBase *s, void *v=0):
         theSet(s), rep(v) { }
   private:
      const SetBase *theSet;   // used just to access virtual
                               //    functions that compare
                               //    two objects, etc.

   };
```

Instances of this wrapper class are maintained by the List used to implement the Set. That means that *all* Lists created for sets will be of the same type—List<ErsatzListElement>—so one list type can be shared across all Sets.

Finally, there is the Set template itself (Figure 7-5). It is parameterized with the type of the objects it contains, but it creates no new types other than List<ErsatzListElement>. It contains private member functions to compare two objects of class T, and whatever operations that Set insists be defined on T. These "scaffold" functions forward their requests to T only after converting the void* parameters to type T with a cast. The cast is safe: Within this parameterized type, it can be guaranteed that the void*s appearing in this code will *always* point to an object of type T. And, of course, all the code—scaffolding and all—is generated automatically from the template by the parameterized type support mechanisms in the compiler.

This ends Set.h. Here is a simple application using a parameterized Set, which in turn uses a parameterized List. Even though there are two kinds of Sets, only one kind of List must be instantiated to support both:

```
#include <iostream.h>

int main() {
    Set<int> foo;
    Set<double> bar;
    foo.add(1);
    foo.add(2);
    cout << foo.get() << "\n";
    cout << foo.get() << "\n";
    bar.add(3.0);
    bar.add(4.0);
    cout << bar.get() << "\n";
    cout << bar.get() << "\n";
}
```

Now the Set abstraction can be managed or marketed as a separate entity; object code for the List<ErsatzListElement> and List abstractions could be provided with the source for Set.

☞ *When to use this idiom*: Use this idiom when templates are extensively used in a program, and particularly when one parameterized class uses one of its type parameters to specify the instantiation of another parameterized class for its own use.

Different installations of C++ may require slightly different sets of administrative procedures to ensure that the List instantiation happens only once. This can be typically achieved by putting the List member function definitions in their own file with a .c suffix.

7.5 Private Inheritance: Does Inheritance Support Reuse?

In Section 6.5, we saw a misapplication of inheritance where Queue was derived from CircularList. Queue ended up having some surprising operations in its signature because of what it inherited from its base class. This is because public derivation was used—that is, we claimed "whatever is public to the base class, I as a derived class claim to be able to do, and wherever a CircularList is expected, I, as a Queue, can stand in." But this is a pretentious claim for a Queue to make.

To solve the problem, we recognize that Queue is just reusing the functionality of CircularList without claiming to be interchangeable with one. Reuse must not violate the abstraction of CircularList, nor mess up the abstraction of Queue. We can achieve this in at least three ways:

1. Put a CircularList inside every Queue (implementation hierarchy)

2. Use a delegate model and have Queue delegate some of its operations to a matching CircularList object

3. Use private inheritance (as Sethi [3] suggests in the source for this example).

```
template <class T> class Set: private SetBase {
    // private inheritance for reuse
public:
    void add(T t2) {
        if (!exists(t2)) {
            ErsatzListElement t(this, new T(t2)); rep.put(t);
        }
    }
    T get() {
        ErsatzListElement l=rep.get(); return *((T*)(l.rep));
    }
    void remove(const T&);
    int exists(const T& e) {
        ErsatzListElement t(this, (T*)&e);
        return rep.element(t);
    }
    Set<T> Union(const Set<T>&) const;
    Set<T> Intersection(const Set<T>&) const;
    int size() const { return rep.size(); }
    void sort() { rep.sort(); }
    Set();
private:
    List<ErsatzListElement> rep;
    int comparelt(const void *v1, const void *v2) const {
        const T *t1 = (const T*) v1;
        const T *t2 = (const T*) v2;
        return *t1<*t2;
    }
    int compareeq(const void *v1, const void *v2) const {
        const T *t1 = (const T*) v1;
        const T *t2 = (const T*) v2;
        return *t1==*t2;
    }
};
template <class T> Set<T>::Set() { }
```

Figure 7-5. A Flexible and Efficient Set Template

The first solution is that advocated by Liskov: It does not violate data abstraction, and it is the intuitive model of reuse. The approach is called *implementation hierarchy*, referring to the hierarchy of instances of reused classes, with "implementation" distinguishing it from the class inheritance hierarchy. Implementation hierarchy is simple *containment* of an object of one class inside another. Use of implementation hierarchy for reuse does not suggest a subtyping relationship as inheritance might; it states that we want to be able to reuse the functionality of a `CircularList` without claiming to be able to be used interchangeably with one. Here is an example using implementation hierarchy:

```
class CircularList {
public:
    int  empty();
    CircularList();
    void push(int);      // push at front
    int  pop();
    void enter(int);     // push at rear
private:
    cell *rear;
};

class Queue {
public:
    Queue() {  }
    void enterq(int x) { l.enter(x); }
    int leaveq() { return l.pop(); }
    long empty() { return l.empty(); }
private:
    CircularList l;
};
```

This is a form of forwarding emphasizing that (1) a `Queue` HAS-A list, (2) the IS-A relationship does not apply, and (3) the `CircularList` in question is not shared (as an object addressed through a pointer might be). The encapsulation of `CircularList` is not violated.

The second approach—delegation—is possible but unnatural in C++ for lack of first-class language support, as was discussed on page 255.

The third approach—private inheritance—might be used as follows:

```
class Queue: private CircularList {
public:
        Queue() { }
    void enterq(int x)    { enter(x); }
    int  leaveq()         { return pop(); }
        CircularList::empty;
};
```

Private inheritance and implementation hierarchy are more or less equivalent from the perspective of efficiency. Each approach has its own advantages. In cases where the derived class can directly use the function of the base class, the programmer has to supply less boilerplate when derivation than when containment is used (namely, the forwarding of the operation to where it will be handled).

A derived class can override virtual member functions called by functions in a private base class, so private inheritance works better than containment for two classes collaborating for reuse. A base class defines overall structure and characterizes obligations on the derived class as pure virtual functions. The base class can depend on an implementation of these pure virtuals in the derived class, as the derived class can invoke (and reuse) the base class member functions. A good example is the `TaxForm` framework in Chapter 11.

But derivation for reuse has drawbacks as well. The client class can access the `protected` members of a private base class, violating its encapsulation: encapsulation is preserved for embedded members. Inheritance has the potential danger of suggesting a subtyping relationship.

A hybrid approach, combining private inheritance and forwarding, is also possible:

```
class Queue: private CircularList {
public:
    Queue() { }
    void enterq(int x) { enter(x); }
    int leaveq()       { return pop(); }
    int empty()        { return CircularList::empty(); }
};
```

Some may find this stylistically cleaner than other options; it incurs a performance penalty of an extra function call for invocations of `empty` (unless the body of `Queue::empty` is expanded inline). This construct must be used instead of the access specifier technique if overloaded functions are present, and the programmer wishes to bestow different access on different base class member functions of the same name.

Diagnostic messages from most C++ compilers flag common errors when private inheritance is expressly used for reuse instead of subtyping. This is important from an architectural point of view. Consider again the above example of `CircularList`, except with virtual functions:

```
class CircularList {
public:
    virtual int  empty();
                 CircularList();
    virtual void push(int);    // push at front
    virtual int  pop();
    virtual void enter(int);   // push at rear
```

```
private:
    cell *rear;
};
class Queue: private CircularList {
public:
        Queue() { }
    void enterq(int x)    { enter(x); }
    int  leaveq()         { return pop(); }
        CircularList::empty;
};

int main() {
    CircularList *alist = new Queue;  // compile-time error
    return 0;
}
```

If it were legal to do this, then a Queue could legally appear in any context where a CircularList was expected. However, the compiler flags the object instantiation as an error, knowing that a Queue cannot be called upon to do the job of a CircularList.

This issue comes into consideration only when virtual functions are used, in the context of pointers or references to class objects.

7.6 Storage Reuse

We sometimes want to be able to share the behaviors of an existing class with several other classes or objects, but without incurring the storage overhead of more than one copy of the shared class. For example, several Window objects may wish to share a single Keyboard object for several input-related functions. Instead of embedding a Keyboard in every Window, all Windows can instead forward their operations to a single, common Keyboard class. That can give every Window the behaviors of Keyboard, while reusing common storage. The handle/body idiom (Chapter 5) can be used to reflect sharing: The body can be shared, and each handle can stand in for that object as an "ambassador" or "surrogate." Sometimes, static members are the best way to share storage between all objects of a given class.

You may also decide to share storage out of more fundamental architectural considerations—for example, by putting an object in memory that is common to more than one CPU. This can be done directly in C++, *provided that the object's class has no pointers*. Explicit pointer variables in a class should either be eliminated or specially treated. Pointers come up in other guises as well: Many implementations of reference members and virtual functions use them. The contents of a pointer must be able to be correctly interpreted in each context that uses it, which is usually the case only if it addresses another shared memory object. Shared pointers cause fewer problems if every processor (or process) maps the shared memory segment to the same logical address in its address space, but many operating systems advise against depending on such mappings.

Making the shared information devoid of pointers, and putting all pointers and virtual function semantics in an envelope class, can make shared memory usable in C++ applications. Classes carefully designed to use relative offsets instead of pointers, and which have no virtual functions, may also be used in shared memory segments.

7.7 Interface Reuse: Variants

A flexibly designed system can incorporate several different implementations of the same design. Each of the implementations may implement what will be thought of as the same type, though the internal algorithms used will differ with context. Some examples include the following:

- Remote procedure call: A "stand-in" class's member functions may forward requests over a network to a remote class that does the actual work. Both the remote and local class can have identical signatures, but the implementations will have little in common: the local class will only ship things off to the remote one. At a high level, the semantics of the operations are identical.

    In a networked application, there may be three distinct variations of a given class:

    1. An implementation to do the work *locally*—that is, a local server class. Consider a file server object: If the object knows the disk is connected to the local machine, it will do the work directly.

    2. An implementation to *forward* requests to a remote machine. Here, a local file server object knows the disk is on another machine and will forward the request over a network medium to another machine, where it will be handled by a remote server class.

    3. A *remote* server class. This class will be logically similar to the local server class (it may embed a local server object in itself), except it will receive its request from the network. It may not be considered a true variant of the other two, since its direct interface is with the network protocol, and not with the user.

- Market dependencies: A class may need to be implemented differently in different contexts. For example, there may be one `Console` class, but we want a different implementation for English-speaking markets than for Arabic-speaking markets.

- Hardware dependencies: For example, a `Stack` class might be written to directly take advantage of stack hardware in one machine, and it might be written in a more portable fashion for other environments. If the class is provided in a library, the class interface definition might be identical for the two implementations, and both implementations can be used equivalently. The same goes for other hardware-dependent primitives such as floating point operations.

- Instrumentation: One version of a class might be a test version that monitors execution progress; another may be tuned for high performance without debugging hooks.

- Performance tuning: An existing concrete data type that is not reference-counted might require a reference-counted counterpart for parts of a system where memory space and real-time are crucial. For an example (which was implemented using simple data abstraction but which could be reimplemented using inheritance), see Section 3.5 (page 69).

What these examples have in common is that the variations have only a weak correspondence to entities in the application; they map more closely onto implementation. However, inheritance is a handy tool to implement them, particularly if abstract base classes are used. Each derived class serves as a particular implementation of the abstract data type, characterized by a shared abstract base class. We reuse a single design, and reflect that design in several different implementations.

Such derived classes are called *variants*. The names of the derived classes are immaterial, and references to such names are localized. Access to objects of these classes is through pointers or references, using virtual functions. Client code is written in terms of the abstract base class.

Another option is to handle alternative cases *within* the parent class, instead of deriving new classes from it. This is a form of encapsulated reuse, and which when used in this context is called an *exemplar*. (This term is unfortunately reused for a related but separate concept, described in Chapter 8). When asked to perform a given operation, an exemplar class may forward the request to one of its own objects, which will itself handle the request using virtual functions. The advantage of exemplars over derivation is encapsulation of the names of the implementations of the variants themselves. For example, our `Stack` class mentioned above might be instantiated in one of two ways: in one case, to contain an object implementing stacks using specific processor hardware, and in another, to use conventional data structure techniques.

Exemplars can be thought of as being implemented in the same way as delegated polymorphic classes (Section 5.5). That is, the inner object may not be physically contained in the bytes of its containing object, but logical containment can be modeled with a pointer from the outer object to the object with specific variant semantics.

7.8 Reuse, Inheritance, and Forwarding

Designers and coders must trade off between completeness and effectiveness of reuse, and design encapsulation of independent classes. Designers working in a more flexible medium than C++ code (e.g., a chalkboard architecture) have the liberty of allocating functionality and data to balance reuse and clean design. Once these designs are reduced to code, language constraints create a tension between the self-containedness of a class, and the ability of another class to reuse its code.

The coupling between two classes may determine if reuse should be implemented using private derivation, or by embedding an instance of one in each instance of the other. With derivation, the encapsulation of the base class can be partially opened to the derived class using `protected` members. Trying to share symbols without private inheritance—using `friends`, for example—leaves the alternative of wholesale visibility of one class to another. Sharing symbols with the benefit of neither `friends` nor inheritance leads to growth of the public interface of a class. Snyder [4] writes:

> The most serious objection to this solution [use of inline functions to efficiently access base class variables directly] is that it requires the cooperation of the designer of the ancestor class that defines the instance variable (as well as the designers of all intervening ancestors), since no access to an inherited instance variable is possible unless appropriate operations have been provided. We claim this is as it should be. If you (as designer of a class) need access to an inherited instance variable and the appropriate operations are not defined, the correct thing to do is to negotiate with the designer(s) of the ancestor class(es) to provide those operations. ([Footnote:] A software development environment might allow you to circumvent this restriction, say by temporarily defining those operations yourself. However, if you seriously intend to leverage off someone else's code, such negotiation is essential.)

A key point here is that reuse can be viewed not just as "taking" code of one class for use in another, but as one class advertising its facilities for reuse by interested parties. Negotiation between the "vendor" and "user" of potentially reusable code is in the interest of all involved, to preserve good design structure while minimizing code volume and duplication of effort.

7.9 Architectural Alternatives for Source Reuse

There are many ways to administer source reuse, or to *conditionally* tune some existing code for a given application. Inheritance is one tool in the toolkit of such devices. There is a time and a place both for inheritance and for traditional techniques. Some tradeoffs between these techniques are highlighted here.

The simplest device is *run-time optioning*, a fancy set of words for if statements and other run-time decisions. Looking at a run-time flag to decide which of two legs of code to execute is well-suited to decisions between small legs of code, both of which are frequently used, and which are architecturally insignificant (that is, they present no interesting operational interface at the level of the system architecture.) We think of the unit of administration as a C statement. An example might be to select at run time whether to activate debugging code based on the contents of a global flag.

Another alternative is *conditional compilation*, familiar to C programmers as #ifdef and friends. This is useful for isolated, small sections of code and only if a decision can be made at compile time about whether the code will be present. It is most useful when the target environment alternatives dictate much different semantics or syntax—for example, selecting between different word lengths for an I/O register depending on the kind of target processor. We think of the unit of administration as a function, though several functions may be packaged in a source file for administrative and configuration convenience. This could also be used for debugging code, with some loss of flexibility, but with less overhead in a production release than if run-time conditionals had been used.

An extreme (but common) approach is to use *separate source*. Starting with a copy of source for an existing class, you tweak it here and there to do what you want. After that, the two copies of the code lead separate lives. If the two classes are to coexist in the same program, then one class must be arbitrarily renamed to keep the classes distinct. The two classes may still have much in common after you made your changes: The class interface might survive largely unchanged, and internal data structures and even entire member functions may go untouched by your improvements. But there are important drawbacks to this approach: If the author of the original applies bug fixes to the original source, you may not find out about them. Even if you are informed of such changes, you have to replicate the original edits; this is a waste of effort, particularly if the updates made by the original author are in member functions that your changes did not touch. This process is error-prone as well. Another drawback is that it leads to unnecessary code growth. If someone ''reuses'' your code this way within the same system, the multiplicity proliferates.

As stated above, if you need a new class that looks a lot like an existing class in its functionality, but whose implementation is a bit different, inheritance is a powerful

```
int SesInterface::saveTty(SGTTY *tty) {
#ifndef USG
#       if sun
                return ioctl(2, TIOCGETP, tty);
#       else
                return gtty(2, tty);
#       endif
#else
        return ioctl(2, TCGETA, tty);
#endif
}
```

Figure 7-6. Source Featuring of Platform Variance. The new code is in *italics*

way to administer that. Inheritance allows you to base a new class on an existing one, while tweaking just what you want to tweak, and *sharing* the rest of the class intact.

However, inheritance as a reuse approach has its liabilities. Assume there is a software product line using objects as its building blocks, and assume that we use derivation to fine-tune the behavior of some software base so it fits individual applications on a variety of hardware and operating system platforms. The product needs to run on a new platform requiring minor changes to the code.

For example, consider the session interface example of Figure 7-6. A `SesInterface` is an example of a class that represents the functionality of a keyboard and window in some interactive application. The `SesInterface` class has a member function, `SesInterface::saveTty(SGTTY*)`, that sets device characteristics for the interface. That member function works by calling primitives in the underlying platform. The primitives used vary as a function of operating system and platform; here, the variance is factored out using source featuring. For systems that are "USG," a call is made to `ioctl` with `TCGETA` as a parameter; for non-USG systems, Suns are a special case, while all other systems use `gtty`.

Another alternative would be to use the inheritance structure of Figure 7-7. Adding the new code just means adding a new class to the inheritance tree in the appropriate place; the new class inherits all the attributes of its parents, save the one member function that changes. Using this approach, there is no source featuring. One supposed advantage might be that the choice between variants can be made at link-edit time (by selecting the right object code files) instead of at compile time. However, there is a trap in this. Somewhere in the system is code of the form

```
    void User::code() {
        SesInterface *si = new SesInterface(keyboard, window);
        . . . .
    }
```

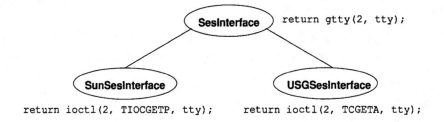

Figure 7-7. Inheritance as a Featuring Alternative

The unwitting designer may not realize that in adding the derived class, all code containing instantiation references to the parent class must *also* be featured to implement the change. Without instantiating the derived class instead of the parent, the change will never be seen. We could take the above code from User and change it to

```
void User::code() {
#ifndef USG
#     if sun
          si = new SunSesInterface(keyboard, window);
#     else
          si = new SesInterface(keyboard, window);
#     endif
#else
          si = new USGSesInterface(keyboard, window);
#endif
          . . . .
}
```

but, of course, that gets us back into source featuring, something we were trying to avoid by using derived classes. We could solve the dilemma by creating three new classes derived from User:

```
class USGUser: public User {
public:
    void code() {
        si = new USGSesInterface(keyboard, window);
        . . . .
    }
};
```

```
class NonUSGUser: public USGUser {
public:
    void code() {
        si = new SesInterface(keyboard, window);
        . . . .
    }
};

class SunUser: public NonUSGUser {
public:
    void code() {
        si = new SunSesInterface(keyboard, window);
        . . . .
    }
};
```

but now we would have to review all code creating a `User` object, and do the same things to the classes containing such code, which means that the change may domino around the system.

In most such cases, it is best to continue to use source featuring. An alternative is to add a level of abstraction to the class, in particular to the end of supporting easier evolution in the area of class object initialization. This is an advanced idiom discussed in Chapter 4.

7.10 Generalizations on Reuse and Objects

The following list is based on the discussion of this chapter and makes a good checklist considering inheritance as a reuse mechanism for C++ code:

- Domain analysis is important to making a class reusable. The application domain should be analyzed for its "pressure points" of parameterization, so that a given class can maximize its breadth of applicability while minimizing the upheaval necessary to achieve it. Classes should not be all things to all people—that makes them formidable to understand and use, and therefore to reuse. But neither should a class cater to the current application.

- Reuse of design, as defined by a class interface, probably has the greatest potential for improving the productivity of large projects. Reuse of an interface may mean throwing away or rewriting parts of an implementation on a case-by-case basis, so there may not be much reuse of code. However, it is still possible to reuse what code it makes sense to reuse, and to allow common evolution of the common parts.

- The power of the object paradigm in supporting reuse lies in abstract base classes. A hierarchy of classes, corresponding to a union of largely disjoint types in problem space, provides a high-level abstraction that generalizes across a wide variety of applications. What makes an abstract class so reusable is the potential breadth of its domain, over that provided by a single implementation of an ADT. This is not to say that abstract base classes alone solve the reuse problem; suitable domain analysis and insight into application needs are still important.

- When using inheritance for the sole purpose of realizing reuse, use private inheritance. Public inheritance reflects subtyping relationships, not reuse.

- If designing for reuse, there is a tradeoff between making many small (fine-grained) classes or fewer large classes suggested by the application domain. Using the coarse granularity suggested by the application at hand makes the abstraction easier to use in that application, but it may be more difficult to use in other applications in the same domain. The small classes are designed to be context-free, increasing the scope of their reusability. Reuse reaches its peak at a fine granularity of classes, in the tradition of the Smalltalk class hierarchy. However, fine granularity is useful only if powerful browsing facilities exist in the programming environment. Also, highly granular reusable classes are likely not to be the items of highest interest and focus in a particular application; the reusable classes act more as background "supporting actors."

- Using delegation-like models to simulate run-time type support does away with many of the compile-time type restrictions that limit reuse. Idioms to support such models are described in Chapters 6 and 8.

Exercises

1. Discuss the following quote: "Reuse is a substitute for thought."

2. Reimplement the `Stack` example of Section 3.5 (page 69) as a variant.

3. List the reusable classes that should come in a library with *every* C++ system. What percentage of these classes should be templates?

4. Note the dependencies between the classes in the previous exercise. (Dependencies include parameterization of one class in terms of another, derivation of one class from another, or any other use of one class's code by another.) How deep is the dependency structure? Is this good (in terms of reuse) or bad (in terms of overhead for the application programmer)?

5. What generally reusable functions should be provided with every C++ system, unrelated to the class library of the preceding two exercises? How many of these functions are templates? How many of these functions use other functions in the library?

6. Write a class template, `CountedClassObject<T>`, that will create a counted class object abstraction for any non-reference-counted class *T*. (Hint: Use the `CountedStack` of Section 3.5 as a model.)

☐

References

1. Tracz, Will. *Software Reuse: Emerging Technology.* IEEE Computer Society Press, 1988.

2. Tracz, Will. "Software Reuse Myths." *Software Engineering Notes (ACM SIGSOFT) 13*,1 (January 1988) 17-20.

3. Sethi, Ravi. *Programming Languages.* Boston, Mass.: Addison-Wesley, 1989, 238.

4. Snyder, Alan. "Encapsulation and Inheritance in Object-Oriented Programming Languages." *SIGPLAN Notices 21*,11 (November 1986).

8

Programming with Exemplars in C++

Most of the C++ type system depends on compile-time constructs. Static type checking promotes early detection of interface errors and makes it possible to produce code more efficient than it would be if typing were deferred to run time or not done at all. However, run-time type support is what lends object-oriented programs their power and flexibility. A program using virtual functions defers part of its typing to run time, which allows objects of multiple classes to be used interchangeably. The cost is some uncertainty of what the program will do until it actually runs. If we apply a `ring` operation to an object from a class in the `Telephone` inheritance hierarchy, we do not know *exactly* what will happen—only that *something* reasonable will happen at run time.

Other object-oriented programming languages, such as Smalltalk and the family of object-oriented languages embedded in Lisp, make further concessions to compile-time typing in the interest of run-time flexibility. The result is usually less efficient code, and the possibility of run-time surprises if an object is asked to perform an operation it does not understand. But the benefit is in flexibility from more extensive and uniform polymorphism. Strongly object-oriented C++ programs commonly need a higher degree of run-time typing than virtual functions alone provide.

For example, assume that we want to read a `Number` object from a disk file. The object may have been written to the disk as a `Complex`, a `BigInteger`, an `Imaginary`, or some other class derived from `Number`, but a programmer dealing with numbers at the level of class `Number` would not know and might not care. We want `Number` to "reconstitute" an instance of itself from the disk image. The object must take on type characteristics (`Complex`-ness, `Imaginary`-ness, etc.) while building itself.

C++ idioms can be applied that approximate such flexibility; the exemplar[1] idiom is one such example and is the subject of this chapter. The exemplar idiom also makes it possible for objects to evolve their type characteristics over the course of execution. For example, the change in a Number's value from the complex quantity *(5−3j)* to *2* may suggest that its type be changed from Complex to Integer. If it retains its Complex identity, it will continue to use complex algorithms to produce results that really could be obtained more simply.

This chapter describes how much of the functionality of compile-time classes can be taken over at run time by special objects, called exemplars, to provide run-time type flexibility beyond what C++ directly supports. To better understand the exemplar idiom, a bit of background on programming languages is in order.

One method of loosely categorizing object-based programming languages is according to whether they have classes as a *basic* and *distinct* construct. C++ is one such language: Classes play a basic role in the language's model of what objects are and how they work; you cannot talk about objects without talking about classes. Languages where classes play a central role in the object model are called *classical languages*.

In C++, classes and objects are different things: Classes behave like types (they implement abstract data types), and objects are the instances created from those types or from built-in types using declaration or new. Classes are fixed at compile time, and objects do not exist until run time. You use a class or built-in type to create new objects; you cannot create a new object from another object alone. A system written in C++ has a collection of classes, usually thought of as being in a hierarchy (in terms of base and derived classes), and it has a separate collection of objects, which may also be thought of as being organized in a hierarchy (in terms of which ones bring which others into existence). Classes are distinct in that they are not "something else." For example, a class is not a function, nor an object, nor a statement. Languages where classes and objects are different things are called *dual-hierarchy languages*, and C++ finds itself in this category.

Some languages, such as self[1] are single-hierarchy languages. Instead of classes serving as the "factories" for objects, some objects are designated by convention as exemplars from which other objects with like properties are copied field for field, or "cloned." After being cloned, they may be modified and fine-tuned by changing properties ordinarily attributed to classes (for example, member function

---

1. This concept is commonly called a *prototype*. The term usually implies language support for delegation, which is lacking in C++. *Prototype* also carries the common meaning of "mock-up" or "throw-away." To avoid the confusion and imprecision of *prototype*, this book uses the term *exemplar* instead.

behavior) as well as those ordinarily associated with object instances (changing the values of instance variables). Exemplar objects are to single-hierarchy languages what classes or types are to dual-hierarchy languages. Their flexibility is useful for program evolution, for iterative development, for update of continuous-running systems, and for certain styles of programming where run-time type support is important (for example, certain AI applications).

Single-hierarchy languages support mechanisms for creating initial exemplar objects from scratch—that is, for creating an initially default or empty object and for adding fields to it and associating member functions with it. C++ has no such facility, or at least provides no way of doing this incrementally at run-time. So the exemplars are bootstrapped from classes that are fixed at compile time. One class may be used to create multiple exemplar objects, each initialized with specific data to customize its type characteristics. For example, a single class used to parse numbers might be instantiated both as a base 8 parser and a base 10 parser. It is possible to use any instance as an exemplar, and any exemplar as an instance, though by convention there is usually a designated single exemplar that serves the role of "type" for some collection of like-structured objects.

For those readers conversant with database concepts, an analogy can be drawn between programming language constructs and database concepts to illustrate a point. Think of classes as the components of a database schema: the things that define the properties, the relations, the layout of tuples, and so forth. The schema tells how new tuples are created and put into the database—for example, what they are "connected" to and how they fit into the overall format or layout of things. The schema is analogous to classes, and the tuples are analogous to objects. As we can flexibly add new tuples to a system, we can readily create a new object from some class on demand. We can change the contents of a tuple or object without disturbing the schema; we have a high degree of flexibility.

But what if the schema itself must change? In the database world, this is called *schema evolution*, and different systems support this with varying degrees of flexibility. If we want to change the schema frequently, we want the same kind of flexibility in schema evolution as we have for modification of tuples—that is, we should be able to add a field to a relation with the same ease that we could add a tuple to the database. In the world of object-based programming, we may want the same kind of flexibility in dealing with changes in the class hierarchy as we have in manipulating objects at run time.

Such flexibility is an important keystone of the object paradigm, as illustrated with class Number above, and has far-reaching ramifications for large system development. For example, assume that a program needs to build a class's behavior bit by bit over the lifetime of a program. This is particularly important for systems that cannot be stopped, recompiled, and restarted to accommodate changes in functionality over time. Included in this class are large, embedded systems such as telecommunications systems and financial market database systems. A brokerage house may use object-oriented design in its software, where each account type is represented by a class: You do not want to have to stop the entire trading community to change behaviors of an existing account type (for example, the function that determines the policy limiting how much stock may be purchased at any given time).

Much of this flexibility comes down to a compile-time versus run-time tradeoff. In C++, the interpretation of class semantics is compile-time intensive: Any change to class characteristics triggers one or more recompilations. Objects, on the other hand, have run-time flexibility. It is the compile-time nature of classes—and the fact that they are "something different" than objects—that trips up program evolution. One way to solve this is by giving classes themselves the characteristics of objects; that is, a class might be just another object whose job is to represent what is common across its "offspring." Exemplars fill this need.

This chapter describes an idiom for approximating the properties of exemplars in a C++ implementation. The style described here is modeled after a single hierarchy, where objects serve the role traditionally played by classes; classes in turn play the role fulfilled by the metaclass concept of, say, Smalltalk.

8.1 An Example: Employee Exemplars

As an example, assume we're building a system that models the activities of members of a business organization; typical classes in this system might include Employee, Manager, VicePresident, etc. We may want to choose an exemplar approach because the definitions of these roles may change over time.

It is a useful programming practice in large projects to derive all classes in a program from a single, common base class. For example, a universal base class can be used for debugging and performance monitoring. Having a single common base class will later serve us well to capitalize on the flexibility of exemplars: We derive all classes in the system from a common base class named Class. Figure 8-1 shows a declaration of the Employee class, thus derived. This declaration looks much as it would ordinarily be written it in C++, with the exception that it has extra member functions named make whose parameter lists parallel those of constructors. Also note that the constructors themselves have been moved out of the public interface of the class. (Here, constructors have been moved into the protected section for use

```
class Employee: public Class {
public:
    Employee(Exemplar);
    Employee *make();
    Employee *make(const char *name, EmployeeId id);
    long printPaycheck();
    void logTimeWorked(Hours);
protected:
    Employee();
    Employee(const char *name, EmployeeId id);
private:
    Dollars salary;
    Days vacationAllotted, vacationUsed;
    String name;
    EmployeeId id;
};

extern Employee *employee;
```

Figure 8-1. An Employee Class for the Exemplar Idiom

by derived classes of Employee.) These make functions supplant constructors when we use this class under the exemplar idiom. The other difference from the "normal" C++ class usage is the gratuitous constructor taking an Exemplar object as a parameter; it is explained below.

Now, we have the class; however, as mentioned above, the main purpose of the class is to be the "type's type," and its instance is used as the factory for manufacturing new instances. So next, we need to create that instance itself. Exemplars can be statically defined as objects with program lifetime extent and file static scope, accessed through a global pointer typed to point to a class high in the inheritance hierarchy:

```
static Employee employeeExemplar(Exemplar());

extern Employee *employee = &employeeExemplar;
```

Another alternative is to allocate an anonymous exemplar on the heap, accessed through a global pointer:

```
extern Employee *employee = new Employee(Exemplar());
```

These definitions can be put in their own source file, or in the same source file where implementation details of the exemplar's class are kept. Declarations of exemplar handles may be published in a global header file.

The exemplar object is initialized with an `Exemplar` object as a parameter; this selects the constructor that is used to build the single prototype object from the class template. The `Exemplar` class conveys no information and has no semantics in and of itself; it is used only to disambiguate the (overloaded) constructor to be used for prototype creation. That is, it really does not matter what the `Exemplar` object does as long as it is well-behaved and has a constructor:

```
class Exemplar {
public:
    Exemplar() { /* null */ }
};
```

The `make` member function can be invoked on an exemplar to create a new object, taking over the role of constructors. In C++, constructors and destructors are "special" and unlike other member functions, in that they are really operations on the *class* itself, instead of operations on *objects* of that class. The `make` member function is like any other member function, except that it is used by convention to request a new object from an exemplar. In the normal case, `make` returns a pointer to a copy of the exemplar as its return value. All new class objects are created by "cloning" from an exemplar. The `make` operation can be overloaded, and the arguments can be used to parameterize the contents of the resultant object (like cloning with mutation). (Each `make` may create new instances simply by calling on constructors of like signature, usually found in the `private` or `protected` interface of the same class.) Here, we make a new `Employee` object by invoking

```
Class *smith = employee->make("Smith","9120784393");
```

Destruction of an object follows the orthodox canonical form, using the destructor of the class used to build the exemplar; the destructor of that class must be declared `virtual`.

We now combine these ideas into an exemplar rendition of a simple `Employee` abstraction. Figure 8-2 shows the declaration of the class itself, including the constructor taking a class `Exemplar` parameter to create the "progenitor" exemplar object. Also in `Employee`'s interface definition are a default `make` operation, and a `make` operation to create a new `Employee` instance from a name and employee identification number. The header file here contains a declaration of the exemplar handle `employee`.

To get the full benefit of separating the exemplar interface from its implementation, we would like user code never to have to depend on a declaration of class `Employee` itself. That means that `Employee`'s protocol to its clients must be in terms of a more general abstraction, such as `Class`. In Figure 8-2, note that the `make` member functions return `Class` object pointers instead of `Employee` object

```
#include "Class.h"
#include "Hours.h"
#include <String.h>

typedef long EmployeeId;

class Employee: public Class {
public:
    Employee(Exemplar /* unused */) { }

    // the make() functions take the place of constructors
    Class *make() { return new Employee; }
    Class *make(const char *name, EmployeeId id) {
        return new Employee(name, id);
    }
    long printPaycheck();
    void logTimeWorked(Hours);
private:
    // note that constructors are private, meaning that
    // ordinary instances of this class cannot be created
    Employee(): salary(0), vacationAllotted(0),
        vacationUsed(0), name(""), id(0) { }
    Employee(const char *emp_name, EmployeeId emp_id):
        salary(0), vacationAllotted(0), vacationUsed(0)
        {
            name = emp_name;  id = emp_id;
        }
    Dollars salary;
    Days vacationAllotted, vacationUsed;
    String name;
    EmployeeId id;
};

// This variable serves as the globally known handle
// to the Employee exemplar object
extern Class *employee;
```

Figure 8-2. File Employee.h Declaring an Employee Exemplar

pointers as they did in Figure 8-1. By duplicating `Employee`'s operations as virtual functions in `Class`, we isolate the user from changes in the layout or private member functions of `Employee` itself:

```
class Class {
public:
    virtual Class *make() = 0;
    virtual Class *make(const char*, EmployeeId) = 0;
    virtual long printPaycheck() = 0;
    virtual void logTimeWorked(Hours) = 0;
    . . . .    // pure virtuals for other derived classes
};
```

The declaration of the exemplar handle, `employee`, would need to be administered separately from the `Employee` declaration itself, potentially by duplication in each client source file. Full access to `Employee` member functions is maintained. To achieve this benefit in general for all exemplars, class `Class` must declare the union of all exemplar member functions, which becomes a potential administrative bottleneck with its own undesirable ripple effects from change. The balance between pushing the member function declarations to the top of the hierarchy and administering application access at levels below `Class` itself is discussed later in this chapter.

The .c file contains only the exemplar itself—declared as a file static so it remains invisible outside of that file—as well as an externally visible "handle" to the exemplar declared as a `Class*`:

```
#include "Employee.h"

// This is the exemplar object itself:  the progenitor
// that creates all other Employee objects
static Employee employeeExemplar(Exemplar());

// Here, the globally known Employee exemplar
// handle is initialized
Class *employee = &employeeExemplar;
```

An alternative form is

```
#include "Employee.h"

Class *employee = new Employee(Exemplar());
```

The member functions might just as well have been defined in this file, had they not been defined as inlines in the header file.

A program uses exemplars a bit differently from the way it would use a purely class-based implementation of the same abstraction (Figure 8-3). Instead of invoking

Class code:

```
#include "Employee.h"
int main() {
    Employee *ted =
        new Employee(
            "ted", 2823763108
        );
    . . . .
    ted->logTimeWorked(8);
    ted->printPaycheck();
    delete ted;
}
```

Exemplar code:

```
#include "Employee.h"
int main() {
    Class *ted =
        employee->make(
            "ted", 2823763108
        );
    . . . .
    ted->logTimeWorked(8);
    ted->printPaycheck();
    delete ted;
}
```

Figure 8-3. Comparison of Orthodox Canonical Idiom with Exemplars

new for a designated class name, the make operation is performed on the exemplar, whose specific type is unknown: it is accessed as a Class*.

If we want stronger type checking, the exemplar pointer can be declared and used as an Employee*, as originally presented in Figure 8-1. The type checking comes at the expense of tighter coupling between the user of Employee and Employee's class interface. In that case, there is no penalty for putting the exemplar handle declaration in the header file. A more "C++-like" style can be adopted, scoping the exemplar handle as a static public member of the class (Figure 8-4). The exemplar is accessed as Employee::exemplar instead of employeeExemplar in application code:

```
Employee *aWorker =
            Employee::exemplar->make("Joe", 123456789);
```

☞ *When to use this idiom*: Use exemplars when you want to change type characteristics at run time; for example, a change to the data of the Employee exemplar might be used to change the behavior (type characteristics) of all extant Employee objects. Exemplars are also useful as object managers for all the objects of a given type: for example, they can be the locus of auditing or resource management attributes and functions for a given class. Their main use is as a foundation for the idioms described in the rest of this chapter and in Chapter 9, all of which have the goals of increased run-time flexibility and reduced impact of change.

File Employee.h:

```
class Employee {
public:
    static Employee *exemplar;
    . . . .
};
```

File Employee.c:

```
Employee *Employee::exemplar = new Employee(Exemplar());
```

Figure 8-4. Exemplar Source File Administration

8.2 Exemplars and Generic Constructors: The Exemplar Community Idiom

Exemplars can be used to add a level of genericity to C++ programming.[2] While C++ allows member functions to be virtual, "virtual constructors" do not make sense in the language. However, the need for something like virtual constructors arises when the *type* of the object being built is a function of the constructor parameters or of global context. Exemplars approximate those semantics, using a technique described here.

Let's say that you have some anonymous data in hand—such as a name or identification number—which itself contains enough information that the Employee class can identify from its context what specific kind of employee is indicated—that is, a manager, a line worker, a stock worker, etc. These data may come from a disk file or from interactive input provided by a human operator. The expertise for interpreting those data lies in the Employee class, where it belongs. Now, we want to build an object suitable to the employee type designated by the data. However, since the code that builds objects is tied to the object's type at compile time, and since the data may not be known until run time, the class system cannot do this directly.

One set of idiomatic solutions was presented earlier in the book under the heading of *virtual constructors* (Chapter 5). Exemplars are also a natural solution for these problems and might be viewed as a generalization of the virtual constructor approaches. Remember that objects are made from exemplars by applying the make

---

2. An alternative approach is covered in Chapter 9.

operation to the exemplar object, and that `make` can be overloaded, just as a constructor might be. If these `make` member functions scrutinize their parameters, they can determine what the appropriate class should be and arrange to return a pointer to a suitably typed or parameterized object.

For example, assume that employees' roles in the company are encoded in their I.D. numbers, such that the first character is **M** for managers, **L** for line workers, **V** for vice presidents, etc. If a common operation is to build `Employee` objects from name/I.D. number pairs, then we might want to have an arrangement as in Figure 8-5. Here, knowledge about all the derived classes of `Employee` is embodied in the `make` operation of that class. `Employee` serves two roles in this context: as the base class tying together the behaviors of its derived classes (i.e., of all kinds of employees), and as an exemplar that is used for part of the management of *all* `Employee` types. Given that arrangement, the program

```
int main() {
    Employee *joe = employee->make("Joe",
                                EmployeeID("M012345678"));
    . . . .
}
```

would create an object of "type" `Manager`.

The management of a collection of related exemplars by a single "mother hen" exemplar is a useful idiom. This idiom is called the *exemplar community idiom*: a community of related exemplars tied together by a single representative called the *community manager*. The community manager serves the "mother hen" function or, being more faithful to the community analogy, serves the role of city manager or mayor for its constituent objects.

☞ *When to use this idiom*: Use exemplar communities when you want to combine the benefits of exemplars, for run-time flexibility, with the benefits of "virtual constructors."

8.3 Autonomous Generic Constructors

The above example works fine if the `Employee` exemplar knows about all the `Employee` derived classes. However, this might be at odds with evolutionary needs:

```
class Class {
public:
    virtual Class *make(const char*,EmployeeID);
    . . . .
};

class Employee:  public Class {
public:
    Class *make(const char*, EmployeeID);
    . . . .
};

Employee *employeeExemplar = new Employee(Exemplar());

class VicePresident: public Employee {
    . . . .
};

class LineWorker:  public Employee {
    . . . .
};

Class *
Employee::make(const char *name, EmployeeID id)
{
    Class *retval = 0;
    switch (id.firstChar()) {
    case 'M':    retval = new Manager(name, id);
                 break;
    case 'V':    retval = new VicePresident(name, id);
                 break;
    . . . .
    }
    return retval;
}
```

Figure 8-5. Generic Employee Constructor

we do not want the addition of a derived class to violate the abstraction of Employee by insisting that something be changed there to accommodate it. What we want to do instead is to distribute knowledge about the system in the appropriate classes, in keeping with good object-oriented design techniques.

We achieve this by doing the following:

1. Identify a collection of related objects that we want to treat as coming from a single generic exemplar (such as the employee classes above).

CLASSES

EXEMPLAR
INSTANCES

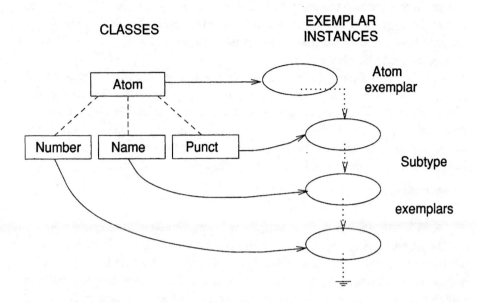

Figure 8-6. Autonomous Generic Exemplars for Atom Classes.

All application requests for new objects are processed by the Atom exemplar instance, which polls exemplars of its subordinate classes to process the request. The first exemplar in the list to be able to parse the string passed to Atom::make gets to process it, and yields an object of its own class as a result.

2. Create a global list accessible to member functions of all those classes, where the elements of the list are pointers to objects of such classes of interest.

3. Arrange for an exemplar to be created for each such class, and for that exemplar to "log" itself into that list.

4. Arrange for each exemplar's make operation to return a zero pointer if it is invoked with an inappropriate parameter.

5. Change the make function of the principal exemplar to loop through the list, iteratively applying make to each exemplar with a copy of its own parameters. Return the first nonzero return value.

We call this approach the *autonomous generic exemplar idiom.* Each exemplar has the intelligence to evaluate its parameters to see if they were intended for it; if not, other exemplars in the same exemplar community are given the same chance. It is as though there were a community bulletin board at which all citizens congregated waiting for want ads to be posted: When a new ad is posted, the citizens line up in a prescribed order to have the chance to respond to the want ad one at a time. The first respondent gets to handle the job.

An example at the end of this chapter applies this approach to a simple parser. Exemplar objects are created as static variables of global extent for each of the derived classes of Atom: Number, Name, Punct, Oper, etc. The instantiation of each of those exemplar objects causes the base class constructor Atom::Atom(Exemplar) to be invoked; this constructor places each of the exemplar objects on the linked list list, a static member of Atom:

```
Atom(Exemplar /* unused */) {
    next = list;  list = this;
}
```

The Atom class stands in for all of its derived classes from the perspective of instantiation. Users of the package construct only new Atoms; that is, they typically do not build Number or Name objects directly. The Atom member function make(String&) passes its parameter to the make operation of each of the objects of list in turn. The first class to find a match between its type and the pattern at the beginning of the String consumes as much of the String as it matches, and returns a nonzero value from its make operation:

```
virtual Atom *make(String &s) {
    Atom *retval = 0;
    extern Atom *atomExemplar;
    if (this != atomExemplar) {    // avoid infinite recursion
        for (Atom *a = list; a; a = a->next) {
            if (retval = a->make(s)) break;
        }
    }
    return retval;
}
```

Each make operation passes on the result of its class's constructor, unless the constructor sets an error flag indicating that the input cannot be recognized as one of its own type. The first nonzero value returned by a derived class make member function is simply passed on by Atom::make as the return value to the user.

Note that for this example, the order in which the derived class exemplars place themselves in the list may be important, because of lexical context sensitivities in the grammar. The exemplars should look for the longest possible matching substrings before trying to match shorter ones.

An advantage of exemplars is that classes lose much of their significance. The only places that need to know about the internals (private members) of a class object are those places where new objects are created, and inside the class's member functions. Since new is no longer used to create objects (make is), we do not need to have class interfaces understood everywhere that objects are being brought into existence. That knowledge is now buried within the make functions of each object. That in turn means that knowledge of the class structure can be limited to the class itself; clients of the class interact through the exemplar mechanism at a higher level, described below.

☞ *When to use this idiom*: Use this idiom as a mechanism to achieve the semantics of "virtual constructors" where you want to avoid centralized knowledge about classes in an exemplar community. Knowledge about object initialization can remain distributed across the participating classes. Example applications include *simple* parsers and scanners.

8.4 Abstract Base Exemplars

Given this approach, how do objects talk to each other? Object communication is still done through object member functions, following C++ conventions (that is, we do not use messages or transactions or anything exotic like that). Any client of an exemplar object must have a declaration of the exemplar's class interface (signature) available at compile time. Since the class interfaces for most exemplar objects are kept in their source files, where does this signature come from?

The answer comes in the use of virtual functions to support high level architectural abstractions called *abstract base exemplars*. Individual implementation classes are derived from higher order classes that are globally available, with declarations in global header files. These high order classes themselves fall into a shallow hierarchy and are few in number. At the apex is the Class class, an abstract base class (Figure 8-6) whose signature reflects most operations for most classes in the system:

```
class Class {
public:
    virtual Class *make() = 0;
    virtual Class *make(const char *, EmployeeID) = 0;
    virtual long printPaycheck();
    virtual void logTimeWorked();
    virtual ~Class();
    . . . .
};

typedef Class *Classp;
```

That is, we gather every member function declaration from a group of related classes, combining them into the signature of `Class`. As an abstract base class, `Class` cannot be instantiated. However, a `Class*` (or its typedefed equivalent, `Classp`) can be used to refer to any object tracing its class parentage to `Class`.

Note that in this approach, the use of classes as a classification mechanism is de-emphasized. By introducing virtual declarations of all member functions into a base class `Class`, we permit access to any object through a `Classp` pointer; it is as though every object were of class `Class`. The programmer works with a few classes that serve as interfaces to all system objects; these classes sit at the apex of a shallow inheritance hierarchy that is wide at the bottom and narrow at the top. So functions, rather than classes, become the major design focus. However, these functions are still polymorphic in that they operate on many forms of `Class` objects. This is a "turning inside-out" of the inheritance approach used by C++, called *inclusion polymorphism*. We think of this form more in terms of *parametric polymorphism*: the polymorphic functions are defined first and collected into an abstract base exemplar, from which all application classes are derived. This is similar to the C++ notion of *function templates* (Chapter 7) from the perspective of design, in that the class structure comprises a wide, shallow hierarchy. Here, we realize no source code reuse as with function templates, but we gain run-time polymorphism that templates can't provide. The difference between abstract base exemplars and the more traditional class-based approach is not in mechanics, but in emphasis. Both have run-time identification of member functions, but with abstract base exemplars there is a collapsing of an elaborate class hierarchy into a simpler structure of classes with larger interfaces.

As these classes fall into a hierarchy, so might their exemplar instances. We want clients of a collection of classes, such as `Employee` or `Atom`, to work with the collection at the highest possible level of abstraction, and that is why the member functions are pushed into the classes nearer the top of the hierarchy. Each application has its own abstract base exemplar; for the parser, it is `Atom`, and for a payroll system, `Employee` is among a few abstract base exemplars. It is, of course, possible to let clients access the same hierarchy at multiple levels, using deeper classes as they need additional specificity. However, this makes client code dependent on the interface of the lower-level classes, and forces such clients to `#include` another header file to access their signatures.

This leads to an important design tradeoff. At one extreme is a "fat" abstract base class at the apex of the hierarchy, through which all member functions can be invoked. The user of such a hierarchy must interface only with the single abstract base class. At the other extreme is a more traditional hierarchy, where specific member functions appear only in the derived classes to which they pertain. Though the abstract base exemplar can be used to invoke common operations on all objects created from the hierarchy, lower level class interfaces must be visible to make all operations available. The tradeoff is between a single, elaborate abstraction and a larger number of simpler abstractions. Evaluate such tradeoffs with an eye to how the software is likely to evolve and the impact of such evolution on recompilation.

The operations on `Class` are all virtual, and most are pure virtual; that is, they serve only as placeholders and have no body. Among the virtual operations defined on `Class` are the `make` member functions. This means that if a program has a pointer p to some prototype object, and if it is compiled using Class.h, it can invoke p->`make` to obtain a pointer to a new object cloned from the prototype. The virtual `make` operation typically calls a constructor of its own class to build a new object.

How does a piece of code get a pointer to a suitable prototype object? As shown above, most exemplars leave a pointer to themselves in a global variable used for that purpose; the pointer is set up when the corresponding `X::X(Exemplar)` constructor is called. An alternative to globally naming these objects is to have a name server object with which every newly formed prototype logs itself.

To summarize: The code for each class and the handle to its exemplar object live together in their own source file. The only globally exported information is a set of global exemplar handles, and a few classes whose interfaces declare the union of the interfaces of all their derived classes. Those abstract exemplars have their interfaces defined in a C++ header file, and that header is `#included` by anyone wishing to construct or use an object of those types.

8.5 Toward a Frame Exemplar Idiom

What we have so far works pretty well to isolate information to the classes where it belongs, and we have solved the problem of violating the encapsulation of a base class when a new derived class is added. However, we still have a serious problem: Addition of a new member function to any of the classes grouped together in a given exemplar community must be reflected in some common parent class (the lowest one accessed by users of these objects). Following simple impact-of-change analysis, that causes the code of all those classes to be unnecessarily recompiled under most C++ implementations.

One way to solve this is through another tradeoff. Assume for a second that each class had exactly one member function named `doit`, which took as parameters a directive indicating a detailed operation, and a list of arguments for that operation. We greatly simplify the class interfaces at the expense of administering a global list of directives, which would be updated every time a new semantic interface was to be added to the system. The use of a semantically weak member function name like `doit` suggests a casual or weak mapping from an application entity to the class used to capture its semantics, and recalls the cautions mentioned in Section 6.5. However, the addition of a new semantic operation to the interface no longer causes the addition of a new member function—it just uses `doit` with a new parameter that is interpreted by the appropriate derived class—so the recompilation impact of change is much smaller than before. Member functions no longer represent the behaviors of the application abstraction; the mapping table used by `doit` does. The class presents a "fat interface," not because the base class has functions that some derived classes may not need, but because the member function parameters can cover an arbitrarily wide range of functions, activities, retrievals or other mappings. These operations are reminiscent of *slots* or *frames* as used by the AI community. A slot is a placeholder for a piece of information; the more of an object's slots (state variables) are filled in, the more completely it describes the abstraction it represents.

Actually, we adopt a level of semantics in our interface that is a level above "doit." There is an exemplar-based example at the end of this chapter that elaborates the `Employee` class above. In that example, class `Class` is used to access most every kind of object, from different kinds of employees to dollars. `Employee` is derived from `Class`, and there are multiple derived classes of `Employee` including `VicePresident`, `Manager`, and other corporate roles.

The exemplar example at the end of this chapter treats all objects as containers with named slots that are filled or whose values are retrieved, and named pushbuttons that are prodded to trigger some work in the context of some parameters. The basic operations on all objects are therefore `at`, which does associative retrieval from a slot; `atPut`, which does an associative store; and functions `getNext` and `putNext`, which are used to treat the object as a serial aggregate (e.g., by scanning its slots in sequence). An `atPut` may also be evaluated just for its "pushbutton" side effects, where the provided parameter is data for the associated activity, rather than something to be stuffed into a slot; the `PrintPaycheck` directive is an example. Here, the key fields are enumerated constants; a less efficient, though more symbolic approach is briefly demonstrated in Chapter 6 using strings as keys (page 233).

Because polymorphism is handled at the level of these access functions—and not at the level of member functions as virtual functions provide—some polymorphism and inheritance semantics must be explicitly coded within the classes themselves. This turns out to be easy to do. In `VicePresident::atPut`, we see a `default` in the `case` statement for those directives not recognized by that exemplar. The semantics of that condition are to forward the operation to the base class of `VicePresident`, namely `Employee`, which acts as a delegate for a subset of the `atPut` operations performed on `VicePresident`. So the behavior is much like method lookup in Smalltalk, where a request percolates up the inheritance chain looking for a class that can handle the "message." This manually administered polymorphism is similar to what virtual functions provide in C++. The only difference is that there is no compile-time type checking, so exceptions can arise at run time. Here, the access functions signal an unhandled request by returning null; more drastic action (e.g., raising an exception) could have been coded instead.

On the pragmatic sides of the function versus slot tradeoff are the variables of flexibility versus convenience. Adding a new exemplar or member function requires little administrative ceremony. Using abstract exemplars, a new class can be added to a program just by compiling the new type and incrementally loading it into existing code. Some environments may allow incrementally link-editing new object code into an existing load module (under UNIX, an a.out file). In a continuous-running system with incremental run-time loading, new exemplars can be incorporated into a *running* program on the fly (see Chapter 9). For example, if the incremental parser described earlier in this chapter were part of the query language processor for an on-line reservation system, we could use the underlying operating system to load new language construct classes into a running, operational system. The software loading mechanism adds the new exemplar to the exemplar list maintained by the exemplar manager in the exemplar community idiom. Placement in this list links the new exemplar into the system. The new software's functionality becomes available immediately, and is installed without disturbing any existing software.

The bad news about the exemplar idiom is that it is not "natural" C++ any more. This makes training more difficult and may require new tool development to effectively administer programs written in this style for a large project. Another down side is that now there are fewer compile-time guarantees that operations will be invoked only on objects of the appropriate type; class implementors must take the responsibility to act appropriately when unexpected requests are applied. Performance will also be poorer than it is using styles more heavily rooted in compile-time binding.

☞ *When to use this idiom*: Use this idiom when the benefit of run-time flexibility outweighs the benefits of compile-time type checking. Use exemplars to reduce the impact of change on recompilation to support rapid iteration for prototyping and exploratory programming.

8.6 A Word About Notation

In Section 6.4, a notation for object and class relationships was described. That notation was based on the "native" C++ model of classes and objects, and exemplars suggest that model should be extended to handle the richer relationships they bring.

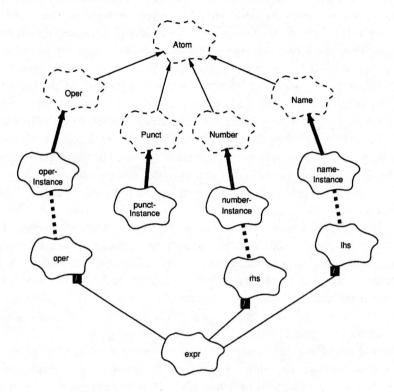

Figure 8-7. A Hybrid Object / Class Diagram

Most of the changes are related more to focus than to basic meaning. For example, IS-A might now apply as a relationship between instances: Any object that starts off as a clone of another bears an IS-A relationship to the original. The clone may have associated with other adjuncts in the meantime, forwarding some of its operations to those objects to change its own functionality. If the signature of the clone retains the basic semantics of the original as described in Chapter 6, an IS-A relationship still exists.

If the exemplar idiom is used, classes are only second-class citizens. Relationships such as the HAS-A relationship no longer have a class sense on one hand, and an object sense on the other hand, with subtly different meanings: Everything is in terms of instances. The CREATES-A relationship loses its characteristic of straddling classes and objects; all is now done in terms of objects.

Classes, of course, are still in the picture, and we can adopt a notation giving them stature if we wish. Exemplars replace classes, and the exemplars' C++ classes are the classes of those "class surrogates." Several languages call the class of a class its *metaclass*. So each exemplar instance is said to have a HAS-METACLASS relationship to its C++ class.

Because exemplars use object instances in a role usually associated with classes, capturing program semantics requires a hybrid presentation of object and class relationships in a single rendering. Figure 8-7 shows this type of diagram for the Atom example; this is mostly a "formalization" of Figure 8-6, using the notation of Booch presented in Chapter 6, in the context of a simple application:

```
extern Atom *atom;
Expr parse(String s) {
    . . . .
    Atom *lhs = (*atom)->make(s);
    Atom *oper = (*atom)->make(s);
    Atom *rhs = (*atom)->make(s);
    Expr expr = (*exprExemplar)->make(lhs, oper, rhs);
    . . . .
    return expr;
}
```

Here, Oper, Punct, Number, and Name are metaclasses for the application. Their metaclass relationship to the exemplar objects operInstance, punctInstance, numberInstance, and nameInstance, respectively, is documented with the metaclass arrows between them. However, Oper, Punct, Number, and Name are implemented as C++ classes, and here they are depicted using the class icon (a dotted blob). The "classes" of the application—operInstance, nameInstance, and other instances—are exemplars, which in C++ are objects, and that is reflected in the figure. The object creation relationships between the application objects (oper, rhs, and lhs) and their exemplars are shown as a special relationship represented by the dotted lines in the figure.

8.7 Exemplars and Program Administration

This style leads to a program structure with few header files. There is typically one source file per class; the class declaration is in the source file itself, *not* in a header file. There are places where a single source file for a class would be too big; in these instances, the class declaration is put in a *local* header file instead of a *global* header. There are places where unusually detailed access of one class is needed by objects of some other class, forcing some class declarations to be in global headers. So class declarations appear in three places: in module source files, in local header files, and in global header files.

Particular attention must be given to the enumerated values used as directives in the frame exemplar idiom. Because the particulars of a concrete subobject's functionality may not appear in the generalized interface of an abstract base class, subprotocols must be established inside those defined by abstract class interfaces. The protocols can be bound at compile time for efficiency. To avoid collision in these protocols, they must be centrally administered. This leads to a long, compile-time-known list of "message types" that are in some sense the moral equivalent of global data. However, because such message types are essentially enumerated types, they can be linearly ordered, and adding a new type at the end does not have a serious ripple effect on the rest of the program, either semantically or in terms of recompilation.

As a slightly less efficient alternative, message type indices can be bound at run time to successive integer values. As exemplars need message types, they can create a new `MessageType` object and bind it to a name in their own name space:

```
class MessageType {
public:
    MessageType(): typeField(nextType++) { }
    operator int() { return typeField; }
    int operator==(MessageType m) {
        return typeField == m.typeField;
    }
private:
    static int nextType;
    int typeField;
};

int MessageType::nextType = 0;

class AssociativeArray {
public:
    AssociativeArray() . . . .
    void atPut(void *element, MessageType key) {
        if (key == size) sizeFrame = *((int*)element);
        else if . . . .
    }
    void *at(MessageType key) {
        . . . .
    }
    static MessageType size, print, . . . .
private:
    int sizeFrame, . . . .
};
```

```
static MessageType AssociativeArray::size,
       AssociativeArray::print ....

int main() {
    AssociativeArray a;
    MessageType AssociativeArrayExample,
        CirclistExample;
    a.atPut((void*)233, AssociativeArrayExample);
    . . . .
    int size = a.at(a.size);
    . . . .
}
```

This approach is less efficient than using enums, but certainly more efficient than the use of Strings in the original example.

Exercises

1. Change the simple parser at the end of the chapter so that the Atom constructor can be invoked several times on the same string, destructively consuming it as tokens are recognized and transformed into objects.

2. Write a name server for an abstract base exemplar application, such as a simple parser. Each exemplar should log itself with the name server (when?). Write a lookup(const char*) member function for the name server providing a name-to-exemplar mapping. Where should you keep the knowledge of an exemplar's symbolic name?

3. Make the above name server efficient so that it does symbolic lookup for any given exemplar, only when lookup is called for the first time with a given string. (Hint: have the user pass a String iterator object to lookup that remembers the association across calls to lookup).

4. Complete the frame-based exemplar example that follows below.

□

Exemplar-Based Simple Parser

This is an exemplar implementation of a simple parser suggested by the examples of
Chapter 5.

```
class Exemplar { public:  Exemplar() { } };

class Atom {
protected:
    static Atom *list;
    Atom *next;
    static char errFlag;
public:   // union of signature of all Atoms
    Atom(Exemplar) { next = list; list = this; }
    virtual Atom *make(String &s) {
        Atom *retval = 0;
        extern Atom *atomExemplar;
        for (Atom *a = list; a; a = a->next) {
            if (a != atomExemplar) {
                if (retval = a->make(s)) break;
            }
        }
        return retval;
    }
    Atom() { next = 0; errFlag = 0; }
    virtual ~Atom() {}
    virtual unsigned long value() { return 0; }
    virtual String name() { return String("error"); }
    virtual operator char() { return 0;}
};

Atom* Atom::list = 0;
static Atom atomInstance(Exemplar());
Atom *atomExemplar = &atomInstance;

class Number: public Atom {
public:
    Number(Exemplar a): Atom(a) { }
    Number(String &s): Atom() {
        sum = 0;
        for(int i=0; s[i] >= '0' && s[i] <= '9'; i++) {
            sum = (sum * 10) + s[i] - '0';
        }
        char c = s[i]; errFlag = !(ispunct(c) || isspace(c));
    }
    Number(Number &n) { sum = n.value(); }
```

```
    Atom *make(String &s) {
        Atom *retval = new Number(s);
        if (errFlag) { delete retval; retval = 0; }
        return retval;
    }
    ~Number() {}
    unsigned long value() const { return sum; }
private:
    unsigned long sum;
};

static Number numberInstance(Exemplar());

class Name: public Atom {
public:
    Name(Exemplar a): Atom(a) { }
    Name(String &s): Atom() {
        for(int i=0; s[i] >= 'a' && s[i] <= 'z'; i++)
            n = n + s(i,1);
        // if this isn't a name, tell caller via errFlag
        if (!isalnum(s[i])) errFlag++;
    }
    Atom *make(String &s) {
        Atom *retval = new Name(s);
        if (errFlag) { delete retval; retval = 0; }
        return retval;
    }
    Name(Name &m) { n = m.name(); }
    ~Name() {}
    String name() { return n; }
private:
    String n;
};

static Name nameInstance(Exemplar());

class Punct: public Atom {
public:
    Punct(Exemplar a): Atom(a) { }
    Punct(String &s): Atom() {
        if (!ispunct(s[0])) errFlag++;
        s = s(1, s.length()-1);
    }
    Atom *make(String &s) {
        Atom *retval = new Punct(s);
        if(!errFlag) { delete retval; retval = 0; }
        return retval;
    }
}
```

```
    Punct(Punct &p) { c = char(p); }
    operator char() { return c; }
    ~Punct() {}
private:
    char c;
};

static Punct punctInstance(Exemplar());

class Oper: public Atom {
    . . . .
};
```

Frame-Based Exemplars

This code shows a simple program framework where diverse classes such as
Employee and Dollars share a common abstract base exemplar Class. Class
Class is a "fat interface" for the classes beneath it in the inheritance hierarchy.

```
extern class Class *dollarsExemplar;   // forward reference
class Class {
public:
    enum Directive { PrintPaycheck, TimeWorked, GiveRaise,
                     Salary, Stock, ToString, Value };
    virtual Class *atPut(Directive key, Class *arg) = 0;
    virtual Class *at(Directive key) = 0;
    virtual Class *getNext() = 0;
    virtual Class *putNext(Class *) = 0;
    virtual Class *make(Class *param) = 0;
    virtual Class *make(int=0, int=0, int=0, int=0);
    virtual int toInt() = 0;
};

class Employee: public Class {
public:
    Class *atPut(Directive key, Class *arg) {
        switch(key) {
        case Salary:    salary = arg->toInt(); return this;
        case Print:     cerr << *this; return this;
        default:        return 0;
        }
    }
    Class *at(Directive key) {
        switch(key) {
        case Salary:    return dollarsExemplar->make(salary);
        . . . .
```

```
            default:          return 0;
            }
        }
    int toInt() { return salary; }
    Class *make(int=0, int=0, int=0,int=0) = 0;
    Class *make(Class param) = 0;
    Class *getNext() = 0;
    Class *putNext(Class *) = 0;
protected:
    Dollars salary;
    Days vacationAllotted, vacationUsed;
};

class VicePresident: public Employee {
public:
    Class *atPut(Directive key, Class *arg) {
        switch(key) {
        case GiveRaise: salary = arg->toInt() + salary;
                        stockOptions *= 1.05;
                        break;
        default:        return Employee::atPut(key, arg);
                        break;
        }
        return this;
    }
    Class *at(Directive key) {
        switch(key) {
        case Stock: return dollarsExemplar->make(stockOptions);
        . . . .
        default:    return Employee::at(key, arg);
        }
    Class *make(Class *param) {
        name = param->getNext()->at(ToString);
        salary = (int)param->getNext()->at(ToInt);
        stock = (int)param->getNext()->at(ToInt);
    }
    Class *make(int i=0, int j=0, int k=0, int l=0) {
        Class * n = new VicePresident;
        n->salary = i; n->stockOptions = j; return n;
    }
    Class *getNext() { return 0; }
    Class *putNext(Class *) { return 0; }
    VicePresident(Exemplar) { }
private:
    Dollars stockOptions;
};
```

```
Class *vpExemplar = (Class *)new VicePresident(Exemplar());

class Dollars: public Class {
public:
    Class *atPut(Directive key, Class *arg) {
        switch(key) {
        case Value:  rep = (int)arg->at(ToInt); return this;
        default:     return Class::atPut(key, arg);
        }
    }
    Class *at(Directive key) {
        switch(key) {
        case Value:  return integerExemplar->make((Class*)rep);
        default:     return Class::atPut(key, arg);
        }
    }
    int toInt() { return rep; }
    Class *make(int i=0, int j=0, int k=0, int l=0) {
        Class * n = new Dollars;
        n->rep = i; return n;
    }
    Class *make(Class *param) {
        Class * n = new Dollars;
        n->rep = (int)param;
        return n;
    }
    Class *getNext() { return 0; }
    Class *putNext(Class *) { return 0; }
    Dollars(Exemplar) { }
private:
    int rep;
};

Class *dollarsExemplar = (Class*)new Dollars(Exemplar());
```

References

1. Ungar, David and Randall B. Smith. "Self: The Power of Simplicity."
   SIGPLAN Notices 22,12 (December 1987).

9

Emulating Symbolic Language Styles in C++

C++ provides the basic machinery to define abstract data types and use them for object-oriented programming. However, the flexibility of a high-level object-oriented programming language like Smalltalk or CLOS is difficult to attain in a language as closely tied to C as C++ is. In both C and C++, a variable name is tightly tied to the *address* of the storage for the object it denotes, instead of being a label that can be peeled off one object and applied to another at will. This strong binding lets the compiler ensure that a given variable always goes with an object of a given type. The compiler uses this property to generate efficient code and to keep the programmer from using objects where they are not expected. Efficiency and type safety come at the expense of run-time flexibility: For example, a variable declared as a float can never be used to address a Complex object at run time, though the two types are behaviorally compatible.

Smalltalk and most Lisp-based object-oriented languages offer two features, based on loose coupling between variables and objects, which are not directly supported by C++ but which can be expressed as idioms using a suitable programming style. The first is automatic memory management (reference counting or garbage collection). In a symbolic language where variables are labels for objects, object lifetimes are independent of the variables that designate them. Symbolic language environments use special techniques based on loose name-value bindings to clean up unreferenceable objects automatically. C++ programs simulate this loose binding by addressing objects through pointers, and this extra level of indirection can be used for automatic memory management, as described in detail in Sections 3.5 and 3.6.

The second important feature of high-level object-oriented programming languages is their high level of polymorphism; idioms to provide such polymorphism are covered in detail in Section 5.5. Such extended polymorphism supports a more pliable software architecture; objects become more loosely coupled, making them easier to maintain independently.

Automatic storage management and extended polymorphism are the two major strengths of Lisp-based systems, Smalltalk, and other object-oriented programming languages in the symbolic tradition. To the degree we can build idioms to emulate those in C++, we bring that flexibility to the C++ programmer as well. The flexibility is not without cost: Run-time performance penalties and storage overhead need to be traded off against this flexibility. Type errors previously detected by the compiler's type system are deferred to run time when these idioms are used, and depend on the integrity of user-supplied type checking code. Rules for this tradeoff are not hard and fast, but experience in design and practice helps the software engineer choose from the idioms in this chapter, or from other chapters, to suit the application at hand.

Three kinds of idioms are combined in this chapter. The first brings together ideas from previous chapters to support an iterative development style through reduced impact of change. A canonical form is provided to reduce the impact of change and to lay a foundation for the other two idioms. The second provides incremental run-time program update through a simple run-time environment. The third is a technique to automate the cleanup and reclamation of deadwood objects. Each idiom can be used independently, or several can be used in combination.

The second idiom may require special expertise and effort to port to a given platform: It depends on implementation details of C++ class data representations. The implementations described here are based on the commentary in the ANSI base document for the C++ language standard [1]. They currently work with Release 3 of the AT&T USL C++ Compilation System and will be found to be portable to many environments using the products of many vendors.

It should be emphasized that it is best not to interpret the techniques described in this chapter as a substitute for Smalltalk or Lisp-based object-oriented programming environments. In addition to having flexibility to support incremental development, symbolic languages have powerful environments with a legacy of incremental development support. The flexibility described here can take C++ several steps in that direction, but not without the costs of extra discipline in coding, and potentially reduced run-time performance. The chapter is intended to foster ideas supporting incremental C++ development, as well as to provide the flexibility to update systems supporting continuously running applications. It may also be used as a model for code automatically generated from a tool, driven by an application generator or very high-level language compiler intended for use in flexible, interactive applications.

9.1 Incremental C++ Development

Why do we want incremental development for C++? We want to be able to turn around changes *quickly* so that continuity of thought is not lost in the process of "test driving" new code. Rapid iteration is an important technique to refine system structure and explore behavior of the application in light of new or changed requirements. The cost of incremental change must be held low to make such iteration effective.

Incrementality and Object-Oriented Design

Incremental development is a natural fit for object-oriented design. The encapsulation of implementation details within classes makes them natural units of iteration; the enforcement of a common protocol to all classes in an inheritance hierarchy eases the addition of a new class as a leaf. All these can be used as design aids in C++, but turn-around time for recompilation and loading may be slow compared to a Smalltalk or Lisp-based system. Although powerful C++ programming environments are emerging that break with traditional software technology to provide incremental modes of development, there will still be platforms for which such technology is not available. For example, much of this flexibility is desirable in a deliverable application platform, running as an embedded system outside the context of any "friendly" operating system or traditional support environment. In this chapter, we explore incremental approaches with less power than would be found in an integrated incremental C++ development environment, but that can support incremental development for many platforms and environments.

Reducing Cost of Compilation

The first step to incremental C++ development is to reduce recompilation cost, and one effective way to do this is to reduce the *need* for recompilation. There is a strong compile-time association between a C++ variable, its type, and the storage to which it is bound. If program evolution changes a variable's type characteristics or displaces its address, code referring to that name must be re-linked or recompiled. Changing one symbol may cause offsets of nearby symbols to shift, making it necessary to recompile everything that references *them* as well. For example, any change to the interface of a class triggers recompilation of all code referencing *any* part of that interface.

Most approaches to compilation avoidance are based on adding a level of indirection to symbol references. The envelope/letter idiom (Section 5.5) and its derivatives, such as the exemplar idiom of Chapter 8, are examples of this approach. The idioms presented in this chapter draw largely from the exemplar approach.

This flexibility for change with minimal compilation brings a performance cost that comes from extra levels of indirection at run-time. In the spirit of most symbolic programming languages, it is also less compile-time type safe than native C++. These two tradeoffs must be carefully evaluated to chart the idioms to be used in a development project.

Reducing Link Editing and Loading Cost

The second step to incremental development is to reduce the time needed for link editing and loading. *Link editing* is the step usually used to build an executable program file from relocatable compiled object files, and *loading* is the act of bringing code from those files into memory for execution. Some systems combine these two steps, and most systems have some degree of symbol-to-address binding in both of them.

The efficiency of linking and loading is particularly important to large system development, and bears attention because it is in large system development that object-oriented techniques have sizable payoff. Most minicomputer and microprocessor operating system traditions are not strong in incremental linking and loading; however, many new releases of UNIX and other systems have incremental linking provisions. Incremental linking results in smaller object modules, and offers substantially faster turnaround than a full link edit.

Even if link editing is fast, reloading can still be a bottleneck. If it takes a long time for a system to initialize, then even incrementally link-edited changes incur that wait time on every iteration. If, however, code can be incrementally loaded into an initialized, running program, then there is potential for even faster turnaround of small changes.

Rapid Iteration in Perspective

Rapid iteration is most effective for early architecture exploration, where throw-away prototypes are built to improve understanding of the application. It can be used as a product development discipline, but only within the constraints of a stable architectural structure. Rapidly iterating upward compatible changes to a system is a potentially successful development technique if properly managed. Leaving major interfaces open to iteration is to invite disaster, fueling entropy and destroying system structure.

9.2 Symbolic Canonical Form

The symbolic idiom offers an alternative to the orthodox canonical form presented in Section 3.1 (page 38). Emulating symbolic paradigms in C++ is "unorthodox," or at least at its own level of orthodoxy, and requires its own conventions and forms. By using this alternative canonical form for C++ classes, C++ code can be used to model many of the properties of symbolic programming languages in general. It loses much of the compact expressiveness that can be achieved using the orthodox canonical form directly.

☞ *When to use this idiom*: Use this idiom where cultural compatibility for C or C++ is desired, but where the flexibility and incrementality of symbolic programming environments are needed. This idiom can also be used as a framework for interfacing between symbolic programming environments and C++ environments. The styles and idioms described here can be used to build a C++ prototyping environment in its own right, provided certain programming conventions are followed in application software. Lastly, the idiom can be used in a continuous running system to support run-time update and long-term evolution.

The canonical form builds on the memory management and polymorphism ideas from previous chapters, and augments them to support additional incrementality. Some of the major aspects of the canonical form are as follows:

- Automatic memory management based on reference counted letter classes (Section 3.5);

- Abolishing end user manipulation of pointers to objects, while giving every object the appearance of having the flexibility of pointers (Section 3.5);

- Dependence on virtual functions for run-time and load-time flexibility; and

- Use of the exemplar idiom (Chapter 8).

A major building block of the symbolic canonical form is a small collection of base classes that are used to build the envelope and letter classes of the application. The declarations of these classes will be placed in a global header file k.h, as shown in Figure 9-1. There are two classes: Top, which serves as a base class for all envelope classes, and Thing, which serves as the base for all letter classes. Class Thing itself is actually derived from Top, which gives an overall system uniformity

```
// include file k.h

class Top {
public:
    // Objects of this class have no data, except __vptr,
    // which is provided by the compiler.  Deriving all
    // classes from this class assures that the __vptr
    // will always be the first element in any object
    // in many implementations.  Some implementations
    // need different mechanisms to access the vtbl. Only
    // the dynamic loading aspect of the symbolic idiom
    // depends on this property.
    virtual ~Top() { /* empty */ }
    virtual Top *type() { return this; }
    // delete is public for run-time update cleanup
    static void operator delete(void *p) {
        ::operator delete(p);
    }
protected:
    Top()  { /* empty */ }
    static void *operator new(size_t l) {
        return ::operator new(l);
    }
};

typedef unsigned long REF_TYPE;

class Thing: public Top {
    // All  "rep" fields are derived from Thing;  it defines
    // the canonical form for all Letter classes
public:
    Thing(): refCountVal(1), updateCountVal(0) { }
    virtual REF_TYPE deref() {        // unbump ref count
        return --refCountVal;
    }
    virtual REF_TYPE ref() {          // bump ref count
        return ++refCountVal;
    }
    virtual Thing *cutover(Thing*); // class update function
    virtual ~Thing() { /* empty */ } // destructor
private:
    REF_TYPE refCountVal, updateCountVal;
};
```

Figure 9-1. The k.h Header File

that models root base classes found in many symbolic programming environments. What is being done with Top and Thing here is somewhat analogous to the roles of classes Object, Class, and Behavior in Smalltalk, though no direct mapping between the two approaches is obvious or useful.

These provide the flexibility, memory management support, run-time update support, and loose type model we desire to adopt from symbolic language environments. Each of the classes is described in detail in the following two sections.

Class Top

Class Top sits at the apex of the system class hierarchy; all classes derive properties from Top. Top has no explicit data; however, most C++ compilers supply one implicit data member to support C++ virtual function dispatching. This data member is called the vptr, and it points to a table of virtual function entries, sometimes called the vtbl. Class Top has a virtual function to ensure that such a pointer is present.

Different implementations of C++ may implement virtual functions differently, but most are variations on the same theme. For example, consider the following three classes [1]:

```
class A {
public:
    int a;
    virtual void f(int);
    virtual void g(int);
    virtual void h(int);
};

class B: public A {
public:
    int b;
    void g(int);
};

class C: public B {
public:
    int c;
    void h(int);
};
```

Given those declarations, an object of class C would look something like this in memory:

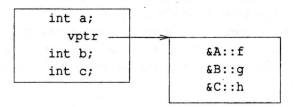

If the apex class has no data, then the vptr is the first thing at the beginning of all objects of interest—that just makes it easy to find. Given a pointer to any such object, any function can find its vptr, and thus can traverse the contents of the vtbl for that object's class. This will be key to replacing functions in a running program on the fly.

Class Top also has a default (argumentless) constructor in its protected section; this prevents objects of class Top from being created directly. It has a virtual destructor, which does nothing; its being virtual ensures that a call to appropriate derived class destructors will be dispatched at run time.

The declaration of operator new for class Top is hidden as a protected field to ensure that no envelope classes are allocated from the heap. Limiting declaration of envelope classes to be objects of local or global extent, or member objects of another class, enables the compiler to completely automate the orchestration of their cleanup. This operator is overridden in letter derived classes so their instances can still be allocated from the heap. Dynamic allocation and deallocation of classes in the letter hierarchy is done from within their letter class, which ensures that their memory is cleaned up when it is no longer needed.

The type member function is overridden in derived classes to return a pointer to the associated exemplar; it is used for run-time class update, which is described later in the chapter.

Class Top is quite compiler-dependent. Most C++ implementations generate code that is a variation on the format described here, but the user should be cautioned that a porting effort may be in order.

Class Thing

Class Thing serves as the base class for all letter classes. Because letter classes contain most of the intelligence of an application, most of the semantics of object dynamics are found in the Thing public interface. In the symbolic idiom, even some memory management functionality—which usually would be found in the envelope class—is implemented in classes under the `Thing` inheritance hierarchy.

The functions `deref` and `ref` manipulate the reference count private member, `refCountVal`. They are virtual so that derived classes can override them; however, a typical application could define them as nonvirtual, inline member functions. These functions exist principally as a notational convenience. The private member, `updateCountVal`, is used to support incremental loading, and its use is described later in this chapter.

The `cutover` function is used to convert an existing object of a given class into an object that reflects a different version of the same class. This allows for conversion of the data of existing objects from their original format to a new class format as the new version of the class is introduced into a running system. The function is usually overridden in the derived class for those occasions it is to be used; its default semantics are to just return a pointer to the original instance. Its use is described later in this chapter.

The virtual destructor is next, existing only as a handle to ensure that the proper derived class cleanup code is executed when `operator delete` is applied to an object of a derived class of `Thing`.

Symbolic Canonical Form for Application Classes

With the framework of the classes in `k.h`, we are now ready to characterize the canonical forms of application classes for use in the symbolic idiom. We use two basic kinds of classes: envelopes, which oversee object creation and assignment, and letters, which embody most of the application semantics of the system.

A given envelope class may be associated with several letter classes. Let's say that the design specifies that type `Number` be a base type for `Double`, `BigInteger`, and `Complex`. The conventional C++ approach using inheritance and virtual functions allows objects of these classes to be used interchangeably, through the `Number` interface: `Number` would be the abstract base class for the other three, and no instances of `Number` would exist. In the symbolic idiom, the user still treats objects of all number classes interchangeably, through the `Number` interface. However, `Number` just serves as an envelope for one of the letter classes `Double`, `BigInteger`, or `Complex`. These latter three letter classes are all derived from a general base class `NumericRep`, a class characterizing the signature of its derived classes: it is a "generic letter" for the numbers application. The `Number` envelope contains a pointer declared to be of type `NumericRep*`, which it uses to "hold" the letter. The generic letter class is in turn derived from class `Thing`, while the envelope (`Number`) is derived from `Top`. This structure adds the appropriate levels of indirection for powerful polymorphism and run-time update.

Note that because the letter is derived from `Thing`, and the envelope from `Top`, we cannot use a common base class for both letters and envelopes as has frequently been the case in earlier examples.

To outline the symbolic canonical form, we will use a generic example, with class `Envelope` being the envelope class and class `Letter` representing a general letter base class. A composite, consisting of one `Envelope` object and one object from among the classes derived from `Letter`, stands in for a single abstraction that can be used as a flexible program building block with the power of the symbolic idiom.

Any program or system may have many envelope classes following the canonical form of `Envelope`, and many letter classes patterned after `Letter`, each customized for its respective semantics. For example, a program may have a `Number` class patterned after `Envelope`, and a `NumericRep` class patterned after `Letter`, with classes `Complex` and others derived from `NumericRep` as described above. The same program may have class `Shape`, also patterned after `Envelope`, and a `ShapeRep` and its associated derived classes in a tree patterned after the `Letter` hierarchy. Although the `Number` and `Shape` object communities are separate, they may live in the same program, each fashioned using the symbolic idiom.

`Envelope` (Figure 9-2) generically describes a class that handles instantiation and assignment (i.e., it handles all "copying" and much of the memory allocation housekeeping); it is often useful to endow it with the full orthodox canonical form (Section 3.1) to make it a concrete data type. The envelope is somewhat like a label that can be attached to different objects. What assignment means is to associate such a label with an object; what it means to peel off the last label is to return the object to free store.

The envelope class behaves like a loosely typed abstraction, and its instances simulate variables that act like typeless labels for objects as in many symbolic languages. For example, the envelope's member functions do not convey detailed semantics of the kinds of objects it holds. However, an envelope object adopts behaviors of its letter class object using the `operator->` mechanism described in Section 3.5, just as a variable in a symbolic language adopts the behaviors of the object to which it is bound. The clue that the interface of an envelope conveys some knowledge of its letter classes is in the return type of `operator->`, namely, a `Letter*`. This is one of the few places in the symbolic idiom where a pointer is visible to the application programmer, but it is only a transitory value not normally captured by the user for later use.

The envelope class has constructors, but most explicit object initialization uses the virtual `make` functions of the letter class; as will be shown later, this is an aid to incrementality. Envelope constructors are "boilerplate" for initializations and conversions performed by the compiler. Two of these constructors come from the

```
#include "k.h"         // from above

#include "Letter.h"   // for Envelope member functions

extern Thing *envelope, *letter; // exemplar pointers

class Envelope: public Top {      // Top defined in k.h
public:
    Letter *operator->() const { // forwards all operations
        return rep;               // to rep
    }
    Envelope()      { rep = letter->make(); }
    Envelope(Letter&);
    ~Envelope() {
        if (rep && rep->deref() <= 0) delete rep;
    }
    Envelope(Envelope& x) {
        (rep = x.rep)->ref();
    }
    Envelope& operator=(Envelope& x) {
        if (rep != x.rep) {
            if (rep && rep->deref() <= 0) delete rep;
            (rep = x.rep)->ref();
        }
        return *this;
    }
    Thing *type() { return envelope; }
private:
    static void *operator new(size_t) {
        Sys_Error("heap Envelope");
    }
    static void operator delete(void *) { }
    Letter *rep;
};
```

Figure 9-2. Class Envelope

orthodox canonical form: a default (argumentless) constructor and a copy constructor. Lastly, there needs to be a conversion constructor to build a new envelope object from instances of the letter classes. This constructor converts the results of computations internal to the letter classes to objects that can be used by general clients of the envelope/letter aggregate object.

The copy constructor, assignment operator, and destructor maintain the object's reference count, as described in Section 3.5. The destructor checks its letter's reference count for zero and reclaims the letter's space if it is the last envelope to relinquish a reference to it.

Last, and perhaps most importantly, is `operator->`, which automatically forwards envelope member function calls to the letter object. The same effect would result if the envelope replicated the letters' signature, with each envelope function just forwarding control to its letter counterpart. However, that leads to a duplication of effort to add new letter class member functions.

Class `Letter` (Figures 9-3 and 9-4) defines the interface to all the classes served by the `Envelope` interface. `Letter` itself is a base class, usually an abstract base class, for a group of classes whose objects are served by the `Envelope` interface. A given `Envelope` object may serve as the interface for several different letter objects during its lifetime. For example, a `Number` object may initially be the interface to a `Complex` letter object, but assignment or another computation may cause that `Number` to replace its original letter with another object, possibly of a different class.

Objects in the `Letter` hierarchy are thought of as being inside an `Envelope` object, with only the `Envelope` object directly visible to the user. The signature of `Letter` is never accessed directly by the user. However, the `Letter` contributes its member functions to the interface of `Envelope` through the workings of `Envelope::operator->`. `Letter` does not need to be a concrete data type since the ''C''-ness of the type is handled at the `Envelope` level.

The `Letter` class serves as a base for the related application classes managed by `Envelope`. The `Envelope` class contains a `rep` field pointing to a `Letter` instance. All the ''real'' work is done in objects of classes derived from `Letter`.

All application member functions are specified in the interface of the letter class, usually as pure virtual functions. Some functions, common to all classes derived from the letter class, may be factored into the letter class itself and have bodies in the base letter class definition. Making the rest of the functions pure virtual ensures that they will be defined in the derived classes. However, we will see later in the chapter that pure virtual functions are disallowed in an extended form of this idiom incorporating properties of exemplar objects.

User-defined functions should return objects either of a built-in or concrete data type (in other words, one adhering to the orthodox canonical form), or of type `Envelope` or of type reference to `Envelope`. The only pointer types that should appear in the signature of `Envelope` are `const` pointers; returning an unprotected pointer to a dynamically allocated block of memory undermines the memory management scheme. Return value declarations may of course be of type `void`.

The `make` function constructs an instance of a class derived from `Letter`, and returns a `Letter*`, as introduced in Chapter 8. There may be several, overloaded `make` functions, each doing all the work necessary to initialize a new object; nothing

```
class Letter: public Thing {
public:
    /* all user-defined operators go here.  Note that, because
     * of the use of operator->, this signature does not have
     * to be mimicked in the Envelope.  However, the Envelope's
     * rep field has to be appropriately typed.  Assignment
     * operators do not go here, but in the Envelope.
     *
     * return_type should either be a primitive
     * type, or of type Envelope, of type Envelope&, or
     * a concrete data type
     */
    virtual void send(String name, String address);
    virtual double postage();
    virtual return_type user-defined-function;
    . . . .
    virtual Envelope make();              // constructor
    virtual Envelope make(double);        // another constructor
    virtual Envelope make(int days, double weight);
    virtual Thing *cutover(Thing*);    // run-time update function
    Letter() { }
    ~Letter() { }
    Thing *type();
protected:
    friend class Envelope;
    double ounces;
    static void *operator new(size_t l) {
        return ::operator new(l);
    }
    static void operator delete(void *p) {
        ::operator delete(p);
    }
    String name, address;
    . . . .
private:
    . . . .
};
```

Figure 9-3. Class Letter

```
/*
 * Put general inlines down here.  This is to support a
 * convention that inlines be broken out of the class
 * declaration.  Also, putting the inlines after both the
 * Envelope and Letter classes helps break some circular
 * dependencies.
 */
inline double
Letter::postage() {
    if (ounces < 2) return 29.0;
    else return 29.0 + ((ounces - 1) * 23.0);
}

inline Thing *
Letter::type() {
    extern Thing *letter;       // exemplar
    return letter;
}
```

Figure 9-4. Inline Functions of Class `Letter`

---

should be left to the constructor to initialize. For example, `Letter::make` might initialize objects of class `OverNight` and `FirstClass` like this:

```
Envelope
Letter::make(int days, double weight) {
    Letter *retval;
    if (days < 2 && weight <= 12) {
        retval = new OverNight;
    } else {
        retval = new FirstClass;
    }
    retval->ounces = weight;
    return Envelope(*retval);
}
```

If the constructor is left with no significant initialization logic, then it never needs to be edited or recompiled: that is of value in an incremental loading environment, where virtual functions (such as `make`) can be incrementally loaded, but constructors cannot.

In general, `Letter` derived classes do not need to follow the orthodox canonical form. There should be a default (parameterless) constructor and a destructor, but no copy constructor or assignment specification is needed.

The derived classes of `Letter` follow next. The `Envelope` may "contain" any of these, and if `Envelope` is designed correctly, any `Envelope` may be assigned to any other transparently. Figure 9-5 shows some simple classes derived from `Letter`. Each of these classes has a default constructor as well.

Following the exemplar idiom, each envelope class has a single, globally accessible object that serves as an exemplar; it may be created using a special constructor to differentiate it from "ordinary" application objects. It is often useful to provide an exemplar for the letter classes, so the envelope exemplar has a letter instance to reference. The letter exemplar fields object creation requests: all `make` invocations are forwarded to the letter object by the envelope's `operator->`. The letter exemplar can be a special instance of the general base letter class (here, `Letter`) if that class is not a virtual base. If it is, a special letter derived class can be constructed, with simple defaults for the pure virtual functions, to create the singleton letter exemplar object.

Classes of the symbolic canonical form are used in the same way that counted pointer and exemplar objects are used—that is, by using `->` instead of the dot operator. Here is a simple application illustrating the use of our pedagogical `Envelope` and `Letter`:

```
static Envelope envelopeExemplar;  // never used directly
Envelope *envelope = &envelopeExemplar;

int main() {
    Envelope overnighter = (*envelope)->make(1, 3.0);
    overnighter->send("Addison-Wesley", "Reading, MA");
    Envelope acrosstown = (*envelope)->make(1.0);
    overnighter = acrosstown;
    acrosstown->send("Angwantibo", "Boston Common");
    return 0;
}
```

Those are the basics of the symbolic canonical form. To underscore and expand on the motivations presented above, here are rules for using the idiom:

1. All references to an `Envelope` class should be via `->`, not through the dot notation. This allows `operator->` to forward the operations to the `Letter` class automatically.

2. Member functions of letter classes should be virtual. Virtual member functions can be incrementally loaded easily, as described in a later section in this chapter.

```
class FirstClass : public Letter {
public:
    FirstClass();
    ˜FirstClass();
    Envelope make();
    Envelope make(double weight);
    . . . .
};

class OverNight : public Letter {
public:
    OverNight();
    ˜OverNight();
    Envelope make();
    Envelope make(double weight);
    double postage() { return 8.00; }
    . . . .
};
```

Figure 9-5. Individual Application-Specific Letter Classes

3. The make member function does the work of the constructor; the constructor itself does little work. This is because we want to be able to replace a class's initialization code at run time, and only virtual functions are run-time updatable. Constructors are still present in classes derived from Thing (they are necessary for C++ virtual function setup), but they should contain **no** user-supplied code.

4. Each class should have a single permanent exemplar present in the program; the exemplar object must be able to identify itself as such (for example, by having been built with a special constructor.) The exemplar should never be accessed directly, but only through a designated pointer variable. The motivation for this will be discussed later.

5. The cutover(Thing*) member functions in subclasses of Thing are used for advanced run-time dynamic loading. These functions are passed a pointer to an object of the class to which they belong; their job is to convert the old class *in place* to accommodate format, layout, and type changes in the new class. If cutover cannot transform an object in place, it may be able to pull some tricks on a per-environment basis to make object cutover work anyhow

(i.e., to simulate the one-way BECOMES facility of Smalltalk). This will be generalized in the next section.

6. Note that a new can never be performed on an envelope class. The operator is made private, and attempts to dynamically allocate an envelope cause a compile-time error. Envelopes should be declared only as automatic variables, members of other classes, and possibly as global variables. Eliminating pointers removes the burden of remembering when to reclaim object storage, which means that even flexible, polymorphic types like Number can be used as concrete data types, just as if they were ints.

To recap where this idiom helps the software engineer: Memory management is largely automated by the envelope class, since it can keep track of when things become unreferenceable. Since access of both functions and data are deferred with an extra level of indirection, clients of this information are one step more distant from being affected by changes to the class. This means that there is less ripple effect when the class changes, and fewer things dependent on the details of the class's implementation need to be recompiled. Given the appropriate link editing and loading tools, this technique can support even incremental changes to classes in a running program, stopping the program just long enough to configure in the new class.

This approach adds another degree of polymorphism to the C++ language, providing run-time parameterized types and a sort of generic class facility. This idiom gives the illusion of changing type characteristics as late as run time. These are explained below, along with some examples.

9.3 An Example: A General Collection Class

Consider, for example, a program that wishes to use three different kinds of containers interchangeably: one based on an array with integer indices, one based on B-trees, and one based on hash tables. To do this, we define an envelope class Collection that contains a pointer to an internal object as above. For additional flexibility, the Collection is made a template so it can be instantiated to hold objects of any desired class. The declaration

```
Collection<Book, Author> library;
```

creates a collection of Book objects we wish to index by author.

The letter objects for this example are created from classes derived from CollectionRep. These classes characterize variants (see Section 7.7) of CollectionRep. Here, three variants of CollectionRep—Array, Btree,

```
#include "k.h"
#include "Collection.h"

// Store items of class T, indexed by values of class S

template<class T, class S>
    class CollectionRep: public Thing {
    public:
        virtual Collection<T, S> make();
        virtual Thing* cutover(Thing *);
        virtual T& operator[](int);
        virtual T& operator[](S);
        virtual void put(const T&);
        CollectionRep() { }
        ~CollectionRep() { }
        Thing *type();
    protected:
        friend class Collection<T, S>;
        static void *operator new(size_t l) {
            return ::operator new(l);
        }
        static void operator delete(void *p) {
            ::operator delete(p);
        }
    private:
        CollectionRep<T, S> *exemplarPointer;
    };
```

Figure 9-6. Base Class for Collection Representation Letters

and HashTable—serve as alternatives for the Collection class to use as a container object. Most of the member functions of CollectionRep and its derived classes should be virtual, so member function calls from Collection through a CollectionRep pointer are dispatched to the appropriate Array, Btree, or HashTable member function. The CollectionRep class interface must declare operations for the union of all these classes' member functions. The only letter class hierarchy operations known to Collection are those declared in CollectionRep itself. Because not all letter derived classes override all these member functions, exception handling may be needed to recover from inappropriate member function invocations. For example, an Array can be accessed only with an integer index; HashTables may use integers for indexed lookup, and character strings for associative lookup. If a Collection object currently holds an Array, then an invocation of operator[](S) should raise an exception. This is the price we pay for the flexibility of a symbolic programming style.

Figure 9-6 shows a skeleton of the declarations for `CollectionRep`, the base class of the letter classes for this example. Classes in the `CollectionRep` hierarchy use an unusual mechanism to implement the `type` member function. Since `CollectionRep` is a parametric class, each instantiation into a new class requires its own (potentially manually administered) exemplar, so the `type` member function cannot simply return a global pointer value. Instead, the exemplar's `make` operation stores away the exemplar's address inside every object it makes (in the `exemplarPointer` field), and the `type` member function simply returns that value. For example,

```
class ClassDerivedFromCollectionRep<T, S>:
    public CollectionRep<T, S> {
    . . . .
    Collection<T, S> make() {
        Collection<T, S> newObject;
        . . . .
        newObject.exemplarPointer = this;
        return newObject;
    }
    . . . .
};

Thing *CollectionRep::type() { return exemplarPointer; }
```

The `CollectionRep` class is a useful abstraction in its own right and could be directly used under another idiom. Logically encapsulating the `CollectionRep` hierarchy inside `Collection` has two advantages. First, it allows `Collection` to change its representation on demand at run time. Dynamic typing makes it possible to assign a collection of one type into a collection of another, so all collection types can be used almost interchangeably. Large collections may use size thresholds or other criteria to change their own type at run time to improve performance (for example, to convert a linear `Array` to a threaded `HashTable`). Second, the `Collection` base class `Top`, using the attributes of the envelope class's base class `Thing`, implements the transparent memory management of the exemplar idiom.

The `CollectionRep` class skeleton illustrates this concept in Figure 9-6. It inherits its reference counting mechanics from its base class, `Thing`.

Class `Collection` itself is shown in Figure 9-7. It does basic memory management—mainly, handling assignment—and otherwise forwards its operations to its letter class. It can create, or reallocate, a letter from a class of its choice, using whatever criteria it chooses. Additional constructors to `Collection` might be provided to give the user control over the data structure used for a given collection.

Subclasses of `CollectionRep` are shown in Figure 9-8. Each `Collection` that is built holds an `Array`, a `Btree`, or a `HashTable` as a letter. Each derived

```
#include "k.h"

template<class T, class S> class CollectionRep;

template<class T, class S>
    class Collection: public Top {
    public:
        CollectionRep<T, S> *operator->() const { return rep; }
        Collection();
        Collection(CollectionRep<T, S>&);
        ~Collection();
        Collection(Collection<T, S>&);
        Collection& operator=(Collection<T, S>&);
        T& operator[](int i) { return (*rep)[i]; }
        T& operator[](S s) { return (*rep)[s]; }
    private:
        static void *operator new(size_t) { return 0; }
        static void operator delete(void *p) {
            ::operator delete(p);
        }
        CollectionRep<T, S> *rep;
    };
```

Figure 9-7. A Collection Class

class overrides those member functions that make sense for what it represents, and the others are left to default to exception handling provided by the placeholders in CollectionRep. Notice that because derived classes selectively override only a subset of the base class functions, these functions cannot be declared as pure virtual in CollectionRep.

To manage storage for such objects, reference counting is generally used. Again, the classes of Section 3.5 are good examples of the application of the letter/envelope idiom as it is used for reference counting. That section shows how the assignment, constructor and destructor member functions manipulate the reference count that is a member of the contained StringRep object, and delete the object when that count falls to zero. Here, the same is true of CollectionRep. In Section 9.5, we will look at alternatives to reference counting for garbage collection.

This approach can be effectively used for an increased degree of polymorphism—for example, to take the union of two collections with arbitrary internal data structures. However, there are many pitfalls to consider. In particular, if the classes being used this way have binary operations (such as merging two collections via operator+), they must cope with the possibility that the two objects that are passed may be of different real types (for example, merging an Array and a

```
template<class T, class S>
    class Array: public CollectionRep<T, S> {
    public:
        Array();
        Array(Array<T, S>&);
        ~Array();
        class Collection<T, S> make();
        class Collection<T, S> make(int size);
        T& operator[](int i);
        void put(const T&);
    private:
        T *vec;
        int size;
    };

template<class T>
    struct HashTableElement {
        HashTableElement *next;
        T *element;
    };
template<class T, class S>
    class HashTable: public CollectionRep<T, S> {
    public:
        HashTable();
        HashTable(HashTable<T, S>&);
        ~HashTable();
        class Collection<T, S> make();
        class Collection<T, S> make(int);
        T& operator[](int i);
        T& operator[](S);
        void put(const T&);
    private:
        int nbuckets;
        virtual int hash(int l);
        HashTableElement<T> *buckets;
    };
```

Figure 9-8. Some `Collection` Implementation Classes

Btree). Design of such classes becomes quite complex, and considerable run-time overhead can be expected in figuring out what kinds of objects have been provided and invoking the right operation. (For analogous examples, see the elaborated Number example in Section 5.5 on page 140 and the discussion of Section 9.7 below.) We could theoretically define these conversions at the level of class Top or

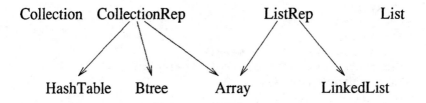

Figure 9-9. Class Hierarchy Using Multiple Inheritance

class Thing, providing full polymorphism. However, the definitions of these classes are very complex and need to be changed whenever any new object operations are added. Multiple inheritance could be used to define more than one external interface class (e.g., a class List that can be an Array or a LinkedList, sharing Array class with class Collection). Figure 9-9 shows the class hierarchy of such an example. Again, this gets complicated quickly.

9.4 Code and Idioms to Support Incremental Loading

If a system's incremental link editor is available, it is often possible to write a loader that can add new code to a running program. Figure 9-10 shows a simple load function that takes the name of a relocatable compiled object file as a parameter, loads it, and runs it. Assume that the object file incr.o contains only a single function, and that its entry point is at the base of the object file's text section. We can then load and execute that function at run time with the following invocation:

```
int main() {
    typedef void (*PF) (...);    // pointer to function
    PF anewfunc = (PF) load("incr.o");
    (*anewfunc)();
    return 0;
}
```

The program works on most Sun Microsystems platforms; the program itself must be loaded using the −n flag. Similar code can be written for most modern operating system platforms.

```
#include <a.out.h>
#include <fcntl.h>
#include <sys/types.h>
caddr_t load(const char *filename) {
    char buf[64];
    caddr_t oadx = (caddr_t)sbrk(0);
    caddr_t adx = ((char*)oadx) + PAGSIZ -
        (((char*)oadx) % PAGSIZ);
    sprintf(buf, "ld -N -Ttext %X -A a.out %s -o a.out.new",
        adx, filename);
    system(buf);
    int fd = open(filename, O_RDONLY);
    exec Exec;
    read(fd, (char *)&Exec, sizeof(exec));
    sbrk(PAGSIZ - (oadx % PAGSIZ));
    caddr_t ldadx = (caddr_t)sbrk(Exec.a_text +
        Exec.a_data + Exec.a_bss);
    read(fd, ldadx, Exec.a_text + Exec.a_data);
    close(fd);
    return ldadx;
}
```

Figure 9-10. Function to Load a Single Function .o File on Sun Platforms

We can put such loader code inside an interactive C++ program and arrange to have it load new functions at run time. When the program is at a wait state, we can compile new code and then ask the program to load in the new relocatable code. Additional work is necessary to bind function references to existing code, and then execution can continue.

☞ *When to use this idiom*: The idioms presented here describe code that can be manually or semi-automatically generated by a development environment to support incremental development. The styles can be used where it is important to be able to change a running program on the fly, often desirable in prototyping exercises. This idiom is also useful for field support of large, continuous-running software applications.

The following sections present idioms and structures that support dynamic loading of code into a running program. The problem can be split into two subproblems: the ability to load new functions, which is described first, and the ability to convert data formats of existing objects.

Loading Virtual Functions

A straightforward application of the loader is to load new versions of functions into a running program. Loading a function is easy, as was demonstrated above, if we can arrange to generate an object file containing nothing other than the new function to be loaded. Some additional work is needed to bind invocations of the existing function to use the new one, and that is what is described here.

Section 9.2 describes a table of pointers to virtual functions that is associated with each class. Furthermore, the exemplar object for any class has as its first element a pointer to that table (its vptr), as guaranteed by the symbolic canonical form. (The details may vary with different compiler implementations.) That is why all envelope classes are derived from Top: It contains the object's virtual function pointer, which can be used to address the vtbl.[1]

Administrative measures must be taken in the C++ environment to guarantee that a program contains exactly one copy of a virtual function table for each class (other than those multiply inherited from other classes). This is straightforward with some C++ compilation systems and may require some retooling in others. Look to your compiler providers to provide help and guidance in this area.

Having a handle to the virtual function descriptor table is not enough: We need to know which element of the table corresponds to the function we wish to update. It would be fortuitous if there were a table in memory mapping the names of functions onto vtbl indices; however, this is not true in most C++ implementations. So some work has to be done from *outside* the program to give the loading empire the information it needs to identify the appropriate vtbl slot.

One way to do this is to write a small *loader helper function* whose only job is to return an aggregate value characterizing the function, including its address and its virtual function table index. This function is hand-coded or automatically generated in preparation for a function update. The update proceeds in two phases. In the first phase, the helper function is loaded by the loader, and invoked to yield the vtbl index of the desired function. Second, the new copy of the function is loaded and its address linked into the right vtbl slot.

---

1. This works only for single inheritance; multiple inheritance is difficult to generalize, and is not covered here.

Before looking at the loading functions, we need to first look at some supporting data structures. First, we need a `typedef` for pointers to functions:

```
typedef int (*vptp)();
```

The `mptr` structure declares what a virtual function table entry looks like in most existing C++ implementations:

```
struct mptr {
    short d;
    short i;
    vptp f;
};
```

This declaration is used by C++ systems based on the `cfront` C++ compiler and is typical of what many systems use. Other compilers may use different structures, and the code in this chapter must be suitably tailored. The two `short`s are offsets used mainly for multiple inheritance and are not discussed here (see Ellis & Stroustrup [1]). What interests us the most is the `f` member, which points to the function for a given table entry.

The loader helper function is easy to write: All it needs to do is return the address of the existing copy of the function that is about to be replaced. Let's call it `functionAddress`; it might look like this:

```
extern vptp functionAddress() {
    // machine- and compiler-dependent code
    return (vptp)&Array::put;
}
```

Every time a function is loaded, a new copy of `functionAddress` is loaded first, either overwriting the previous version—returning the text space to a text memory manager—or leaving it as uncollected garbage if memory reclamation is not a serious concern.

The `functionAddress` function can resolve ambiguity when loading a function with an overloaded name, using suitable casts. For example, assume class `Array` had multiple `put` functions:

```
class Array {
public:
    . . . .
    void put(int, double);
    void put(int, int);
};
```

Assignment into a suitably typed left-hand side can be used to select the function whose second parameter is a `double`:

```
extern vptp functionAddress() {
    // machine- and compiler-dependent code
    typedef void ((Array::*TYPE)(int, double));
    TYPE retval = &Array::put;
    return (vptp)retval;
}
```

The next group of functions is added to the `Top` class to support incremental loading and function replacement. The first, `compareFuncs`, is used to compute whether two function descriptions designate the same function:

```
int
Top::compareFuncs(int vtblindex, vptp vtblFptr, vptp fptr) {
    // machine- and compiler-dependent code
    return vtblindex == (int)fptr;
}
```

The first pair of arguments conveys information about a virtual function table entry, the `int` is its index, and the `vptp` argument is the contents of the function pointer (the `mptr::f` member) found in that entry. The second parameter is the address of the function to be replaced. If, from the first two parameters, `compareFuncs` can determine that the function indicated is the same as the one indicated by the last argument, it returns a nonzero value. Whichever of the parameters is actually used in this comparison is implementation-dependent. Here, we know the compiler yields a virtual function's virtual table index when its address is taken, so comparison with the index parameter is all that needs to be done.

The second function is `findVtblEntry`:

```
mptr *
Top::findVtblEntry(vptp functionAddress) {
    // machine- and compiler-dependent code
    mptr **mpp = (mptr**) this;
    register mptr *vtbl = *mpp;
    for(int i = 1; vtbl[i].f; ++i ) {
        if (compareFuncs(i, vtbl[i].f, functionAddress) {
            return vtbl + i;
        }
    }
    return 0;
}
```

It simply looks in the virtual function table of the current object (pointed to by the first word in the object, its `vptr`) for an entry corresponding to the function about to be updated, which is passed as a parameter. It returns a pointer to the corresponding virtual function table entry (mptr) if such is found.

All that remains is to load and bind the new virtual function; this is coordinated by Top::update:

```
extern "C" vptp load(const char *);

void
Top::update(const char *prepname, const char *loadname) {
    vptp findfunc = load(prepname);
    mptr * vtbl = findVtblEntry((*findfunc)());
    vtbl->f = load(loadname);
}
```

It is called with the name of the file containing the loader helper function, and the name of the file containing the function to be loaded. Using previously defined functions (with load retyped to return a vptp instead of a caddr_t) it finds the virtual function table entry and replaces the function pointer field with a pointer to the newly loaded function. All following invocations of this virtual function are bound to the new version.

With a little more work, the code can accommodate the addition of new virtual functions to a class (see the exercises at the end of this chapter). However, full support for such a facility requires more sophistication in configuration management tools to preserve both semantic correctness and incrementality. For example, adding a new virtual function entails more than just growing the vtbl and ensuring that the ordering of previous entries is preserved. Consider adding a new virtual function whose name hides a previously existing global function: How do you evaluate what gets recompiled and reloaded?

Class Layout Update and the cutover Function

Broadening incremental update techniques to deal gracefully with data layout changes greatly extends the flexibility of a development or product support environment. The problem is more difficult than a function update: virtual functions afford a level of indirection not found in data. However, the letter/envelope idiom has just the extra level of data indirection we are looking for, and it can be used to effect data changes smoothly. This section describes an approach to support incremental data changes in letter classes. Since most application code lives in the letter classes, a letter class update technique handles most member data changes.

What it means to update a class's data layout, or to reload a class, is to reload its member functions; there is no code that corresponds to the class layout itself, but knowledge of the layout is distributed through the text of its operations. The previous section described how to do such incremental function loading. But reloading a class is more than just reloading all the member functions, since extant objects must be converted to the new class layout.

To support this capability, every exemplar keeps track of each object it is asked to create. This way, it can convert each of its letter class data representations when their class is changed. An exemplar can conveniently keep track of its instances using a simple, general purpose List class from a C++ library. The List object can be declared as a static member in the Exemplar's class.

The user must supply a cutover member function that knows how to convert existing objects in memory to new versions, changing their format but preserving semantics. This function, like any other function, can be independently loaded. Invoking the cutover function after loading is complete is up to the infrastructure of the application itself. The application may choose to invoke cutover when the system is in a known, quiescent state—for example, at such a time that it knows that activation records cannot possibly be open for any of the functions being updated.

Many approaches can be used to craft cutover functions, the following examples will illustrate the kinds of things that need to be done.

Adding a New Field to a Class

Adding a New Field to a Class Let's say we want to add a new field, an overflow bucket list, to our HashTable class:

```
template<class T, class S>
    class HashTable: public CollectionRep<T, S> {
    public:
        HashTable();
        HashTable(HashTable<T, S>&);
        . . . .
        Thing *cutover();
    private:
        int nbuckets;
        virtual int hash(int l);
        HashTableElement<T> *buckets;
        HashTableElement<T> *overflow;     // new
    };
```

Notice that the new datum has been added at the *end* of the class; this often has some advantage in that code compiled against the old interface can still use objects built from the new interface. It may also simplify the cutover algorithm. Note, too, that the cutover function has been overridden in the new class.

If the data layout of the original elements is unchanged by the addition of a new datum, then the cutover function is straightforward:

```
Thing *
HashTable::cutover() {
    HashTable *object = (HashTable*) this,
              *retval = new HashTable;
    // copy base class part
    (*(CollectionRep *)retval) = (*(CollectionRep *)this);
    // copy this class's fields
    retval->buckets = object->buckets;
    // initialize new fields (from old ones, if need be)
    retval->overflow = 0;
    // delete old one
    object->buckets = 0;
    delete object;
    // return new object
    return retval;
}
```

Although the changes here are made to the HashTable template itself, the template needs to be re-instantiated for each parametric use within the program. That is, each instantiation of HashTable needs to be updated separately, though the source conversion must be done only once.

Substantial Changes in Class Representation If the internals of a class are substantially reworked, then more advanced measures are necessary to update existing instances. New instances need to be forged from old ones. The cutover function needs access both to the old and new declarations of the class interface. We need to have a copy of the old class interface declaration with all appearances of the class name changed to some temporary name. Both that interface and the new one are used by the cutover function, so cutover is unrestricted in how it builds the new object from the old.

As an example, consider class Point:

```
class Point: public ShapeRep {
public:
    Shape make(double x, double y);
    void rotate(Shape& p);   // rotate about a point
private:
    double x, y;
};
```

We want to change `Point` to work in radians to take advantage of some new graphics hardware. This does not change its interface, so we can convert existing objects and still have the system work. The new class looks like this:

```
class Point: public ShapeRep {
public:
    Shape make(double r, double theta);
    void rotate(Shape& p);  // rotate about a point
    Thing *cutover();
private:
    double radius;
    Angle theta;    // easily built from a double
};
```

We recast the old header file in terms of a temporary class name, yielding the following interface. Note that `Point` is made a `friend` so that `cutover` can directly address its fields. Most of the time, `cutover` should be able to get what it needs from the public signature of the old class; however, after the update, the old functions may not be available any more!

```
class OLDPoint: public ShapeRep {
friend Point;
public:
    Shape make(double x, double y);
    void rotate(Shape& p);  // rotate about a point
private:
    double x, y;
};
```

Next, we write the `cutover` function for the new class:

```
Thing *
Point::cutover() {
    OLDPoint *old = (OLDPoint *)this;
    Point *newPoint = new Point;
    newPoint->radius = ::sqrt(old->x*old->x + old->y*old->y);
    if (::abs(old->x) < .000001) {
        newPoint->theta = ::atan(1) * 2;
    } else {
        newPoint->theta = ::atan2(old->y, old->x);
    }
    if (y < 0) newPoint->theta += ::atan(1) * 2;
    return newPoint;
}
```

Orchestrating Function Loading and Object Cutover   The application itself must orchestrate the loading and conversion activities. For example, it needs to know when it is safe to perform updates (to avoid updates in the middle of crucial computations), or it may need to get user input (to obtain the names of files containing new object code, etc.). Such "orchestration code" can be automatically generated in many applications. This section discusses some considerations for the design of such code. Using `Point` as an example, let's walk through an update.

With the source conversion of `Point` complete, all `Point` member functions need to be recompiled against the new interface. A loader helper function is written for each virtual member function of `Point`, and then the existing `Point` exemplar invokes its `Top::update` member function to load the new functions into memory. They are loaded one at a time, each paired with a helper function for the corresponding call to `Top::update`.

Now all the functions are loaded. Among the new functions is a `cutover` function to convert existing instances into their new representations. All exemplars keep track of all their living instances, so the job of converting existing objects of classes derived from the letter is straightforward. Remember letter classes are conceptually scoped within a corresponding envelope class, so we know that only one class of envelope objects can have its `rep` pointer reference any given object of a class in the letter hierarchy. The exemplar of that envelope class can track all its instances, and can investigate each in turn to see what type of letter it holds. Any such letter whose `type` member function returns a pointer to the exemplar of the letter being updated is a candidate for update. This means that it can perform the `cutover` operation on each of those objects in turn, updating the `rep` field of each so it points to a converted instance.

For example, say that we are replacing `Point`, which is derived from `ShapeRep`. The exemplar for `Shape` has a record of all `Shape` objects made; it knows that the `rep` field for each one points to some object in the `ShapeRep` hierarchy. Going through each `Shape` instance *s*, the update algorithm focuses on those for which *s.rep–>type() == point* is true, where *point* points to the `Point` exemplar. For each such *s*, it replaces the value of *s.rep* by *s.rep–>cutover*. Now, all the envelope objects will be updated to reference objects of the new class, converted from objects of the old.

One more adjustment is necessary. If multiple envelopes share the same letter, then old and new versions get confused and the conversion goes awry. We want to update each shared letter just once. To accomplish this, we put a counter in each `Thing` object that can be used to shadow a reference count. As each object is visited, the shadow counter is checked for zero (its initialized value): if it is zero, the counter is set to the value of the reference count. The shadow value is then decremented: if it is zero, then the cutover is performed; otherwise, it is skipped. So each shared letter object is converted the last time it is visited in the update scan.

Much of this orchestration can be put inside a new Thing member function named docutover:

```
int
Thing::docutover() {
    if (!updateCountVal) {
        updateCountVal = refCountVal;
    }
    return !--updateCountVal;
}
```

The Shape::dataUpdate function of Figure 9-11 orchestrates an update for data changes in classes derived from ShapeRep, the letter base class. Its parameters are the exemplar pointer for the letter class being updated, and a pointer to an exemplar that is to take its place. After executing the algorithm described above, it also updates the exemplar object, leaving the program completely changed to reflect a newly loaded version of the class. The dataUpdate function assumes that the virtual functions for the new version of the class have been previously loaded.

Incremental Loading and Autonomous Generic Constructors

Incremental loading is an effective tool when used with the autonomous generic constructors described in Section 8.3. Autonomous generic constructors allow specialized exemplars (e.g., Number, Name, Punctuation) to register themselves with a more abstract general exemplar (Atom), which we call an *autonomous generic exemplar*. The registrants are usually derived from the class of the autonomous generic exemplar. The autonomous generic exemplar serves as the agent for all its registrants; the set of registrants can change over the life of the program.

With incremental loading, we can add new derived classes during the life of the program, create exemplars for them and register them with the abstract base exemplar as they appear. So, for example, we could add classes BinaryOp and UnaryOp to the parser of a running system, create exemplar objects for them using the appropriate constructor, and register those new exemplars with class Atom. The system would thereafter accept and parse binary and unary operator expressions in new strings from its user interface, incoming data links, or wherever the Atom exemplar is used for syntactic analysis.

```
typedef Thing *Thingp;
void
Shape::dataUpdate(Thingp &oldExemplar,
                  const Thingp newExemplar) {
    Thing *saveRep;
    Shape *sp;
    for (Listiter<Shape*> p = allShapes;
         p.next(sp);  p++) {
        if (sp->rep->type() == &oldExemplar) {
            if (p->rep->docutover()) {
                saveRep = sp->rep;
                sp->rep = (ShapeRep*)sp->rep->cutover();
                delete saveRep;
            }
        }
    }
    saveRep = oldExemplar;
    oldExemplar = newExemplar;
    delete saveRep;
}
```

Figure 9-11. Example Code Controlling a Full Class Update Cycle

9.5 Garbage Collection

A popular property of symbolic programming environments is that they free programmers from the burden of managing memory: unreferenced objects are automatically reclaimed by the run-time environment (with help from the operating system, the hardware, or both). This is called *garbage collection*. Garbage collection gives the illusion of an infinitely large storage space, so application programmers can just forget about objects that have served their purpose and are no longer needed. If the system can determine that an object is unreachable from anywhere else in memory, then its space can be reclaimed and made available for later allocation requests. The mechanics and timing of an object's reclamation are transparent to the end user.

The reference counting idioms presented in Section 3.5 are a weak form of garbage collection. In particular, the counted pointer idiom (page 65) offers the level of memory management transparency found in symbolic environments. However, reference-counted reclamation algorithms cannot reclaim memory for circularly referential data structures unless they employ expensive recursive scanning techniques. The garbage collection schemes employed by high-level object-oriented programming environments avoid this limitation, and therefore seldom use reference counting. The garbage collection idiom described in this section is an alternative to reference-counted techniques.

Non-reference-counted techniques also have advantages for real-time embedded systems, where exceptional events such as memory or processor failure may trigger levels of application recovery where memory resources cannot be easily reclaimed. If a process goes insane and needs to be killed, it may not get the chance to execute its destructors. If that process shares reference-counted objects with other processes, then those objects' reference counts never go to zero and the objects are never reclaimed. Scavenging acts as a memory resource audit that is more resilient in light of these failures, in terms of its ability to return more unusable resources to a free pool than reference counting can.

Most symbolic programming environments hide garbage collection details in the implementation of the compiler and run-time support environment. Although some early Smalltalk environments used reference-counted memory reclamation algorithms, application programmers wrote no reference-counting code. This can be contrasted with the C++ approach described in Section 3.5, where memory management was implemented as an idiom within the language instead of as an algorithm hidden *inside* the compiler and environment. Some garbage collection schemes rely on specialized hardware to tell whether a word in memory is an active pointer to an object, or just a piece of data. Whether through compiler support, operating system facilities, or specialized hardware, symbolic language memory management is handled at a level below source code written by application programmers. Such transparency is usually implied when the term "garbage collection" is used. C++ is so close to the machine that there is no level "underneath" to accommodate a completely transparent and general garbage collection mechanism. By adhering to simple conventions and providing code that establishes an environment for garbage collection, C++ programs can provide largely transparent garbage collection for selected classes.

The technique described here is equally transparent to the reference counting approach of Section 3.5, but separates the reclamation of object storage from its "unbinding" from its last reference; however, it does not reclaim circularly referential structures. Its real-time performance is a little worse than that of reference counting, though the magnitude of the comparison varies with patterns of usage and implementation details. Variations on the technique presented here support incremental garbage collection, so normal processing does not have to be suspended for long periods of time to reclaim memory. And, unlike conventional garbage collectors, this one allows the programmer to associate some activity with the reclamation of an object: The garbage collector can invoke destructors to clean up reclaimed objects.

Several algorithms have been developed for garbage collection. One early approach was *mark-and-sweep* [2]: all objects in memory are analyzed to see what other objects they reference, and the referenced objects are marked. After all objects have been processed, another pass is made to discard unmarked objects.

Semispace copying is a technique that guarantees complete cleanup of unreferenced objects, as well as cleanup of communities of objects that have no clients external to themselves. The prototypical implementation of semispace copying, Baker's algorithm [3], avoids the impractical delays incurred by mark-and-sweep at the expense of memory space. In Baker's algorithm, memory is divided into half A and half B. The A space is usually called the "to space," and B the "from space," for reasons that will become clear below. New objects are created in half A. At some point in time (such as when half A fills up or the system is idle), all reachable objects in half A are compacted into one end of half B. Pointers to one object from another are adjusted to reflect the relocation. At that time, A is known to contain no reachable objects: it is all "garbage." The roles of A and B are reversed, and processing continues for another cycle.

Baker's algorithm (and most non-reference-counted garbage techniques) relies on being able to differentiate between data values and object references (pointers) in memory. It is impossible to look at an arbitrary word in C++ memory and determine if it is being used as a pointer or an integer. A recent family of garbage collection techniques have been published that do *almost* complete garbage collection using techniques based on mark-and-sweep. These garbage collectors may fail to reclaim memory because of *pointer aliasing*, the appearance of a data value in memory whose contents coincide with the address of an object, though the value represents an integer quantity or something else unrelated to its interpretation as an object address. However, these algorithms do not leave dangling references as long as the programmer follows reasonable conventions. For an example of such an algorithm, see Caplinger [4].

However, in the constrained world of symbolic envelopes and letters, we *can* identify all the objects of a given envelope class (by looking in the list in its exemplar), so we can find all references to any given letter class. If we change the letter class memory allocation algorithm to use a fixed pool (Section 3.6), then the types of all objects in the pool are known (they are all of the same type). We also know every possible address where we might find an object of the letter class, so there is hope of marking those that are used and cleaning up the rest. Because the objects in a class pool are all of the same size, we do not need to worry about memory fragmentation; the tradeoff is that the amount of memory used by the objects of each garbage-collected class must be preengineered.

☞ *When to use this idiom*: Use garbage collection to relieve users from concerns about memory management—for example, to support a rapid prototyping environment. Garbage collection is also a powerful technique to audit systems with real time exceptions. It helps guarantee that all memory resources are reclaimed even in light of exceptional circumstances.

Using `Triangle` as an example, let's consider an approach to garbage collection for the symbolic envelope/letter idiom. To support this technique, the letter base class `ShapeRep` must be augmented with a "mark" bit that can be checked off to designate the object as "reachable" as the algorithm executes. These objects also need an "in use" bit that designates whether the space is free for use; this bit could also be put to use by `ShapeRep::operator new` to find unused space to satisfy an object creation request. Initially, all "in use" and "mark" bits are reset; when an object is allocated, the "in use" bit is set as well. In addition to these bits, each object has A and B bits that correspond to the object being in the A and B spaces of the Baker algorithm.

An Example: Geometric Shapes with Garbage Collection

Appendix E presents an example of a shape-drawing package using the symbolic idioms described in this chapter. It demonstrates the incremental loading capabilities described earlier in this chapter, and uses an advanced form of garbage collection. The garbage collection technique is not based on reference counting, but it is in the spirit of mark-and-sweep and Baker's algorithm.

The garbage collection algorithm examines the objects listed in the `Shape` exemplar's list of extant objects, looking at the `rep` field of each to see if it points to a `Triangle` object (by applying the `type` member function and checking its return value for equality with the address of the `Triangle` exemplar). For each such object that it finds, it sets the "mark" bit. That pass complete, the algorithm steps through the fixed vector from which `Triangle` objects are allocated, looking for those whose "mark" bit is not set. If an object's "mark" bit and "in use" bit are both reset, then the `Triangle` destructor is called to clean up that object, and its "in use" bit is reset. Lastly, the object's "mark" bit is reset to prepare for the next garbage collection cycle.

This algorithm would be cycled to process all `Triangle` objects, followed by all `Line` objects, then all `Circle` objects, and so on, until all classes derived from `ShapeRep` had been covered, and then the sequence would restart. At a higher level, the algorithm would be applied for each application area (e.g., `Shapes`, `Collections`, and others) in turn. The scheduling of the reclamation cycles would be done by the run-time environment, and may need to be tuned for each application. Use of the Baker techniques even makes it possible to do garbage reclamation incrementally (see the exercises at the end of this chapter).

We can take a look at the details of the implementation of the algorithm in Appendix E. The class structure is as described above, with the inheritance hierarchy shown in Figure 9-12. All the detailed implementation is in classes derived from `ShapeRep`, while all the user perceives is instances of `Shape`.

Some global data structures are initialized by the static member function `Shape::init`. This initialization is done through explicit coding, rather than through the default mechanisms provided with the C++ environment, so that the order of initialization can be controlled. `Shape::init` first initializes two list objects, one named `allShapes`, which tracks the creation of all `Shape` instances, and another named `allShapeExemplars`, which tracks all exemplar objects created for classes derived from `ShapeRep`.

`Shape::init` next invokes the `init` operation on each of the classes derived from `ShapeRep`, which in turn construct their respective exemplar objects. Each exemplar logs its creation with `Shape` through `Shape::register`, which stores a pointer to each exemplar in the `allShapeExemplars` list. This is why it is important for `Shape`'s lists to be initialized before exemplar initialization takes place. The drawback of this initialization scheme is that `Shape` must have compile-time knowledge of the existence of all `ShapeRep` derived classes.

Initialization done, the user can generate a request to create a `Shape`, using the autonomous generic constructor idiom:

```
Shape object = (*shape)->make(p1, p2, p3);
```

The `make` operation is invoked on the `Shape` exemplar, yielding an object that conforms to the user-supplied parameters. The user supplies a set of points that define the shape and may supply an exemplar pointer if the number of points alone does not unambiguously specify a shape—for example, two points may define a rectangle or a line segment, so a third parameter is necessary to specify which should be chosen. The default for three points is a triangle, which will result from the above invocation.

Notice that the above invocation of `make` could alternatively be expressed as

```
shape->operator->()->make(p1, p2, p3)
```

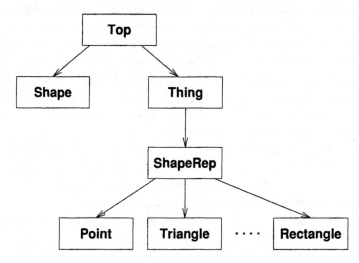

Figure 9-12. Symbolic Shapes Class Structure

That is, the `Shape` exemplar yields its internal representation pointer, which points to a `ShapeRep` instance, as the operand to which `make` is applied. In the envelope/letter idiom of Section 5.5, all memory management—including `make` operations—was handled by the envelope. Here, we manage memory from within the letter. Because `make` is a virtual function in the letter class, a new version of it can be incrementally loaded using the techniques described earlier in this chapter.

This invocation calls `ShapeRep::make`, which is an overloaded function. There are two kinds of `make` functions in `ShapeRep`. The first is called with an exemplar pointer for the desired type of object, along with coordinates specifying the details of the object representation. The second takes only coordinates as parameters and makes a reasonable default assumption about what kind of shape is desired; it simply calls the more general `make` function with the appropriate parameters. Using the above invocation, it is the second kind of `make` function that is invoked:

```
Shape ShapeRep::make(Coordinate pp1, Coordinate pp2,
        Coordinate pp3) {
    return make(pp1, pp2, pp3, triangle);
}
```

This in turn invokes

```
Shape ShapeRep::make(Coordinate pp1, Coordinate pp2,
        Coordinate pp3, Thingp type) {
    return ((ShapeRep*)type)->make(pp1, pp2, pp3);
}
```

which in turn causes an invocation of `Triangle::make` with the three specified vertices as parameters:

```
Shape Triangle::make(Coordinate pp1, Coordinate pp2,
        Coordinate pp3) {
    Triangle *retval = new Triangle;
    retval->p1 = pp1;
    retval->p2 = pp2;
    retval->p3 = pp3;
    retval->exemplarPointer = this;
    return *retval;
}
```

This make function first requests a new `Triangle` object using new. That object is then filled in with the the appropriate data for the triangle vertices. The object's `exemplarPointer`—that is, its type field—is filled in to point to this, which points to the triangle exemplar (this in this context has the same value as the global triangle exemplar pointer, `triangle`). Lastly, the `return` statement passes the new object back to the caller. The `return` causes the `Shape` constructor `Shape(ShapeRep&)` constructor to be called to convert to the proper return type.

When `Triangle::make` calls new to get a new `Triangle` object, `Triangle`'s own `operator new` is invoked:

```
void *Triangle::operator new(size_t nbytes) {
    if (poolInitialized - nbytes) {
        gcCommon(nbytes, poolInitialized, PoolSize, heap);
        poolInitialized = nbytes;
    }
    Triangle *tp = (Triangle*) heap;
    while (tp->inUse) {
        tp = (Triangle*)(((char*)tp) + Round(nbytes));
    }
    tp->gcmark = 0;
    tp->inUse = 1;
    return (void*) tp;
}
```

`Triangle::operator new` returns a pointer to an available `Triangle` object-sized block of memory from the pool of `Triangles`. On the first time through, the `poolInitialized` variable is zero; it was initialized at compile time. The comparison with nbytes, which has value `sizeof(Triangle)`, will show a difference, causing `ShapeRep::gcCommon` to be called. This routine is used both for garbage collection and, as a special case, for initialization of memory pools at program startup or when class cutover takes place. Among other things, the initialization phase of `gcCommon` gives initial values to all the memory allocation bits in the pool. On return from `gcCommon`, the `new` operator steps through the blocks in the `Triangle` memory pool (pointed to by `Triangle::heap`) looking for a block whose `inUse` bit is reset; it returns the first one it finds. Code to handle freelist exhaustion is left as a proverbial exercise to the reader.

All newly allocated `Shape` objects follow the same pattern. Initialization of a new `Shape` from an existing one, or assignment of one shape to another, invokes the appropriate overloaded constructor or assignment operator:

```
Shape::Shape(Shape &x) {
    Thing tp = this;
    allShapes->put(tp);
    rep = x.rep;
}

Shape& Shape::operator=(Shape &x) {
    rep = x.rep;
    return *this;
}
```

Multiple `Shape` objects may therefore point to a common object of a class derived from `ShapeRep`.

Following the counted pointer idiom (page 65), no `Shape` objects are allocated from the heap; that just prevents worrying about having to deallocate them. Any `Shape` object allocated as an automatic cleans up after itself when it goes out of scope. Any `Shape` that is a class member is cleaned up when any object of that class is cleaned up. `Shapes` of global extent are cleaned up at program termination. We still must worry about reclaiming the storage for, and cleaning up after, objects of classes derived from `ShapeRep`. That's where the garbage collector comes in.

Garbage collection can be invoked at any time. In the example in Appendix E, it is invoked manually at several points in the program. A more transparent though costly approach would be to invoke garbage collection every time a new object was allocated. Another strategy would be to reclaim unused memory only when `operator new` is unable to find any free entries. The garbage collection phases can even be split up across time to do incremental memory reclamation in a real-time environment, if large real-time breaks for garbage collection are an issue (see the exercises at the end of this chapter). Garbage collection is orchestrated by `Shape::gc`, which does the mark phase itself and which delegates the sweep phase to the individual letter objects:

```
void Shape::gc() {
    Listiter<Topp> shapeIter = *allShapes;
    for (Topp tp = 0;  shapeIter.next(tp); ) {
        ((Shape*)tp)->rep->mark();
    }
```

```
Listiter<Thingp> shapeExemplarIter = *allShapeExemplars;
for (Thingp anExemplar = 0;
        shapeExemplarIter.next(anExemplar); ) {
    ShapeRep *thisExemplar = (ShapeRep*) anExemplar;
    thisExemplar->gc(0);
}
}
```

The first loop goes through *every* extant `Shape` object and sets its "mark" bit, through the `mark` member function. All objects of classes derived from `ShapeRep`, that are referenced by an existing `Shape`, are thus marked. The second loop goes to each exemplar for the letter classes—there is one such exemplar for each class derived from `ShapeRep`—and lets it process the sweep phase of the algorithm.

Since each `ShapeRep` derived class exemplar manages its own memory pool from which all its dynamic objects are allocated, each such class can easily locate and scan all its dynamically allocated instances. In the `Shape` example here, the pool is a contiguous block of memory; however, it is necessary only that the exemplar be able to trace all its instances.

The sweep work is done by a static, common routine in `ShapeRep` named `gcCommon` (Figure 9-13). The routine is passed the number of bytes per object (`nbytes`), the number of bytes known to be in each object on the last garbage collection pass (`poolInitialized`), the number of objects in the pool (`PoolSize`), and a reference to a pointer to the arena (`heap`). These parameters can be provided from a simple `gc` routine in the derived class, which in turn can be called from `Shape` with no parameters.

As alluded to before, `ShapeRep::gcCommon` performs both a memory arena initialization function and a memory reclamation function. The garbage collection logic is in the zero branch of the case statement inside the loop. This logic saves objects that have been marked, or that are already in "to space," per the Baker algorithm. The space membership check is not critical in the implementation as shown, but is important if incremental memory reclamation is to be done as alluded to earlier. Objects that are unmarked in "from space" are reclaimed: their in-use bit is zeroed, returning them to the pool for future use by `operator new`.

Note that we have tied object cleanup (destructor invocation) to memory reclamation (garbage collection). Object cleanup is a semantic action related to the application, and garbage collection reclaims one particular resource that happens to be interesting and worrisome in many applications: namely, memory. It is possible to separate these two operations (Section 3.7), but then programmers are burdened with manually finalizing the objects after determining they should no longer be used, but before the garbage collector reclaims them. For example, if an object carries a file

```
void
ShapeRep::gcCommon(size_t nbytes, const size_t poolInitialized,
        const int PoolSize, Char_p &heap) {
    size_t s = nbytes? nbytes: poolInitialized;
    size_t Sizeof = Round(s);
    ShapeRep *tp = (ShapeRep *)heap;
    for (int i = 0; i < PoolSize; i++) {
        switch (nbytes) {
        case 0:    // normal garbage collection case
            if (tp->inUse) {
                if (tp->gcmark || tp->space != FromSpace) {
                    // don't sweep it away
                    tp->space = ToSpace;
                } else if (tp != tp->type()) {
                    // object needs to be reclaimed
                    tp->ShapeRep::~ShapeRep();
                    tp->inUse = 0;
                    printf("ShapeRep::gcCommon ");
                    printf("Reclaimed Triangle object %c\n",
                      'A' + (((char *)tp-(char *)heap)/Sizeof));
                }
            }
            break;
        default:    // initialization of memory arena
            tp->inUse = 0;
            break;
        }
        tp->gcmark = 0;
        tp = (ShapeRep*)(Char_p(tp) + Sizeof);
    }
}
```

Figure 9-13. Per-Type Sweep Phase for Memory Reclamation

descriptor for an open UNIX file, reclaiming the object's memory resources alone is not enough to reclaim the resources associated with the file. To avoid this user-level housekeeping, the two functions are unified here.

This approach assumes the user can afford to defer finalization for an indefinite period. To elicit finalization, the user can invoke the garbage collector immediately after relinquishing the last reference to an object.

9.6 Primitive Type Encapsulation

In most symbolic environments, instances of *every* data type are objects, as contrasted with C++ where some types close to the machine—int, char, long, short, and so forth—are more primitive than full class objects. We may want to use objects of these types as if they had the flexibility of symbolic types: For example, we want them to be garbage collected. We want to be able to do the same for concrete data types as well: classes that have all the flexibility of "real" types, but which have not yet been endowed with the properties of symbolic types.

For each primitive type that is to be used in the symbolic environment, we can make a new class that acts as a wrapper around it, and so build up a library of classes that parallel their primitive counterparts. Though tedious to set up, such types are not conceptually difficult to create. An example is the Number collection of classes described in Section 5.5. With minor changes to the Number code based on envelopes and letters—mainly, deriving the appropriate classes from Top and Thing—fully polymorphic, garbage-collected numbers can be used where int, double, long and the like were used with more conventional idioms.

The main challenge of incorporating indigenous types in the symbolic idiom is how to place them in the inheritance hierarchy. The Number example is intended to subsume the functionality of all numeric types, but at the expense of not distinguishing between double and float, or between char and int and unsigned int and others. Should String be a symbolic type in its own right, as was assumed in Chapter 3, or should it be placed under ArrayedCollection, under SequenceableCollection, under Collection, after the Smalltalk hierarchy? As emphasized in Chapter 6, these decisions should be driven by analysis of the application and the application domain.

9.7 Multi-Methods under the Symbolic Idiom

Consider for a moment what it means to perform addition on two number objects, particularly when the operands are of different types. The traditional way of handling this has been for the compiler type system to know enough to arrange for type conversion. But that approach breaks down with dynamic run-time typing, so another solution is needed for symbolic programming. Assume every number appears to the programmer as an instance of a Number class, with invisible letter classes such as

Complex and BigInteger. The Number objects change type characteristics at run time, so the compiler does not have enough type information to generate type conversion code. The conversion, and selection of the right addition operation, must be done at run time.

How do we select the algorithm to add a given pair of numbers? One possibility is to give the job arbitrarily to the first number. Another way of saying that is that the operator+ selected is based on the type of the first operand; that's exactly what would happen if we used virtual functions. But that burdens each type with knowledge about all types that might be added to it, and the numeric types become less autonomous, self-contained, and independent.

We ideally would like to select an algorithm based on the types of *both* operands. C++ virtual functions do not support this, but some symbolic program languages do. Using the types of multiple operands to choose a member function or operator at run time is called a *multi-method* in object-oriented programming languages embedded in Lisp.

Simulating multi-methods in C++ requires idioms based on an object type field as described in Chapter 4. Type fields are ordinarily discouraged; virtual functions are the preferred mechanism to select between variant derived class implementations. We will discuss below why virtual functions are not a suitable solution.

In Section 5.6 (page 175), we saw the definition of an operator on class LPF, a low-pass filter:

```
Value *
LPF::operator()(Value *f) {
    switch (f->type()) {
    case T_Data:
        myType = T_Data;
        cachedInput = f;
        return evaluate();
    case T_LPF:
        if (f->f1() > f1()) return this;
        else return f;
    case T_HPF:
        if (f->f1() > f1()) return new Notch(f1(), f->f1());
        else return new BPF(f->f1(), f1());
    case T_BPF:
        if (((Filter*)f)->f2() < f1()) return f;
        else return new BPF(f->f1(), f1());
    case T_Notch:
        cachedInput = f;
        return this;
    }

}
```

It was noted at that point that this case analysis could be transformed into a collection of virtual functions definitions. That would cause public virtual functions to proliferate as the number of filter types grew, and would not simplify the code anyhow.

The semantics of `Filter::operator()(Value*)` are to return a value or one of several different kinds of filters, depending on context. The context includes the type of filter for which the member function is invoked, *and* the type of the object passed as a parameter. That is, there is an input filter, and an output filter, and the types of both determine which algorithm should be applied, and what type of result is produced. In the example in Section 5.6, the logic to parcel out the work is distributed through the derived classes of `Filter`. As in the code for class `LPF` above, this work is distributed into the output filters. If a virtual function approach were taken, and `Filter::operator()(Value* input)` simply called a member function of the input filter to do the job, then the intelligence to handle the operation would be in the input filters.

Neither of these approaches is totally satisfying. We want to handle these requests as hybrid operations that do not belong solely to one class or the other. This is reminiscent of `friend` functions, using global overloading, as described in Section 3.3:

OLD:	NEW:
	`Complex operator+(Complex c,`
	`    Imaginary i) { . . . . }`
`class Complex:`	`class Complex {`
`public:`	`friend Complex operator+(`
`   Complex operator+(Imaginary);`	`    Complex, Imaginary);`
`   operator double();`	`public:`
`   . . . .`	`    operator double();`
`   . . . .`	`    . . . .`
`};`	`};`

Here, the operator is chosen at compile time from the *declared* types of the arguments; there is no direct way to choose a function at run time based on the *actual* types of the arguments. That is what we want multi-methods to do.

Let's look first at the `Number` class as a simple example, and in particular at the addition operator. To implement the multi-method `operator+`, we take advantage of the commutativity of addition, cutting the number of special cases in half. For the type field, we use the virtual function `Top::type`. Though it is a virtual function, it acts as a public, enumerated class type field.

We start by adding a new member function to class `Number` and each of its derived classes: `isA(const Top *const)`. This function returns true when invoked on an object of class *A* with an argument pointing to an object of class *B* if it is true that *B* IS-A *A*. This is used to determine which of two operands is the more general, and therefore which gains control of the operation.

We also add a single `promote` member function, which replaces the conversion operators of earlier examples. The `promote` member function converts an argument of any `Number` type, to the type of the object for which `promote` is invoked. Given that `promote` is called to perform all conversions, it is no longer necessary to overload addition in the signature of each envelope class; each class has a single `add` function. (The name is changed to `add` from `operator+` to avoid ambiguity introduced by a new `operator+` below.) Nor is it necessary to switch on the type of the parameter passed, since each envelope's `add` member function can assume it always receives a parameter of its class's own type:

```cpp
class Number {
public:
    . . . .
    virtual Number *type() const;
    virtual int isA(const Number *const) const;
    virtual Number promote(const Number&) const;
    virtual Number add(const Number&) const;
    friend Number operator+(const Number&, const Number&) const,
    . . . .
};

class Complex: public Number {
public:
    . . . .
    int isA(const Number *const n) const {
        return n->type() == complexExemplar;
    }
    Number promote(const Number& n) const {
        // always returns a Complex
        if (n.type() == imaginaryExemplar) {
            return Number(0, n.magnitude());
        } else if (n.type() == integerExemplar) {
            return Number(n.magnitude(), 0);
        } else . . . .
            . . . .
    }
    // this operator must deal only with Complexes
    Number add(const Number&) const;
};
```

```
class Imaginary: public Complex {
public:
    . . . .
    int isA(const Number *const n) const {
        return n->type() == imaginaryExemplar ||
            Complex::isA(n);
    }

    // no promote:  nothing is promoted to an Imaginary

    // this operator must deal only with Imaginaries

    Number add(const Number&) const;
};
```

We provide multi-methods by adding a globally overloaded `operator+` that the compiler applies to the definition of any two Numbers:

```
Number operator+(const Number &n1, const Number &n2)
    throw(NumberTypeError)
{
    if (n1.isA(&n2)) {
        Number temporary = n2.promote(n1);
        return n2.add(temporary);
    } else if (n2.isA(&n1)) {
        Number temporary = n1.promote(n2);
        return n1.add(temporary);
    } else {
        throw NumberTypeError();
    }
}
```

Note that this offers some advantages over the approach in Section 5.5 on page 140. Member functions are more cohesive: All the promotions to a given type are localized, and all binary arithmetic operators work on operands of homogeneous types (there is no need to overload the operators). There are no longer `switch` statements in the definition of the class member functions.

The approach outlined here approximates that followed by symbolic languages. In some Smalltalk implementations, specific numeric classes directly handle arithmetic operations if both operands are of the same type. If the types do not agree, then the message is handed off to Number to handle the necessary conversions and promotions, and eventually to dispatch the right subclass method. What was presented as a globally overloaded

```
operator+(const Number&, const Number&)
```

above, would be

```
Number::operator+(const Number&)
```

if we were to follow that Smalltalk scheme (and there is no harm in doing that). Some Lisp environments implement multi-methods as cascades of virtual function calls, dynamically finding a path to a method determined by the types of multiple arguments.

Exercises

1. Change `Top::update`, and other code as necessary, so that *new* virtual functions can be added to a letter class. Keep in mind that the original `vtbl` for a class is statically allocated in memory. Assume that the compilation environment can arrange to sort entries for new functions to the bottom of the `vtbl`. What limitations does this imply for inheritance from letter classes and how virtual functions can be added to them?

2. Add a member function `Thing::backout(Thing*)` that causes a class to revert to the data layout and virtual member functions it had previous to the most recent update.

3. Modify the program of Appendix E so that garbage collection is performed for every new object allocation.

4. To spread out garbage collection over time, change the garbage collection algorithm of Appendix E so that any single invocation of `Shape::gc` will cause collection of garbage from only one derived class of `ShapeRep`.

5. To make the garbage collection even more incremental, arrange for `Shape::gc` to relinquish control in the middle of marking of objects, with subsequent calls to gc picking up where the marking was left off. Hints: do the mark phase indivisibly, and split the work of the sweep phase over several invocations. Successive sweeps resume at the point in the memory pool where the previous one left off. Swap the roles of the A and B spaces only after the entire sweep phase is complete. What combination of the states of the `inUse`, `gcmark`, and `space` fields should trigger reclamation of an object?

6. Repeat the previous exercise, except arrange for the postponement of the sweep phase of the Baker algorithm instead of the mark phase.

7. Combine the previous two exercises into a single strategy.

8. Write a memory allocation system where all classes of the same size share the same memory pool and are managed under the same garbage collection cycle. The mapping of classes onto pools should be done at run time.

9. *Generation scavenging* [5] is a garbage collection technique that maintains separate memory pools for objects segregated by age. Pools containing young objects are scavenged more frequently than pools for old objects, based on the observation that young objects have a higher probability of imminent mortality than old objects do. Write a generation scavenging algorithm replacing the single class memory pool with pools for three different generations. Determine suitable object ages (measured in mark/sweep cycle counts) for each of the generations.

10. Rewrite the Number classes in Section 5.5 following the constructs of the symbolic idiom.

11. Write a symbolic String class based on the String of Section 3.5.

□

References

1. Ellis, Margaret A., and B. Stroustrup. *The Annotated C++ Reference Manual.* Reading, Mass.: Addison-Wesley, 1990, sect. 10.5.

2. McCarthy, J. "Recursive Functions of Symbolic Expressions and Their Computation by Machine," *Communications of the ACM 3* (1960), 184.

3. H. G. Baker, "List Processing in Real Time on a Serial Computer," A.I. Working Paper 139, MIT-AI Lab, Boston (April 1977).

4. Caplinger, Michael. "A Memory Allocator with Garbage Collection for C," *USENIX Association Winter Conference*, (February 1988), 325-30.

5. Ungar, David. "Generation Scavenging: A Non-Disruptive High Performance Storage Reclamation Algorithm." *SIGPLAN Notices 19*,5 (May 1984).

10

Dynamic Multiple Inheritance

The main purpose of inheritance in C++ is to capture the relationship between two similar application abstractions, where one is a specific case of the other. Inheritance structures can be viewed as classification trees. These trees are usually strict hierarchies, because our mind naturally imposes a hierarchical organization on complex systems.

There are times when we want to view a class as inheriting properties from multiple parents. An object may take on aspects of multiple roles at the same time. For example, we might combine the behaviors of a window designed for text editing (EditWindow) with behaviors of a specific window technology (XWin or MSWindow), yielding a new class combining the behaviors of both parents.

C++ supports static multiple inheritance—that is, the ability of a class to inherit behaviors from multiple base classes. However, the inheritance structure is fixed at compile time and many real-world examples suggest that run-time context is necessary to determine how multiple classes should be combined to create a new class to serve an application. For example, if a system contains a "kit" of different Window classes, we might want to create the appropriate derived class of Window on-the-fly and then instantiate it. After looking at command line options or other data available in the environment, a program might want to mix together an EditWindow and an XWin window in one case, and an EditWindow and a MSWindow in another. The alternative would be to pre-declare all possible class combinations at compile time, with the program choosing from among the available classes to build a window at run time. The combinatorial explosion of classes resulting from all possible combinations of window types can lead to an unnecessarily complex and tedious software architecture.

Multiple inheritance has been proposed as a mechanism for objects that play different roles during their lifetime. Consider a class `SeaPlane`, which is derived from `Plane` and `Boat`;[1] such an example is often cited as a justification for the use of multiple inheritance (see page 163). However, the resulting `SeaPlane` abstraction does not at any given time display a combination of the behaviors of its parents; it takes on the role of a plane while in the air, and a boat while in the water. Static multiple inheritance does not capture this relationship properly. Consider, for example, that the classes `Plane` and `Boat` have a member function called `mpg`, which returns the vehicle's miles per gallon figure. (Or assume that both of these classes are in turn derived from `Vehicle`, which itself has a pure virtual `mpg` function.) This `mpg` member function for `SeaPlane` must ascertain the role being played by the object at the time it is called, and choose between the `mpg` member functions of its `Boat` part and its `Plane` part to compute its own result. Managing inheritance dynamically is an intuitively more satisfying solution.

☞ *When to use this idiom*: Use the dynamic multiple inheritance idiom when decisions about an object's type properties must be deferred until run time, when there are multiple parent classes involved. Dynamic multiple inheritance is weakly analogous to the mix-ins concept found in object-oriented programming languages embedded in Lisp.

So multiple inheritance hierarchies are needed, and there is a need to give the illusion of building and modifying such hierarchies at run time. Through an example, this chapter will present one way to simulate dynamic multiple hierarchies using tricks that can be isolated to the internals of classes in the hierarchy. Ordinary C++ class derivation, virtual functions, and the envelope/letter idiom are the tricks that are combined to make limited dynamic multiple inheritance possible.

As a note of history, this technique was originally applied to provide multiple inheritance in early versions of C++ before multiple inheritance was part of the language.

---

1. Thanks and a tip of the hat to Tom Cargill and Andrew Koenig for this example.

10.1 An Example: A Multi-Technology Window System

The example in Figure 10-1 is taken from the multiple inheritance example in Chapter 3 (page 179). As in the original example, the idea is that an object of class CursesWindow or XWindow can be instantiated and then used throughout the editor as though it were of class Window. Other C++ programs could be written to use the portable Window interface.

Though one goal is to provide a general Window facility for use by many programs, it is also desirable to tailor class Window to the needs of an editor. An EditWindow is a Window with attributes peculiar to an editor: knowledge of the source line numbers of the first and last lines on the screen, the ability to handle line wrap-around, and so forth. EditWindow should be a derived class of Window but should also behave like a CursesWindow or an XWindow as appropriate. How do we set up the derivation?

We can consider several approaches to this problem. One would be to generate the full combinatorial explosion of classes resulting from combining those discussed above:

EditCursesWindow	EditXWindow
EditWindow	CursesWindow
XWindow	Window

These classes could be generated either by using static multiple inheritance or by embedding objects of one class inside another to perform services on its behalf. This seems unpleasant and inflexible for the addition of either new window technology classes or other new window functionality classes. Another idea might be to avoid derivation altogether, but to have separate classes (and therefore, objects) of type Window, CursesWindow, XWindow, and EditWindow. The objects could access each through a friend relationship if necessary. However, friends are considered dangerous, and this approach does not encapsulate change well.

Another idea would be to derive EditWindow from Window, and to derive both CursesWindow and XWindow from it. This has the disadvantage of burdening users of Window with the baggage of the EditWindow class, and tends to degeneralize the use of Window for more than only the editor.

Instead, a variation of envelope and letter classes can be used. The original derivations of CursesWindow and XWindow from Window would be preserved, making Window usable by developers as a generic window interface. The class EditWindow would contain a pointer to Window, which would really be a pointer

```
class Window {
public:
    virtual void addch(char);
    virtual void addstr(string);
    virtual void clear();
    . . . .
private:
    Color curColor;
};

class CursesWindow : public Window {
public:
    void addch(char);
    void addstr(String);
    void clear();
    . . . .
private:
    WINDOW *cursesWindow;
};
```

Figure 10-1. Using Inheritance for Windowing Technologies

to either XWindow or CursesWindow at run time (Figure 10-2). All Window operations on EditWindow would invoke Window's (virtual) member functions, using the stored internal pointer as the passed this variable.

This trick is well known as a work-around to the dynamic multiple inheritance problem. But to this approach we add another twist: EditWindow would still be derived from Window, so that routines in the editor that know just about Windows could operate on an EditWindow:

```
class EditWindow : public Window {
    . . . .
};

. . . .

Window *screen = new EditWindow;
screen->addch('A');
```

This is a simple variation on the envelope/letter idiom.

Of course, here the EditWindow class is making the decision about what the hierarchy should be. Adding arguments to the EditWindow constructor allows the

```
class EditWindow {
public:
    void addch(char x)        { window->addch(x); }
    void addstr(string x)     { window->addstr(x); }
    void clear()              { window->clear(); }
    . . . .
    EditWindow()              { if (this_is_an_X_environment) {
                                    window = new XWindow;
                                    . . . .
                                } else {
                                    window = new CursesWindow;
                                    . . . .
                              } }
private:
    Window *window;
    short topLine, bottomLine;
};
```

Figure 10-2. Another Level of Indirection for Another Level of Polymorphism

creator of EditWindow to specify more detail of the derivation hierarchy:

```
enum wType { Apollo, Curses };

EditWindow::EditWindow(wType t) {
    switch (t) {
        case Apollo:
            window = new XWindow; . . . .
            break;
        case Curses:
            window = new CursesWindow; . . . .
            break;
    }
}

. . . .
Window *window = new EditWindow(Curses);
```

A final adjustment is necessary. The derivation must be done in such a way that the constructors for EditWindow cause the base (Window) class constructor to be effectively skipped. If it were to execute, it may create a window on the screen. The creation of the window should be left to EditWindow, in a sense, which calls the constructor for `CursesWindow` or `XWindow` and puts the return value in the `Window*` pointer in its private data. The constructor trick is done using argument defaulting:

```
Window::Window(bool doConstructor=true) {
      if (doConstructor) {
          . . . .
      }
   }

   . . . . .

   EditWindow::EditWindow() : Window(false);

   . . . .

   Window      *ordinaryWindow = new Window;
               // same as "new Window(true)"

   Window      *editorWindow = new EditWindow;

   . . . .
```

If there are base classes above the `Window` class, some additional work may be needed to add special cases to their constructors. For example, derivation of all classes from `Class` when using the exemplar idiom (Chapter 8) requires special measures. The `Class` constructor is still called in spite of the "if" statement, but that, of course, does nothing in the way of executing window initialization software. Such base class initializations are usually harmless, but should be scrutinized to avoid surprises.

10.2 Caveats

This approach is not as general as the dynamic multiple inheritance in languages that support it directly. It *does* provide a multiple inheritance simulation capability for many interesting cases, and experience has proven it useful.

As an example of the limitations of the approach, let's again consider the `Window` example discussed above. We showed that an object's effective derivation chain could be specified at construction time:

```
Window *window = new EditWindow(Curses);
```

This scheme does not generalize to make the following legal, unless special measures are taken ahead of time:

```
Window *window = new Curses(EditWindowType);
```

This order of derivation may be preferred over the other to achieve a different hierarchy of name hiding (for example, to have a function in Curses hide one in EditWindow instead of the other way around). The above scheme can probably be realized with additional coding, but an even nastier example might be

```
Window *window = new Window(EditWindowType);
```

This would be difficult to achieve without making information about EditWindow available to someone who wanted to use only the Window class.

It is also noteworthy that the code *can* get a bit tricky for the owner of a class that's involved in multiple derivations. The good news is that most of the tricks are transparent to users of those classes.

11

Systemic Issues

The preceding chapters in this book have looked at tools, conventions, and idioms using objects and classes as basic system building blocks. Object-oriented programming was shown to be a useful reuse and abstraction tool in Chapters 5 and 7; it turned out to be a natural expression of the principles of the design philosophy discussed in Chapter 6. A combination of object-oriented programming and other techniques can lead to implementations that are manageable, extensible, and maintainable; Appendix A discusses the issue of mixing paradigms at the implementation level.

In this chapter, we step back to get a broader perspective. The object paradigm deals well with the structural aspects of large systems, but there are innumerable other design considerations behind system construction that deserve attention as well. Exception handling, scheduling, packaging, and the management of communities of objects are among those issues. This chapter looks at a subset of these considerations. Although this chapter, combined with Chapter 6, cannot embrace the full spectrum of design considerations, it does cover those areas where the programming language offers little guidance, or where C++ has special opportunities or special needs to deal with system level issues. The chapter does not cover its material in great depth and is not prescriptive, but it is intended to serve as a starting point for project-specific constructs and practices.

These systemic constructs can be divided into two categories: those relating to the static system structure and those relating to its dynamic structure. Static structure includes the relationships captured by the class diagrams of Chapter 6, but also includes abstractions at a higher level and in different dimensions. Different static structures reflect the way we think about design, system delivery, and packaging.

A dynamic structure viewpoint includes what is in object diagrams but also must capture how structure changes over time as well as some traditional notions such as processor scheduling, parallelism, and exception handling. Such considerations reflect how we think about the system performing robustly in an application. This chapter studies systemic issues from these two perspectives in turn.

Readers familiar with operating system implementations might think of this chapter as "the object paradigm's answer to operating systems" for embedded system design. Many design techniques in common use today focus on processes as the units of abstraction: objects are the counterpart in object-oriented design. Those processes are the units of scheduling: What are the units of scheduling under the object paradigm? Operating systems provide common services such as input/output, resource allocation, and fault tolerance: What framework should provide such services in an object-oriented program? Some of the approaches described here can be used with or instead of a traditional operating system in applications having special resource allocation, timing, and service needs.

11.1 Static System Design

There are things grander in scope than objects. In an abstract sense, it is possible to use objects to reflect even the highest level conceptual entities in a system: one could build arbitrarily deep object hierarchies by wrapping a collection of related objects inside a bigger object, then wrapping *that* object and its collaborators together, and so forth.

This presents some problems from the perspective of the design guidelines of Chapter 6, however. Consider the design of the autopilot software for an airplane: We need to consider abstractions like ailerons, rudders, engines, and the operations on them. Can we aggregate these as an airplane object? Looking at our design rules of thumb, we ask whether there are good, crisp, intuitive operations we can assign to it. What would these be? Take-off, cruise, bank, and turn? From the perspective of a flight control system, these are not primitive operations. Each of these is an orchestration of dozens, hundreds, or thousands of interactions between other objects in the system, not something easily designed as an algorithm or implemented as a member function. Higher order abstractions are necessary.

A critical corallary to this is that the addition of a single functional capability to a system will rarely map on to the addition of a single piece of software. For example, the addition of "barrel roll" to an autopilot will require widely dispersed changes in code implementing existing system functionality. Changes in functionality cut across *any* design or implementation paradigm. (We might take exceptions in narrowly defined applications, using application-specific languages or libraries, but we are more interested in large, complex systems here.) If procedures are the units of organization, most end user requests will cut across them. Objects tend to encapsulate change because they reflect what domain experts hold to be the most inviolate abstractions, but they, too, are subject to this problem. The isomorphism between the application structure and the solution structure does help minimize impact of change over what would be found in a procedural structuring of a system. But it is not perfect, as some changes will inevitably outstrip even very broad assumptions about the design domain and can be accommodated only through class restructuring. There is no free lunch here. If there is any guarantee, it is in the spirit of large changes having large impact, and small changes having small impact: the principle of least surprise.

Here we look at several abstraction mechanisms above the object level. Two of them—transaction diagrams and frameworks—are static design tools for the front end of the development process. Modules, subsystems and libraries are used to organize software already designed and written (though they, of course, can serve as input to downstream designs).

Transaction Diagrams

Although object-oriented design focuses on the natural building blocks of a system, it appeals to our intuition to think of some systems in terms of the functions they perform, even though those functions are not implemented as primitive operations. Consider an editor for a graphical design language. It has boxes, circles, and other shape types as its classes, as well as lines used to connect the shapes. We want the editor to support a moveline command, such that the relocation of a line will cause its connected shapes to follow its endpoints; other lines follow the shapes to which they are connected.

The moveline command will be supported by appropriate data structures and member function code for the objects. Where does the member function code go? Moving a line involves active collaboration between a Mouse object, the Screen object, individual shape objects, and the Line object itself. So moveline is less a well-defined, crisp operation on a single object than it is an orchestration of objects working together toward a common goal. Such complex interactions are called *transactions* in the sense of "business transactions." The collection of objects which together provide a transaction or a related collection of transactions is called a *mechanism* by Booch[1]. A transaction is not the responsibility of any given object; it is what happens as the result of a mechanism's objects interacting with each other to perform the system's functions.

Many large system activities fall into the transaction category and are better treated as such than as member functions. We can draw examples from telephony: features like call waiting, call forwarding, and even billing should not be cast as objects or as member functions on objects, but as transactions. An aviation example follows below.

BUSINESS TRANSACTIONS

	Takeoff	Climb	Cruise	Right	Left	Descent	Land
Flaps	Raise						Lower
Left Aileron				Lower	Raise		
Right Aileron				Raise	Lower		
Left Elevator		Raise		Raise	Raise	Lower	
Right Elevator		Raise		Raise	Raise	Lower	
Rudder	Right			Right	Left		
Throttle	Increase	Increase		Increase	Increase	Decrease	Decrease

(OBJECTS, left vertical label)

Figure 11-1. Transaction Diagram for an Airplane System

Should object-oriented techniques be put aside when analyzing high-level transactions like forwarding of a phone or landing an airplane? What if each transaction were treated as a procedure, and stepwise refinement (functional decomposition) applied? Objects that characterize system resources still tend to encapsulate change best in the long run. Abandoning object-oriented techniques and allowing the transactions to drive the system structure is likely to lead to erosion of the system structure over time. Taking a procedural approach distributes knowledge in the wrong places; most procedures depend on internal details of data structures external to themselves. That makes code hard to understand and evolve. An object-driven approach distributes knowledge about individual transactions—but if a designer understands what a transaction needs to do, it is clear what objects are involved, so the loci of change are easier to identify.

A design tool called a *transaction diagram* is used to help identify the appropriate objects and their interactions with the application. Often, customers want to interact with designers at a level of business transactions that are too abstract to be member functions. However, these business transactions are what the system *does* when its objects interact through specific member functions, and it is important to capture that mapping to accommodate the user's view of system functionality.

Transaction diagrams describe the functionality of a mechanism as a whole. That mechanism may be an entire *system* or just a *subsystem*. Here, the terms "system" and "subsystem" are used to describe the parts of an application that are self-contained and that are separately deliverable as independent wholes; subsystems are explored further below.

Each column in the transaction diagram is a transaction, or mechanism. Each row corresponds to an object. The ordering of the rows and columns is important: Logically related functions and abstractions should be kept adjacent in the table. The left edge should be thought of as being logically adjacent to the right edge, and the top edge adjacent to the bottom. As one moves across the transaction diagram from left to right, one might be progressing through successive transactions in the life of the system; this is true of the example in Figure 11-1.[1]

The elements of the table are the member functions a given object performs for a given transaction. We want to look for patterns in the diagram: clusterings of similar functions that are applied to related objects for related transactions. These similarities point to similarities in object structure that can be factored into common base classes. For example, we note that both elevators are raised when an airplane climbs; this suggests that both elevators have something in common. A class Elevator might serve as the base class for both kinds of elevators and would have a climb member function to carry out what elevators need to do when the airplane climbs.

We also see that the throttle needs to be increased for both left and right turns. That suggests that some global function should be called for both left and right turns, containing logic common to both transactions that belongs to no single object.

Taking a more global view, we see that we can do one better. Since both left and right elevators behave identically, we do not need to treat each of them differently at the design level. Each elevator is an individual object of a common class, and the class Elevator we identified above as handling *some* elevator operations in common, can handle all of them. The two elevator rows can be collapsed into one.

There are some member functions that do not cluster together, such as the right operation on the rudder during takeoff to compensate for propeller spin. These are

---

1. Many thanks to Neil Haller and Suzan Scott for helping change this into a design that would fly.

directly implemented as simple member functions instead of being folded with other member functions into transactions.

It should be emphasized that the transaction notation is not a formalism: It is a tool to help identify patterns and commonality. It is similar in approach to a formal tool used in sequential hardware circuit design called a *Karnaugh map*.

Modules

A module is a unit of configuration. C++ supports modules only to the same extent C does—namely, through the organization of code into separate source files. A module may contain a single class or several classes; it may export other types and constants as well.

There are two parts to a module: the symbols it exports for use by clients and its private implementation. The exported part of a module is specified in a header file (also called a "#include" file) that usually has a .h or .hpp suffix, and most of the private part is in a code source file (one with a .c or .cpp suffix). Some of the private implementation is in the header file as well.

The header file should consist primarily of declarations to satisfy the type system and notational conveniences. Typical declarations in a header file include declarations of the classes used in the module, and declarations of global variable names defined within the module but accessible to clients of the module. Other associated type definitions and enumerations for the module appear in the header file as well. Some definitions are useful to put in a header file, particularly definitions of symbolic constants, whether global or scoped within a class.

The code source file contains the definitions of member functions for the module's classes, and definitions of global functions and global objects.

The contents of the code source file should be invisible to clients of the module; the header file is #included by module clients to obtain access to the module interfaces. This creates a dilemma for functions that are to be inline expanded; these are best maintained in a separate code source file, each declared using the inline keyword. The file can be #include at the end of the module header file if the functions are to be inline expanded, or can be separately compiled if inline expansion is not desired. For an example class `Stack`, Stack.h might look like this:

```
#ifndef _STACK_H
#define _STACK_H
class Stack {
public:
     int pop();
     . . . .
};

#ifndef inline
#include "StackInlines.c"
#endif
#endif
```

and StackInlines.c might look like this:

```
#ifndef _STACKINLINES_C
#define _STACKINLINES_C
#include "Stack.h"
inline int Stack::pop() {
     . . . .
}
#endif
```

and Stack.c, containing noninline member functions of `Stack`, would look like this:

```
#include "Stack.h"
#ifdef inline
#include "StackInlines.c"
#endif

Stack::Stack() {
     . . . .
```

Now, by defining the `inline` macro to be the null string when compiling the system, a single closed copy of each `Stack` member function will be generated instead of multiple inline expansions:

```
CC -Dinline="" *.c
```

Subsystems

A *subsystem* is a collection of modules that stands as an independent deliverable, with functionality that is both rich enough and general enough that the collection could generate revenues as a product. For example, one organization or company could contract for the design and delivery of a subsystem to another.

Some abstractions that start as types in early system design may be good candidates for subsystems in implementation. Good designers broaden the scope of their abstractions to accommodate the needs of most applications in a given domain; as this broadening takes place, care should be taken to identify modules and collections of modules that might be reused across applications (see Section 6.3). Such abstractions are worthwhile to package as subsystems, to take extra pains to document for use external to the project at hand, and to organize in repositories where they can be found by projects looking for reusable code.

A subsystem often implements a mechanism: a collection of classes providing high-level application functions that may transcend member functions. Run-time support environments, database managers, and network interfaces are examples of subsystems.

A class can be used to group a collection of functions as static member functions, with the resulting abstraction behaving like a subsystem. These functions are usually more weakly bound to each other than ordinary (non-static) member functions are, and need no polymorphic treatment. A subsystem usually does not correspond to a single resource that would be characterized as an object-oriented analysis entity or type. It is a singleton entity: There is only one of a given subsystem in any system. A subsystem is usually conceptually larger, has more disparate and decoupled internal states, and has less semantic cohesion than an object does. An operating system interface serves as a simple example:

```
class OperatingSystemInterface {
public:
    static int reboot();
    . . . .
    class Process {
        . . . .
    };
};
```

However, what is considered a subsystem at one level may be an object at another level, and static member functions may be "instance" (non-static) member functions at another level. Whether an abstraction should be an object or a subsystem depends largely on how cohesive it appears from a system perspective, and how intuitively it relates to the application domain. If the system view indicates that such a resource should be an object instead of a subsystem, then static member functions should be avoided.

The class enclosing the static functions might be compared to an Ada package. In addition to static functions, such a class can export other classes, enumerations, and constants.

Frameworks

A *framework* defines a subsystem or mechanism that is customizable or extensible. The subsystem *design* is encapsulated by a set of classes, though the *implementation* may be only partially specified. Framework abstract base classes leave some member function definitions to the application. Examples of object-oriented frameworks are the X Toolkit, MacApp, and the Smalltalk Model-View-Controller.

A framework provides utility services commonly associated with operating systems. Unlike most operating systems, frameworks provide services specific to some domain. A framework goes beyond the simple services of an operating system to characterize the major abstractions of an application; a framework user supplies the code to fill in the abstractions to make a complete system.

C++ templates are one way of parameterizing software to customize it for the application at hand. Frameworks tend to be broader, more general abstractions than can be conveniently captured by templates. General frameworks can be built as collections of abstract base classes, which constrain the "shape" of a design while giving the user liberty to customize the semantics to a particular application. One useful framework idiom is to flesh out the public member functions of base class abstractions, leaving the implementation details to private, virtual functions that are overridden by the user in a derived class. A framework results in base classes with few, if any, public member functions (Figure 11-2). Most of the public operations are handled in a general way in the base class. Base class member functions take care of the sequencing of implementation-dependent routines supplied as private virtuals in the derived class.

A framework can be packaged as a library for distribution.

Libraries

A library is an organized collection of software, from which an application may pick and choose pieces to meet its needs. It is similar to a subsystem, but it is more a packaging unit than a unit of software organization or abstraction.

```
class TaxFormFramework {
public:
    TaxFormFramework(int numberOfLines) {
        . . . .
    }
    void draw() {
        makeField(loc1, taxpayer.name());
        makeField(loc2, taxpayer.ssn());
        . . . .
        addFields();
    }
private:
    void makeField(Point, const char *const);
    // derived class must have its own version of addFields
    virtual void addFields() = 0;
    Point loc1, loc2, . . . .
    . . . .
};
class ScheduleB: public TaxFormFramework {
public:
    ScheduleB(): TaxFormFramework(14) { }
private:
    Point locA, . . . .
    void addFields() {
        // add the lines for Schedule B
        makeField(locA, mortgage.income());
        makeField(locB, other.income());
        . . . .
    }
    . . . .
};
```

Figure 11-2. A Form Framework

Libraries are usually packaged in two parts: an object code part and a collection of header files. The packaging is done in such a way that part of the abstractions from a library can be used without incurring the overhead of unused parts of the library.

Each library should be built around a theme or topic, just as a genealogical library has books and other materials on family history, and an agricultural library has reference materials on the use of life sciences to produce consumer goods. A library is like a subsystem in that it is a separately purchasable deliverable. But, again, it is like a library of books in that it does not need to be incorporated in its entirety to meet the need at hand.

Each library has a certain set of rules or expectations, which must apply uniformly across all its abstractions. Consistency of memory allocation techniques, exception handling strategies, and class extension mechanisms (using templates or derived classes) makes a library easier to comprehend and apply. It would be ideal if all libraries used within a project displayed such a degree of coherence and consistency, but this is difficult to achieve in practice. A collection of simple interface classes can be put around classes of an existing library to conform to local interface standards or preferences. Bringing memory allocation techniques into alignment is a more serious problem, and most application-independent libraries rely only on the allocation and deallocation support manifest in the language. Users wishing to use more exotic techniques—for example, the garbage collection technique described in Chapter 9— should build handle classes around those library classes to manage their memory. Happily, most such conversions can be done without editing or recompiling the source files for the original library.

Special attention must be used when creating dependencies between libraries. Handling conversions between related library classes should be done by using the conventions and rules of thumb presented in Section 3.4 (page 56). Care must be taken to create class template libraries that avoid instantiating redundant copies of templates they use in turn. Chapter 7 discusses some approaches to reduce this code redundancy (page 262).

Subject to these guidelines, libraries can be used to package the code for an individual concrete data type, for a collection of base classes, or for an entire framework. For consistency's sake, they can be used to package and deliver subsystem code as well. However, a subsystem is usually incorporated in an application as a monolithic collection of code, so the selective loading advantages of library packaging are seldom exercised for subsystem libraries; a single relocatable file could be delivered just as well.

Most library design is a footnote to the principles of software reuse, and all the guidelines of Chapter 7 apply here. Good programming techniques and software organization facilitate the organization and management of libraries; for some good examples, see Coggins and Bollela [2] and Stroustrup [3].

11.2 Dynamic System Design

Most design techniques focus on static design. Dynamic system characteristics receive some design consideration, but full treatment of system dynamics requires feedback from a prototype or early implementation. These dynamic issues include patterns of collaboration between individual instances at run time, the ability of scheduling disciplines to meet system real-time constraints, and the effects of distributed processing. These are all traditional operating system concerns but bear revisiting in light of object-oriented principles.

Scheduling

Scheduling is an important design issue, because processes as units of scheduling dominate much of how we think about software modularization. Scheduling receives no explicit C++ language support. This is not to say that the scheduling issue is foreign to the C++ community; C++ was originally created as a language to support discrete event simulation like that of Simula 67, and it used a task library to support event dispatching. Many installations continue to use a descendant of this task library in current C++ environments.

In a discussion of scheduling, several terms need to be explored as a basis for understanding. The terms *process*, *multiprocessing* and *parallel processing* are in common use, and bear scrutiny in light of what they mean to objects. The terms will be used as follows in this chapter:

> *Process*: A process is a unit of *scheduling*, and may also be a unit of protection, and of address space or name space. The units of *structure* that are scheduled are usually *programs*.

> *Multiprocessing*: Multiprocessing is a scheduling technique based on processes as units of scheduling. Multiprocessing may be done on a single processor, giving the illusion of a virtual processor for each process. A uniprocessor multiprocessing environment is also called a *time-shared* environment. There is no true asynchrony between processes in such an environment, though a "pseudo-parallelism" arises from the simulated asynchrony.

> *Parallel processing*: Parallel, or distributed processing, involves more than one processor or, more precisely, more than one concurrent thread of control (program counter). Most multiprocessing disciplines apply to parallel processing; however, additional consideration must be given to *true* asynchrony that does not arise in the uniprocessor case.

Software applications cover an enormously broad spectrum of real-time and scheduling characterizations. No single scheduling approach will suit all applications. Language support for multiprocessing is hard to make general enough to be a good fit for a broad base of applications, and narrowly conceived scheduling models are often difficult to apply in a particular application. For example, some applications may need multiprocessing without parallelism (for example, a simulation of autonomous entities) while others may need preemptive resumption. Support for distribution must be done on a case-by-case basis as well. Some environments may support concurrency with a low level network protocol, others may not support it at all, and still others may support it through shared memory. Such variety makes it difficult to provide language support or even idiomatic constructs supporting a single, reusable model of concurrency. Individual projects will want to fine-tune an existing scheme (such as the C++ task library) or create entirely new approaches. Language support for concurrency nonetheless exists; see Gehani and Roome [4] for one example.

In Chapter 6, we noted that an important design principle underlying the object paradigm is to strive to create parallels between the structure of the application domain and the class and object structure of the solution; we called this property the isomorphic structure principle. This "structure" in both worlds is characterized by a collection of related behaviors. Is there an analogous underlying principle for scheduling?

Experience, and a bit of introspection, suggest the answer: maybe. If the model of computation is an essential and clear part of the application characteristics, then the answer is "yes," in the spirit of the isomorphic structure principle. As an example, consider the design of an object-oriented database, with objects living on a shared medium where they are accessed from multiple processors. Objects would be the units of synchronization, and the scheduling mechanism would need high-level design consideration to protect data integrity. That is a good example of where parallelism relates directly to the problem to be solved; it appears in the vocabulary of the problem statement.

By contrast, there may be places where the problem is not intrinsically parallel but where parallelism suggests itself as part of the solution. A simple example is graphics rendering for a computer-generated animation. Another good example is a telephone call abstraction in a switching network control system: while "call" is a single conceptual entity, parts of it may need to live on one switching control processor close to an originating terminal, while other parts might live on control processors associated with called parties. Here, the need for distribution not only raises the issue of scheduling but changes the structure as well.

It makes no difference in most applications whether they are implemented using a particular kind of scheduling or whether there is a single CPU or multiple CPUs. Scheduling usually pertains to implementation engineering, rather than to the characteristics of the application itself. Some applications are intrinsically parallel; others may have stringent performance constraints forcing an implementation to use distributed processing. Coexistence with existing software, or use of special application-specific processors (signal processors, graphics accelerators, math processors) may also constrain the solution to specific scheduling regimens. Much of the distinction between problem domain specifications and application domain constraints is artificial; many of the application domain constraints are implicit in the structure of the problem.

Can each object in an object-oriented design be treated as a process? The context switching overhead and message dispatching costs of most multiprocessing environments are too high to treat all objects as units of scheduling. Think what it would mean to do an operating context switch, or to literally send an operating system message to a string every time you wanted to look at another character. (What Smalltalk calls messages, by the way, have only weak ties to processor scheduling and imply no asynchrony.) Furthermore, it is a poor semantic fit to most applications. Multiprocessing exists to give multiple processes the illusion of running on their own processors; there is no need to provide this illusion between a string and its client, and serial program counter execution is adequate.

On the other side of the coin: If we have need for a process abstraction, can `Process` be an object? The answer lies in whether the design leads to crisp, semantically clear member functions for such an abstraction. If we want to treat these objects for their process-ness, then the answer is yes. Consider a highly distributed processing environment with hundreds of processors. If we frequently want to take processors into or out of the computation, then we truly may want to manage the units of scheduling as architectural components. These objects may be derived from a base class `Process`; such objects are called *Actors*, like the performers in a play carrying out their own roles independently. Each object has its own program counter.

As mentioned above, the C++ language itself has no support for Actors or any other scheduling discipline; however, environments can be put underneath a C++ application to support such a model. For examples, see Agha [5] and Kafura and Lee [6]. The Actors model is also closely approximated by a C++ task library in popular use and in common distribution with many C++ environments; a brief description follows below, and a more detailed description can be found in Shopiro [7].

Actors unify the units of structure and scheduling into a single abstraction. It is less constraining on design if these can be treated as two separate, loosely coupled abstractions. One downfall of process-based architectures has been that the units of structure, address space, and scheduling have been so closely coupled. In contrast, we might let the scheduling structure cut across objects, running in finite bursts of computation that pass indivisibly through the member functions of several different objects. These bursts are called *threads*, and will be discussed below.

C++ Tasks   A commonly used C++ library supports *tasks* as units of scheduling in a way that can closely model the Actors approach. Task objects serve as units of scheduling as well as units of structure. They are also units of name space—they have their own scope. The C++ task package was initially designed for discrete event simulation, but it can be used for any scheduling application needing nonpreemptive scheduling.

Library classes provide multitasking support:

> task: Objects of classes derived from task represent active system resources. Each behaves as though it had its own program counter and was running on its own processor. The constructor of a task object acts as its "main" routine. Like a process, a *task* object has its own private data and its own locus of control. A task may temporarily relinquish control by blocking on the status of an object resource (below) or by invoking delay (*n*) to give up the processor for *n* time ticks.

> object: Class object serves as a base class for passive system resources. These resources can either be *pending* or *ready*, and a task can block its own execution on the status of one or more object instances. If multiple instances are being waited for, the task is resumed as soon as any one of them undergoes a status change to *ready*.

> queue: Tasks communicate with each other through general-purpose queues. A queue has attributes called a *head* and a *tail*; these are of classes qhead and qtail, respectively. Both qhead and qtail are derived from object, so a task can block on a queue's head waiting for data to be supplied.

Notice that though tasks may invoke each others' member functions directly, such invocations are synchronous and do not follow task semantics. In the Actors paradigm, interaction between objects is typically through message interfaces, and the contents of a message are examined by the receiver at run time to interpret its semantics. The interface of one task object is not directly accessed by another, so class signatures do not figure strongly in the design of a task-based system. Virtual functions are effectively inoperative for task objects: the polymorphism comes in the (user-defined) run time interpretation of message contents.

The task library provides low-level synchronization. First, there is no true asynchrony since the tasks all run on a single processor with a single underlying thread of control. Second, and more to the point, synchronization of user-level activities is done through the blocking mechanism in object and queue objects; the details of the implementation are hidden from the user.

A priority-driven dispatching scheme can be added to a task object system; for example, it may schedule requests based on priorities attached either to the requests or to the queues containing them. Priorities are most useful in I/O-intensive systems, where peripheral activities can be initiated at high priority to run in parallel with ongoing computation.

☞ *When to use this idiom*: Task objects are useful for discrete event simulations and other uniprocessor applications where simulated parallelism is desired. Use this idiom when the units of scheduling constitute abstractions germane to the application itself, instead of being artifacts of the solution.

Threads   Threads are a natural scheduling mechanism for objects, providing an alternative to the Actors model. Where Actors unify the units of scheduling and structure, threads allow the two abstractions to be treated differently. For someone whose knowledge of scheduling is based on the process model, threads will appear unusual in the same sense that classes as abstractions are unfamiliar to someone whose experience is steeped in functional decomposition. Threads have some attractive properties for real-time systems using object-oriented techniques.

Figure 11-3 demonstrates how thread scheduling is done. A thread of execution is started off by a *request* or a *stimulus*. Assume that the stimulus labeled ⊡ comes from an externally generated message. All stimuli and requests are dispatched by a dispatcher object, which maps request types to the objects that are to receive them and the member function that is to be invoked. Most requests will have this information embedded in them, provided by another system object that originated the request: in that sense, these requests act like messages or like the entries in the `task` library's queues.

The dispatcher object sends the message for stimulus ⊡ to a member function of object A, which starts executing. That member function calls a member function of B, which in turn calls a member function of C. C's member function returns; control is eventually returned to the dispatcher immediately following the point where it passed control to A, and the thread is complete. The thread runs *without interruption* from beginning to end: no code in a thread ever blocks on a resource or relinquishes the processor until the thread is complete. As a policy issue, system timers may be used to guarantee that a given thread executes within a specified amount of time; the dispatcher starts the timer at the beginning of a thread, and extinguishes the timer when the thread terminates. If the timer fires during the thread, the current thread might be deemed insane and recovery action can be instigated.

A thread's execution may generate other stimuli or requests to the dispatcher. When the dispatcher regains control at the end of a thread, it will start a new thread from a request generated by a previous thread; if there are none, it will idle until an external stimulus restarts execution. The execution of thread ⊡ may have created request ⊡ which will start its own thread of execution.

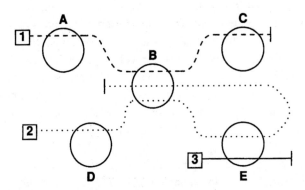

Figure 11-3. Thread Scheduling of Object Member Functions

Synchronization is greatly aided by threads because there is no explicit blocking. Between threads, no object is in a "partially computed" state because one of its member functions is blocked waiting on a resource.

Thread scheduling generalizes in a natural way to distributed, multiprocessor environments. Any single thread runs within a processor; all interprocessor communications take place as the passing of a stimulus from one processor's run-time support environment to that of another processor.

Threads can be driven by a priority scheme based on stimulus type, where the dispatcher might shuffle the order in which stimuli are handled, based on the type of stimuli or on any other convenient criteria.

☞ *When to use this idiom*: Use threads in real-time applications where response times to real-time events are critical. Threads are useful for distributed architectures where the binding of objects onto processors needs to be done late in design or as part of implementation.

Contexts

All interesting problems in computer science can be reduced to what's in a name. In object-oriented designs, the names of most classes and their member functions are global, as are the handles for many system objects. Trying to find objects, evaluate impact of change, and manage run-time resources becomes difficult in systems with dozens or hundreds of top-level classes.

If we review the abstractions of static system structure—classes, modules, subsystems, frameworks, libraries (and to a lesser degree, transactions)—we find that each has an intuitive relationship to some collection of source code. Contexts describe relationships between extant, running objects, which means that the relationship to static abstractions, and therefore to source structure, is much looser. It is important to recognize such abstractions as units of run-time administration, for much the same reason that processes are important abstractions for design techniques in popular use today.

Entities in most applications congregate into communities; that is, most objects interact closely with only a few other objects. These communities can often be treated as local empires that can be independently initialized, administered, and delivered. An object hierarchy—the encapsulation of object instances within other objects—is one example of such an aggregation. Other aggregations of objects reflect abstractions that themselves are not good objects, and object hierarchies do not properly capture the relationships between them. For example, Mouse, Menu, Keyboard, Screen, and Window classes are clearly related, but they do not all belong inside any single class abstraction (though Screen, Keyboard, and Mouse may be aggregated as a Terminal). To that degree, these communities are just subsystems. But it is possible for an object to belong to *multiple* communities: a Window may belong to a community of objects implementing a graphical editor, but it may also belong to a window manager. The Telephone and Call objects in a phone call represent a locality of reference; however, any given phone may live simultaneously in two such communities if it uses call waiting to put one party on hold while talking to another. Neither ''large objects'' nor subsystems can express these relationships in a satisfactory way. We coin the term *context* for a community that may overlap another.

Each context has a *server object* that acts like its own mini-operating system; objects access each other only through a server, and a server is accessed only from within the context it manages. The server functions are rudimentary, supporting *name serving* and perhaps some basic memory management. The name server function maps symbolic names onto objects; these ''symbolic'' names may be strings, or just enumerated constants. They make objects within a context accessible to each other without cluttering the name space of the whole program. An object may log itself with one or more servers when it comes into existence.

A context is reminiscent of a traditional process in that it defines a name space. Other traditional process functions can also be folded into contexts such as memory management and fault handling. (Scheduling will probably be handled at a higher level than contexts, at a level of abstraction that more closely maps onto processors.)

All objects created for a context, or created from code within a running context, might be allocated by the server for that context.

Interaction Across Name Spaces

A distributed environment should supply common support for communication between objects in different processes and in different processors. If distributed communication is integrated with the mechanisms underlying object communications within a process, then the environment can support distribution transparency. The overhead of object context switches should be minimized as well, by customizing remote interactions as needed instead of using a single, general dispatching mechanism with uniformly high overhead. This section investigates C++ idioms providing distribution transparency, and a balance of generality and efficiency.

Processes Versus Objects Revisited   Whether an architecture uses processes or objects as its major abstractions, the abstractions must communicate with each other. When one abstraction yields control to another—voluntarily or otherwise—we call it a *context switch.*

In a process architecture, a context switch often involves a message. If passing the flow of control is not as important as passing data, then shared memory can be used instead of messages, without the overhead of message formatting. In both cases, the operating system must save process state when control passes from one process to another. This includes the information normally saved by a function when called from another: the program counter and miscellaneous registers. The operating system must also dispatch another process: restore its state, and branch to where the process left off when it was preempted, or where it is to resume as the result of a stimulus or change in its state (e.g., receipt of a signal). All interprocess communication incurs the overhead of least one of these context switches, and potentially a message creation.

If objects instead of processes are the units of architecture, then they must have a context switch mechanism as well. The context switching mechanism between ordinary C++ objects is an ordinary function call. The dispatching is direct, instead of through a message mapping table. The function call stack protocol saves the context of the invoker, which is restored on return. Instead of being passed in messages, arguments are pushed on the stack. All interobject communications incur the overhead of a single function call.

Each approach has its advantages and disadvantages. Processes can be dispatched in an arbitrary order, making it easier to implement dispatching schemes based on priority independent of the order of message arrival. Processes can be distributed across processors more easily than objects can; the function call mechanism used to communicate between objects does not extend to multiprocessor configurations. The generality comes at a price, and the overhead of context switching and message formatting can be substantial.

In an object-oriented world, we would like to reap the benefits of direct function calls where possible, and pay for use of messages where we must (for distributed processing). We would also like as high a degree of distribution transparency as possible. The following section examines this tradeoff.

Distribution Transparency

As a system evolves, the number of processors may grow and objects may be migrated from processor to processor. Changes in technology or requirements may force a change in the partitioning of objects across processes or processors. Such changes occur not only over the course of long-term maintenance but during initial implementation as tradeoffs are considered and experienced. Using threads and special handle and body classes, these objects can be remoted across processors with a minimum of effort.

Each interaction between a pair of objects can be thought of as having two parts: a request and a dispatch. Each object has two parts: its *handle*, and its *body*, per the idiom of Section 3.5. To provide distribution transparency, the handle class object can field requests and dispatch them to the body. Within a single processor, the handle is simply an envelope class, and the body is the letter class or the class served by the handle; the two classes are joined by a pointer (Figure 11-4). Any given body instance is fully contained by a single processor, but that body may have *ambassadors* on several processors, including the one hosting the body. Even when referenced from multiple processors (or from multiple name spaces), the body (letter class) remains unchanged. Handle classes on the same processors as the body reference the body directly as a letter class, as in the uniprocessor case. Remote access to the object is through handle classes as always, but the handle class forwards requests to an ambassador instead of to a body class.

What the ambassador does is package the arguments into a message and transmit them transparently to the "real" body class in the foreign name space. For example, the ambassador `RemoteDiskRep` packages `read` and `write` requests from the handle objects `C` and `D` and sends them to `DiskRep` on another processor. An operating system dispatcher routes the message to a communications link and sends the message to the remote processor. The dispatcher then starts another thread on the sending end. The operating system on the receiving end dispatches the message to the body object `DiskRep`. The body object may be dispatched through a member function dedicated to that purpose, which decodes the message and performs the proper operation on `DiskRep`.

Note that member functions with return values are not easily distributed, since calling them across a processor boundary would require a real-time break between the

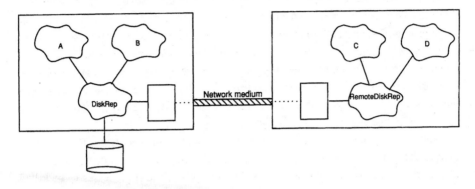

Figure 11-4. Ambassador Classes

call and the return. A thread scheduling environment has no explicit provision for saving the return address and other dynamic thread data (automatic variables) during such a real-time break. One important property of threads is that most system state resides in object data instead of on the stack, which can be a boon to error analysis and recovery.

If return values are necessary, they can be implemented as callbacks. The original service requester can specify a callback routine as a function pointer or functor when it originates the request for service. When the body object DiskRep finishes its task, it can send a message back to the invoking processor. The message is dispatched to the ambassador object, which can invoke the callback. If a handle class object satisfies the request through a body object on the same processor (e.g., from A), then the body can invoke the callback directly on completion of the request. If the body can satisfy the request without a real time break, then the callback is invoked on the same thread of control as the original request. If the request is satisfied remotely or with a real time break, the callback is on a different thread. Except for timing, the difference is transparent to the caller invoking the service on A, B, C, or D.

Exception Handling

An *exception* is an event caused by some abnormal condition requiring special attention. Examples of exceptions include traps (such as division by zero), interrupts (for example, to signal arrival of data from a peripheral interface), and a variety of other software errors (for example, attempting to invoke a virtual function that does not exist). Exception handling is application specific, and no single approach can fit all needs. This section explores some typical exception handling approaches and conveys some insights to aid in the design of fault tolerant software.

In programs such as editors, compilers, games, and the like, it may be sufficient to clean up or "finalize" resources, print a message, and then exit. Examples of resource finalization include closing open files, releasing semaphores, adjusting reference counts on shared resources, and so forth. Such cleanup is usually performed automatically from within objects' destructors, so the right cleanup happens if all objects are cleaned up properly on an exception.

There is an important question in establishing an exception handling model is: what is the unit of recovery? In traditional minicomputer environments (and many others), the unit of recovery is a process, and exceptions cause processes to be killed or restarted. Because processes give way to Actors or threads as more natural scheduling disciplines for objects, a new recovery abstraction must be found. One model of exception handling is to make functions (member functions or global or static functions) the units of recovery. Such an exception handling mechanism has been proposed for the C++ language standard, as described in Ellis and Stroustrup [8].

Because exception handling is an immature feature in the language, and there is not a base of experience to draw on in the creation of advanced idioms, the topic is dealt with only superficially in this chapter. It is also likely that a given application will need its own mechanisms and constructs to deal with exceptions, and domain experience will yield some ideas that can be used as starting points.

The main issue in function-based exception handling is how to clean up automatics (local function variables) when an exception occurs. If an exception occurs while the program is executing several function calls deep, objects need to be cleaned up for all the functions with activation records on the stack. The currently executing function should be given the opportunity to recover from the exception; the function that called it should likewise recover at its level, and so on, until a high enough level function is reached so that the error is propagated no further.

In the C++ exception handling scheme, every piece of code that is to be given fault tolerant treatment must be executed in a try block:

```
void foo() {
    try {
        // calls in here will be given
        // fault-tolerant treatment
    }
    // calls here will NOT be given
    // fault-tolerant treatment (unless
    // foo was called from within another
    // try block)
}
```

Exceptions may be generated by the run-time environment (such as division by zero) or may be explicitly generated with the `throw` statement, which contains an expression designating the type of exception to be thrown. Exceptions generated by code in a `try` block, or by code in functions called from within the block, cause control to be transferred to a handler. Exception handlers are coded as `catch` statements, which declare the type of exception they handle and specify statements to be executed when the handler gains control. Here is a simple example:

```
void foo() {
    try {
        bar();
    }
    catch (const char *message) {
        // gets a pointer to the throw parameter
    }
    catch (const List<String> &message) {
        // gets a temporary copy of the throw parameter
    }
}
void bar() throw(List<String>, const char*) {
    List<String> errorReport;
    . . . .
    throw errorReport;    // invokes second catch above
    . . . .
    throw "Help!";        // invokes first catch above
    . . . .
}
```

Note that `bar` declares, as part of its interface, which exceptions it will throw. There is no resumption of execution at the point the exception occurred.

This mechanism works fine to recover objects local to those functions that are active when an exception occurs, and it is well-suited to simple container classes, strings, and other classes commonly found in general-purpose libraries. But C++ exception handling does not address the issue of finalizing objects allocated off the heap. Nor does it deal with asynchronous or cascaded errors; these are the domain of signal handling. Presumably, those objects would be cleaned up by explicit code in the exception handlers.

In practice, complex fault-tolerant systems need a more global recovery strategy. First, they need to be able to deal with events not commonly associated with programming language abstractions, such as memory parity errors and service-affecting device failures. Such errors are asynchronous with respect to the "main" thread of execution, and their recovery does not relate to what the software is doing at the time they occur. Such fault tolerance relates to things that happen "behind the scenes'', and can be categorized as *subparadigmatic recovery* (for low-level interrupts such as memory parity failures) or *superparadigmatic recovery* (recovery at the context, process, or processor level). There is a rule of thumb that recovery in continuously running systems needs to be addressed at the lowest accessible level of technology.

Second, where the `try/throw/catch` mechanism recovers a nesting of function calls (or, equivalently, a set of adjacent stack frames), there are places we would like the unit of recovery to be an object instead. Exception handling routines might defer such reinitialization to higher levels of error handling. A damaged or insane object can be restored by invoking its constructor on the object in place (Section 3.7), or by other suitable techniques.

Third, a system level view is needed to handle system-level errors such as memory exhaustion. A system recovery scheme might remove the least critical resources from service to enable the ongoing functionality of the system as a whole. Some resource may be brought back into service using redundant or checkpointed system state information. C++'s exception handling can be thought of as a checkpointing technique that is short-term (e.g., to recover a thread if a thread scheduler is used) and local (only local data are ''recovered;'' the need to recover global resources must be inferred from context). Different recovery approaches are suitable for different systems and, as with scheduling, programming language cannot offer a single, universally satisfactory solution.

Finally, some errors are not caught just as they occur. If an error is detected through a second-, third- or fourth-order effect on some distantly related data, an exception handling routine will not have the context to repair the problem. Repair must be escalated to software with a more global view. Exception handling is one mechanism to provide that escalation, but it is not the only such mechanism and must be coupled with a global recovery strategy to be effective in continuously running systems.

Most C++ environments do not support exception handling at this writing. Surrogate techniques have been developed anticipating implementation of the exception handling proposal; for example, see Miller [9].

Garbage Collection as an Aid to Reliability

Garbage Collection as an Aid to Reliability   Garbage collection of unreferenceable memory, coupled with automated finalization (destructor invocation) of unreferenceable objects can be an important part of recovery. Idioms for such a technique are described in Chapter 9. If an object is judged insane, it is a dubious proposition to trust its destructor to release all the resources it allocated. It is often better to just return the memory of such objects to the free pool; invoking their destructors may actually start an avalanche of errors from wild or undefined pointers. That has the potential of leaving valid, extant objects unreferenced, a problem that garbage collection techniques address. Subparadigmatic fault handlers may not be able to "do the right object-oriented things" when they are activated, so they, too, may deallocate objects without properly finalizing them. As an analogy, a process on a time-sharing system may not properly close out open files if it terminates abnormally as a result of a division by zero.

Garbage collection does three things to aid recovery:

1. It frees the memory associated with unreferenceable objects.
2. If garbage collection invokes the destructors of unreferenceable objects, then resources other than memory (file descriptors, virtual memory registers, semaphores, etc.) are also freed.
3. If destructors are invoked by the garbage collector, then objects referenced only by unreferenceable objects are freed, and so forth, potentially collapsing whole trees of resources.

If such resources are not reclaimed, creeping entropy may eventually exhaust a system resource and total system failure will ensue. Again, this needs to be traded off against the potential from an avalanche of errors that might result from calling the destructor for an insane object.

Garbage collection can be a costly technique and requires sometimes tedious coding. However, it is suitable for C++ code produced from application generators, and still can be used in hand-coded portions of the system having extreme reliability requirements.

Contexts as Units of Recovery   When using threads, there is no longer a concept of process. A process cannot be killed and restarted as a recovery measure. However, contexts manage their own resources and can be treated as units of recovery. The server object can be called on to reinitialize all local context objects, perhaps treating shared context objects specially.

Zombie Objects

Even in the best-designed recovery schemes, accidents still happen. What would happen if an attempt were made to access an object that had disappeared? General insanity would likely ensue, triggering errors for which root cause analysis would be difficult. A solution is to replace deleted objects by *zombie objects*, objects with controlled, fail-safe behavior.

What a zombie object looks like will depend on the C++ environment you are using. Most zombie objects should be constructed as a list of virtual function table pointers. The objects contain nothing but such pointers, and all pointers point to the same virtual function table. That table is allocated to be at least as large as the largest virtual function table in the system, and it is filled with pointers to a recovery function. Such a zombie object can appear in place of any other object and will channel all its virtual function calls to the recovery function.

Zombie objects can be overlaid on newly deleted objects by the system `operator delete`, or by overloaded `operator delete` member functions.

The recovery function referenced from the virtual function tables either does nothing (totally passive fail-safe operation), raises an exception (to let the caller know it dereferenced a dangling pointer), or makes arrangements in the recovery system to deem the current object insane. Which alternative is chosen is a function of system recovery policy.

Little can be done in general to thwart nonvirtual member function invocations through dangling pointers.

References

1. Booch, Grady. *Object-Oriented Design with Applications.* Redwood City, Calif.: Benjamin/Cummings, 1991.

2. Coggins, James M., and Gregory Bollela. "Managing C++ Libraries." *SIGPLAN Notices 24*,6 (June 1989), 37.

3. Stroustrup, B. *The C++ Programming Language*, 2nd ed. Reading, Mass.: Addison-Wesley, 1991, ch. 12.

4. Gehani, N., and W. D. Roome. *Concurrent C Programming Language.* Summit, New Jersey: Silicon Press, 1989.

5. Agha, Gul A. *Actors: a model of concurrent computation in distributed systems.* Cambridge, Mass.: MIT Press, 1986.

6. Kafura, Dennis, and Keung Hae Lee, *ACT++: Building a Concurrent C++ with Actors*, TR89-18. Blacksburg, Va.: Virginia Polytechnic Institute and State University, Department of Computer Science.

7. Shopiro, Jonathan E. "Extending the C++ Task System for Real-Time Control," *Proceedings of the USENIX C++ Workshop.* Santa Fe: USENIX Association Publishers (November 1987).

8. Ellis, Margaret A., and B. Stroustrup. *The Annotated C++ Reference Manual.* Reading, Mass.: Addison-Wesley, 1990, Chapter 15.

9. Miller, W. M. "Exception Handling Without Language Extensions," *Proceedings of the C++ Workshop.* Denver: USENIX Association Publishers (October 1988).

A

C in a C++ Environment

C++ is C—that is, most of what you see in a C++ program comes directly from C, and many C programs require only minor conversion to become C++ programs.[1] This section looks at what minimal conversions are necessary to give a program the C++ "style." It does not attempt to teach the full C language. For an excellent reference on C, see Kernighan and Ritchie [2].

A.1 Function Calls

C++ introduces an additional level of scoping beyond what is found in C. The scoping is provided by a language facility called the *class*. Classes are the language constructs used to create *abstract data types*, or user-defined types. So whereas in C most any symbol could be local or global, in C++, symbols can be local, global, or in a class. It is true that in C, variables can also appear inside multiple levels of nested curly braces inside functions, and names inside a struct can duplicate names occurring in local and global scopes. However, in C, this is not true of functions: All functions are either global or static (which just means "global to a source file"). In C++, functions may also be declared inside classes: Such functions are called *member functions* of the class containing them. This means that if there is a global function foo, and a class F containing a function foo, the two exist as distinct and unrelated functions. In order to talk about them, we refer to F's foo as F::foo, and to the global one as ::foo or sometimes just foo.

---

1. For a detailed discussion of the differences between C++ and C, see Koenig and Stroustrup [1].

If there is code inside class F that looks like this,

```
foo();
```

we cannot can't easily tell from inspection whether the programmer *intended* to call the foo inside class F, or intended to call the global foo. Readers of code must work their way out from the call, through the class, and finally to the global scope to determine where the call will transfer to. To help in the reading and understanding of such code, we can adopt a convention that clarifies things a bit for C++ programs that use classes. The convention is that functions of global scope should be called by using the C++ global scope qualifier:

```
::foo();
```

This is just a notation, a coding standard, that does not (for this example) change the code generated or make the compiler any happier when no ambiguity exists. It does avoid confusion, and for that reason it is followed in this book and is offered as a notation for use by the reader.

A.2 Function Parameters

C++ asks that you declare your function parameters in a style a little different from that used in Classic C. Pascal programmers will find the style familiar:

C code:	C++ code:
```int main(argc, argv)int argc;char *argv[];{ . . . .}int func(){ . . . .}```	```int main(int argc, char *argv[]){ . . . .}int func(){ . . . .}```

A single syntactic form specifying the interface to a function serves two purposes. First, it heads the function body in the function definition. Second, it is used as a function interface specification called a *function prototype* (see below), which must appear prior to the call of a function.

A.3 Function Prototypes

Good C program source files start with declarations of the functions that are to be used by the code in that file, even though those functions may not be defined in that file. Some programmers put these declarations inside every function to indicate the external functions to be used by that function; some collect them at the top of a file, and still others put all the declarations in a header file that is #included at the top of the file.

The best way to organize these in C++ is to put the declarations in header files. If you are the provider of some function or class, then you usually provide a declaration of that function or class in a header file, which usually has a .h suffix and which resides in a specially designated header file directory. Users of your software #include the header file, and thereby are given type-checked access to your routines. Having the declaration in a header file not only helps ensure type safety, but also avoids the tedium of having to redeclare a function or class every time you need to reference it.

In most C++ environments, all system functions are declared for you in header files that come with the compiler. For example, in a UNIX Operating System installation, the C++ environment would have header files containing declarations of the kernel and library functions you find in Sections 2 and 3 of your UNIX Operating System manual. To get the declaration for the function, you should #include the appropriate header file. To find out which header file you should pull in, you can either ask your administrator where the header files are, and peruse them yourself, or ask your administrator or consultant to help you find the right header file.

In Classic (Kernighan and Ritchie) C, if you do not declare functions before using them, the compiler usually issues no warnings and generates code anyhow. The compiler assumes that all undeclared functions return integers, and it assumes that such functions expect *exactly* the type of parameter that you are supplying it.

On the other hand, C++ makes no such assumptions but forces you to be explicit: all identifiers and functions need to be declared before use. Here are some examples comparing Classic C with C++:

C code:	C++ code:
```extern double myfunc();```	```extern double myfunc(int,char);```
```extern double cos();```	```extern "C" double cos(double);```

ANSI C follows the same convention set by C++ in the above example, except that it does not have "extern C" linkage.

Note that the *linkage*—that is, the language of the referenced routine (extern "C" designates the C language)—may be an explicit part of the declaration. In general, a linkage directive is needed for all symbols, both functions and data, that are to be accessed from code of another programming language. In most implementations, specifying C linkage for data has no effect, though a function with C++ linkage usually has a different name in the object code than one with C linkage. If no explicit linkage is specified, C++ linkage is assumed (as for myfunc).

Being explicit about return types and parameter types helps in two ways: (1) It ensures that you pass the types of arguments expected by the function, so the function does not unknowingly try processing something it did not expect, and (2) it gives the compiler enough information to convert one object type to another, where necessary, on your behalf. For example, C++ knows how to convert integers to floats automatically, which leads to the following:

C code:	C++ code:
| ```
extern double sin();

sin(1);  /* undefined */
sin((double)1);
sin(2.0);
sin(3.0);
``` | ```
extern double sin(double);

sin(1); // converts to double
sin(2); //    automatically
sin(3.0);
``` |

A.4 Call-by-Reference Parameters

The normal semantics of parameter passing in C (and in C++) are to make a copy of each parameter for use by the called function. This is called *call-by-value*. The copy is discarded when the function returns. Occasionally, a C program will pass the address of a variable as the parameter to a function, with the understanding that the function will always access that parameter with a "*" to read or write the variable. This lets the function change the value of the variable supplied by the caller. In C++, a *call-by-reference* parameter obviates the need for pointers and explicit pointer dereferencing. Consider the following incr functions, which return the old value of their argument, while incrementing the argument itself:

C code:	C++ code:
| ```c
int incr(i)
int *i;
{
    return (*i)++;
}

int main()
{
    int i, j = 5;
    i = incr(&j);
     /* i = 5, j = 6 */
    . . . .
}
``` | ```cpp
int incr(int &i)
{
    return i++;
}

int main()
{
    int i, j = 5;
    i = incr(j);
     /* i = 5, j = 6 */
    . . . .
}
``` |

The C++ syntax int &i means pass a *reference* to the variable i. The function's formal parameter (i) becomes another name for the same value, or object, that was passed as the actual parameter in main (j). Both i and j are names for the same object; that is what "reference" means in general, and what "call-by-reference" means in this case. In general, reference variables can always be created to name an object that is already named:

```cpp
int m = 5;
int &n = m;      // n means m, and m means n
n = 6;           // both m and n are now 6
```

References are more commonly used for call-by-reference. Another common idiomatic use is return-by-reference, which can save a memory copy when returning a value from a function. This is particularly useful for frequently copied, large objects (Appendix C).

A.5 Variable Number of Parameters

Occasionally we want to define a function that can take any number of any type of arguments, and let the function determine from context what was passed and how to deal with it. A common example of such a function is the printf function in C. Here, we will briefly look at how to declare, call, and implement such a function.

A function taking an unknown number of arguments of unknown type is declared as follows:

```
extern "C" int printf(...);
```

The ellipsis ("...") means that the type or number of the parameters to be supplied is variable or not compile-time knowable. Ellipses circumvent the type system so the caller can pass any number of arguments of any type. A variant of this form lets you declare the types of any fixed number of initial parameters, followed by an unknown number of parameters of unknown type:

```
extern "C" int printf(const char *, ...);
```

Such declarations are typically published in header files that are #included by applications. Header files for operating system primitives and C library primitives are provided with most C++ compilers.

A function taking a variable number of parameters is called in C++ just as it might be called in C:

```
#include <stdio.h>
// stdio.h declares printf
int main() {
    printf("hello world\n");
    int i = 1, j = 1;
    printf("%d plus %d equals %d\n", i, j, i+j);
    return 0;
}
```

Defining a function that takes an unknown number of parameters of unknown types is done much as it is in C. The facilities of stdarg.h, which is an adaptation of varargs.h, allow code taking a variable number of parameters to be written in a portable way. C++ usage differs from Classic C in that at least one formal parameter of known type must be part of the function declaration. That parameter's presence is the only guaranteed portable way to access actual arguments from within the body of the called function:

```
#include <stdarg.h>
#include <stdio.h>
int printf(const char *p1, ...) {
    va_list ap;
    va_start(ap, p1);
    . . . .
    switch(fmt) {
    case 'f':
        double d = va_arg(ap, double);
        . . . .
```

```
    case 's':
        char *string = va_arg(ap, char);
        . . . .
    case 'd':  case 'c':
        int val = va_arg(ap, int);
        . . . .
    }
    va_end(ap);   // call before returning
}
```

The use of the standard argument package shown here for C++ differs from some programming practices occasionally found in Classic (Kernighan and Ritchie) C programs, where tricks of the stack layout or assumptions about stack adjacency of lexically adjacent arguments drive the implementation. The only safe, guaranteed portable way of accessing actual arguments passed to a routine taking a variable number of arguments is through the mechanism used by stdarg.h.

Good programming practices discourage use of variable numbers of parameters for reasons of portability and readability of code. Use of the above stdargs package maximizes portability and provides programming convenience, and the ellipses declaration provides more notational convenience than was available in Classic C. The need for stdargs can often be alleviated by function overloading and argument defaulting, with increased type safety and convenience. For more information, see your local system's manual page on varargs or stdargs.

A.6 Function Pointers

Pointers to functions work almost the same as they do in C. The difference is that argument typing information must be provided:

C code:	C++ code:

`void error(p) char *p;`
`{`
`    . . . .`
`}`
`void (*efct)();`
`int main()`
`{`
`    efct = &error;`
`    (*efct)("error");`
`    efct("also calls error");`
`    return 0;`
`}`
	`void error(const char *p)`
	`{`
	`    . . . .`
	`}`
	`void (*efct)(const char *);`
	`int main()`
	`{`
	`    efct = &error;`
	`    (*efct)("error");`
	`    efct("also calls error");`
	`    return 0;`
	`}`

Another example is that of the familiar `signal` system call. This declares `signal` as being a function that takes two parameters, the first an `int` and the second a `SIG_PF` (a typedef provided in a header file). The function itself returns a pointer to a function taking an integer parameter:

C code:	C++ code:
`int efct2();`	`int efct2(int);`
`typedef int (*SIG_PF) ();` `SIG_PF fptr;`	`typedef int (*SIG_PF) (int);` `SIG_PF fptr;`
`extern (*signal())();` `fptr = signal(3, &efct2);`	`extern (*signal(int, SIG_PF))(int);` `fptr = signal(3, &efct2);`

This is like the above example, but with more specific argument types:

C code:	C++ code:
`extern (*f())();`	`extern int` `        (*f(int,char,long)) (double,int);`

`(*f(1,'a',123)) (1.0,2);`
`(*(f(1,'a',123))) (1.0,2);`
`f(1,'a',123) (1.0,2);`
	`(*f(1,'a',123)) (1.0,2);`
	`(*(f(1,'a',123))) (1.0,2);`
	`f(1,'a',123) (1.0,2);`

Function pointer declarations are often done with typedefs. Here is the `signal` example redone using more of the power of typedef:

C code:	C++ code:
`typedef int (*SIG_PF) ();`	`typedef int (*SIG_PF) (int);`
`extern (*signal())();`	`extern SIG_PF signal(int, SIG_PF);`

And here is the "gory" example done with `typedef`:

C code:	C++ code:
`typedef int (*FP)();` `extern FP (*f)();`	`typedef int (*FP) (double,int);` `extern FP f(int,char,long);`
`f(1,'a',123) (1.0,2);`	`f(1,'a',123) (1.0,2);`

A.7 The const Type Modifier

C++ lets you define a "variable" to be constant by using the const type modifier. Use of this modifier can replace the use of #define directives for *manifest constants* (so called because their value is obvious or "manifest" on inspection). A const modifier allows the compiler to enforce checks against assigning to pointers (or what they point to), or writing to a variable after it has been initialized. Three examples follow.

Example 1: Using const in place of #define

The #define directive in C is often used to create (hopefully) mnemonic, symbolic names for manifest constants. Referring to them by a given name helps document their intended use, and helps centralize the definition and administration of constants used repeatedly throughout a program. In C++, const declarations can be used in place of #define to associate names with such values. The const approach has the advantage of stronger compile-time type checking than #define offers, and in some systems it may offer better symbolic debugging capabilities.

C code:

```
#define CTRL_X '\030'
#define msg "an error"
```

C++ code:

```
const char CTRL_X = '\030';
const char *msg = "an error";
```

Either:

```
int main() {
    char c;
    . . . .
    if (c == CTRL_X) { . . . .}
    printf("%s\n", msg);
    return 0;
}
```

Symbols defined this way are guaranteed by the C++ compiler to be immutable; you cannot accidentally change the value of a constant. Purposefully changing the value of a constant requires an explicit cast (Section 2.9).

Example 2: Constant Pointers

Pointers have been called "the gotos of data." Unfortunately, pointers have an important role in C and C++ programs, serving as a way to efficiently pass large data records or arrays between functions. It is sometimes the programmer's intent to use pointers as a "read-only handle" to the data.

The const keyword can be used to control modifications to data, both directly and through pointers. Consider first the example:

```
char *const a = "example 1";
```

Here, we declare a, the pointer, to be a constant; that is, the contents of a cannot be changed. But what "contents of a" means is the *address* of some block of storage that contains a null-terminated block of characters. So this declaration asserts that we cannot change *where* a points, although it says nothing about changing the contents of *what* a points to:

```
a = "example 2";      // flagged as illegal at compile time
a[8] = '2';           // creates "example 2" successfully
```

An expression that can legally appear on the *left*-hand side of an assignment is called an *l-value* (the *l* is for "left" in "left-hand side"). Here, a is an illegal *l-value*, while a[8] still is a legal left-hand side.

To prevent a pointer from being used as an *l*-value to modify the data it references, we change the declaration to make the thing pointed to itself a constant. The declaration of b below makes the contents of the string "example 2" immutable, while the declaration of c prevents modification of the pointer itself as well as what it points to. The symbol c can be thought of as an immutable constant.

```
const char *b = "example 2";
const char *const c = "example 3";
```

Although a is not an *l*-value, *a is. The pointer b is an *l*-value, but *b is not. Neither c nor *c are *l*-values. Note that the term const strongly associates with the immediately following declarator:

```
a = "ex4";    // not O.K., declared char *const blah
*a = 'E';     // O.K., a is an l-value, declared blah *
b = "ex4";    // O.K., b is an l-value, declared char * blah
*b = 'E';     // not O.K., b is declared const blah * blah
c = "ex4";    // not O.K., c is declared char *const blah
*c = 'E';     // not O.K., c is declared const blah *blah
```

Example 3: Declaring Functions With const Arguments

To propagate the const-ness of an object across function call boundaries, the declarations of formal function parameters must be designated const. If an attempt is made to pass a const actual parameter to a function expecting a non-const formal parameter, the compiler issues an error message. Closure of function declarations is used by the compiler to guarantee the "constancy" of a const value wherever it is passed in the program.

Consider the following declaration:

```
extern char *strcpy(char*, const char*);
```

If we have declarations

```
char a[20];
const char *b = "error message";
char *c = "user prompt> ";
```

then C++ will allow

```
::strcpy(a, b);      // copy const to non-const memory
::strcpy(a, c);      // okay for const char* argument
                     //    to be non-const
::strcpy(c, b);      // like ::strcpy(a, b)
```

but it will not allow

```
::strcpy(b, c);   // not okay for non-const argument
                  //    to be passed a const char*
```

Of course, we can defeat this checking with a cast:

```
::strcpy((char *) b, c);   // okay now
```

but then why did we declare b to be const char*?

The const keyword plays an important role in canonical forms described elsewhere in the book. For a complete list, look in the index under const.

A.8 Interfacing with C Code

Many systems contain their share of low-level code, or of legacy code with its roots in a long project history. Even new systems may use a mixture of C and C++ for historical or sociological reasons. For these reasons, the C++ language has provisions for interfacing with C language modules. This section looks at external linkages from the C++ perspective: how to make C++ coexist with other languages in the same program. We look first at design considerations, followed by syntax and program administration issues.

A.8.1 Design Considerations

Combining C and C++ code in a program takes insight beyond the syntax and mechanics of sharing declarations and getting the program to link. C, C++, and other languages must be evaluated for their suitability to a problem, the role they will play in solving a problem, and their compatibility with project tools.

A major reason for using C++ is its ability to express implementations of designs using abstract data types and objects. C code rarely reflects these programming styles; it is more often used to support functional decomposition design, or as output from an automatic code generation tool such as a parser generator or CASE tool. So mixture of C code and C++ code means mixing at least two different design styles.

Such mixtures are frequently artifacts of organizational or product history. C++ can be used to write new code both for object-oriented designs and procedural designs. It is usually because of existing code, deemed too expensive to rewrite, or because of a pre-existing C code generator (for example, yacc), that the two are mixed. The designer's chore is to decide when and how to mix different styles.

Here are some typical examples of when C and C++ code might be mixed:

- **Object Libraries in a C Environment**: Consider an existing database manager written in C++, largely for C++ applications. A longstanding C application needs to be converted to communicate with the database. That C program needs to invoke C++ member functions on the objects in the database manager, and the C and C++ software need to share data structures. So the "main" part of the program is in C, using the C++ objects as a passive library of server objects.

- **C Libraries in a C++ Environment**: There is a wealth of software written in C, both in the public and private domains. C++ programs can build on this software with little effort. They need to be able to call C functions and to access C data structures; these are two of the easiest interfaces to arrange between C and C++. One example of this is a C++ program written on top of an existing graphics library on a work station or a PC; another is the use of operating systems interfaces from new C++ code.

- **Reverse Engineering**: In some cases, a project wants to rewrite its mature C code in C++ to gain the benefits of type checking, software structure, and advanced features. A C++ class might be used to encapsulate a piece of existing C code, either by converting the existing C code to C++, or by providing interfaces that allow the existing code to be called transparently from the new C++ abstraction.

  Some large base of software may have been designed using Jackson System Design [4], Yourdon dataflow analysis [3], or some other technique with origins either in the literature or in a project's own local culture. A project may wish to retarget this code to an object-oriented architecture, to take advantage of the object paradigm's support for evolution, containment and protection, or for its support of update. Here we review two major divisions of approaches to convert a non-

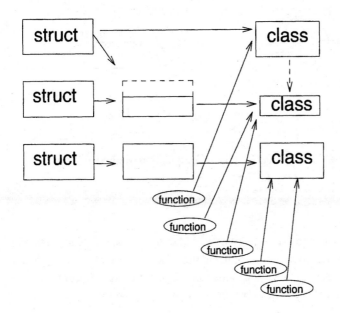

Figure A-1. A Data-Driven Inductive Class Composition Method

object-oriented software base to use the object paradigm:

- **Inductive**: Starting with specific information about low-level components of an existing architecture, such as functions, data structures, and variables, we can conceivably identify clusters of these components that will be the classes and objects of a new system.

    Inductive methods may be either data-driven or procedure-driven. A data-driven method looks to the system data structures (`structs`) as the dominant architectural entities that define what classes are (Figure A-1). Inheritance structures are inferred from commonality between data structures. Functions that interact closely with those structures become the corresponding class member functions. Note that although this approach often results in a reasonable inheritance structure, factoring of common data is not in itself the definition of inheritance. More important is the relationship between the

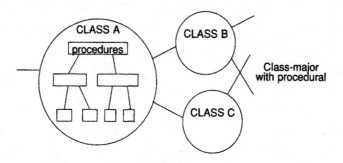

Figure A-2. A Deductive Class Composition Method With
Internal Stepwise Refinement

semantics of base and derived classes (Chapter 6). An adequate understanding
of such semantics often is not available until the class member functions have
been identified. Getting the structure right requires insight into the
application, and refinement over time through prototyping.

- **Deductive**: Deductive methods start with abstractions and converge on
  specifics, and as such are more applicable to implementing new systems from
  specifications than to evolving current systems. However, if a system has the
  right identifiable high-level abstractions (for example, general and specific
  nouns), then we can work from those to derive the class and object structure
  that will be used in the object-oriented system (Figure A-2).

  These abstractions may be discovered by an analysis of early project
  design documents; such abstractions are not likely to be found in code written
  in a language where procedures are the primary abstraction. However, an
  understanding of the design can guide the designer to pieces of code that came
  from a common design structure. Existing pieces of code may be used intact
  in a new structure that captures and strengthens the constructs of the original
  design.

  Inheritance precipitates more naturally from a deductive approach than
  from an inductive approach. Deductive approaches are more in the spirit of
  the method outlined in Chapter 6. There are some dangers to this reverse
  engineering approach—for example, identifying abstractions such as processes
  that are not problem domain nouns, but rather solution domain nouns, as the
  classes for the new system.

One paradigm can be used to create refined structures within the abstractions of another, as we might use functional decomposition within a class. Independent clusterings of mutually coupled functions might be found in a traditional design. The functions at the tops of these hierarchies might make good public member functions of a class, or private utilities that can be hidden inside a single class for use by other member functions of the same class. Lower-level functions in the hierarchy are made private member functions of the class, or are hidden using the structured programming techniques described in Appendix F.

Both these approaches have the flaw of trying to extract design information from implementation, like trying to recreate three-dimensional information from a two-dimensional picture. For implementations originally based on object-oriented techniques or on data modeling, this is at least a tractable exercise; for designs based on procedural decomposition, it is dubious at best. Instead of trying to derive an architectural model from the code, every attempt should be made to return to the original system specification and use it to define system classes. Having done so, it is likely that existing implementation components can be folded into the class structure with some modification. There is no guarantee that existing procedural code derived from the Yourdon techniques will map directly into an object orientation, but some software is likely to survive the transition. The Jackson System Design method seems well suited to the early phases of object-oriented design, and systems built on that model may lead to easier migration paths toward the object paradigm. However, Jackson techniques offer no clear advice on how their abstractions might be used in inheritance structures.

An existing body of C code may be encapsulated in a ''C++ module.'' This involves no redesign and is only a packaging technique; however, it provides a convenient mechanism for interfacing a logically cohesive collection of C software to new C++ code.

In general, conversion of stable C code to C++ is a bad idea: There is little or no long-term benefit, and there certainly is a short-term cost. For large projects, a one-time total conversion is unmanageable; incremental conversion has the cost of maintaining multiple support environments and cultures, and managing the complexity of interfaces between converted and unconverted software.

A.8.2 C Language Linkage

C++ supports name overloading; that is, two functions may have the same name if the intended function can be unambiguously selected from the context of a call, based on the types of the parameters supplied. Multiple declarations for a single function name may appear in program header files, each with distinct parameter lists, provided that the types of their return values agree. A separate function body is provided for each such declaration in a C++ source file.

Using C++ 1.2, it was possible to get into trouble depending on what order you specified #include lines at the top of a file. For example, let's say that both cookie.h and cake.h contain declarations of the function print:

```
cookie.h:          extern void print(Cookie*);
cake.h:            extern void print(Cake*);
```

The programmer uses these functions as follows:

```
overload print;    // C++ 1.2 overloading construct

#include "cookie.h"
#include "cake.h"

int f1() {
    Cookie c;
    Cake d;
    print(&c);     // calls function internally named print
    print(&d);     // calls function with encoded name
}
```

The internal name of the first print is print, and the second one has a suffix in its internal representation that distinguishes it from the first. This would work fine, unless code in another part of the system did this:

```
overload print;

#include "cake.h"
#include "cookie.h"

int f2() {
    Cookie c;
    Cake d;

    print(&c);     // calls function with encoded name
    print(&d);     // calls function internally named print
}
```

The ordering of the two #include directives affects which functions are called! One possible solution would be to require that all overload declarations be put in a single #include file. That is an unreasonable solution for common names like print that recur in many libraries.

Most current C++ compilers generate a unique internal name for each distinct function, encoding the function argument types in a suffix appended to the source name of the function. The overload keyword is now vestigial in C++. But this creates a second problem; a call to `read` would map to an internal name of `read__something`, where the suffix "`__something`" is derived from the types of the function's arguments. This works if the function `read` is itself written in C++. But if all that was intended was to call the `read(2)` function, which is written in C, then the program will not link.

To solve this, functions need to be tagged as belonging to a "foreign" language if they are not written in C++. For example, if we intend to call the C version of `read`, we must say

```
extern "C" int read(int, char*, int);
```

One can declare several functions at once as being C functions:

```
extern "C" {
    int read(int, char*, int);
    int open(char*, int, int=0);
    int write(int, char*, int);
}
```

These declarations may *not* be used inside a class or function scope; they must be at the outermost scope level. It is best to put them in the header files that users are expected to `#include` to get the declaration for the routine.

Some existing ANSI C language header files may have exactly what is needed for C++, except for the `extern "C"` construct to define the function linkages. A C++ program wishing to use one of these header files can simply wrap the `#include` inside a linkage directive:

```
extern "C" {
#include <cfuncs.h>
};
```

If the header file contains constructs other than function declarations (e.g., structure or constant declarations), it is of no consequence; they will be processed as they should be. For example, this construct has no effect on the encoding of class member functions declared in the scope of the `extern "C"`.

A.8.3 Calling C++ from C

A C++ class member function should not be called directly from C code; it should instead go through an intermediate global C++ function that bridges the two worlds.

A bad practice is to work the problem at the level of how the C++ compilation system maps C++ names onto C names, calling the "mangled" names directly at the source level:

```
struct Stack {
    . . . .   // C declaration simulating
    . . . .   //   C++ class Stack structure
};
struct Stack s;
. . . .
push__5StackFi_v(&s, 10);   /* not recommended */
```

This creates code that (1) is not portable; (2) requires more knowledge about compiler internals than is available to most people; (3) is not guaranteed to work in a future compiler even if it works in the one you have, and (4) is difficult to understand.

A much better approach is to write C language interface functions inside C++ compilation modules. These C language interface routines may be called from ordinary C functions:

C++ code:
```
class Stack {
    . . . .
};
extern "C" void CStackPush(Stack *s, int v) { s->push(v); }
```

These interface functions can be thought of as being the "firewalls" between two different paradigms. They need to be designed with care, and they are most successful when invisible.

A.8.4 Sharing Header Files between C and C++

The most important role played by function declarations in header files is to provide a single reference point for function argument and return types. If both the provider and user of a function #include the same header file, then type safety is guaranteed, even for overloaded functions. We want this to work for C-compatible functions, both as they are called from other C functions and as they are called from C++ code. However, ANSI C declarations

```
extern char *foo(short, long);
extern void bar(char, const char*);
#define SIZE 10
extern char *text[SIZE];
```

differ from the Classic C syntax

```
extern char *foo();
extern void bar();
#define SIZE 10
extern char *text[SIZE];
```

which in turn may differ from C++:

```
extern "C" char *foo(short, long);
extern "C" void bar(char, const char*);
const unsigned char SIZE = 10;
extern char *text[SIZE];
```

How can a single, common header file be structured for use with both C and C++ clients? Sometimes, we can use a single syntax that is the least common denominator to all three languages. For example, the C++ specification of SIZE and text could have used the C style. However, C++ may be able to take advantage of its own declaration style to provide better debugging information or more efficient code. We use *conditional compilation*—provided by the preprocessor macros #if, #ifdef and other related directives—to combine different language styles in a single header file.

Only ANSI C compilers pre-define the preprocessor definition __STDC__; only C++ compilers define __cplusplus. In an environment with only ANSI C and C++, you might take this approach:

```
#if __cplusplus
extern "C" {
#endif
    extern char *foo(short, long);
    extern void bar(char, const char*);
#if __STDC__
#define SIZE 10
#endif
#if __cplusplus
const unsigned char SIZE = 10;
#endif
extern char *text[SIZE];
    . . . .
#if __cplusplus
}
#endif
```

That is a bit ugly: the literal constant *10* appears in two places, so there is a chance that C and C++ code may lose synchronization as the program evolves. One might prefer to adopt the following style so that changes to the value represented by SIZE need to be made only in one place:

```
#if __cplusplus
extern "C" {
#endif
    extern char *foo(short, long);
    extern void bar(char, const char*);
#define COMMON_SIZE 10
#if __STDC__
#define SIZE COMMON_SIZE
#endif
#if __cplusplus
    const unsigned char SIZE = COMMON_SIZE;
#endif
char *text[SIZE];
    . . . .
#if __cplusplus
}
#endif
```

Sharing as much text as possible helps keeps updates coordinated.

Another frequent combination is an environment where Classic C is being used with C++:

```
#if __cplusplus
extern "C" {
#endif
    extern char *foo(
#          if __cplusplus
                short, long
#          endif
    );
    extern void bar(
#          if __cplusplus
                char, const char*
#          endif
    );
#define COMMON_SIZE 10
#if __cplusplus
    const unsigned char SIZE = COMMON_SIZE;
#else
#    define SIZE COMMON_SIZE
#endif
extern char *text[SIZE];
    . . . .
#if __cplusplus
}
#endif
```

If you have a mixture of all three, the file starts getting complicated:

```
#if __cplusplus
extern "C" {
#endif
    extern char *foo(
#           if __cplusplus||__STDC__
                short, long
#           endif
    );
    extern void bar(
#           if __cplusplus||__STDC__
                char, const char*
#           endif
    );

#define COMMON_SIZE 10

#if !__cplusplus
#     define SIZE COMMON_SIZE
#else
    const unsigned char SIZE = COMMON_SIZE;
#endif

extern char *text[SIZE];
    . . . .

#if __cplusplus
}
#endif
```

Based on the rule of thumb that code is read ten times more often than it is written, the problem of redundant maintenance may be traded off against readability by using a single #ifdef for each language, duplicating everything for each one.

There are also places where a single, common syntax can express a declaration equally well in both ANSI C and in C++. For example, a common form can be used in C++ and ANSI C to declare parameterless functions:

```
return-type function(void);
```

This makes it clear in ANSI C programs that no parameters are expected; if the void were not there, the ANSI compiler would accept calls with any number of parameters of any type. While the void is optional in C++, it is legal and has the same semantics as in ANSI C. Another form common to the two languages can be used as the core of symbolic constant declarations:

```
#if __cplusplus
extern "C" {
#endif
static const type symbol1_name = initializer;
extern const type symbol2_name;
#if __cplusplus
}
#endif
```

Making the static and extern explicit is the key to agreement between the two languages.

These are just rules of thumb, and each application and administrative environment should apply them as common sense dictates, and invent their own conventions as more suitable alternatives are found.

A.8.5 Importing C Data Formats to C++

We've talked about how functions access each other between C and C++. How about data? If you have a C structure that you want to access from C++, you can often share the same header file, declaring the layout of the structure, between the two languages. Provided a structure declaration adheres to C syntax, "objects" of that structure can be shared between C and C++ code in a single program with no problem.

A.8.6 Importing C++ Data Formats to C

Although upward compatibility works for us when writing C++ code to use existing C data formats, the converse works against us here. You cannot in general add C code to an existing C++ application and expect the C code to use the C++ data formats. Some explicit conversion is necessary.

If the data structure found in the C++ program is a simple C struct with no member functions, then it can be treated as a C structure, #included by C and C++ programs alike, as described above.

There are two basic approaches to handling the more complex case:

1. *(Not recommended)*: Determine what the data layout of a C++ class is, and duplicate its structure in a C struct. A class with virtual functions may have some surprise fields in it for which a filler (dummy member) must be provided in the struct. The location and size of this field are implementation dependent. If your C++ environment allows the generation of C object code from C++ source, you may be able to automatically generate a C header file from the C++ header file containing the class declaration, by running it through

```
extern "C" const char *EmployeeRecordName(void*);
extern "C" short EmployeeRecordYOS(void*);
extern "C" double EmployeeRecordSalary(void*);

class EmployeeRecord {
friend const char *EmployeeRecordName(void*);
friend short EmployeeRecordYOS(void*);
friend double EmployeeRecordSalary(void*);
public:
    EmployeeRecord(const char*, short, double);
    EmployeeRecord();
    void giveRaise(double);
    virtual void disbursePay();
private:
    char name[NAME_SIZE];
    short yearsOfService;
    double monthlySalary;
};

extern "C" {
    void aCFunction(void *RecordPtr);

    const char *EmployeeRecordName(void *RecordPtr) {
        return ((EmployeeRecord *)RecordPtr)->name;
    }

    short EmployeeRecordYOS(void *RecordPtr) {
        return((EmployeeRecord *)RecordPtr)->yearsOfService;
    }

    double EmployeeRecordSalary(void *RecordPtr) {
        return((EmployeeRecord *)RecordPtr)->monthlySalary;
    }
}


    . . . .
    EmployeeRecord aRecord;
    aCFunction(&aRecord);      // call of C application routine
                               // giving C land a pointer into
                               // some C++ data
    . . . .
```

Figure A-3. C++ Code Accessed by C Code

your compiler or translator with appropriate options. However, this can produce a header file having funny field names, and some knowledge of compiler-proprietary algorithms may be required by the C programmer to make this work. Keeping the two interfaces in synchronization is a manual, and therefore error-prone, procedure.

2. Access the data through functions provided in C++ for that purpose, adopting some of the "firewall" tricks described above.

Figure A-3 shows an example in which some C code can access the data members of an `EmployeeRecord` class written in C++. The C code is given an anonymous handle (`void*` pointer) as a parameter; it uses that handle as a parameter to the data dereferencing functions:

```
extern char *EmployeeRecordName(void*);
extern short EmployeeRecordYOS(void*);
extern double EmployeeRecordSalary(void*);

void aCFunction(void *RecordPtr) {
    char *name = EmployeeRecordName(RecordPtr);
    short YOS = EmployeeRecordYOS(RecordPtr);
    double salary = EmployeeRecordSalary(RecordPtr);
    . . . .
}
```

Exercises

1. Write a simplified version of the `printf` function that processes only **%d** and **%s** formats.

2. Write a `qsort` routine that has the following interface:

```
void qsort(void *base, int nel,
                int elementSize, int(*compar)(void*, void*));
```

Assume the following: `base` points to the element at the base of the table to be sorted; `nel` is the number of elements in the table; `elementSize` is the size of a single table element; `compar` is a pointer to a function that compares two elements and returns an integer less than, equal to, or greater than zero depending on whether the first argument is to be considered less than, equal to, or greater than the second. Feel free to borrow from the source for any existing sorting function.

3. Write declarations for the familiar UNIX functions `printf`, `malloc`, `read`, `write`, `pipe`, `open`, `close`, and `signal`.

□

References

1. Koenig, A, and B. Stroustrup. "C++: As Close as Possible to C—But No Closer," *C++ Report 1*,7 (July/August 1989).

2. Kernighan, Brian W., and Dennis M. Ritchie. *The C Programming Language*, 2nd ed. New York: Prentice-Hall, 1988.

3. DeMarco, T. *Structured Analysis and System Specification*. New York: Yourdon Press, 1978.

4. Jackson, M. A. *Principles of Program Design*. London: Academic Press, 1975.

Shapes Program: C++ Code

```
#include "Shapes.h"
/*------------------------------------------------------------*/
/* File main.c -- Driver program for Shapes example           */
/*------------------------------------------------------------*/
const int XSIZE = 800;
const int YSIZE = 1024;

void
rotateList(Shape *s, Angle a)
{
    for (Shape *f = s;   f;   f = f->next())
        f->rotate(a);
}

int
main()
{
    Coordinate origin (0,0);

    /*
     * windowBorder is not only the frame for the screen,
     * but also serves as list head for the list of shapes
     */

    Rect windowBorder(origin, XSIZE, YSIZE);

    Shape * t = new Triangle(
       Coordinate(100, 100),
       Coordinate(200, 200),
       Coordinate(300, 100)

    );
```

```
    windowBorder.append(t);

    Shape * c = new Circle(Coordinate(500,652), 150);
    t->insert(c);

    rotateList(&windowBorder, 90.0);
    return 0;
}




#include <math.h>
#include <X11/X.h>

/*
 * File Shapes.h
 * Author:  J. O. Coplien
 *
 * This header file contains declarations for classes used in
 * a demonstration Shape library.  Many member functions are
 * defined herein as inlines.
 */

/*-------------------------------------------------------------*/
/* class Angle is an angle in degrees or radians.  It is a     */
/* class so that it can be easily ported to systems using      */
/* either degrees or radians, and also so arithmetic           */
/* precision(float, double, or int) can be changed.            */
/*-------------------------------------------------------------*/

class Angle {
friend double cos(Angle);
friend double sin(Angle);
public:
    Angle(double d)        { radians = d; }
    Angle ()               { radians = 0; }
    Angle(const Angle& a) { radians = a.radians; }
    inline Angle &operator=(const Angle& a) {
        radians = a.radians;
        return *this;
    }
    Angle operator+(const Angle&) const;
private:
    double     radians;
};
```

```
/*-----------------------------------------------------------*/
/* class Coordinate describes a point on the Cartesian plane.*/
/*   It can be in micrometers, pixels, inches, or any other  */
/* convenient units and scale.                               */
/*-----------------------------------------------------------*/

class Coordinate {
public:
    inline long x() const        { return x_rep; }
    inline long y() const        { return y_rep; }
    Coordinate    &operator=(Coordinate &c) {
        x_rep = c.x_rep;
        y_rep = c.y_rep;
        return *this;
    }
    Coordinate(long x, long y) {
        x_rep = x; y_rep = y;
    }
    Coordinate(const Coordinate &c) {
        x_rep = c.x_rep;
        y_rep = c.y_rep;
    }
    Coordinate()         { x_rep = y_rep = 0;}
    ~Coordinate()        { }

    void rotateAbout(Coordinate,Angle);
private:
    long x_rep, y_rep;
};


/*-----------------------------------------------------------*/
/* These functions overload the normal trig functions,       */
/* arranging so that they can be called with Angle as an     */
/* argument.  Since overloading cannot be done on the basis  */
/* of return value--only on the basis of argument            */
/* type--the trig function atan, which needs to be able      */
/* to return an object of type Angle, cannot be overloaded   */
/* and must be made a whole new function.                    */
/*-----------------------------------------------------------*/

inline double cos(Angle a)       { return ::cos(a.radians); }
inline double sin(Angle a)       { return ::sin(a.radians); }
inline Angle Angleatan(double t) {
    Angle a(::atan(t)); return a;
}
```

```
/*-----------------------------------------------------------*/
/* Class Color encapsulated the implementation of color      */
/* encoding for the graphics package being used; its         */
/* internals can be accessed just by low-level interface     */
/* routines, while high-level routines deal at a more general*/
/* level.  This makes porting possible across a wide variety */
/* of machines.                                              */
/* Flashing is an attribute of color.  The commonly used     */
/* constants Black and White are predeclared as constant     */
/* global color objects.                                     */
/*-----------------------------------------------------------*/

enum Flash { FlashBlack, FlashWhite, FlashOff };

class Color {
public:
    inline    double    red()        { return red_rep;  }
    inline    double    green()      { return green_rep;  }
    inline    double    blue()       { return blue_rep;  }
          Color(double r=0.0, double g=0.0,
                double b=0.0, Flash f=FlashOff) {
        red_rep = r;
        green_rep = g;
        blue_rep = b;
        flashing = f;
    }
    inline    Color&    operator=(const Color& c) {
        red_rep = c.red_rep;
        green_rep=c.green_rep;
        blue_rep = c.blue_rep;
      return *this;
    }
          ~Color()        { }
private:
    double    red_rep, green_rep, blue_rep;
    Flash    flashing;
};

const color Black, White = Color(1.0, 1.0, 1.0);
```

```
/*---------------------------------------------------------------*/
/* Shape is the base class for all of the graphical shapes.  */
/* It defines the signature (operations) possible on a shape,*/
/* and also provides the actual implementation of operators  */
/* common to all shapes (like move, common to all with some  */
/* exceptions).                                              */
/*---------------------------------------------------------------*/

class Shape {
public:
    // rotate about center
    virtual   void    rotate(Angle a)          { }
    virtual   void    move(Coordinate xy) {
        erase(); center_val=xy; draw();
    }
    virtual   void    draw()   = 0;      // renderer
    virtual   void    erase() {
        color = Black; draw();
    }

    virtual   void    redraw() {
        erase(); draw();
    }
    Shape();
    virtual   ~Shape();
    virtual   Coordinate origin() const  { return center_val; }
    virtual   Coordinate center() const  { return center_val; }
    inline    Shape   *next() const   { return next_pointer; }
    inline    Shape   *prev() const   { return prev_pointer; }
    inline    void    insert(Shape* i) {
        i->next_pointer= this;
        i->prev_pointer=prev_pointer;
        prev_pointer->next_pointer=i;
        prev_pointer = i;
    }
    inline    void    append(Shape* i)     {
                      i->next_pointer=next();
                    i->prev_pointer = this;
                    next_pointer->prev_pointer=i;
                    next_pointer = i;
                }
protected:

    /*
     * These are protected instead of private so they can be
     * accessed by routines in the derived classes
     */
```

```
    Coordinate    center_val;    // nominal center
    Color    color;          // shape's color

    /*
     * These class static variables are used by the underlying
     * window package (e.g., X) for general graphics setup.
     */

    static        Display       display;
    static        Window        window;
    static        GContext      gc;

private:
    Shape    *next_pointer;    // pointer to next in list
    Shape    *prev_pointer;    // pointer to previous in list
};

/*----------------------------------------------------------------*/
/* Line is a special shape, since it is usually the               */
/* rendering component of all other shapes. It alone among        */
/* shapes has a rotateAbout member function which is used as       */
/* the primitive for rotating other shapes.  The rotate          */
/* operation is a degenerate form of rotateAbout. The center      */
/* is defined as the average of the endpoints; the origin is      */
/* the first endpoint.                                            */
/*----------------------------------------------------------------*/
class Line : public Shape {
public:
    void    rotate(Angle a)      { rotateAbout(center(),a); }
    void    rotateAbout(Coordinate,Angle);
    void    draw();
    inline Line &operator=(const Line &l) {
        p=Coordinate(l.p); q=Coordinate(l.q); return *this;
    }
    Line(Coordinate,Coordinate);
    Line(Line& l) {
        p = l.p; q = l.q;
        center_val = l.center_val;
    }
    Line()                  { p = Coordinate(0,0);
                              q = Coordinate(0,0); }
   ~Line()                  { erase(); }
    inline  Coordinate      e() const    { return q; }
    inline  Coordinate origin() const    { return p; }
private:
    Coordinate    p, q;                     // line endpoints
};
```

```
/*-----------------------------------------------------------*/
/* Rect is made up of four lines. Origin is upper-left hand  */
/* corner, and is established from the constructor's first   */
/* parameter. Center is geometric center, as expected. The   */
/* operation erase is inherited from Shape. Reps are         */
/* protected instead of private so that subclass Square can  */
/*  use them.                                                */
/*-----------------------------------------------------------*/

class Rect : public Shape {
public:
    void      rotate(Angle);
    void      draw();
    void      move(Coordinate);
              //upper left corner, x size, y size
              Rect(Coordinate,long,long);
              ~Rect()                 { erase(); }
    inline    Coordinate  origin() const { return l1.origin(); }
protected:
    Line      l1, l2, l3, l4;
};


/*-----------------------------------------------------------*/
/* Ellipse's center is geometric center; origin is center.   */
/* Ellipse is unimplemented.                                 */
/*-----------------------------------------------------------*/

class Ellipse : public Shape {
public:
    void      rotate(Angle);
    void      draw();
              // center, major axis, minor axis
              Ellipse(Coordinate,long,long);
              ~Ellipse()      { erase(); }
protected:
    long      major, minor;
};
```

```
/*-------------------------------------------------------------*/
/* A triangle is made up of three lines.  Its center is        */
/* calculated as the average of all points.                    */
/*-------------------------------------------------------------*/

class Triangle : public Shape {
public:
    void      rotate(Angle);
    void      draw();
    void      move(Coordinate);
          Triangle(Coordinate,Coordinate,Coordinate);
          ~Triangle()      { erase(); }
private:
    Line      l1, l2, l3;
};


/*-------------------------------------------------------------*/
/* A square is just a degenerate rectangle.  All member        */
/* functions are inherited from Rect; only the constructor     */
/* is customized, and it does nothing but call Rect's          */
/*  constructor.                                               */
/*-------------------------------------------------------------*/

class Square : public Rect {
public:
          Square(Coordinate ctr, long x):
            Rect(ctr, x, x)           { }
};
```

```
/*--------------------------------------------------------------*/
/*                                                              */
/* File Shapes.c, containing Shape code for example program     */
/*                                                              */
/*--------------------------------------------------------------*/

#include "Shapes.h"

extern "C" {
    extern void doXInitialization(Shape&);
    extern void
      XDrawLine(Display, Window, GContext, int, int, int, int);
}

/*
 * CLASS ANGLE
 */

Angle
Angle::operator+(const Angle& angle) const {
    Angle retval = angle;
    retval.radians += radians;
    return retval;
}

/*
 * CLASS COORDINATE
 */

void
Coordinate::rotateAbout(Coordinate pivot, Angle angle)
{
    long xdistance = pivot.x()-x(), ydistance = pivot.y()-y();
    long xdistsquared = xdistance * xdistance,
      ydistsquared = ydistance * ydistance;
    double r = ::sqrt( xdistsquared + ydistsquared );
    Angle newangle = angle +
                Angleatan(double(ydistance)/double(xdistance));
    x_rep = pivot.x() + long(r * ::cos(newangle));
    y_rep = pivot.y() + long(r * ::sin(newangle));
}
```

```
/*
 * CLASS SHAPE
 */

/* flag for underlying graphics package */

static int X_initialized = 0;

Shape::Shape() {
    center_val = Coordinate(0, 0);
    next_pointer=prev_pointer=0;
    color = White;
    if( !X_initialized) {
       doXInitialization(*this);
       X_initialized = 1;
    }
}

/*
 * CLASS LINE
 */

void
Line::rotateAbout(Coordinate c, Angle angle) {
    erase();
    p.rotateAbout(c, angle);
    q.rotateAbout(c, angle);
    draw();
}

void
Line::draw() {
    if (p.x()-q.x() && p.y()-q.y()) {
       XDrawLine(display, window, gc, p.x(),
                                    p.y(), q.x(), q.y());
    }
}

Line::Line(Coordinate p1, Coordinate p2) {
    p = p1; q = p2;
    center_val = Coordinate((p.x()+q.x())/2, (p.y()+q.y())/2);
    color = Color(White);
    draw();
}
```

```
/*
 * CLASS RECTANGLE
 */

void
Rect::rotate(Angle angle) {
    erase();
    l1.rotateAbout(center(), angle);
    l2.rotateAbout(center(), angle);
    l3.rotateAbout(center(), angle);
    l4.rotateAbout(center(), angle);
    draw();
}

void
Rect::draw() {
    l1.draw();
    l2.draw();
    l3.draw();
    l4.draw();
}

void
Rect::move(Coordinate c) {
    /*
     * Argument is center.  Move center there; find out how far
     * center moved and displace all points by the same amount.
     */

    erase();
    long xmoved = c.x() - center().x();
    long ymoved = c.y() - center().y();
    center_val = c;
    l1 = Line(Coordinate(l1.origin().x()+xmoved,
                                        l1.origin().y()+ymoved),
        Coordinate(l1.e().x()+xmoved,l1.e().y()+ymoved) );
    l2 = Line(Coordinate(l2.origin().x()+xmoved,
                                        l2.origin().y()+ymoved),
        Coordinate(l2.e().x()+xmoved,l2.e().y()+ymoved) );
    l3 = Line(Coordinate(l3.origin().x()+xmoved,
                                        l3.origin().y()+ymoved),
        Coordinate(l3.e().x()+xmoved,l3.e().y()+ymoved) );
    l4 = Line(Coordinate(l4.origin().x()+xmoved,
                                        l4.origin().y()+ymoved),
        Coordinate(l4.e().x()+xmoved,l4.e().y()+ymoved) );
    draw();
}
```

```
Rect::Rect(Coordinate topLeft, long xsize, long ysize) {
    Coordinate    a(topLeft);
    Coordinate    b(a.x()+xsize, a.y());
    Coordinate    c(a.x(),a.y()+ysize);
    Coordinate    d(b.x(),c.y());
    l1 = Line(a,b);
    l2 = Line(b,c);
    l3 = Line(c,d);
    l4 = Line(d,a);
    center_val = Coordinate((l1.origin().x()+l2.e().x())/2,
                    (l4.origin().y()+l4.e().y())/2);
    draw();
}

/*
 * CLASS TRIANGLE
 */

void
Triangle::rotate(Angle angle) {
    erase();
    l1.rotateAbout(center(), angle);
    l2.rotateAbout(center(), angle);
    l3.rotateAbout(center(), angle);
    draw();
}

void
Triangle::move(Coordinate c) {
    /*
     * Argument is center.  Move center there; find out how far
     * center moved and displace all points by the same amount.
     */

    erase();
    long xmoved = c.x() - center().x();
    long ymoved = c.y() - center().y();
    center_val = c;
    l1 = Line(Coordinate(l1.origin().x()+xmoved,
                                    l1.origin().y()+ymoved),
        Coordinate(l1.e().x()+xmoved,l1.e().y()+ymoved) );
    l2 = Line(Coordinate(l2.origin().x()+xmoved,
                                    l2.origin().y()+ymoved),
        Coordinate(l2.e().x()+xmoved,l2.e().y()+ymoved) );
    l3 = Line(Coordinate(l3.origin().x()+xmoved,
                                    l3.origin().y()+ymoved),
        Coordinate(l3.e().x()+xmoved,l3.e().y()+ymoved) );
    draw();
}
```

```
void
Triangle::draw() {
    l1.draw(); l2.draw(); l3.draw();
}

Triangle::Triangle(Coordinate a, Coordinate b, Coordinate c) {
    l1 = Line(a,b);   l2 = Line(b,c);   l3 = Line(c,a);
    center_val =
                Coordinate((l1.e().x()+l2.e().x()+l3.e().x())/3,
                           (l1.e().y()+l2.e().y()+l3.e().y())/3);
    draw();
}
```

C

Reference Return Values from Operators

A reference variable is not a pointer, nor is it really an object or variable in the pure sense of the term. Rather, it is the *name* of an object. A reference is brought into existence to give a new name to some pre-existing object.

The high-level answer to "why `operator=` and `operator[]` return reference values" is that being a reference allows the return value to act like a variable name. That is, anywhere a variable name can occur, a variable reference (of the same type) can also appear legally. A name, for example, can occur as an *l*-value (something that can appear on the left-hand side of an assignment), but in general, expressions cannot. Having `operator=` and `operator[]` return references means that such expressions can appear as *l*-values. This is particularly important in the case of vectors, where we want to do vector assignment (Section 3.3).

The following idiom (from Appendix A) illustrates a simple use of call-by-reference:

C code:		C++ code:
```int incr(i)```		```int incr(int &i)```
```int *i;```	=	```{```
```{```		``` return i++;```
``` return (*i)++;```		```}```
```}```		
```int main()```		```int main()```
```{```		```{```
``` int j = 5;```	=	``` int j = 5;```
``` incr(&j);```		``` incr(j);```
```}```		```}```

The idiom can be extended to function return value types, including those of operator overloading functions. In fact, many built-in binary operators should return reference values to support associativity. Consider the following example:

C code:		C++ code:

```
struct String {            1    class String {
    char *rep;             2    public:
};                        3        char operator[](int i) {
                          4            return t[i];
char index(t, i)          5        }
struct String *t; int i;  6    private:
{                         7        char *t;
    return t->rep[i];     8    };
}                         9
                          10
int main()                11   int main()
{                         12   {
    struct String x; char c;  13       String x; char c;
    . . . .               14       . . . .
    c = index(x, 5);      15       c = x[5];
    index(x,6) = 'a';     16       x[6] = 'a';
    return 0;             17       return 0;
}                         18   }
```

Here, the C version yields the compile-time error message

```
"t2.c", line 16: addressable expression required
```

and the C++ version gives the error message

```
"t2.c", line 16: error: assignment to generated function call
    (not an lvalue)
```

However, if we add a level of indirection to the C version—and make the analogous change to use a reference return value in the C++ version—all works out well:

C code:	C++ code:
```c\nstruct String {\n char *rep;\n};\n\nchar *index(t, i)\nstruct String *t; int i;\n{\n return t->rep + i;\n}\n\nint main()\n{\n char x[80], c;\n c = *(index(x, 5));\n *(index(x,6)) = 'a';\n return 0;\n}\n```	```cpp\nclass String {\npublic:\n char &operator[](int i) {\n return t[i];\n }\nprivate:\n char *t;\n};\n\nint main()\n{\n String x; char c;\n c = x[5];\n x[6] = 'a';\n return 0;\n}\n```

D

Why Bitwise Copy Doesn't Work

In versions of the C++ translator before release 1.2, structure (and class) assignment were done just as they are in C: The contents of the source were simply copied to the destination. We call this *bitwise copy*.

Usually, a programmer defining a C++ class uses the canonical form (Section 3.1) to thwart bitwise copy by "catching" all the operations that cause copying: assignment (`operator=`) and argument passing and return values (`X::X(X&)`). The user can then do the same thing a bitwise copy would, or can do more elaborate processing, such as keeping track of reference counts. It is particularly important that this special processing be done when objects hold a *pointer* to any dynamically allocated storage; otherwise insanity can ensue.

Consider our (now sadly overworked) `String` example:

```
class String {
public:
    String(int n)              { rep = new char[size = n]; }
    ~String()                  { delete rep; }
    inline int length() const  { return size; }
private:
    char *rep;
    int size;
};
```

Now consider the following program that declares two `Strings`, then assigns one to the other:

```
int main() {
    String s1(10), s2(20);
    s1 = s2;
    return 0;
}
```

This program first calls the constructor `String(int)` for each of s1 and s2; each object in turn allocates a character vector and stores a pointer to that vector into its respective `rep`. Then when assignment takes place, each of the fields in s1 takes on exactly the same value as its corresponding field in s2. This leaves both s1.`rep` and s2.`rep` pointing to the same twenty-element vector in memory, and leaves the ten-element vector originally associated with s1 unreferenced! That alone is at least confusing. But now, when the program exits, the destructors for both s1 and s2 are automatically called (the compiler arranges to do so). Each will invoke `delete` on their `rep` field, which means the same block of memory will be freed twice. This generally results in heap arena insanity, and ultimate abnormal program death.

By catching assignment and either making a local copy of the vector in s1, or by keeping a reference count, the problem can be avoided. That is why every non-trivial class should have an `operator=` and an `X::X(const X&)` constructor, as in the orthodox canonical form.

D.1 Why Member-by-Member Copy Isn't a Panacea

C++ automatically provides a reasonable `operator=` and `X::X(const X&)` constructor for classes in which you omit them. `X::X(const X&)` initializes the current object member-by-member from its parameter's members; `operator=` assigns its object's members from its parameter, one at a time. However, these are not always done as bitwise copies: `X::X(const X&)` initializes members using *their* `X::X(const X&)` constructor, and assignment likewise applies assignment recursively. Those routines may increment reference counts for dynamically allocated memory owned by those contained objects, or may do other housekeeping to avoid the kind of insanity discussed with the `String` example above.

This adaptation works well in situations where everything is a class object. However, if *anything* is a pointer—particularly, a pointer that is `delete`d by a destructor—then the approach breaks down and we're back to the same problem we started out with: doubly deleting dynamically allocated memory. So in any class where the destructor performs a `delete` on one of its members, it is important to define an `operator=` and a `X::X(X&)` constructor.

One motivation behind overloading `operator->` (see the discussion of counted pointers in Section 6.5) in C++ 2.0 was to make everything a class object; this means that the automated member-by-member copy would always be sufficient, since pointers would go away. This has not yet matured as a well understood idiom in the C++ programming community, and other approaches are being developed in its stead.

E

Symbolic Shapes

```
//**********************************************************************//
//                                                                    //
//     F I L E :     M P T R . H                                      //
//                                                                    //
//        Declarations of C++ compiler data structures               //
//                                                                    //
//**********************************************************************//
// These data structures support the C++ virtual function
// mechanism.  vptp is a general function pointer;  it
// is used to address (but not call) member functions.
// vvptp is a pointer to a function returning a pointer
// to a function;  it is used in some setup idioms in the
// cutover empire.  mptr describes an entry in the
// virtual function table;  it can be derived from your
// C++ compilation system's object code.

typedef int (*vptp)();
typedef vptp (*vvptp)();
struct mptr {short d; short i; vptp f; };
```

```
//*********************************************************************//
//                                                                     //
//        F I L E :   K . H                                            //
//                                                                     //
//        Declarations for classes Thing and Top                      //
//                                                                     //
//*********************************************************************//
#ifndef _MPTR_H
#       include "mptr.h"
#endif
#define _K_H
#include <String.h>

//  MACHINE AND COMPILER DEPENDENT
const unsigned int WRDSIZE = sizeof(void*);

inline size_t
Round(size_t s) {
    return (size_t)((s + WRDSIZE - 1)/WRDSIZE)*WRDSIZE;
}

// commonly used character pointer type
typedef char *Char_p;

// dummy type, simply used to disambiguate between
// constructors of ShapeRep derived classes
enum Exemplar { };

//  MACHINE AND COMPILER DEPENDENT

class Top {
public:
    // This class has no data, except __vtbl which is
    // provided by the compiler.  Deriving all classes
    // from this class assures that the __vtbl will
    // always be the first element in any object.
    // If that is not true for the compiler being
    // used, then other mechanisms will be necessary
    // to find the __vtbl, and the implementation
    // here may need to change (viz., findVtblEntry).

    // This also reserves a __vtbl slot for system
    // internal use

    virtual ~Top() { }
    mptr* findVtblEntry(vptp);
    void update(String, String, const char *const = "");
    static void operator delete(void *p) {
        ::operator delete(p);
    }
    // doit is a general-purpose function to help users
```

```
    // to orchestrate update.
    virtual Top *doit();
protected:
    Top()   { }
    static void *operator new(size_t l) {
        return ::operator new(l);
    }
private:
    // compare two function pointers for equality
    int compareFuncs(int, vptp, vptp);
};

typedef Top *Topp;

class Thing: public Top {
    // All  "rep" fields are derived from Thing;  it defines
    // the canonical form for all Letter classes
public:
    virtual Thing *type() { return this; }
    Thing() { }
    virtual Thing *cutover();        // field update function
    virtual ~Thing() { }             // destructor
    int docutover();
};

typedef Thing *Thingp;
```

```
//**********************************************************************//
//                                                                      //
//       F I L E :     K . C                                            //
//                                                                      //
//            Code for class Thing                                      //
//                                                                      //
//**********************************************************************//
#include "k.h"

Thing *
Thing::cutover() {
    // placeholder for cutover function.  This function is
    // provided by the user on a case-by-case basis to
    // orchestrate the conversion between an old class
    // data format and a new one.  The function is
    // invoked on an instance of the old class, and should
    // return an instance of the new one.
    return this;
}

int
Thing::docutover() {
    // the user may choose not to cut over some objects
    // on a class data conversion.  This function returns
    // true or false on an object-by-object basis to tell
    // whether the object should be converted to the new
    // format.  This is done mainly for objects shared
    // by multiple envelope classes:  the object needs
    // to be converted exactly once, NOT once per
    // envelope, and docutover can orchestrate when that
    // shared object is converted (by looking at its
    // reference count, keeping a shadow counter, etc.)
    return 1;
}
```

```
//**********************************************************************//
//                                                                      //
//      F I L E :    T O P . C                                          //
//                                                                      //
//              Code for class Top                                      //
//                                                                      //
//**********************************************************************//
#include "k.h"
#include <sys/types.h>

Top *
Top::doit() {
    // unused function provided as a handy,
    // user-loadable hook to help orchestrate
    // class update
    return 0;
}

int
Top::compareFuncs(int vtblindex, vptp, vptp fptr) {
    // this compares two function pointer abstractions
    // for equality.  The first function pointer is
    // characterized by its vtbl index and a function
    // pointer;  the second, by just a function pointer.
    // The use of these parameters may be system dependent;
    // here the first pointer's function address is
    // unused
    return vtblindex == (int)fptr;
}

mptr *
Top::findVtblEntry(vptp f) {
    // Look in "this" object's virtual function table
    // for a function pointer equal to the f parameter,
    // and return the address of its mptr structure
    // (the full contents of the virtual function table
    // entry)

    // mpp will be the address of the vtbl pointer;  we
    // are guaranteed by the inheritance structure that
    // the vtbl pointer will be at the beginning of
    // every object of interest (all objects are derived
    // from Top)
    mptr ** mpp = (mptr**) this;

    // dereference the pointer address to get the
    // vtbl address which is sitting in the beginning
    // of this object
    mptr * vtbl = *mpp;
```

```
    printf("Top::findVtblEntry(%d):   vtbl = 0x%x\n", f, vtbl);

    // go through my own vtbl;  a zero entry is an end
    // sentinel, and the zeroth entry is unused.  Look
    // for the requested function
    for(int i = 1; vtbl[i].f; ++i ) {
        if (compareFuncs(i, vtbl[i].f, f)) {
            return vtbl + i;
        }
    }
    return 0;
}

// declaration of external "load" function from C land
extern "C" vptp load(const char *);

void
Top::update(    String filename,
                String fname,
                const char *const TypedefSpec) {

    // Get function fname from file filename and
    // load it into memory.  The last parameter
    // optionally specifies the type of a pointer
    // to the function;  it is necessary if the
    // function is overloaded.  The virtual function
    // table is updated accordingly.  Only virtual
    // functions can be updated.

    const String temp = "/tmp";

    printf("Top::update(\"%s\", \"%s\", \"%s\")\n",
        (const char *)filename, (const char *)fname,
        (const char *)TypedefSpec);
    String prepname = temp + "/" + "t.c";
    String Typedef, cast = "";
    if (strlen(TypedefSpec)) {
        Typedef = String("// TYPE used to disambiguate\
        overloaded function\n\t\t\ttypedef ") + TypedefSpec;
    } else {
        Typedef = "typedef vptp TYPE";
        cast = "(vptp)";
    }
    // make prepname:  helper function to return address
    // of the function being updated
    FILE *tempFile = fopen(prepname, "w");
    fprintf(tempFile, "#\
        include \"includes.h\"\n\
        extern vptp functionAddress() {\n\
            %s;\n\
```

```
                    TYPE retval = %s&%s;\n\
                    return (vptp)retval;\n\
            }\n",
            (const char*)Typedef,
            (const char *)cast,
            (const char*)fname);
        fclose(tempFile);

        // Compile the helper function
        String command = String("DIR='pwd'; cd ") + temp + ";\
            CC +e0 -I$DIR -c -g " + prepname;
        system(command);
        unlink(prepname);
        String objectname =
                prepname(0, prepname.length() - 2) + ".o";

        // Load the helper function.  Recall that load
        // returns the new function's address
        vvptp findfunc = (vvptp)load(objectname);
        unlink(objectname);
        printf("Top::update: calling findVtblEntry(%d)\n",
                        (*findfunc)());

        // Now find the correct vtbl entry within this
        // class vtbl. The helper function is called to
        // tell findVtblEntry which function it is
        // looking for
        mptr *vtblEntry = findVtblEntry((*findfunc)());

        // Now load the new version of the function and store
        // its address in the vtbl entry
        printf("Top::update: old vtblEntry->f = 0x%x\n",
            vtblEntry->f);
        printf("Top::update: calling load(\"%s\")\n",
            (const char *) filename);
        vtblEntry->f = load(filename);
        printf("Top::update: complete, new vtblEntry->f = 0x%x\n",
            vtblEntry->f);
}
```

```
//**********************************************************************//
//                                                                      //
//     F I L E :     C O O R D I N A T E . H                            //
//                                                                      //
//             Interface for struct Coordinate                          //
//                                                                      //
//**********************************************************************//

#define _COORDINATE_H

// This is a simple public class that represents a Cartesian
// coordinate on the graphics screen

struct Coordinate {
    int x, y;
    Coordinate(int xx = 0, int yy = 0) { x = xx; y = yy; }
};
```

```
//**********************************************************************//
//                                                                      //
//      F I L E :    S H A P E . H                                      //
//                                                                      //
//          Interface for class Shape                                   //
//                                                                      //
//**********************************************************************//
// Class Shape is the user interface to the entire graphics
// package--all other classes are just used for internal
// implementation
#define _SHAPE_H
#      include "k.h"
#endif
#include "List.h"

// forward reference declaration
class ShapeRep;

class Shape: public Top {      // Top defined in k.h
public:
    // forwards all operations to rep
    ShapeRep *operator->() const {
        return rep;
    }
    // constructors and orthodox canonical form
    Shape();
    Shape(ShapeRep&);
    ~Shape();
    Shape(Shape& x);
    Shape& operator=(Shape& x);

    // yield type of letter object
    Top *type();

"
```

```
    // replace one exemplar with a new version,
    // updating its instances using the user-
    // provided cutover function
    void dataUpdate(Thingp&, const Thingp);

    // general purpose function that can be loaded
    // by a user to do whatever they want
    Top *doit();

    // garbage collector for Shape empire
    void gc();

    // routines for exemplars to register and
    // unregister themselves with Shape
    void Register(ShapeRep*);
    void UnRegister(ShapeRep*);

    // initializes class variables
    static void init();     // class initialization
private:
    friend ShapeRep;
    // operator new is called only from ShapeRep.
    // operator delete is unused
    static void *operator new(size_t s) {
        return ::operator new(s);
    }
    static void operator delete(void *) { }
    // keep a list of all instances of myself
    static List<Topp> *allShapes;

    // keep a list of all exemplars of things
    // derived from ShapeRep
    static List<Thingp> *allShapeExemplars;

    // pointer to the business end of an actual Shape
    ShapeRep *rep;
};
// pointer to the Shape exemplar, dynamically
// created by Shape::init
extern Shape *shape;            // exemplar

// users shouldn't have to know about, or include,
// the header file for ShapeRep

#ifndef _SHAPEREP_H
#    include "ShapeRep.h"
#endif
```

```
//*********************************************************************//
//                                                                   //
//     F I L E :     S H A P E . C                                   //
//                                                                   //
//         Code for class Shape                                      //
//                                                                   //
//*********************************************************************//
#include "Shape.h"
#ifndef _SHAPEREP_H
#     include "ShapeRep.h"
#endif
#ifndef _TRIANGLE_H
#     include "Triangle.h"
#endif
#ifndef _RECTANGLE_H
#     include "Rectangle.h"
#endif
#include "List.h"

// Class Shape does much of the memory management work for
// all Shapes.

// Handles to all extant Shape instances everywhere
List<Topp> *Shape::allShapes = 0;

// List of all Exemplars that are made for subclasses
// of class ShapeRep
List<Thingp> *Shape::allShapeExemplars = 0;

// Shape exemplar
extern Shape *shape = 0;

void
Shape::init() {
    // initializes all global data structures for
    // Shapes, so main can orchestrate order of
    // initialization
    allShapes = new List<Topp>;
    allShapeExemplars = new List<Thingp>;
    shape = new Shape;

    // orchestrate initialization of ShapeRep types
    ShapeRep::init();
    Triangle::init();
    Rectangle::init();
}

Top *
Shape::doit() {
    // handy function that can be reloaded by users
```

```
    // and used as a utility
    return 0;
}

Shape::Shape() {
    // default shape constructor
    Topp tp = this;

    // log self in allShapes list
    allShapes->put(tp);

    // we don't know what kind of Shape:
    // just make it a dummy for now
    rep = new ShapeRep;
}

Shape::~Shape() {
    Listiter<Topp> tp = *allShapes;
    Topp t;
    for ( tp.reset(); tp.next(t); ) {
        if (t == (Thingp)this) {
            tp.remove_prev(t);
            break;
        }
    }
    if (allShapes->length() == 0) {
        // last gasp garbage collection
        gc();
    }
}

Shape::Shape(Shape &x) {
    // copy constructor
    Thingp tp = (Thingp) this;

    // log self with allShapes list
    allShapes->put(tp);

    // just point to parameter's rep
    rep = x.rep;
}

Shape::Shape(ShapeRep &x) {
    // build a Shape from a ShapeRep:  used
    // mainly to convert the ShapeReps built
    // by Triangle, Rectangle, etc., into
    // Shapes that are returned to the users
    // (users never see the inner classes)
    Topp tp = this;

    // log self with allShapes
    allShapes->put(tp);
```

```
        // note:  no ->ref();  caller must yield copy!
        rep = &x;
}

Shape&
Shape::operator=(Shape &x) {
        // assignment of shapes.  Don't worry about what
        // rep used to point to:  garbage collection
        // will get it.
        rep = x.rep;
        return *this;
}

Top *
Shape::type() {
        // A Shape's type is its own exemplar
        return shape;
}

void
Shape::dataUpdate(Thingp &oldExemplar,
                                const Thingp newExemplar) {
        // This function allows class replacement of a subclass
        // of ShapeRep.  It assumes that all virtual functions
        // have been recompiled and incrementally loaded
        // against the new class definition.  It also assumes
        // the programmer has provided a cutover function
        // which, when invoked on an old instance of the
        // shape, will return a pointer to a semantically
        // equivalent copy.

        ShapeRep* savedExemplar = (ShapeRep*) oldExemplar;
        Topp tp = 0;

        // get a static copy to iterate over;  we don't
        // want to catch new things as they are added!
        // The copy will be reclaimed on return from this
        // member function
        List<Topp> staticCopy = *allShapes;

        // change exemplars
        oldExemplar = newExemplar;

        // cut over all subobjects for this exemplar
        Listiter<Topp> shapeIter = staticCopy;
        for ( shapeIter.reset(); shapeIter.next(tp);  ) {
            Shapepointer sp = (Shapepointer)tp;
            if (sp->rep->type() == (Thingp)savedExemplar) {
                if (sp->rep->docutover()) {
                    ShapeRep *oldrep = sp->rep;
                    printf("\tchanging shape 0x%x to new format\n",
```

```
                        oldrep);
            sp->rep = (ShapeRep*)sp->rep->cutover();

            // must manually clean up old rep here:
            // garbage collector won't get it, as it's
            // about to go out of the arena
            oldrep->ShapeRep::~ShapeRep();
        }
    }
}

// Remove this exemplar from Shape's list of all exemplars
// in the world--it is no longer participating as part
// of this abstract base exemplar
UnRegister(savedExemplar);
}

void
Shape::gc() {
    // Shape garbage collector: orchestrates collection
    // of unreachable objects for all subclasses of
    // ShapeRep.  Uses Baker's algorithm

    // First half of Baker:  mark all reachable shapes
    Listiter<Topp> shapeIter = *allShapes;
    shapeIter.reset();
    for ( Topp tp = 0; shapeIter.next(tp);  ) {
        Shapepointer sp = (Shapepointer)tp;
        if (sp->rep) {
            sp->rep->mark();
        }
    }

    // Second half of Baker:  sweep.  Let individual
    // subtypes each do their own sweep of their own
    // pools, using their own gc member function.
    Listiter<Thingp> shapeExemplarIter = *allShapeExemplars;
    shapeExemplarIter.reset();
    for ( Thingp anExemplar = 0;
                shapeExemplarIter.next(anExemplar);  ) {
        ShapeRep *thisExemplar = (ShapeRep*)anExemplar;
        thisExemplar->gc(0);
    }

    // Baker swap of To and From spaces
    ShapeRep::FromSpace ^= 1;
    ShapeRep::ToSpace   ^= 1;
}

void
Shape::Register(ShapeRep *s) {
```

```
    // routine by which ShapeRep exemplars
    // register themselves with Shape
    Thingp tp = s;
    allShapeExemplars->put(tp);
}

void
Shape::UnRegister(ShapeRep *s) {
    // Allows an exemplar to unregister itself
    // (as when it is replaced by a new version)
    Thingp tp = 0;
    Listiter<Thingp> shapeIter = *allShapeExemplars;
    for ( shapeIter.reset(); shapeIter.next(tp); ) {
        if (tp == (Thingp)s) {
            shapeIter.remove_prev(tp);
        }
    }
}
```

```
//**********************************************************************//
//                                                                    //
//      F I L E :     S H A P E R E P . H                             //
//                                                                    //
//            Interface for class ShapeRep.                           //
//                                                                    //
//**********************************************************************//
#define _SHAPEREP_H
#ifndef _SHAPE_H
#     include "Shape.h"
#endif
#ifndef _COORDINATE_H
#     include "Coordinate.h"
#endif

class ShapeRep: public Thing {
public:
    /* all user-defined operators go here.  Note that, because
     * of the use of operator->, this signature does not have
     * to be mimicked in the Shape class.  However, the Shape's
     * rep field has to be appropriately typed.  Assignment
     * operators do not go here, but in the Shape class.
     *
     * return_type should either be a primitive
     * type, or of type Shape, of type Shape&, or
     * a concrete data type
     */
    virtual void rotate(double);
    virtual void move(Coordinate);
    virtual void draw();
    virtual void erase();

    // constructors
    Shape make(Coordinate,Thingp);
    Shape make(Coordinate,Coordinate,Thingp);
    Shape make(Coordinate,Coordinate,Coordinate,Thingp);

    // these are overridden in the derived classes;
    // their default action is to call the ones above,
    // with Thingp suitably defaulted
    virtual Shape make();
    virtual Shape make(Coordinate);
    virtual Shape make(Coordinate,Coordinate);
    virtual Shape make(Coordinate,Coordinate,Coordinate);

    // routine to mark this object as used for the
    // Baker algorithm
    virtual void mark();
```

```
    // type returns a pointer to an object's exemplar
    Thing *type();

    // Do garbage collection.  If the argument is zero,
    // sweep the current pool;  if non-zero, build a
    // new pool to hold objects of the designated size,
    // and forget about the old pool
    virtual void gc(size_t = 0);

    // class constructors
    ShapeRep();
    ~ShapeRep();
    ShapeRep(Exemplar);

    // used to orchestrate order of initialization of
    // static, class-specific information
    static void init();
protected:
    friend class Shape;
    Coordinate center;

    // this is the "type field"
    Top *exemplarPointer;

    // memory management state variables:  Space
    // is FromSpace or ToSpace; gcmark is the mark
    // bit for marking objects under Baker;  inUse
    // means that this object has been returned to
    // a caller for use, but that it hasn't yet been
    // reclaimed by the garbage collector
    unsigned char space:1, gcmark:1, inUse:1;
protected:
    // do common processing for (the sweep phase of)
    // Baker garbage collection
    static void gcCommon(size_t nbytes,
        const size_t poolInitialized,
        const int PoolSize, Char_p &h);

    // These two "constants" designate From space and
    // To space for the Baker algorithm.  They are flipped
    // every garbage collection cycle
    static unsigned char FromSpace, ToSpace;

    // general memory management operators, which use the
    // pool operated on by gc
    static void *operator new(size_t);
    static void operator delete(void *);

    // a typeless shape usable as a default return value
    static Shape *aShape;
};
```

```
//*********************************************************************//
//                                                                   //
//      F I L E :      ShapeRep.c                                    //
//                                                                   //
//            Code for class ShapeRep                                //
//                                                                   //
//*********************************************************************//


// ShapeRep is the base class for all letter classes that
// use Shape as an envelope.  It is in the derived classes
// of ShapeRep where all the shape intelligence is
#include "ShapeRep.h"
#ifndef _RECTANGLE_H
#      include "Rectangle.h"
#endif
#ifndef _TRIANGLE_H
#      include "Triangle.h"
#endif

// "constant" used as a degenerate return value
Shape *ShapeRep::aShape = 0;

// bits designating From space and To space for Baker's
// algorithm;  are flipped on every cycle
unsigned char ShapeRep::FromSpace = 0, ShapeRep::ToSpace = 1;

void ShapeRep::init() {
    // initializes class data structures
    aShape = new Shape;
}

void *
ShapeRep::operator new(size_t l) {
    // overridden in derived classes
    return ::operator new(l);
}

void
ShapeRep::operator delete(void *p) {
    // overridden in derived classes
    ::operator delete(p);
}

Thing *
ShapeRep::type() {
    // type of any derived class of
    // ShapeRep is kept in exemplarPointer
    return (Thingp)exemplarPointer;
}
```

```
Shape
ShapeRep::make() {
    // default ShapeRep manufacturer
    return *aShape;
}

Shape
ShapeRep::make(Coordinate c1, Thingp) {
    // one constraint: Point object
    return point->make(c1);
}

Shape
ShapeRep::make(Coordinate c1, Coordinate c2, Thingp type) {
    // exemplar constructor for Shape objects with two
    // constraints:  Lines and Rectangles
    return ((ShapeRep *)type)->make(c1, c2);
}

Shape
ShapeRep::make(Coordinate c1, Coordinate c2, Coordinate c3,
          Thingp type) {
    // exemplar constructor for Shape objects with three
    // constraints:  Triangles, Arcs, Parallelograms
    return ((ShapeRep*)type)->make(c1, c2, c3);
}

Shape
ShapeRep::make(Coordinate c1) {
    // make a Shape from one coordinate
    // default is to return a Point
    return make(c1, point);
}

Shape
ShapeRep::make(Coordinate c1, Coordinate c2) {
    // make a Shape from two coordinates
    // default is to return a Rectangle
    return make(c1, c2, rectangle);
}

Shape
ShapeRep::make(Coordinate c1, Coordinate c2, Coordinate c3) {
    // make a Shape from three coordinates
    // default is to return a Triangle
    return make(c1, c2, c3, triangle);
}

void
ShapeRep::gcCommon(size_t nbytes, const size_t poolInitialized,
        const int PoolSize, Char_p &heap) {
```

```
// Garbage collection common to all ShapeReps.  This
// is where most of the "sweep" of the second half
// of Baker's algorithm happens.  It is called by
// the derived class gc routines, who call it
// directly with appropriate parameters.

// calculate s to be the size of the object.  If
// nbytes is specified, use it:  it designates
// a change in size (or is given at initialization
// time to get things rolling).  Otherwise, use
// the value saved in poolInitialized.
size_t s = nbytes? nbytes: poolInitialized;

// round up for alignment constraints
size_t Sizeof = Round(s);

// if a non-zero parameter was given, it is the size
// of an object;  it indicates we are to discard the
// old pool and allocate a new one.  This is done at
// startup and after class update.
if (nbytes) heap = new char[PoolSize * Sizeof];

ShapeRep *tp = (ShapeRep *)heap;

// sweep through the pool
for (int i = 0; i < PoolSize; i++) {
    switch (nbytes) {
    case 0:    // normal garbage collection case
        // If still earmarked, but not checked off, and
        // in FromSpace, nuke it.
        if (tp->inUse) {
            if (tp->gcmark || tp->space != FromSpace) {
                // don't sweep it away
                tp->space = ToSpace;
            } else if (tp != tp->type()) {
                // object needs to be reclaimed
                tp->ShapeRep::~ShapeRep();
                tp->inUse = 0;
                printf("ShapeRep::gcCommon ");
                printf("Reclaimed Shape object %c\n",
                  'A' + (((char *)tp-(char *)heap)/Sizeof));
            }
        }
        break;
    default:    // initialization of memory arena
        tp->inUse = 0;
        break;
    }
    tp->gcmark = 0;
    tp = (ShapeRep*)(Char_p(tp) + Sizeof);
```

```
    }
}

ShapeRep::ShapeRep(Exemplar) {
    // constructor to build ShapeRep's exemplar
    // (not very important)
    //
    // Recall that Exemplar is a dummy type used
    // to disambiguate this and the default constructor
    exemplarPointer = this;
    shape->Register(this);
}

void
ShapeRep::rotate(double) {
    // acts like pure virtual function
    printf("ShapeRep::rotate(double)\n");
}

void
ShapeRep::move(Coordinate) {
    // acts like pure virtual function
    printf("ShapeRep::move(Coordinate)\n");
}

void
ShapeRep::draw() {
    // acts like pure virtual function.  For now,
    // draw routines will just print the type's
    // name
    printf("<Shape>");
}

void
ShapeRep::erase() {
    // acts like pure virtual function
    printf("ShapeRep::erase()");
}

void
ShapeRep::gc(size_t) {
    // acts like pure virtual function
}

void
ShapeRep::mark() {
    // used by Shape in mark phase of Baker
    gcmark = 1;
}

ShapeRep::ShapeRep() {
```

```
    // default constructor
    exemplarPointer=this;
    gcmark=0;
    space=ToSpace;
    inUse=1;
}

ShapeRep::~ShapeRep() {
    // destructor does nothing
}
```

```
//*******************************************************************//
//                                                                 //
//    F I L E :    L O A D . C                                      //
//                                                                 //
//         Code for C function loader function                     //
//                                                                 //
//*******************************************************************//
```

```cpp
#include <a.out.h>
#include <fcntl.h>
#include "mptr.h"
#include "String.h"

static String symtab;
static char y = 'a';

extern "C" vptp load(const char *filename) {
    // load first link edits the specified file into
    // a new a.out, using a previous a.out file as
    // the base to resolve symbolic references.
    // load then opens the new file, figures out its
    // .text and .data sizes, and reads them into a
    // newly allocated block of memory.  It functions
    // as a dynamic loader, designed to work with an
    // outboard incremental link editor.  C linkage
    // is just so it can be called from C, too.

    int errcode = 0;
    String newfile;
    char buf[256];
    long adx, oadx;
    unsigned char *ldadx;
    struct exec Exec;
    int fd, wc;

    // use reasonable defaults first time through;  a.out will
    // be the file supplying the symbol table.  Each time we do
    // an incremental load, change the name of the file that
    // the link editor will produce.  Clean up old files as
    // we go along.

    if (!symtab.length()) {
        symtab = "a.out"; newfile = "b.out";
    } else {
        symtab = String(++y) + ".out";
        newfile = String(y+1) + ".out";
    }

    // find current memory high, and pad things so memory high
    // is on an even page boundary.
    oadx = (long)sbrk(0);
```

```
    adx = oadx + PAGSIZ - (oadx%PAGSIZ);

    // create load command to do an incremental link edit
    // of the provided .o against the current a.out, specifying
    // that the new code be linked at memory high
    sprintf(buf, "ld -N -Ttext %X -A %s %s -o %s",
        adx, (const char*)symtab, filename,
        (const char*)newfile);
    printf("<%s>\n", buf);
    if ((errcode=system(buf)) != 0) {
        printf("load: link edit returned error code %d\n",
            errcode);
    }
    if (symtab != "a.out") unlink(symtab);

    // open it up to load it into memory
    fd = open(newfile, O_RDONLY);
    if (fd < 0) {
        printf("load: open of \"%s\" failed\n", newfile);
        return 0;
    }

    // read the relocatable file header to get text,
    // data sizes
    read(fd, (char *)&Exec, sizeof(struct exec));

    // now do the memory pad, and allocate space for the
    // new program text
    sbrk(int(PAGSIZ-(oadx%PAGSIZ)));
    ldadx = (unsigned char *)
        sbrk(int(Exec.a_text + Exec.a_data + Exec.a_bss));

    // read the newly linked file into the running
    // process at the address just calculated
    wc = read(fd, (char *)ldadx,
        int(Exec.a_text + Exec.a_data));
    close(fd);

    // return load address
    return (vptp) ldadx;
}
```

```
//*********************************************************************//
//                                                                   //
//      F I L E :     M A I N . C                                    //
//                                                                   //
//          Sample driver code for geometric shapes example          //
//                                                                   //
//*********************************************************************//
#include <a.out.h>
#include <fcntl.h>
#include "Shape.h"
#ifndef _COORDINATE_H
#     include "Coordinate.h"
#endif
extern void doClassUpdate();
extern int compile(const String &fileName);
extern int mkfile(const String &fileName,
                               const String &contents);

int main2() {
    Shape::init();
    Coordinate p1, p2, p3;
    Shape object = (*shape)->make(p1, p2, p3);
    printf("object is "); object->draw(); printf("\n");

    // demonstrate virtual function update
    object->move(p1);
    compile("v2Triangle.c");
    String include = "includes.h";
    mkfile(include,
        "#include \"k.h\"\n#include \"v2Triangle.h\"\n");
    object->update("v2Triangle.o", "Triangle::move");
    object->move(p1);
    doClassUpdate();
    object->move(p1);
    {
        Shape object3 = (*shape)->make(p1, p2, p3);
        printf("object3 is "); object3->draw(); printf("\n");
    }
printf("main: making object2\n");
    Shape object2 = (*shape)->make(p1, p2, p3);
    shape->gc();          // do a gc now and then
    printf("object2 is "); object2->draw(); printf("\n");
printf("main: made object2, calling object2->move\n");
    object2->move(p1);
    shape->gc();          // do a gc now and then
printf("exiting\n");
    return 0;
}
```

```
int main() {
    int retval = main2();
    shape->gc();
    return retval;
}

void
doClassUpdate() {
    extern Shape *triangle;
    const String include = "includes.h";
    mkfile(include,
        "#include \"k.h\"\n#include \"v2Triangle.h\"\n");

    compile("v3TriangleA.c");
    (*triangle).update("v3TriangleA.o", "Triangle::make",
        "Shape (Triangle::*TYPE)()");

    compile("v3TriangleB.c");
    (*triangle).update("v3TriangleB.o", "Triangle::make",
        "Shape (Triangle::*TYPE)\
            (Coordinate,Coordinate,Coordinate)");

    compile("v3TriangleMove.c");
    (*triangle).update("v3TriangleMove.o", "Triangle::move");

    compile("v3TriangleCutover.c");
    (*triangle).update("v3TriangleCutover.o",
                                "Triangle::cutover");

    mkfile(include, "#include \"k.h\"\n\
        #include \"v3Triangle.h\"\n");

    mkfile("v3doit.c",  "#include \"k.h\"\n\
        #include \"v3Triangle.h\"\n\
        Top * Shape::doit() {\n\
            printf(\"v3 Shape::doit (new) called\\n\");\n\
            Thingp Ttriangle = triangle;\n\
            shape->dataUpdate(Ttriangle,\n\
                new Triangle(Exemplar(0)));\n\
            triangle = (ShapeRep*) Ttriangle;\n\
            printf(\"Shape::doit: did data update\\n\");\\
            return 0;\n\
        }\n\n\
        Triangle::Triangle(Exemplar e): ShapeRep(e) { }\n");

    compile("v3doit.c");
    printf("doClassUpdate:\
        calling shape->update(\"v3doit.o\",\
        \"Shape::doit\")\n");
    shape->update("v3doit.o", "Shape::doit");
    shape->doit();
```

```
    shape->gc();            // do a gc now and then
    unlink("v3doit.c");
    unlink("v3doit.o");
}

#include <sys/stat.h>

int compile(const String& fileName) {
    struct stat dotC, dotO;
    String fileNameDotO =
            fileName(0,fileName.length()-2) + ".o";
    stat(fileName, &dotC);
    stat(fileNameDotO, &dotO);
    if (dotC.st_mtime < dotO.st_mtime) {
        printf("\"%s\" is up to date\n", (const char*)fileName);
        return 0;
    } else {
        String command = String("CC +e0 -c -g ") + fileName;
        printf("compile: <%s>\n", (const char*)command);
        return system(command);
    }
}

extern int mkfile(const String &fileName,
                                const String &contents) {
    FILE *inc = fopen(fileName, "w");
    printf("mkfile: creating <%s>\n", (const char *)fileName);
    fprintf(inc, (const char*)contents);
    return fclose(inc);
}
```

```
//***********************************************************************//
//                                                                       //
//      F I L E :    T R I A N G L E . H                                 //
//                                                                       //
//            Interface for class Triangle                              //
//                                                                       //
//***********************************************************************//

// This is the interface for the code implementing the
// semantics for the geometric shape, Triangle

#define _TRIANGLE_H
#ifndef _SHAPEREP_H
#     include "ShapeRep.h"
#endif
#ifndef _COORDINATE_H
#     include "Coordinate.h"
#endif

class Triangle: public ShapeRep {
public:
    // exemplar constructors
    Shape make();
    Shape make(Coordinate, Coordinate, Coordinate);

    // memory management
    void *operator new(size_t);
    void operator delete(void *);
    void gc(size_t = 0);

    // user application semantics
    void draw();
    void rotate(double);
    void move(Coordinate);

    // class routines
    Triangle(Exemplar);
    Triangle();
    static void init();
private:
    // these should never be called
    Shape make(Coordinate);
    Shape make(Coordinate, Coordinate);
private:
    // instance state variables
    Coordinate p1, p2, p3;
private:
    // memory management data
    static char *heap;
    static size_t poolInitialized;
```

```
    enum { PoolSize = 10 };
};
```

```
// Triangle exemplar pointer declaration
extern ShapeRep *triangle;
```

```
//***********************************************************************//
//                                                                     //
//      F I L E :     T R I A N G L E . C                              //
//                                                                     //
//           Interface for class Triangle                             //
//                                                                     //
//***********************************************************************//
#include "Triangle.h"

// class-specific variables
ShapeRep *triangle = 0;
char *Triangle::heap = 0;
size_t Triangle::poolInitialized = 0;

void
Triangle::init() {
    // initialize Triangle-specific statics and globals.
    // Some data structure initialization is done
    // the first time ShapeRep::gcCommon is called
    triangle = new Triangle(Exemplar(0));
}

Shape
Triangle::make()
{
    // make a default (degenerate) triangle
    Triangle *retval = new Triangle;
    retval->p1 = retval->p2 = retval->p3 = Coordinate(0,0);
    retval->exemplarPointer = this;
    return *retval;
}

Shape
Triangle::make(Coordinate pp1, Coordinate pp2, Coordinate pp3)
{
    // set up and return a new Triangle
    Triangle *retval = new Triangle;
    retval->p1 = pp1;
    retval->p2 = pp2;
    retval->p3 = pp3;
    retval->exemplarPointer = this;
    return *retval;
}

void
Triangle::gc(size_t nbytes) {
    // pass Triangle memory data structures to common
    // garbage collection (sweep) routine in base class
    gcCommon(nbytes, poolInitialized, PoolSize, heap);
```

```
}
void
Triangle::draw() {
    // for now, just print out a name corresponding
    // to the triangle's position in the pool
    int Sizeof = poolInitialized? poolInitialized:
        Round(sizeof(Triangle));
    printf("<Triangle object %c>",
        'A' + (((char *)this-(char *)heap)/Sizeof));
}
void
Triangle::move(Coordinate) {
    // . . .
}
void
Triangle::rotate(double) {
    // . . .
}
void *
Triangle::operator new(size_t nbytes) {
    // if pool has not yet been initialized, or if we just
    // updated the Triangle class, give garbage collector
    // control
    if (poolInitialized - nbytes) {
        gcCommon(nbytes, poolInitialized, PoolSize, heap);
        poolInitialized = nbytes;
    }

    // find a free one
    Triangle *tp = (Triangle *)heap;
    // need to add memory exhaustion test
    while (tp->inUse) {
        tp = (Triangle*)(((char*)tp) + Round(nbytes));
    }

    // initialize memory bits appropriately
    tp->gcmark = 0;
    tp->inUse = 1;
    return (void*) tp;
}
void Triangle::operator delete(void *) {
    // this should never be called, but C++ insists
    // on its being here if new is
}

Triangle::Triangle() { }  // size and vptr knowledge are in here
```

```
Triangle::Triangle(const Triangle& t) {
    // copy constructor
    p1 = t.p1;
    p2 = t.p2;
    p3 = t.p3;
}

Triangle::Triangle(Exemplar e) : ShapeRep(e) {
    // build a Triangle exemplar
}

Shape
Triangle::make(Coordinate) {
    // dummy function--should never be called
    return *aShape;
}

Shape
Triangle::make(Coordinate, Coordinate) {
    // dummy function--should never be called
    return *aShape;
}



//************************************************************************//
//                                                                      //
//      F I L E :     V 2 T R I A N G L E . C                           //
//                                                                      //
//          Modified code for class Triangle (Version 2)                //
//                                                                      //
//************************************************************************//
#include "v2Triangle.h"

void
Triangle::move(Coordinate)
{
    printf("version 2 Triangle::move of size %d\n",
        sizeof(*this));
}
```

```
//*********************************************************************//
//                                                                   //
//     F I L E :     V 2 T R I A N G L E . H                         //
//                                                                   //
//         Modified interface for class Triangle (Version 2)   //
//                                                                   //
//*********************************************************************//
#define _TRIANGLE_H
#ifndef _SHAPEREP_H
#    include "ShapeRep.h"
#endif
#ifndef _COORDINATE_H
#    include "Coordinate.h"
#endif
class Triangle: public ShapeRep {
public:
    // Just like Triangle.h, except set up for a
    // new definition of Triangle::move
    Shape make();
    Shape make(Coordinate, Coordinate, Coordinate);
    Triangle();
    void draw();
    void move(Coordinate);
    void rotate(double);
    void *operator new(size_t);
    void operator delete(void *);
    void gc(size_t = 0);
    Triangle(Exemplar);
    static void init();
private:
    static void poolInit(size_t);
    Shape make(Coordinate) { return *aShape; }
    Shape make(Coordinate, Coordinate) { return *aShape; }
    Coordinate p1, p2, p3;
private:
    static char *heap;
    static size_t poolInitialized;
    enum { PoolSize = 10 };
};
extern ShapeRep *triangle;
```

```
//**********************************************************************//
//                                                                      //
//      F I L E :      V 3 T R I A N G L E . H                          //
//                                                                      //
//           Data structures for version 3 Triangle class              //
//                                                                      //
//**********************************************************************//
#define _TRIANGLE_H
#ifndef _SHAPEREP_H
#       include "ShapeRep.h"
#endif
#ifndef _COORDINATE_H
#       include "Coordinate.h"
#endif

// This is the declaration of the NEW (Version 3) triangle
// class--it has a color attribute

class Triangle: public ShapeRep {
public:
    Shape make();
    Shape make(Coordinate, Coordinate, Coordinate);
    Triangle();
    void draw();
    void move(Coordinate);
    void rotate(double);
    void *operator new(size_t);
    void operator delete(void *);
    void gc(size_t = 0);
    Thing *cutover();
    Triangle(Exemplar);
    static void init();
private:
    static void poolInit(size_t);
    Shape make(Coordinate) { return *aShape; }
    Shape make(Coordinate, Coordinate) { return *aShape; }
    Coordinate p1, p2, p3;
    enum Color { Black, White } color;
private:
    static char *heap;
    static size_t poolInitialized;
    enum { PoolSize = 10 };
};

extern ShapeRep *triangle;
```

```
//**********************************************************************//
//                                                                      //
//      F I L E :     V 3 T R I A N G L E A . C                         //
//                                                                      //
//          Code for version 3 of class Triangle                       //
//                                                                      //
//**********************************************************************//
#include "v3Triangle.h"

Shape
Triangle::make()
{
    printf("Triangle::make() entered\n");
    Triangle *retval = new Triangle;;
    retval->p1 = retval->p2 = retval->p3 = Coordinate(0,0);
    retval->exemplarPointer = this;
    color = Black;
    return Shape(*retval);
}

// this will get statically expanded for use by make above
Triangle::Triangle() {  }  // size and vptr knowledge are in here
```

```
//*********************************************************************//
//                                                                   //
//      F I L E :      V 3 T R I A N G L E B . C                     //
//                                                                   //
//          Code for version 3 of class Triangle                    //
//                                                                   //
//*********************************************************************//
#include "v3Triangle.h"

Shape
Triangle::make(Coordinate pp1, Coordinate pp2, Coordinate pp3)
{
    Triangle petval = new Triangle;
    retval->p1 = pp1;
    retval->p2 = pp2;
    retval->p3 = pp3;
    retval->exemplarPointer = this;
    return *retval;
}

Triangle::Triangle() {  }  // size and vptr knowledge are in here
```

```
//*********************************************************************//
//                                                                   //
//     F I L E :    V 3 T R I A N G L E C U T O V E R . C    //
//                                                                   //
//         Cutover control code for version 3 Triangle code    //
//                                                                   //
//*********************************************************************//
#include "v3Triangle.h"
#include "Map.h"

// -----------------------------------------------------------------

class v2Triangle: public ShapeRep {
public:
    Shape make();
    Shape make(Coordinate, Coordinate, Coordinate);
    v2Triangle();
    void move(Coordinate);
    void *operator new(size_t);
    void operator delete(void *);
    void gc(size_t = 0);
    void draw();
    v2Triangle(Exemplar);
    static void init();
private:
    friend Thing *Triangle::cutover();  // put in for conversion
    static void poolInit(size_t);
    Shape make(Coordinate) { return *aShape; }
    Shape make(Coordinate, Coordinate) { return *aShape; }
    Coordinate p1, p2, p3;
};

// -----------------------------------------------------------------

// Use this map to keep track of all old objects we are
// asked to convert, and of the new ones they were converted to.
// That way, if we are asked to convert the same object
// several times, we map all requests onto the same return
// value.

Map<Thingp, Thingp> objectMap;

Thing *
Triangle::cutover() {
    // we are going to return a pointer to a converted triangle
    Triangle *retval = this;

    // instance passed in is really old triangle
    // the old triangle declaration is preserved
    // under the name v2Triangle;  class Triangle
```

```
    // is the version 3 one
    v2Triangle *old = (v2Triangle *)this;
    Thingp oldtp = this;
    ShapeRep *oldsr = (ShapeRep*)this;

    if (objectMap.element(oldtp)) {
        // if we've converted it already, don't
        // convert it again--just return old
        // converted value
        retval = (Triangle*)(objectMap[oldtp]);
    } else {
        // create a new (version 3) triangle to return
        // store it in several different kinds of pointers
        retval = new Triangle;
        ShapeRep *newsr = retval;
        Thingp newtp = retval;

        // copy over just the base class (ShapeRep) part
        *newsr = *oldsr;

        // now set up the fields of the new object
        retval->exemplarPointer = triangle;
        retval->p1 = old->p1;
        retval->p2 = old->p2;
        retval->p3 = old->p3;
        retval->color = Black;

        // save converted one for later
        objectMap[oldtp] = newtp;
    }
    return retval;
}

Triangle::Triangle() { }
```

```
//**********************************************************************//
//                                                                      //
//      F I L E :      V 3 T R I A N G L E M O V E . C                   //
//                                                                      //
//          Code for version 3 Triangle's move implementation           //
//                                                                      //
//**********************************************************************//
#include "v3Triangle.h"

void
Triangle::move(Coordinate)
{
    printf("version 3 Triangle::move of size %d\n",
        sizeof(*this));
}
```

F

Block-Structured
Programming in C++

Top-down design is a mature software engineering discipline that underlies most structured design techniques that have been in use over the past two decades. Object-oriented design is offered as a replacement for these techniques, especially when dealing with the complexities of large systems. However, top-down design techniques such as functional decomposition are still applicable where the algorithms are well understood or when the problem is self-contained and its solution structure foreseen.

Block-structured programming is a programming language feature that supports top-down design. This appendix will show how some C++ idioms provide an interesting variant of block-structured programming. The idiom requires more explicit scope qualification than is necessary in Pascal or Modula-2, owing to the scoping properties of the C++ language. The result may or may not be wholly satisfying, depending on the tastes and inclinations of the reader. But the approach can be adjusted to taste, and a few variations are presented here.

C preprocessor macros are defined as part of the C++ language. This chapter will also give the reader a flavor of how to mix macros with C++ constructs to achieve a degree of functionality and expressiveness not possible with the "base C++" language alone.

F.1 What Is Block-Structured Programming?

Top-down design is perhaps the dominant software structuring technique in use today. Perhaps the most frequently used top-down design technique is *functional decomposition,* or *stepwise refinement,* first proposed by Niklaus Wirth in the early 1970s. In functional decomposition, the system is initially characterized by the high-level function it is to perform, and then that function is broken down into constituent pieces, each of which is likewise decomposed, and so on. The eventual result is a set of modules with well-defined semantics that can be directly implemented.

Data play a decidedly secondary role in functional decomposition. At each level of refinement, a data design is done for each procedural entity. The data design drives the design of the modules that are decomposed from it. Procedures are thought of as "owning" these data. The lifetime of a data block is that of the activation record of the procedure owning it. A data block's scope is likewise defined by the procedure structure.

Top-down design has come to enjoy language support over the years. An important language feature supporting top-down design is *block-structured programming.* Block-structured programming languages have scoping constructs that allow procedures to nest within each other. Languages like C and C++ are called block-structured, but only in a weak sense. Although they separate local variables from globals and allow nesting of declaration blocks inside procedures, their block nesting constructs do not extend to procedures. By this definition, neither C nor C++ qualify as block-structured programming languages, whereas Algol 68, PL/1, Modula-2, Ada, and Pascal do.

Simple facilities of C++, creatively applied, provide the scaffolding to build block-structured programs. We call the styles and techniques used to give this illusion of block-structuring the *block-structured idiom.* The idiom will be introduced in a limited form that allows access of symbols between neighboring scopes, and then extended to a more general form.

☞ *When to use this idiom:* Block-structuring is well-suited to straightforward problems where algorithm and procedure dominate over data relationships and structure. Use this approach for problems where control flow is sequential, the solution requires at most a few hundred lines of code, and algorithms of the solution are well understood.

F.2 Basic Building Blocks for Structured C++ Programming

What is necessary to give C++ a block-structured feel is to build a new scope, or name space, inside each function, which itself can contain its own functions. A `struct` fits the bill nicely. In C++, unlike in C, `struct` declarations may contain functions, and functions local to a structure which is itself local to a function are scoped accordingly. Also, `structs` can be used to encapsulate the data designs for each level of functional decomposition. We will see that this encapsulation makes C++ block-structured programs easier to analyze than their Algol-based counterparts.

Although `structs` provide the right level of semantics to support block structuring, their syntax is cluttered and foreign compared with the Algol and Pascal constructs for procedural blocks. Preprocessor macros are used to make the programmer's design intent clearer to the casual reader. These macros are used to delineate the contents of the new scopes created in each function body. We put these macros in a header file, block.h, which appears as follows:

```
// file block.h

#include <generic.h>

#define LocalScope(function)                              \
     struct name2(function,ForLocalScope) { public
#define EndLocalScope } local
```

The `LocalScope` declaration just sets up the opening phrase of a `struct` declaration. The `name2` macro, defined in generic.h, catenates its two arguments together into a single new name. By convention, the parameter to the `LocalScope` macro should be the name of the function in which it is embedded. The `EndLocalScope` macro closes the `struct` declaration, and declares an instance of the `struct` named `local` that is used as a handle for the context set up by this `struct`.

Figure F-1 is an example of a simple block-structured bubble sort implementation [1]. The bubble sort algorithm is decomposed to the point where one module, `CompareExchange`, has been precipitated as a function in its own right, abstracted inside `BubbleSort`. `BubbleSort` orchestrates the invocation of `CompareExchange`, and fills out the sorting algorithm.

Note that although `BubbleSort` is accessible as an ordinary function, `CompareExchange` is not visible from outside `BubbleSort` itself. Block structuring provides information hiding in the procedural dimension, and algorithmic details are encapsulated in their higher order abstractions.

Here is an example of use of the bubble sort implementation:

```
char *records[] = {
    "Stroustrup, Bjarne",
    "Lippman, Stan",
    "Hansen, Tony",
    "Koenig, Andy"
};
```

```
#include <block.h>
#include <iostream.h>
#include <string.h>

void BubbleSort(int n, char *records[], char *keys[])
{
    // Bubble Sort from Knuth, Vol. 3
    LocalScope(BubbleSort):
        int bound, t;
        void CompareExchange(int j, char *records[],
                                        char *keys[]) {
            if (::strcmp(keys[j], keys[j+1]) > 0) {
                char *temp = records[j];
                records[j] = records[j+1];
                records[j+1] = temp;
                temp = keys[j];
                keys[j] = keys[j+1];
                keys[j+1] = temp;
                t = j;
            }
        }
    EndLocalScope;

    local.bound = n;
    do {
        local.t = -1;
        for (int j = 0; j < local.bound-1; j++) {
            local.CompareExchange(j, records, keys);
        }
        local.bound = local.t + 1;
    } while (local.t != -1);
}
```

Figure F-1. A Block-Structured Bubble Sort Implementation

```
char *keys[] = {
    "bs",
    "stan",
    "hansen",
    "ark"
};

int main() {
    for (int i = 0; i < 4; i++) {
        cout << records[i] << endl;
    }
    BubbleSort(4, records, keys);
    for (i = 0; i < 4; i++) {
        cout << records[i] << endl;
    }
    return 0;
}
```

When designing a procedural decomposition hierarchy, one is well advised to keep a few engineering rules in mind. One rule of thumb is to declare a function's local variables within its own LocalScope block. Putting "local" variables in these blocks causes them to be in scope both for the function creating the block and for the functions at the next layer of functional decomposition. For example, t and bound are in BubbleSort's scope in the above program; they are "owned" by BubbleSort but are accessible to CompareExchange. Note that access from within BubbleSort is qualified with the local prefix and the dot operator, a syntactic anomaly arising from the C++ implementation of the idiom.

The rationale of this approach is that block-structured languages allow a function in an inner scope to access and change variable values in the surrounding scope, including variables local to the enclosing function. In one sense, this violates the encapsulation of the enclosing function. Functional decomposition naturally results in coupling directed from the top of the hierarchy toward its leaves, and the lower abstractions are dependent on the higher ones. Nevertheless, we do not want the higher level abstractions to be overly sensitive to those below them. A procedure's variables should be its own, and any access to them by lower-level, more refined routines should be easy to discover from inspection of the code. Access of local variables from a deeply nested scope would violate a "principle of least surprise" in program evolution and maintenance.

The approach presented here limits access to variables in a block so that only the "owning" scope, or at most one level deeper, can see them. The next deepest level (that of CompareExchange) is directly visible from the current level (that of BubbleSort), which means that an extensive search is not necessary to study the domain of a scope's variables.

Notice that some trivial variables (for example, loop variables) do not receive this treatment. They are not part of the data design and can be informally treated with normal C++ conventions.

Another rule of thumb is to use parameter passing as the preferred method to access the data of one level from another. It is possible to pass data between nested blocks through global data or data within a `LocalScope`, but that can cause maintenance headaches when the time comes to find all the places that such data are referenced. Localizing the data to a nested block helps, but a datum in a block still can be accessed from any of the functions inside that block. A cleaner interface results from passing data through parameters, and returning results through return values. This is in fact necessary for variables that are not made part of the `LocalScope`; for example, `BubbleSort`'s parameters are not directly accessible to `CompareExchange`. To be made accessible, the variables must be passed as parameters, as they are in the bubble sort example. This is in keeping with good design, maintaining well-defined, explicit interfaces between modules.

F.3 An Alternative for Blocks with Deeply Nested Scopes

The block-structured idiom allows access only to the neighboring scope, albeit with some syntactic awkwardness. Most block-structured languages grant symbols visibility to all scopes enclosed by their own scope, but the idiom described here does not support that. Here, symbols can be accessed only from their "owning" scope (as `bound` and `t` are accessible from `BubbleSort` using the `local.` prefix) and from the next lower level of functions contained within that scope (as those same symbols can be accessed from `CompareExchange`). It is difficult to achieve the full nested scope generality of block-structured languages within the confines of C++ scoping constructs. We might argue that the approach presented above results in code more readable than in, say, Pascal: Use of a symbol cannot appear very far from its declaration. In Pascal or Modula, a symbol may be declared several levels of scope removed from its use. However, if we can make full nested scope access possible, expressed in a way that helps the reader find the declaration of a referenced symbol, and implement it within the confines of C++, then we will have achieved an idiom with balance between explicit scope resolution and nested scope structures. The *dynamic block-structured idiom* is presented here as such an approach.

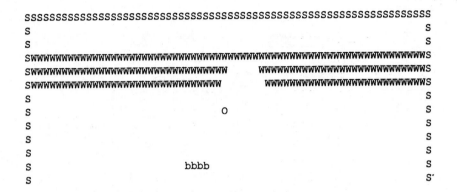

Figure F-2. Description of Video Game.

From Bell et al., Software Engineering: A Programming Approach,
Englewood Cliffs, N.J.: Prentice Hall, ©1987, 43. Reprinted by permission.

The game makes use of a keyboard and a crude visual display that can display characters (but no other graphics) at any position on the screen. [See figure] ...portrays a wall, built from 'w' characters, a bat ('b' characters) and a ball (the letter 'o'). The ball bounces around the screen, moving up, down or diagonally, changing direction conventionally when it hits the wall, the sides or the bat. The player can move the bat left or right by keying 'l' or 'r' on the keyboard. The objective is to make the ball knock down the wall and so break out [2].

☞ *When to use this idiom*: Use this idiom where you would use the block-structured idiom (page 478), where access to symbols from deeply nested scopes is necessary. This is often necessary in functional decomposition, as the nesting of the data design abstractions often cuts across the grain of the procedural abstractions.

For an approach that is both more dynamic and more type-safe, see the exercises at the end of this appendix.

Consider the example program at the end of this appendix, which partially implements the design of a simple video game. The rules of the game are shown in Figure F-2 [2]. This is a more ambitious top-down design than the bubble sort; its structure is shown in Figure F-3. In this program, we add facilities so the user can gain explicit access to outer scopes.

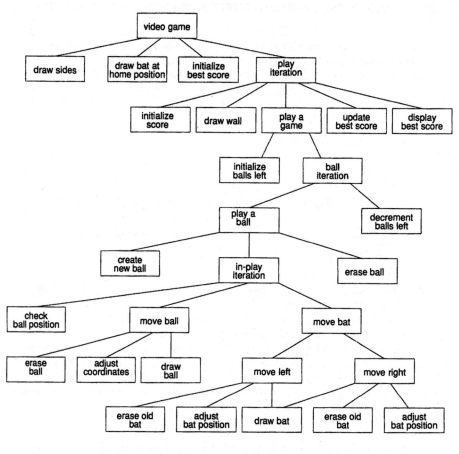

Figure F-3. Hierarchy Chart for Video Game

We start by building a crude scope mechanism into the macros. The scope mechanism maintains a *dynamic chain*, or call history list, of the functions in this nested scope structure. The programmer can walk back this list to get to any of the nested function scopes up the chain, and access any of their data or call any of their functions. We accomplish this trick by letting the `LocalScope` macro define a constructor for the scope, which is called automatically whenever the scope is opened (see Section 2.3). By convention, the name of a constructor function is the same as the name of the `struct`, and its job is usually to initialize the state of new variables created from a given structure type. This constructor function takes a single parameter, which is the variable `this`, set up by the compiler to point at the enclosing object. So the .new block.h file starts like this:

```
#include <generic.h>

#define LocalScope(function)                     \
    struct name2(function,ForLocalScope) {       \
        void *parent;                            \
        name2(function,ForLocalScope)(void *p)   \
            { parent = p; }                      \
    public

#define EndLocalScope                            \
    } local(this)
```

The LocalScope macro has been expanded to include the declaration of parent, which is a pointer to a parent scope, and a constructor function that initializes the value of parent. The macro invocation

```
LocalScope(SomeFunction)
```

expands into code equivalent to

```
struct SomeFunctionForLocalScope {
    void *parent;
    SomeFunctionForLocalScope(void *p) { parent = p; }
```

The EndLocalScope macro ends the declaration of the struct containing the scope information and defines a variable named local which will hold the scope state information. The variable local is initialized with the value of this by the EndLocalScope part of the declaration. The variable this refers to the enclosing scope because the inner class sits inside a member function of the enclosing scope. The value of local will in turn be passed as a parameter to the constructor for any enclosed scopes. It is this parameter that establishes a link from a given scope to its enclosing scope (that is, to the enclosing local object).

The outermost level receives special treatment because it has no enclosing LocalScope object. The outermost LocalScope block still has one level of scope outside it—the global scope—but no formal link is maintained between those two levels. Global variables are not subject to the regular block scoping restrictions: they can always be accessed, unqualified, from anywhere. Because the outermost LocalScope block cannot create a scope link from the this pointer of the enclosing block, it needs its own "end scope" macro that just sets the parent scope pointer to the null pointer; it is called EndOuterScope:

```
#define EndOuterScope } local(0)
```

```
int main() {
    LocalScope(main):
        int a;
        int b;
        void foo() {
            LocalScope(foo):
                int a, b;
                void bar() {
                    local.a = 3; local.b = 4;
                    a = 5; b = 6;
                    printf("bar: a=%d, %d, %d; b=%d, %d, %d\n",
                        a, local.a,
                        Parent(main,this)->a,
                        b, local.b,
                        Parent(main,this)->b);
                }
            EndLocalScope;
            local.bar();
            printf("foo: a=%d, b=%d\n", a, b);
        }
    EndOuterScope;
    local.a = 1;
    local.b = 2;
    local.foo();
}
```

Figure F-4. Access Across More than One Level of Scope

To access parent scopes, the `Parent` macro is provided; it is little more than syntactic sugar to apply a type cast to the `void*` parent scope pointer and dereference one of its fields:

```
#define Parent(type,c)        \
        ((name2(type,ForLocalScope)*)(c)->parent)
```

To access an enclosing scope, the `Parent` macro is invoked with the name of the enclosing scope's function as its first parameter, and `this` as its second parameter. Its return type is a pointer to the scope object for the desired function:

```
outerProcLocalScope *scopePtr = Parent(outerProc,this);
```

The `Parent` macro returns the `this` pointer of its enclosing scope. The macro can be applied iteratively to access successively more global scopes:

```
PlayGameLocalScope *p = Parent(PlayGame, this);
BallGameLocalScope *p2 = Parent(BallGame, p);
int &y = p2->ball.yposition;
```

To illustrate how this scoping works, a simple program is presented in Figure F-4. As output, it produces:

```
bar: a=5, 3, 1; b=6, 4, 2
foo: a=1, b=2
```

F.4 Implementation Considerations

There is no syntax in C++ to separately define or compile the body of a class member function for any class nested inside a function. The function definition must therefore be inside the class declaring it. This means that the bodies of these functions may be interpreted as inline functions by your C++ compilation system. Many C++ compilation environments will inline expand only functions that are reasonably simple; the more complex ones are compiled as static functions and incur the overhead of an ordinary function call.

If your C++ compilation system allows, you might consider turning off inline expansion when using this idiom. If you do not, function calls will expand into code many times their size, and the object code size will quickly become unwieldy. If your compilation system has heuristics to keep it from expanding large functions, then such action may not be necessary.

One might also consider it a handicap not to be able to compile nested functions separately; they can indeed be compiled only at the expense of compiling their enclosing function as well. This is not a prohibitive restriction in practice; most block structured language compilers have separate compilation of nested functions only as a significantly advanced feature, or as an ugly hack, if at all.

Exercises

1. Because the idiom presented in this appendix is based on casting `void*` values to various classes, it is not type-safe. Giving the wrong `struct` name to a macro will cause the wrong value to appear at run time, with no warning at

either run time or compile time. Run-time results will be undefined and almost
certainly wrong. Consider the following alternative to block.h:

```
#include <generic.h>
#include <string.h>
#include <iostream.h>

struct Scope {
    Scope *parent;
    virtual char *ScopeName() = 0;
};

#define LocalScope(function)                                    \
struct name2(function,ForLocalScope):public Scope {             \
  char *ScopeName() { return "function"; }                      \
  name2(function,ForLocalScope)(Scope *p) { parent = p; } \
  public
#define EndLocalScope } local(this)
#define EndOuterScope } local(0)
#define Parent(type,c)                                          \
  ((name2(type,ForLocalScope)*)_Parent("type",c))

inline Scope *_Parent(const char *type, Scope *c)
{
    register Scope *s = c;
    while(s && strcmp(s->ScopeName(), type)) s = s->parent;
    if (!s) cerr << "couldn't find scope " << type << endl;
    return s;
}
```

Use this version of the header file to compile and run the example program at
the end of the appendix. What protection does it offer that is not offered by the
previous version of block.h?

2. Modify the macros of exercise (1) to provide a run-time execution trace facility
   that can be turned on and off at run time.

3. Redo block.h using m4 [3] macros instead of C preprocessor macros (or use
   any suitably powerful macro processing language). Using the advanced power
   of m4, minimize the number of Parent macro calls necessary to access a
   given scope, and minimize the number of parameters to the Parent macro.

□

Block-Structured Video Game Code

```cpp
#include <block.h>
#include <iostream.h>
#include <curses.h>

int main()
{
    LocalScope(BallGame):
        void DrawSides() {
            for(int i = 0; i < 66; i++) mvaddch(0, i, 'S');
            for(i = 0; i < 13; i++) {
                mvaddch(i, 0, 'S');
                mvaddch(i, 65, 'S');
            }
            leftWall = 0;
            rightWall = 65;
        }

        struct Ball {
            int yposition, xposition;
            int yspeed, xspeed;
            Ball() {
                yposition = 6;
                xposition = 33;
                yspeed = 1;
                xspeed = 1;
            }
        } ball;

        struct Bat {
            int yposition, position, length, xspeed;
            Bat() { position = 40;
                yposition = 11;
                length = 4;
                xspeed = 0;
            }
        } bat;

        void DrawBat() {
            for (int i = bat.position;
                        i < bat.position + bat.length; i++) {
                mvaddch(bat.yposition, i, 'b');
            }
        }

        void EraseBat() {
            for (int i = bat.position;
                        i < bat.position + bat.length; i++) {
                mvaddch(bat.yposition, i, ' ');
```

```
      }
   }

   short leftWall, rightWall;

   int score;

   void DrawWall() {
      for(int i = 0; i < 66; i++) {
         mvaddch(3, i, 'W');
         mvaddch(4, i, 'W');
         mvaddch(5, i, 'W');
      }
   }

   char ballIsInPlay() {
      return ball.xposition < rightWall &&
         ball.xposition > leftWall &&
         ball.yposition <= bat.yposition;
   }

   void PlayGame() {
      LocalScope(PlayGame):
         char key;     // from keyboard

         short ballsLeft;
         void PlayABall() {
            LocalScope(PlayABall):
               void CheckBallPosition() {
                  PlayGameLocalScope *p =
                                    Parent(PlayGame, this);
                  BallGameLocalScope *p2 =
                                    Parent(BallGame, p);
                  int &y = p2->ball.yposition;
                  int &x = p2->ball.xposition;
                  if (x <= p2->leftWall+1 ||
                                    x >= p2->rightWall-1) {
                     p2->ball.xspeed = -p2->ball.xspeed;
                  }
                  if (y <= 0) {
                     p2->ball.yspeed = -p2->ball.yspeed;
                  }
                  char c = mvinch(y+p2->ball.yspeed,
                                    x + p2->ball.xspeed);
                  switch (c) {
                  case 'W':
                     mvaddch(y + p2->ball.yspeed,
                                    x + p2->ball.xspeed, ' ');
                     p2->score++;
                  case 'b':
```

```
            p2->ball.yspeed = -p2->ball.yspeed;
            p2->ball.xspeed = ->bat.xspeed;
            break;
    }
}

void MoveBall() {
    PlayGameLocalScope *p =
                    Parent(PlayGame, this);
    BallGameLocalScope *p2 =
                    Parent(BallGame, p);
    mvaddch(p2->ball.yposition,
                    p2->ball.xposition, ' ');
    p2->ball.xposition += p2->ball.xspeed;
    p2->ball.yposition += p2->ball.yspeed;
    mvaddch(p2->ball.yposition,
                    p2->ball.xposition, 'O');

}

void MoveBat(char key) {
    LocalScope(MoveBat):
        void MoveLeft(Bat& bat) {
            PlayABallLocalScope *p =
                    Parent(PlayABall, this);
            PlayGameLocalScope *p2 =
                    Parent(PlayGame, p);
            Parent(BallGame, p2)->EraseBat();
            if (bat.position >
              Parent(BallGame, p2)->leftWall) {
                bat.position--;
            }
            Parent(BallGame, p2)->DrawBat();
        }

        void MoveRight(Bat& bat) {
            PlayABallLocalScope *p =
                    Parent(PlayABall, this);
            PlayGameLocalScope *p2 =
                    Parent(PlayGame, p);
            Parent(BallGame, p2)->EraseBat();
            if (bat.position <
                Parent(BallGame, p2)->rightWall -
                bat.length) {
                bat.position++;
            }
            Parent(BallGame, p2)->DrawBat();
        }
    EndLocalScope;
```

```
                         PlayGameLocalScope *p =
                                   Parent(PlayGame, this);
                         switch (key) {
                         case 'l':
                            local.MoveLeft(
                                        Parent(BallGame, p)->bat);
                            Parent(BallGame, p)->bat.xspeed = -1;
                            break;
                         case 'r':
                            local.MoveRight(
                                        Parent(BallGame, p)->bat);
                            Parent(BallGame, p)->bat.xspeed = 1;
                            break;
                         default:
                            break;
                         }
                    }
              EndLocalScope;

              while (Parent(BallGame,this)->ballIsInPlay()) {
                 local.CheckBallPosition();
                 local.MoveBall();
                 refresh();
                 key = getch();
                 local.MoveBat(key);
              }
         }
      EndLocalScope;

      local.ballsLeft = 4;
      while (local.ballsLeft > 0) {
         refresh();
         local.key = getch();
         local.PlayABall();
         --local.ballsLeft;
      }
   }

EndOuterScope;

int bestScore = 0;

initscr();
cbreak();
noecho();

local.DrawSides();
local.DrawBat();
```

```
for (;;) {
   local.score = 0;
   local.DrawWall();
   local.PlayGame();
   if (local.score > bestScore) {
      bestScore = local.score;
   }
   cout << "best score is " << bestScore << "\n";
}
}
```

References

1. Knuth, Donald E. *Sorting and Searching*. Reading, Mass.: Addison-Wesley, 1973.

2. Bell, Doug, Ian Morrey, and John Pugh. *Software Engineering: A Programming Approach*. Englewood Cliffs, N.J.: Prentice Hall, 1987, ff. 43.

3. American Telephone and Telegraph Company, *UNIX System V Release 4 Programmer's Guide: ANSI C and Programming Support Tools*. Englewood Cliffs, N.J.: Prentice-Hall, 1990.

Index

- B -

- C -

- E -

- F -

- G -

- H -

- I -

- O -

- P -

- R -

- S -